CONFIDENCE GAMES

CONFIDENCE
GAMES
MARK C.
TAYLOR

MONEY AND MARKETS
IN A WORLD WITHOUT
REDEMPTION

The University of Chicago Press
Chicago and London

RELIGION AND POSTMODERNISM
a series edited by
Mark C. Taylor and Thomas A. Carlson

MARK C. TAYLOR is the Cluett Professor of Humanities at Williams College and
visiting professor of architecture and religion at Columbia University. His numerous
books include, most recently, *Grave Matters*;
*About Religion: Economies of Faith in Vir-
tual Culture*; and *The Moment of Complexity: Emerging Network Culture*, the last
two published by the University of Chicago
Press. He is also the cofounder of the Global
Education Network (GEN.com).

The University of Chicago Press,
Chicago 60637
The University of Chicago Press, Ltd.,
London

13 12 11 10 09 08 07 06 05 04   1 2 3 4 5

ISBN: 0-226-79166-1 (cloth)

LIBRARY OF CONGRESS
CATALOGING-IN-PUBLICATION DATA
Taylor, Mark C., 1945–
  Confidence games : money and
markets in a world without redemption /
Mark C. Taylor.
      p. cm. — (Religion and
postmodernism)
  Includes bibliographical references
and index.
  ISBN 0-226-79166-1 (cloth : alk. paper)
    1. Economics—Religious aspects.
  2. Art—Economic aspects.
  3. Money—Religious aspects.
  4. Economics—Religious aspects—
Christianity. I. Title. II. Series.
    HB72.T32 2004
    332′.01—dc22
                        2004001200

⊗ The paper used in this publication
meets the minimum requirements of
the American National Standard for
Information Sciences—Permanence
of Paper for Printed Library Materials,
ANSI Z39.48-1992.

FOR

AARON S. TAYLOR

AND

KIRSTEN J. TAYLOR

Money is a kind of poetry.

———————————————————

God is a symbol for something that
can well take other forms, as, for
example, the form of high poetry.

Wallace Stevens

———————————————————

CONTENTS

PREFACE

This book has its origin in two events separated by sixteen years: President Nixon's suspension of the gold standard on August 15, 1971, and the stock market crash of October 19, 1987. In the fall of 1971, I traveled to Copenhagen for a year to write my doctoral dissertation on Søren Kierkegaard. The previous three years had been especially tumultuous at Harvard. Student protests had disrupted Harvard as well as many other colleges and universities in the United States and abroad. With the drug culture and political activism raging in Cambridge, serious study was not high on the agenda of many students. A strange mix of despair and hope filled the air: despair because of the injustice of the war in Vietnam and continuing racism, yet hope brought by the relaxation of long-sanctioned repressions and by the belief that real change was possible. Human liberation—sexual and political—was the rallying cry, Freud and Marx the prophets.

As bombs continued to fall in Southeast Asia and more and more bodies returned in bags, disillusion with American capitalism spread like a virus. In Harvard classrooms, many students and faculty believed Marxism was the way of the future. I vividly remember the first session of a class on Marx taught by a well-regarded analytic philosopher who had recently discovered his long-dormant political conscience. Since I was not sure where the classroom was, I arrived early only to discover over four hundred students in Harvard Yard clamoring to get into Emerson Hall. At the Divinity School, where I took most of my courses, everyone was enthralled with Marxist-inspired liberation theology. My journey to Harvard had started with philosophy and theology rather than politics. While an undergraduate at Wesleyan University, I had discovered new worlds in the writings of G. W. F. Hegel, Søren Kierkegaard, and Karl Marx. Having lost my draft deferment for a war I believed was unjust, I read the demanding works of these authors religiously during the fateful spring of 1968. Their

ideas seemed not only timely but also prescient; indeed, these philosophers implicitly and explicitly framed the terms of debate both in classrooms and in halls of power. Philosophy and theology on the one hand and
politics and economics on the other, I learned, are inseparable. The questions protesters on the street were raising were extensions of questions
Hegel, Kierkegaard, and Marx had asked: Can war be just? What is the political role of religion? What is the relation between the individual and the
state? Is communism or democracy a better political system? Is socialism
or capitalism a more effective economic system? As I left for my first trip
to Europe, these were some of the questions circulating in my mind.

I was not prepared for what greeted me in Copenhagen. Though the
Danes were extremely cordial, they were vehemently opposed to American
foreign and domestic policies. Then, as now, they believed the war was
an unjustified expression of American imperialism. With the images of
America's racial strife bombarding them daily, Danes from every walk of
life viewed the U.S. as a country torn apart by social and economic in-
equities at home and intent on ruthless expansion abroad. Coming from
citizens of a country with a homogeneous population of only five million,
many of these charges seemed to be cheap shots. Moreover, it was clear
that, while the Danes relentlessly criticized American military power, neither Denmark nor the rest of Europe could survive without it. In the U.S.,
I usually felt left of center; but as I tried to respond to my Danish friends
and colleagues, I felt far to the right. Until I learned to read and speak Danish, my only source for daily news other than the *International Herald Tri-
bune* was Radio Moscow. At midnight, I could pick up the news. Night after night, reporters and commentators rushed through daily events so they
could recount and analyze every detail of the activities of the "California
communist" Angela Davis. When I told the Danes how slanted Radio Moscow was, they invariably responded: "To us it sounds no more slanted than
Radio Free Europe." But there *were* differences and these differences *were*
important.

A few months after arriving in Denmark, I saw how deep these differences were and how much they mattered. In October 1971, my wife, Dinny,
and I decided to drive through East Germany to Berlin. Since we were arriving from Denmark, we did not take the major east-west highway but followed the much less-traveled route from Warnemunde to Berlin. Not until
we made our way through East German customs did I realize how deeply
the rhetoric and images of the Cold War had been seared in my mind. We
were completely alone and it felt as if we were going behind enemy lines.

There were no other tourists anywhere, and we had no way of contacting the "outside" world. The route was poorly marked with faded signs, and we had been repeatedly warned of the dire consequences of straying from approved roads. Words from a journal I kept that year capture the experience better than I can now express it.

October 18, 1971. Berlin.

It's hard to know just what to write tonight. We left Copenhagen with some anxiety, suddenly realizing all the ideas that had been drilled into us for years about the Communists were surprisingly fresh in our minds. Drove to Gedser and took a two-hour ferry to Warnemunde. Though there were only 5 cars on the boat, it took us an hour to get through all the "red" tape. Before allowing us to proceed, border guards thoroughly searched the car with military precision. After clearing customs, we cautiously wound our way along the two-lane road through the bleakest, gloomiest villages and towns I've ever seen. Houses and buildings looked like they had not seen paint since the Second World War. The few cars we saw were old and belched clouds of sooty exhaust. Rather than trucks, produce was hauled in carts with big tires pulled by old and tired horses. What a contrast from Denmark! It is turnip harvesting time but instead of using modern tractors like the Danes, the fields were filled with peasant women in long black dresses and stockings, digging and topping the turnips before tossing them into their horse-drawn carts. The transit road was filled with military vehicles and village sidewalks were crawling with East German and Soviet soldiers. At the edge of every town, there was a big military installation. As we approached Berlin with night falling, we drove along extensive military facilities extending about 10 kilometers. At the Berlin border crossing, we were subjected to another thorough search. They looked under the car with big mirrors and even put a probe down the gas tank. Leaving East Germany behind, we entered a bright and bustling city that seemed thoroughly modern. The differences between East and West could not have been greater. We found a pension for the night and tuned in the Armed Forces radio station, which, we soon discovered, is blocked in East Germany. What else to say? It has been a sobering and thought-provoking day.

The next morning we began by exploring West Berlin's rich museums, art galleries, and stores. Our day ended at the Berlin Wall, where we met a man staring blankly toward East Berlin. In my fumbling German, I learned that he had been born in what is now East Berlin and still has two daughters who live there whom he had not seen in ten years. He said he often comes to the Wall to look for them. Near the point where his eyes had been fixed there was a sign: "Sixty-three people died here trying to escape."

The following morning we rose early to visit East Berlin. We decided to pass through the famous Checkpoint Charlie. Waiting for more than an hour to get across the border, childhood memories of scurrying to get under my desk during air raid drills in elementary school during the 1950s flashed through my mind. Once in East Berlin, we headed straight for Alexander von Humboldt University, where Hegel and Friedrich Schleiermacher, the father of modern theology, both had lectured at the height of their fame. As I entered the central building, my eyes fell on a huge brown marble wall emblazoned with one of Marx's most famous proclamations in large gold letters:

THE PHILOSOPHERS HAVE ONLY INTERPRETED THE WORLD;
THE POINT IS TO CHANGE IT.

Since I had studied and written about this text, I understood its philosophical, political, and economic importance. As I took out my camera to photograph the wall, four armed guards descended on me, grabbed my camera, and ripped out the film before roughly throwing me out of the building. Startled and confused, I was glad nothing worse had happened. Marx was right, I thought; the point *is* to change the world, but his followers were wrong about which world needed to be changed. I did not get my photograph of Marx's maxim on the university wall until I returned to Berlin in 1991.

During those autumn days in 1971, it became perfectly clear to me that, even though Marx was sometimes an insightful philosopher, the political and economic system he promoted turned out to be a dismal failure. From the streets of Berlin, the Marxist students back in Cambridge looked naïve and misguided. This is not to suggest that all of their criticisms of American foreign and domestic policies were wrong but that the alternatives they preferred were politically more repressive and economically less viable. It would be another eighteen years before I dragged my protesting daughter out of bed to watch the Berlin Wall collapse. Today a fragment of the Wall sits in my living room as a reminder of the lessons I learned more than three decades ago.

When we returned to Copenhagen, the $2,000 check for my second-semester fellowship was waiting for me. Harvard had given me the choice of receiving $2,500 to stay in Cambridge and work as a teaching assistant or $4,000 to study abroad. It had not been a difficult decision. Since we had no savings and were not allowed to work in Denmark, we had planned to live the entire year on $4,000. When I went to our Danish bank to exchange the $2,000, I received the equivalent of approximately $200 less in Danish kroner than I had in July. With all of the travel and without my regular news sources, I somehow had missed Nixon's suspension of the gold standard in August. When you are trying to live abroad on $4,000 for the whole year, $200 is a lot of money. With the stroke of a pen, my $200 had vanished. Where had the money gone?

Our dinner table conversations were as often about the large as the small issues of the day. This question returned sixteen years later. On October 20, 1987, we were having a discussion about money and markets. The previous day had been "Black Monday," when the Dow Jones Industrial Average fell from 2,246 to 1,738, losing 22.6 percent of its total value. Between Tuesday, October 13, and Monday, October 19, the Dow fell by almost one third. Outstanding stocks lost approximately one trillion dollars during this brief period. The October crash seemed to mark the end of the bull market, which had begun with the Dow at 776.92 in August 1982. "You know," I said, "the past few days have been pretty amazing."

Aaron, who was fourteen at the time, asked, "Why, what's going on?"

"The stock market has crashed and billions and billions of dollars have vanished."

"Really? Where'd the money go?"

Once again, I had no answer. But by this time, I had come to suspect that the issue was not merely a matter of economics.

In the years between 1971 and 1987, I discovered that many of the problems that interested me in the writings of Hegel, Kierkegaard, and Marx were at the heart of the debates then swirling around postmodernism and poststructuralism. The more I studied how these movements had developed in areas ranging from philosophy and literature to art and architecture, the more convinced I became that culture and economics are interrelated in much more complicated ways than traditional reductive analyses suggest. This impression was reinforced by an unexpected turn of events. In the fall of 1998, at the height of the dot-com boom, Herbert Allen, an influential New York investment banker who specializes in media, entertainment, and technology, and I founded Global Education Network (GEN.com). The goal of our company is to provide high-quality on-

line education in the liberal arts, humanities, and sciences to people of
all ages throughout the world. My work with Herbert and our colleagues
has been a combination of fieldwork and an extended tutorial on business
and finance. This extraordinary experience has allowed me to look behind
a curtain very few outsiders are allowed to lift. The more I have learned,
the clearer it is that contemporary culture can no more be understood
apart from recent changes in money and markets than money and markets can be understood apart from the cultural history that has made them
possible.

Since that dinner table conversation, I have been attempting to develop
a philosophy of culture that, I believe, can account for the interplay of natural, cultural, and socioeconomic processes. In many ways, this book represents the culmination of an argument I have been developing for more
than three decades. This is not to imply that I imagined this end at the outset of the journey. To the contrary, like the systems I am analyzing, the argument has proven to be a self-organizing system that I have been able to
understand only after it has emerged. I suspect that when we eventually
look back on the beginning of the twenty-first century, it will appear to be
one of those critical periods of transition when more suddenly becomes
different. We are entering a new territory and need new maps. One of the
morals of the tale unfolded in the following pages is that in an increasingly
networked world where information is the currency of the realm, models
matter. If we try to move into the future with models and visions drawn
from the past, we court the very disaster we are trying to avoid.

Conversations, like books and courses, have unpredictable consequences. While I have been reading, writing, and teaching, Aaron has
graduated from college, picked up a Ph.D. in geochemistry, and begun
working as a Wall Street specialist in structured finance. Kirsten, who was
too young to join the conversation in 1987, obviously was listening. After
graduating from college and working with the Boston public schools, she
came to understand that the problems of education are inseparable from
the legal and policy issues. She will soon graduate from law school and
join a prestigious New York law firm specializing in corporate finance.
Both of them approach their work differently because of those hours of
conversation. Aaron understands that the pressing environmental issues
that threaten our future can be addressed only through global financial
markets, and Kirsten understands that the children upon whom our future depends will never receive the education they need and deserve without the leverage of the law. As the years have passed, our roles have been

reversed: Aaron and Kirsten have become my teachers. I could not have completed this book without the lessons they have taught me. Whether or not others find the map I have developed useful in understanding the new world emerging in our midst, I hope Aaron and Kirsten will accept it as my belated answer to the question "Where'd the money go?"

mct

ACKNOWLEDGMENTS

Like many of my previous works, this book has taken me into new territory for which I have no formal training. Though I read extensively for several years in business, finance, and economics, I would not have been able to complete this book without the willingness of my remarkable colleagues at Williams College to answer my questions patiently, read my drafts carefully, and teach me many things I did not understand. I express my sincere appreciation to Ralph Bradburd, John Chandler, Thomas Garrity, Chris Geiregat, Catherine Hill, H. Ganse Little, and William Wootters. Roger Bolton read every page of the manuscript with extraordinary care and offered extensive comments and corrections—often more than I wanted but never more than I needed. In the course of completing this book, I became his student and now understand why he has had such an impact on his other students at Williams over his long and distinguished career. Morton O. Schapiro and Thomas A. Kohut continue to offer the personal and professional support without which much of what I do would be impossible. The ongoing assistance of Margaret Weyers continues to be critical for all of my work. Ray L. Hart and William Doty read the manuscript with great care and offered unusually helpful suggestions. My friends and colleagues at Allen & Company and the Global Education Network have given me a business education I never expected to receive: Herbert Allen III, Steve Greenberg, Kim Wieland, Paul Gould, Jon Newcomb, Alexander Parker, and Ian Huschle. I offer a special word of thanks to Herbert A. Allen for our countless conversations and e-mails in which he has drawn on his vast experience in the worlds of finance, media, and entertainment to provide insights few are privileged to share. Nothing has contributed more to my understanding of the complex trajectories I have attempted to track than Herbert's remarkable Sun Valley Conferences. While Herbert Allen and his colleagues have taught me much about business, Thomas Krens, director of the Guggenheim Museum, has taught me much of what I know about the art world. No one understands the relation between art and business better than Tom. I have known Tom Krens for more than twenty years and have worked with him at both Williams College and the Guggenheim. During the 1990s, I ran the Guggenheim's Critical Issues Forum for several years. Just as my involvement with Herbert Allen has taught me lessons about Wall Street, so my long association with Tom has taught me lessons about the art world. It is difficult to imagine two better—and more different—teachers. David Schulte is a good enough friend to tell me when I don't know what I'm talking about. For more than two decades, Alan Thomas, editorial director at the University of Chicago Press, and I have worked together on most of the books I have published. Alan is a writer's dream editor: smart, savvy, and dedicated to intellectual excellence, he knows how to encourage and when to push back. As every author knows, work does not end when the manuscript is complete. For years Randy Petilos has offered invaluable assistance throughout the publication process. The first two people with whom I always share whatever I write are Jack Miles, senior advisor to the president, The J. Paul Getty Museum, and Edith Wyschogrod, professor emerita, Rice University. I know I can have complete confidence in their assessments and responses. Finally, my family: Dinny S. Taylor, who is, I believe, the only person who has read everything I have written; Kirsten J. Taylor, whose new ventures take me places I never expected to go; and Aaron S. Taylor, who, by a series of life's unexpected twists, finds himself in the midst of the complex currents I have tried to understand. This book is a belated response to a question he asked me more than twenty-five years ago.

INTRODUCTION

In recent years, American society has undergone a disturbing crisis of confidence in many of the individuals and institutions responsible for the country's well-being. Priests, politicians, and financiers as well as the press, media, courts, and schools no longer seem trustworthy. Looking back on the 1990s, many people see a period of undisciplined excess not unlike the 1960s. As fundamental truths and values faded or disappeared, it no longer seemed possible to be sure what was real and what was fake. While the stock market was rising, people did not seem to be concerned about the ground slipping from beneath their feet. By the end of the decade, however, the party every one knew could not last forever was over. The traumatic events of the new millennium announced a world that appeared to be spinning out of control. Shaken from their nondogmatic slumber and terrified by overwhelming insecurity, the search for religious certainty, moral clarity, and national purpose became urgent.

The longing for clarity and simplicity in the face of overwhelming complexity is as understandable as it is misguided. There are no simple answers or clear alternatives in a world whose growing interconnectedness renders it ever more complex. The current crisis of confidence is the result of neither the isolated events nor the aberrant actions of misguided individuals but is the symptom of a profound crisis of representation that is endemic to modern and postmodern society and culture. For the past two centuries, the line separating appearance and reality, truth and illusion, the material and the immaterial, the real and the virtual has been gradually eroding. As new information and networking technologies have rapidly proliferated, the tutored eye has been able to discern growing anxiety, doubt, and uncertainty shadowing the frenzied spectacles and accelerating speculation of the era. Postmodern religion, art, architecture, and philosophy are, in large measure, the cultural articulation of a crisis of confidence created by the crisis of representation.

1

While it has long been clear that the cultural movement known as post-modernism is inseparably bound to developments in the economy and financial markets during the last four decades, the complex dynamics joining money, markets, and culture have not been adequately examined. In the following pages, I argue that postmodern culture simultaneously reflects and promotes economic changes that result in what can only be described as a postmodern economy. With the continuing expansion of the global networks and world-wide webs increasingly forming the fabric of contemporary experience, culture and markets are joined in loops of co-determination and coevolution. The general trajectory of development is toward increasing dematerialization and growing complexity. While cultural production becomes a process of reproduction in which original work gives way to the recycling of signs, financial assets become insubstantial information backed by virtual assets circulating ever faster on global markets whose complexity exceeds our grasp. *Confidence Games: Money and Markets in a World without Redemption* provides a map for the baffling new territory we have entered at the beginning of the twenty-first century. By coming to a better understanding of how and why this crisis of confidence has emerged, we might better understand our current situation and come to a more realistic assessment of the extraordinary challenges we face.

I frame the argument of *Confidence Games* in terms suggested by William Gaddis's remarkable novels: *The Recognitions* (1955) and *JR* (1976). Taken together, these two overlooked works provide an interpretation of the latter half of the twentieth century that is more insightful than any theoretical treatment of this period. Recounting the story of an erstwhile Protestant minister who spends his life forging paintings by Flemish masters, *The Recognitions* presents an extended meditation on the problem of forgery and counterfeiting in a world where everything has become a copy of a copy or a sign of a sign. The forger is a latter-day confidence man whose artful deceits create a crisis of confidence. Just as a century earlier Herman Melville had offered an analysis of emerging industrial society and a diagnosis of the perils of paper currency in *The Confidence-Man* and *Moby-Dick*, so Gaddis presents an examination of emerging network culture and the uncertainties digital currencies and virtual capital engender in *The Recognitions* and *JR*. In chapter 1, "Paper Trails," I argue that the fictive worlds Gaddis and Melville explore have become our historical destiny.

In an effort to understand how we have arrived at what I have described elsewhere as "the moment of complexity," I return to the work of Hegel.

By recasting his speculative philosophy, I develop a dialectic without synthesis in which religion, art, and economics progressively displace but do not replace each other. Religion first gives way to art, which then is displaced by economics. Throughout the 1960s and early 1970s, theologians, philosophers, and social scientists consistently argued that modernization and secularization are inseparable. The culmination of the process of secularization appeared to be the death of God and the birth of the secular city. As the cultural significance of religion appeared to be fading, art—especially so-called fine art—gradually became the focus of spiritual expression and aspiration: artists became the high priests and museums the cathedrals of modernism. By the middle of the twentieth century, however, art had become thoroughly entangled with economics. Pop art collapsed high into low by aestheticizing consumer culture, while at the same time marketing itself with strategies that were often indistinguishable from advertising. The initial site of this transformation was the urban display window of department stores. In response to these developments, Minimalists and Conceptualists tried to break the alliance between art and commerce by transforming the work of art into either an industrially produced mechanical product or a plan or program whose material realization was less important than its conceptual formulation. Though apparently opposite, Pop art on the one hand and Minimalism and Conceptualism on the other share more than they acknowledge. Both promote the dematerialization of the work of art in a play of signs grounded in nothing other than itself. While Pop art creates images of other images, conceptualists identify artistic production with the creation of a program that functions like an algorithm.

In the following decades, the play of signs prefigured in late modern and postmodern art and architecture expands to encompass the world of finance. As the financial economy displaces so-called real economy, money becomes increasingly virtual and markets morph into webs circulating images and information. The critical perspectives of structuralism and poststructuralism, which were emerging at the same time, both reflect these economic and financial developments and provide an interpretive perspective from which to assess their significance.

Having considered the interplay of religion, art, and economics in the contemporary culture of signs as well as the information economy, chapter 2, "Marketing Providence," analyzes the historical and psychological origins of money and considers the importance of religious beliefs and practices for the emergence of markets. As the embodiment of oppositions like valuable/worthless, material/immaterial, rational/irrational, and useful/useless, money has always been fraught with an ambiguity that has led to its association with God as well as the Devil. From its earliest appearance in the West, money has been related to the divine. In Greek and early Christian rituals, gold figures served as tokens exchanged for divine favors. In these divine economies, redemption depends upon a token of exchange that sustains the relationship between believer and deity. From ancient Greece through the Middle Ages and Reformation and into the modern period, the formation and operation of markets are inseparable from religious rituals, ecclesiastical regulation, and theological speculation.

Though rarely recognized, the relation between the divine and the human lies at the heart of the modern understanding of markets. Calvinism not only prepared the way for a flourishing economy but also provided principles for understanding and justifying market activity. The first person to use the image of the invisible hand was not Adam Smith but John Calvin. For Calvin, God's providence is the invisible hand that sustains the order of the world even when it is not immediately evident. Smith appropriated Calvin's doctrine of providence to explain the machinations of the market. Emphasizing aesthetic aspects of Calvin's theology that were important for Scottish philosophers in the eighteenth century, Smith brought together religion, art, and economics to form the modern theory of markets. Just as the beautiful work of art is characterized by the harmonious interrelation of its parts, so the market functions as an integrated system in which individuals pursuing their own interests also promote the good of the whole. With Smith's translation of theology and aesthetics into economics, the source of order shifted from an external agent, i.e., God, to internal relations among individual human actors. From this point of view, the market is a self-organizing system that regulates itself. F. A. Hayek has gone so far as to claim that for Smith the market is, in effect, a cybernetic system that operates by processing information. The market, in other words, works like a computer. By the seventeenth century, the Amsterdam stock exchange had already become a thriving speculative market where investors were using financial instruments remarkably similar to the sophisticated products promoted during the 1980s and 1990s in New Amsterdam, i.e., New York City.

The bridge between the eighteenth and twentieth centuries is formed by post-Kantian theology, philosophy, and aesthetics. Chapter 3, "Figuring Capital," is devoted to an examination of how Kant's notion of beauty prepares the way for Schleiermacher's aesthetic theology as well as Hegel's rational system. Hegel translates Kant's account of the beautiful work of art into speculative terms to form his interpretation of the Absolute, which, he believes, constitutes the logical structure of reality. The self-referentiality of Kant's work of art becomes the principle of self-reflexivity of Hegel's Idea in and through which differences are mediated and oppositions overcome. This logic of self-referentiality discloses what many modernists regard as the definitive structure of the work of art. Instead of referring to something beyond itself, true art refers only to itself; art, in other words, is about art. Marx turns aesthetic theory to economic ends. While claiming to invert Hegel's idealism in a dialectical materialism, he actually develops his analysis of capital and money by appropriating Hegel's logic. Money, Marx argues, is the general equivalent, which serves as the medium of exchange by establishing the relative value of differences. In its most developed form, capital is a self-reflexive process with no purpose beyond its own self-replication. The intersection of religion and aesthetics in Marx's view of capital suggests unexpected similarities between his position and Smith's account of the market. The trajectory that begins with Kant's *Critique of Judgment* reaches closure with Georg Simmel's monumental *Philosophy of Money*. By extending Hegel's dialectical analysis and Marx's understanding of capital, Simmel develops an interpretation of aestheticized money that anticipates structuralism's recasting of meaning and value in terms of relation rather than reference. As the "incarnation" of relationality, money reveals the economic absolute, which is both an aesthetic and an ontological principle. Unlike Hegel and Marx, Simmel realizes that the paradoxes of self-reflexivity create what mathematicians call "strange loops," which never close on themselves. With this insight, he anticipates what complexity theorists now describe as complex adaptive systems. Chapter 3 concludes with a consideration of the way in which different forms of currency entail different cultural formations and vice versa.

What the nineteenth century theorized, the twentieth century realized. After we have examined the unexpected role of religion and art in the genealogy of the classical understanding of markets, the scene of analysis shifts to economic developments during the past four decades. The economy of the 1980s and 1990s would not have been possible without political, economic, and technological developments in the 1970s. In chapter 4, "Money Matters," I argue that two pivotal events in the 1970s—President Nixon's 1973 abandonment of the gold standard and Paul Volcker's 1979 shift in monetary policy—were critical for financial markets and the world economy in the following decades. The rise of the neoconservative politics of the Reagan and Thatcher administrations and neoliberal economics of

Milton Friedman and supply-siders in the 1970s created the conditions for the extraordinary market of the 1980s and 1990s. While many factors contributed to the shifts in the political and economic climate, one of the most important was the 1971 suspension of the Bretton Woods agreement, which had brought stability to the global economy after the end of World War II. In addition to creating the International Monetary Fund and the World Bank, Bretton Woods reestablished a modified version of the gold standard by linking the dollar to gold and establishing the value of other currencies in relation to the dollar. After suspending gold convertibility, Nixon tried to maintain fixed exchange rates, but eventually was forced to allow currencies to float. About the same time, Reuters installed the first electronic system for international currency trading. Floating currencies circulating in electronic networks created a new economic condition.

Though not immediately apparent, the abandonment of the gold standard had broad cultural significance. It is no exaggeration to insist that going off the gold standard was the economic equivalent of the death of God. God functions in religious systems like gold functions in economic systems: God and gold are believed to be the firm foundations that provide a secure anchor for religious, moral, and economic values. When this foundation disappears, meaning and value become unmoored and once trustworthy symbols and signs float freely in turbulent currents that are constantly shifting.

In retrospect, it is clear that God did not simply disappear but was reborn as the market. In contemporary society, the market has become God in more than a trivial sense. The terms many economists and analysts use to describe the market implicitly suggest language once reserved for God: the market is omniscient, omnipotent, and omnipresent. Since the market knows best, it should be allowed to operate according to its own principles with minimal interference from humans, whose knowledge is unavoidably limited. By the late 1970s, belief in the market had become a widely accepted orthodoxy.

This emerging orthodoxy contributed to the second major event in the 1970s. In 1979 Paul Volcker, then the chairman of the Federal Reserve Bank, launched a sustained attack on inflation by shifting to a policy of controlling the money supply and allowing the market to determine interest rates. This decision marked a move away from accepted Keynesian orthodoxy, in which a healthy economy and orderly markets require regular government action in the form of fiscal policies (taxation) and federal expenditures, to monetary policies long supported by Milton Friedman and his followers, whose faith in the market led to suspicions about too much

government intervention. In the early 1980s, President Reagan began promoting policies to deregulate and privatize banking, financial services, information and network technology, and telecommunications. With the
world increasingly wired, actions originating in Washington quickly rippled through the national and global economy in unexpected ways. The political and economic decisions made in the 1970s set the stage for the transformation of markets and accompanying economic boom in the 1980s and
1990s.

Since the dawn of trading, technological innovation has transformed
markets. When things are exchanged, new transportation networks create
new markets that require different investment strategies. As bits become
more valuable than stuff, communication networks become more important than railways, highways, seaways, and airways. In recent decades,
news, information, and network technologies have both created new products and markets and changed the way material commodities are produced, marketed, and distributed. While much has been written about
the shift from a manufacturing to an information economy, the most important development is usually overlooked: *the distinctive characteristic of
our age is not simply the spread of computers but the impact of connecting
them.* When computers are networked *everything* changes. What has occurred in the past four decades is the emergence of a new network economy that is inseparable from a new network culture. The constantly changing networks that increasingly govern our lives have a distinct logic that we
are only beginning to understand.

Chapter 5, "Specters of Capital," explores the complex interplay among
three critical factors: government policies of deregulation and privatization of the financial and technology industries; innovations in information, telecommunications, and networking technologies; and new forms
of money, financial products, and investment strategies. The abandonment
of the gold standard, shift in monetary policy, and deregulation of the
banking and financial industries combined with the rapid expansion of
trading networks to increase the volatility of global financial markets. As
markets became more volatile, investors sought ways to manage risk. To
meet this growing demand, financial institutions developed new versions
of established products as well as novel financial instruments like swaps,
options, and options on options, designed to take advantage of emerging
technologies for the real-time distribution of news and information as well
as online trading through proprietary and open networks.

As the bull market, which began in 1982, continued to flourish, individuals and institutions began to borrow money to invest in increasingly

speculative derivatives. Many financial firms, startups, and traditional businesses that were the target of mergers and acquisitions deals became more highly leveraged than ever. Furthermore, the nature of their collateral changed. Instead of securing loans with cash or material assets like factories, equipment, and inventory, investors used securities purchased with the borrowed money as collateral for loans. Deregulation even transformed the traditionally cautious savings and loan industry. With the fever of speculation spreading, new products and the investment strategies with which they were traded created a crisis in which more and more financial assets rested on a dwindling collateral base. As derivatives became more abstract and the mathematical formulas for the trading programs more complex, markets began to lose contact with anything resembling the real economy. To any rational investor, it should have been clear that markets were becoming a precarious Ponzi scheme. Contrary to expectation, products originally developed to manage risk increased market volatility and thus intensified the very uncertainty investors were trying to avoid. As derivatives, virtual currencies, and e-money circulated across ethereal nets at ever-greater speed, financial markets began to resemble a postmodern play of signs indistinguishable from the digital signs on display along the Vegas Strip. Though the mounting risks were clear, investors did not seem to care. Having checked reason at the door, they continued to party; the more dicey the game, the bigger its draw. By the middle of the 1990s, the market had become as fashionable as the overpriced clothes investors bought at Barneys and the overvalued art they purchased in downtown galleries and hung on the walls of their redecorated uptown apartments.

Nowhere was the frenzy of the market more evident than in the dot-com mania of the 1990s. In chapter 6, "Yahoo Nation," I reconsider this remarkable period by reflecting on my own experience of cofounding a dot-com company with New York investment banker Herbert Allen. My experiences as a participant-observer in the worlds of investment banking and dot-coms have given me a rare opportunity to look behind the curtain of the financial world. What I have seen makes me all the more convinced that Wall Street has become as postmodern as philosophy, art, and architecture, which are often dismissed as irrational and even nihilistic.

I begin this chapter with a tour of today's Times Square. While one cannot understand Wall Street in the 1970s and 1980s if one does not understand the signs of Las Vegas, it is impossible to understand Wall Street in the 1990s without understanding the signs of Times Square. Times Square is where the real becomes virtual and the virtual becomes real in a play of screens screening other screens. One of the most important nodes in the new finance-entertainment complex rapidly transforming our lives, "the crossroads of the world" is bordered by Lehman Brothers and Morgan Stanley on the north and Reuters and NASDAQ on the south. In between, all the major television networks as well as ESPN, MTV, and leading financial networks broadcast daily. To understand the far-reaching implications of this finance-entertainment complex, I return to Gaddis's *JR*.[1] *JR* is the story of an eleven-year-old who, using phones and faxes to implement sophisticated financial transactions, creates a paper empire that eventually becomes big enough to threaten the global economy. Two decades after the publication of Gaddis's novel, Jonathan Lebed became a real-life JR; he created a virtual empire by trading stocks and publicizing his picks on his Web site, Stock-Dogs.com. If one can understand the worlds of JR and JL, one can understand the Internet economy and the dot-com boom and bust.

Neither the dot-com phenomenon nor the economy of the 1990s would have been possible without NASDAQ. Established in 1971, the National Association of Securities Dealers introduced the first computer network capable of providing investors with access to real-time quotes for over-the-counter stocks. By 1991, NASDAQ had become a computerized trading network on which individuals, professional traders, brokerage houses, and financial institutions could trade online without going through a financial intermediary. This new trading network not only changed the way Wall Street does business but actually transformed the global economy. For many entrepreneurs, analysts, and investors, the old rules did not seem to apply to the new economy. In a world where companies generated no revenues and produced no products, it was not clear how to establish the value of securities. Instead of continuing to rely on long-trusted fundamental analysis, new methods of assessing companies were developed that resulted in completely unrealistic evaluations. While analysts and investors both realized the dot-com economy was spinning out of control, everybody was reluctant to get out of the game. Analysts hyped companies they knew were all image and no substance in the hope of persuading them to do their IPOs through the investment banks for which the analysts worked. The media further fueled the frenzy with new television shows, glitzy magazines, and online publications. By the end of the decade, Wall Street had become even more exciting than Vegas—the stakes were so much higher and the game so much faster. Nonetheless, an inescapable specter hung over the markets: almost all the players quietly admitted that investing had become more of a confidence game than ever. From Wall Street to Main Street, people knew the boom was not real but, after two decades of a bull market, no one was any longer sure what was.

I introduce the analysis of financial economics in chapter 7, "Difference Engines," with a discussion of the Guggenheim Museum. There is no better laboratory for understanding the complex relations between art and finance in the 1990s than the Guggenheim. The rise and fall of the museum's fortunes coincide exactly with the rise and fall of NASDAQ. For director Thomas Krens, art is always business and business is necessarily an art. In the late 1980s, he already understood that in "the new world order," culture would be one of the most important currencies of the realm. With media and information networks rapidly extending their reach, art and cultural institutions would assume greater political and economic significance. In an effort to develop a global institution for the global economy, Krens has established a worldwide network of museums in which the real and the virtual are seamlessly integrated. While changing economic conditions have made it impossible to realize important aspects of this vision, Krens understands the future better than his critics.

There is no more telling sign of the intersection of the old and new financial markets than the New York Stock Exchange's 1998 commissioning of Asymptote, the same architectural firm that had designed the Guggenheim Virtual Museum and Guggenheim.com, to create a virtual trading floor. When NASDAQ went live with online trading for both individuals and institutions in 1991, the grand old market remained committed to its real trading floor and face-to-face trading. By the late 1990s, however, even the NYSE was forced to admit that the future would be digital. Their virtual trading floor created an immaterial data space in which news and information circulate and trades can be executed in real time 24/7. The NYSE Virtual Exchange is as visually engaging as NASDAQ's spectacular digital sign in the heart of Times Square.

As technologies change, markets are transformed. The networking of markets for trading financial instruments that are more virtual than real led to greater volatility, uncertainty, and risk; this, in turn, created the need for different market strategies. Traditionally, market analysts and traders and academic economists have paid little attention to each other. By the 1980s, however, the growing complexity of computerized exchanges and network technology made it necessary to develop mathematically sophisticated models and techniques for trading. As early as the 1950s, a new breed of academic economists began to formulate theories that three decades later seemed to be just what investors needed to manage risk. Though the close interrelation of markets, models, and computers appears to be a recent phenomenon, it can actually be traced to the origin of the computer. The structure of markets and the architecture of computers have always mirrored each other. The prototype of the modern computer was developed by Charles Babbage in the nineteenth century. Babbage invented a mechanical device called "the Difference Engine" to execute calculations previously done by women clerics known as computers. The inspiration for the structure and function of this early mechanical computer was borrowed from the principle of the division of labor, which Adam Smith developed to explain the operation of markets. As if to reverse process, late twentieth-century financial theorists understand markets as so-called difference engines, which function like information-processing machines.

For mathematically inclined economists, the privileged science has always been physics. In an effort to create models for managing risk, economists have used the physics of equilibrium systems and Brownian motion to develop a theory of the market as a random walk. Random processes are subject to the laws of probability and therefore are not completely uncertain or unpredictable. The physics of equilibrium systems and probability statistics contributed to the formulation of the efficient market hypothesis (EMH), which assumes that rational investors with equal access to information will create orderly markets that are not subject to catastrophic disruptions. As new products were marketed, financial economists developed theories, models, and computer programs for trading on increasingly interconnected markets. However, these developments created as many problems as they solved. Just as new financial products created to decrease risk increased volatility, so financial theories that were supposed to provide models for managing risk brought the global economy to the verge of meltdown in 1998. Multiple factors contributed to the reversal of economic fortunes in the closing years of the decade: unchecked financial speculation, the growing dot-com frenzy, and the world debt crisis. No less important, however, was the fact that the models and programs investors were using were better suited to the bipolar world that was passing away than to the interconnected world that is emerging. The mistakes financial economists made were philosophical as well as mathematical. Unlike Newton's rational world governed by the laws of equilibrium, the networked economy is not always rational and episodically tends toward disequilibrium, which results in unpredictable disruptions.

One of the most remarkable things about the 1990s is that so many people were so wrong about so much for so long. In retrospect, it seems painfully obvious that the reality of the emerging network economy completely disappeared in the abstract models driving many on Wall Street. The efficient market hypothesis was less the product of much-touted rea-

son than the expression of an understandable yet irrational desire for order in a world that seemed chaotic. As the world becomes increasingly volatile and uncertain, the longing for order, reason, and predictability grows.
In their effort to find order, economic theorists, financial analysts, and investors created the very disorder they feared. The failure of the huge hedge
fund, Long-Term Capital Management, with Nobel Prize–winning financial economists at its helm, revealed the new market dynamics that have
emerged in the past four decades. In chapter 8, "In-Securities," I draw on
recent work in the emerging field of complexity studies to develop a more
adequate model for understanding markets in a network economy. In contrast to the efficient market hypothesis, which presupposes negative feedback and automatically corrects imbalances and restores equilibrium,
complex adaptive systems also involve positive feedback, which can increase imbalances and can push markets far from equilibrium where unpredictable changes occur. Rather than occasional disruptions caused by
exogenous forces, intermittent instability and discontinuity are inherent
features of complex networks. Unlike isolated molecules, investors are interrelated agents whose interacting expectations make volatility unavoidable but not completely incomprehensible. When the economy is understood as a complex adaptive system, it appears to be a relational web in
which order and disorder emerge within and are not imposed from without. This picture of an emerging self-organizing system brings the argument full circle by returning to a version of the vision of the market first
proposed by Adam Smith when he used theology and aesthetics to rethink
economics. Just as Smith translated transcendent purpose into immanent
order, so current theorists suggest that markets are self-organizing systems
in which order emerges from the interactions of individual agents acting
in their own interests without any reliable understanding of the market as
a whole.

I conclude *Confidence Games* by returning to religion, which I never really leave. In chapter 1, I pointed out that during the 1960s and 1970s, conventional wisdom was that modernization always brought secularization
in its wake. By the late 1970s, it was becoming clear that, contrary to expectation, postmodernism and religion are inseparable.

In chapter 9, "Rustling Religion," I consider the reasons for and implications of the return of the religious. During the past two decades, the
spread of global capitalism has been accompanied by the rise of global
fundamentalism. Religious fundamentalism takes different forms in different historical, social, political, and cultural contexts. In the most general
terms, outside the United States, religious fundamentalism frequently pro-

vides a way to resist the expansion of global capitalism and American power, while within the U.S., religious fundamentalism tends to legitimize market fundamentalism and sanctify American power. In other words, religious neofundamentalism, political neoconservatism, and economic neoliberalism are closely related. After considering the rise of the religious right to a position of significant political power, I suggest an alternative understanding of the critical role of religion in contemporary society. Extending and expanding Paul Tillich's analysis in his well-known essay "Two Types of the Philosophy of Religion," I identify three types of the theology of culture—monistic, dualistic, and complex—which enable us to understand contrasting religious alternatives and their relation to corresponding artistic practices and currency regimes. Neofundamentalists East and West remain committed to closed dualistic ideologies, which are, in the final analysis, self-destructive. While new economic realities require new models of complex adaptive systems, overcoming the current religious and ideological impasse requires fashioning a religious, ethical, and political vision as complex as the world in which we find ourselves. Instead of providing certainty, clarity, and security, religion can engender creative uncertainty, which leaves things productively fuzzy. If reality turns out to be virtual, who can really be sure what is real and what is not? Far from posing a threat to be avoided, uncertainty and insecurity are traces of the openness of the future, which keeps desire in play. Life in all its complexity remains a confidence game in which the abiding challenge is not to find redemption but to learn to live without it.

1

PAPER TRAILS

—It's all over, he shuddered. —I swear, by all that's ugly it's done. But you

. . . He'd suddenly begun pinching up rolls of flesh on the back of one hand. —Why are you doing this to me? he demanded without looking up. —When you know it doesn't exist? to ask me to copy it? Like he . . . restoring an empty canvas, yes. He scratched me a bit, I'll tell you. Until today, God! that damned table. God's watching? Invidia, I was brought up eating my meals off envy, until today. And it was false all the time! He spoke with more effort than he had yet made to control his voice. —Copying a copy? is that where I started? All my life I've sworn it was real, year after year, that damned table top floating in the bottom of the tank, I've sworn it was real, and today? A child could tell it's a copy, he broke off, wrenching at the folds of flesh and veins on his hand, and he dared look up.

Valentine was watching him closely, the watery blue of his own eyes hardened, the narrowed lids sharpening interest into scrutiny: he saw what appeared as a weak attempt at a smile, but no more, a quirk on that face and it was gone while the voice picked up again. —Now if there was no gold? . . . continuing an effort to assemble a pattern from breakage where the features had failed. —And if what I've been forging, does not exist? And if I . . . if I, I . . .

William Gaddis, *The Recognitions*

COUNTERFEIT DETECTORS ⟩   In 1955, William Gaddis published *The Recognitions*. This important, though much overlooked, novel can be read as a prescient parable of our time. While critics initially dismissed it as "unreadable," Gaddis's work could not have been more timely for understanding postwar America. If *The Recognitions* is unreadable, it is unreadable in the same way *Finnegans Wake* is. Indeed, it is no exaggeration to say that Gaddis has done for postmodernism what Joyce did for modernism. What makes this accomplishment all the more astonishing is that Gaddis developed his analysis *before* postmodernism actually emerged. *The Recognitions* is long, difficult, and complex—but no more so than the era whose shifting currents it attempts to fathom. Not until the publication of *JR* twenty years later did Gaddis's work begin to receive some of the critical attention and acclaim it deserves. There is no better perspective from which to approach developments during the last half of the twentieth century than these two demanding novels.

Gaddis's remarkable work presents a penetrating interpretation of the intricate interrelation of religion, art, and economics. From Gaddis's perspective, it is impossible to comprehend the profound social and cultural transformations that accompany modernity without an appreciation for how art first displaces religion and then both art and religion are subsumed by market forces. The title of the book is borrowed from an unlikely source—a work by Clement of Rome, the second-century bishop and theologian. The novel is filled with lengthy theological and philosophical debates ranging from Plato, Aristotle, Origen, and Augustine to Aquinas, Calvin, Marx, and Nietzsche. References to a virtual pantheon of gods—Hermes, Hercules, Gaia, Dionysus, Osiris, Marduk, Brahma, Vishnu, Siva—as well as religious traditions East and West—Christianity, Judaism, Buddhism, Hinduism, Manichaeism—are scattered throughout the book. The names of many of the characters carry mythic and even theological overtones. The central figures in the drama are a Calvinist pastor—Reverend Gwyon—and his son Wyatt.[1] The opening lines of the book identify the themes that preoccupy Gaddis in all of his work. On All Saints' Day, Gwyon and his wife Camilla left their infant son in Protestant New England and set sail for Catholic Spain. When Camilla suffers an attack of appendicitis seven days later, the ship's surgeon botches the operation and she dies. The story begins with an account of Camilla's funeral procession.

> Even Camilla had enjoyed masquerades, of the safe sort where the mask
> may be dropped at that critical moment it presumes itself as reality. But
> the procession up the foreign hill, bounded by cypress trees, impelled
> by the monotone chanting of the priest and retarded by hesitations at
> the fourteen stations of the Cross . . . might have ruffled the shy counte-
> nance of her soul, if it had been discernible.[2]

The question Gaddis implicitly poses and relentlessly probes for the 956 pages that follow is whether there are masquerades in which the masks cannot be dropped because they have become indistinguishable from reality. Distraught by having to bury his wife in "Catholic soil," Gwyon searches until he at last finds a cemetery on the edge of a village named San Zwingli.[3] As Gwyon recounts the story of Camilla's death, he explains that the person to whom he had entrusted his wife's life actually "was not a surgeon at all" but a confidence man, Frank Sinisterra (a sinister character who is anything but frank), who "was a fugitive, traveling under what, at the time of his departure, had seemed the most logical of desperate expedients: a set of false papers he had printed himself. (He had done this work with the same artistic attention to detail that he gave to banknotes, even to using Rembrandt's formula for the wax ground on his copper plate)" (5). This fatal encounter with a counterfeiter and forger shakes Gwyon's faith in both God and his fellow man so much that he retreats to a Catholic monastery, where he reads and meditates until he feels ready to return to the United States and once again take up his ministerial responsibilities. When he finally arrives back in New England, his bags are packed with "un-Protestant" relics and his head filled with "pagan" myths. The change in Gwyon is immediately evident to his parishioners: his sermons, sprinkled with allusions to the strange myths and rituals of so-called "primitive religions," become more and more bizarre. When Gwyon eventually mimics the Crucifixion by performing a ritual sacrifice of an ape he had brought back from Europe, the congregation finally loses patience and insists on his institutionalization.

Throughout his youth, Gwyon's son, Wyatt, copes with his father's growing madness by withdrawing into the world of his own. A gifted artist, Wyatt spends hours studying painting and doing drawings by copying images from the books in his father's library. While Wyatt's preoccupation with art seems to be a quiet rebellion against the austere world embodied in his Aunt May, he actually accepts, without fully understanding, the prohibitions with which Calvinism supposedly surrounds art. According to Gwyon, "the romantic disease of originality" is the work of the Devil through which man attempts to take the place of God. Since God is the sole creator, human creativity is sin; art is acceptable only if it is not original. Wyatt manages to pursue his artistic vocation without violating his aunt's theological prohibitions by making copies of copies, which, he insists, have no originality. In these images of images, the original is never present but is always missing.

Though he finds "the Christian system suspect," Wyatt follows his father and grandfather to divinity school. But he does not last long and soon flees to Paris and settles in an area where "activity centered around the stock exchange" (21, 67). He supports himself by restoring the deteriorating works of medieval masters. As word of Wyatt's consummate skill quickly spreads throughout the city, it draws the attention of an entrepreneurial art forger, Recktall Brown, whose scatological name suggests Freud's association of money and excrement. Attempting to disabuse Wyatt of any lingering romantic notions of art's redemptive power, Brown insists that art is, in the final analysis, about money—nothing more and nothing less.

> —I talk business to people. Recktall Brown drew heavily on his cigar, watched the cigarette stamped out, the brandy finished.
> —But . . . you're talking to me. You're listening to me.
> —We're talking business, Recktall Brown said calmly.
> —But . . .
> —People work for money, my boy.
> —But I . . .
> —Money gives significance to anything.
> —Yes. People believe that, don't they. People believe that.
> Rectall Brown watched patiently, like someone waiting for a child to solve a simple problem to which there was only one answer. The ciga-

rette, like across from him, knit them together in the different textures
of their smoke.

—You know . . . Saint Paul tells us to redeem time.

—Does he? Rectall Brown's tone was gentle, encouraging.

—A work of art redeems time.

—And buying it redeems money, Recktall Brown said. (144)

For Gaddis, a world in which the only redemptive power is money is a
world without redemption.

Whether as the result of financial exigencies or a complete loss of faith,
Wyatt eventually cuts a deal with Brown to produce forgeries of Flemish
masterpieces. Wyatt's fakes are so convincing that the forgery business
quickly becomes profitable. As the enterprise continues to thrive, it becomes apparent that art forgery is not the only game in town. Fakes and
counterfeits of all kinds proliferate until it is impossible to tell what is real
and what is not. At one point, one of the characters observes that con men
had gone so far as "counterfeiting poker chips, to be cashed in gambling
palaces" in the capital of faux—Las Vegas (946). Halfway through this
enormous novel, Frank Sinisterra reappears.

> Mr. Sinisterra kept his copy of Bicknall's *Counterfeit Detector* for 1839
> as a professional curiosity, much as a noted surgeon may exhibit a copy
> of Galen's *Anatomy*. And just as the noted cardiac surgeon may admire
> Galen's discovery that the arteries contain blood . . . so Mr. Sinisterra
> mused over the ingenious devices of the century before him in Bick-
> nall's, which listed 20 issues of money on fictitious banks, 43 banks
> whose notes were worthless, 54 banks which were bankrupt, 254 banks
> whose notes were counterfeited, and 1395 varieties of counterfeit notes
> in circulation. Thus he was becoming proud of his tradition, which he
> had brought to the land of opportunity to exercise in the early part of
> the century, when the proportion of Italians to immigrants from less
> imaginative lands was about five to one: he whose consecration had
> helped to raise New York to its present reputation for being the greatest
> modern center of counterfeiting money of every currency in the world.[4]

Frank Sinisterra is the dark double of another confidence man, Frank Goodman, who plays an important role in Hermann Melville's *The Confidence-
Man: His Masquerade,* published, not insignificantly, April 1, 1857.[5] From
the opening sentence of Gaddis's work, echoes of Melville's masquerade re-
sound throughout *The Recognitions.*

The distance between Melville's New York of the 1850s to Gaddis's New York of the 1950s is not as great as it initially seems. Indeed, the world Melville imagines in 1857 has become a reality by 1955. The year 1857 marked a turning point in Melville's life. Though he had suffered depression for many years, his mental condition steadily worsened during the months he was completing *The Confidence-Man.* The anchors mooring his fragile mind seemed to vanish, leaving him floating as freely as the beguiled passengers aboard the Fidèle, whose meanderings Melville's tale follows. The crisis Melville was undergoing was simultaneously religious, artistic, and economic. Long haunted by a God who is inescapable yet inaccessible, Melville transformed his religious doubt into an artistic quest. The sea became his library, literature his scripture. His early works *Typée* (1846) and *Omoo* (1847) were travel tales mixing fact and fantasy, which brought him considerable fame and were financially profitable. Popularity, however, proved to be a curse. As his concerns grew more serious, his fiction became less popular. Responding to pressure from publishers, Melville, like Edgar Allan Poe, attempted to write double-coded narratives in which popular adventure stories asked serious philosophical and spiritual questions. When these works were neither critically nor financially successful, Melville began to doubt his artistic ability and finally gave up the hope of making a living by writing. With the exception of several volumes of poetry, *The Confidence-Man* was the last work he published.[6] After moving from Arrowhead in the Berkshires to New York City, he labored anonymously as a customs inspector in the New York Custom House. When he died in 1891, the country had literally forgotten his name.[7] For the last thirty-four years of his life, America's greatest writer remained wrapped in silence.

For Melville, money was more than a practical interest. With the country standing on the cusp of an agrarian past and an industrial future, he realized the far-reaching implications of the economic transformation the country was undergoing. The prism through which he viewed the problem of theological and artistic representation was the question of paper currency. While paper money first appeared in China in 910 CE and various European countries briefly experimented with it, America was the first country where it gained wide acceptance. From colonial times, the issue of paper currency has been a highly charged political issue that separates people with different economic interests. In 1751, England passed the Currency Act, prohibiting New England colonies from issuing bills of credit. This ban was extended to all the colonies in 1764. It remained a source of conflict after independence, bursting into violence in Shays's

Rebellion in Massachusetts (1786–87).[8] By the mid-1780s, seven states were issuing paper money. Debtors, many of whom were farmers, tended to favor paper money because it made credit cheaper and created inflation, which enabled them to repay loans with less valuable money. Creditors, by contrast, opposed cheap credit and feared inflation because it eroded their wealth. (In some cases, of course, farmers were also creditors with contradictory interests. In the following chapters, we will see that the conflict between debtors and creditors was largely responsible for the decisive policy changes enacted by the Federal Reserve Bank in 1979, which, among other things, created the conditions for the bull market of the 1980s and 1990s.) Throughout the 1820s and 1830s, soft money grew rapidly. Private banks and insurance companies were largely unregulated and freely issued different forms of paper currency whose value fluctuated wildly. As a result of these economic uncertainties, debate about the gold standard raged from 1825 to 1875. When efforts to curb or prohibit paper currency failed, the expanding economy of the 1850s combined with growing industrialization to create irresistible pressure on the United States government to expand the money supply by printing currency. On February 25, 1862, Congress authorized the "issuance of notes that were lawful money and legal tender in the payment of all debts public and private."[9] These notes, known as greenbacks, were not convertible to gold or specie and in fact were backed by nothing other than the word of the government. The value of this paper currency was created by something like a performative utterance proffered by Congress and sustained by the confidence of people who used the money. In the absence of gold, the economy was more than ever a matter of faith.

Melville was among the first to realize that the emerging industrial economy created a crisis of confidence, which reflected a crisis of representation, extending from religion and art to business and finance. When signs and symbols—be they monetary, religious, artistic—are no longer grounded in anything other than themselves, they become insubstantial and float freely in currents, which often become turbulent. Toward the end of Melville's cautionary tale, the confidence man appears in the guise of a cosmopolitan named Frank Goodman.[10] Descending below deck, Goodman stumbles on an old man anxiously reading the Bible while hoarding his money. As he is about to engage the miser in conversation, the cosmopolitan is interrupted by a *marchand* selling wares designed to protect travelers' valuables. When the elderly man, frantic for anything that promises security, eagerly buys a money belt, the young peddler throws in as a bonus a copy of *Counterfeit Detector,* a magazine that enjoyed wide circu-

lation in Melville's day. With every imaginable forgery circulating throughout the latter-day ship of fools, the miser tries to use the counterfeit detector to distinguish real from fake currency. But the signs are not clear and
he quickly drifts into doubt.

> "I don't know, I don't know," returned the old man, perplexed, "there's
> so many marks of all sorts to go by, it makes it a kind of uncertain. Here,
> now, is this bill," touching one, "it looks to be a three dollar bill on the
> Vicksburgh Trust and Insurance Banking Company. Well, the Detector
> says—"
> "But why, in this case, care what it says? Trust and Insurance! What
> more would you have?"
> "No, but the Detector says, among fifty other things, that if a good
> bill, it must have, thickened here and there into the substance of paper,
> little wavy spots of red . . ."
> "Well, and it is—"
> "Stay. But then it adds, that sign is not always to be relied on; for
> some good bills get so worn the red marks get rubbed out. And that's the
> case with my bill here—see how old it is—or else it's a counterfeit, or
> else—I don't see right—or else—dear, dear me—I don't know what else
> to think."[11]

"So many marks of all sorts to go by, it makes it a kind of uncertain." *Inescapably uncertain.*

A century later, Melville's uncertainty becomes pandemic. Just as *The
Confidence-Man* presents an analysis of emerging industrial society and a
diagnosis of the perils of paper currency and all it does or does not represent, so *The Recognitions* and *JR* examine emerging network culture and
the uncertainties digital currencies and virtual capital engender. When
what we deem real is inaccessible, dead, or irretrievably lost, Melville and
Gaddis warn, all that remains is an "empire of signs" with "naught beyond." By the end of the second millennium, the capital of this virtual empire is New York City, where everything seems to have become a confidence game.

Gaddis shares Melville's uncertainty; *The Recognitions* remains "en-
gulfed in the sense of something lost" (821). Attempting to articulate this
lack, Wyatt explains to his lover, Esther:

> —There's always the sense, he went on,—the sense of recalling some-
> thing, of almost reaching it, and holding it . . . She leaned over to him,

her hand caught his wrist and the coal of tobacco flowed, burning his
fingers. In the darkness she did not notice.
—And then it's . . . escaped again. It's escaped again, and there's only a
sense of disappointment, of something irretrievably lost.
He raised his head.
—A cigarette, she said. C—Why do you always leave me so quickly af-
terward? Why do you always want a cigarette right afterward?
—Reality, he answered. (119)

Wyatt's answer is deliberately ambiguous: Is the cigarette reality or is reality what is always slipping away, leaving disappointment in its wake?
The issue is more than a matter of words—it is a matter of life and, it turns
out, death. What is not ambiguous is Gaddis's insistence that the only hope
for escaping our counterfeit world is to stop trading.

—You got to stop trading in some time. You trade in your goddam car
you trade in your goddam wife, and the minute you get used to the
goddam thing some bastard puts out a new model. Just go to the goddam bank. Eye-bank. Blood-bank. Bone-bank.
—That's a nice idea for a show. . . . C—Banks as a symbol of progress.
Money-banks. Bone-banks. Eye-banks. Blood-banks. (752)

But, of course, trading cannot be stopped; indeed, in the decades after the
publication of *The Recognitions,* not only did the regime of commodification expand to include religion, art, and even ideas, but new trading
networks accelerated exchange until speed seemed to become an end in
itself.

While *The Recognitions* stages a prolonged process of mourning the disappearance of what once seemed real, *JR* gives up nostalgia in all of its
guises and explores a world governed by floating signs and fungible currencies, where nothing is fixed and everything is in play. JR is an eleven-
year-old schoolboy who purchases and resells army surplus plastic forks
and, using phones and faxes, parlays his investment into a "paper empire,"
which grows to millions of dollars before it inevitably collapses. Though
only a child, he is a latter-day confidence man who shrewdly plays a confidence game that has become global. While we can never be sure whether
Melville's masks conceal a single impostor or many confidence men, Gaddis's novel consists entirely of conversations in which it is often difficult
or even impossible to be sure who is speaking. JR is supposed to be the
central character, but he is so lacking in substance that his personality and

masks become indistinguishable. This strangely characterless character reflects a new world disorder in which reality has dematerialized and has been dispersed through the invisible communication, entertainment, and financial networks transforming who we are and changing how we do business. Rather than the exception, recurrent crises of confidence in long-held beliefs and long-established institutions ranging from government, the press, and media to the church, markets, and financial institutions have become the rule. This loss of confidence is symptomatic of an often inconspicuous crisis of representation, which occurs when the referents that once provided secure foundations for thought and action are "liquefied" and begin to circulate freely in worldwide webs whose dynamics we do not yet understand.

DISPLACEMENTS) During the past thirty years, the pace of technological innovation has greatly accelerated processes of dematerialization and virtualization in all spheres of life. These changes have not emerged de novo, but are the culmination of developments that have been unfolding throughout the modern period. To understand the significance of what now is occurring, it is not sufficient to examine recent trends in business, finance, and technology; rather, we must follow the lead of Gaddis and Melville by exploring the intricate interplay of religion, art, and economics. Since the end of the nineteenth century, the history of Western culture has been characterized by a series of subtle displacements. Beginning with post-Kantian idealists and romantics in Europe and America, art began to displace religion as the focus and expression of spiritual aspiration. First literature and then the visual arts provoked the desire and fulfilled the need for order, meaning, and purpose that religion traditionally had satisfied. In ways that were not immediately obvious, these developments simultaneously reflected and promoted broader economic changes taking place at the time. Hegel was the first to recognize the complex interrelation of culture and history. His monumental philosophical system is best understood as a comprehensive philosophy of culture in which representations, ideas, and concepts influence and are influenced by history. Neither arbitrary nor directionless, the course of history, according to Hegel, follows a strict dialectical progression in which later stages bring to fruition and replace preceding stages. Within this trajectory, religion gives way to art, which, in turn, culminates in philosophy. Having become free from images and representations, philosophy brings nature, history, and self-consciousness to conceptual clarity and perfect transparency.

With four important modifications, Hegel's philosophy of culture still provides rich resources for understanding our era. First, instead of Hegel's dialectic of negation in which one stage replaces another, it is necessary to develop *dialectic without synthesis* in which later stages *displace without replacing* earlier stages. Rather than representing distinct historical moments, religion, art, and philosophy fold together in such a way that each shadows the other. The displaced does not disappear but is temporarily repressed and can always return to disrupt what seemed to have overcome it. Second, the course of history is not programmed or determined; on the contrary, temporal development is repeatedly interrupted by aleatory occurrences, which can be neither anticipated nor avoided. Third, the process of development is open rather than closed. History, therefore, does not come to an end but is an ongoing process of becoming, which is an end in itself. Finally, it is necessary to extend Hegel's analysis beyond religion, art, and philosophy to the domain of economics. Though anticipated in surprisingly similar ways in the eighteenth century by Adam Smith's musings on the beauty of markets and in the nineteenth century by Marx's analysis of art and money, economics does not actually displace religion and art until the last half of the twentieth century. In the 1960s, the so-called death of God creates the conditions for the correlative commodification of the work of art and aestheticization of commodities. As the business of art morphs into the art of business, capital is virtualized and a return of the displaced becomes all but inevitable.

The 1960s marked a decisive turning point in American history as well as Western society and culture as a whole. In the two decades following World War II, America became the acknowledged military and economic leader of the Western world. The conversion from a wartime to a consumer economy created unprecedented prosperity throughout the 1950s. By the 1960s, however, things were rapidly changing at home and abroad. The civil rights movement and widespread opposition to the Vietnam war fueled unprecedented social unrest. The much-maligned counterculture of the 1960s was, for many who participated in it, a critical response to a country that seemed to have forgotten its founding values and thus to have lost its way. It is no exaggeration to say that the past four decades are in large measure simultaneously an extension of and a reaction to the turbulence of the 1960s.

Though less often noted than these important social, political, and cultural currents, developments in economics and technology were unfolding during the 1960s and 1970s, which, in retrospect, have proven to be even more decisive for our era. This is not to imply, of course, that economics and technology can be separated from broader social and cultural trajectories; on the contrary, I will attempt to show how cultural, economic, and technological threads have been woven together to fashion the tapestry of contemporary experience. By the late 1960s, tensions between domestic and foreign policies combined to create an economic crisis, which has had lasting effects. Throughout the Johnson years, the financial strain resulting from the effort to fund both extensive Great Society programs and the expanding war in Vietnam led to growing inflation, a weakening dollar, and an extended bear market that made the boom days of the 1950s little more than a distant memory. The transition from the financial disarray of the late 1960s and early 1970s to the booming economy of the 1980s and 1990s turns on events during two pivotal years: 1971 and 1979. In 1971, the Bretton Woods agreement, which had ensured the stability of the global economy since the end of World War II, broke down. In an unrelated event that anticipated things to come, NASDAQ (National Association of Securities Dealers Automated Quote System) introduced the first computerized system for stock prices the same year (I will consider the history and significance of NASDAQ in chapter 4). While the use of computers in financial markets was not widespread until the end of the decade, the impact of the end of Bretton Woods was immediate. With the economy in steep decline, President Nixon suspended the convertibility of the dollar to gold in August of 1971 and, after a period of fixed exchange rates, allowed the dollar to float in relation to other currencies. This action, which transformed the global economy, marked the end of the postwar era and contributed significantly to creating the conditions for the excesses of the 1980s and 1990s. In the absence of either the gold standard or fixed exchange rates, markets were suddenly subjected to a new volatility, which required novel financial products and strategies. Nixon's economic reforms did not, however, restore the health of the American economy. Throughout the 1970s inflation and unemployment remained stubbornly high. Economic policy continued to be governed by more or less orthodox Keynesian theory. By the end of the decade, it was clear that this approach was not working. Thus, on October 6, 1979, Paul Volcker, chairman of the Federal Reserve Board, announced a policy shift that played a significant role in shaping the economic climate for the next two decades. In an effort to slow inflation, the Fed now would attempt to control the money supply more closely and would allow market forces to determine interest rates. The predictable result was a rapid rise in interest rates. This change in policy had important implications for people who held financial assets. Since bond prices go down as interest rates go up, institutions and individuals who had loaned money in the form of buying bonds or fixed rate mortgages *before* the Fed's decision suffered considerably. However, anyone who loaned money *after* October 6 reaped much higher profits. In the long run, the net effect of the Fed's decision was a major tilt in favor of people and institutions with significant financial assets. By 1982, inflation was under control and the longest bull market in the nation's history had begun.

These developments alone would not, however, have brought about the economic changes that have occurred in the past thirty years. No less important was the technological revolution in the computer and communications industries. New technologies have become so ubiquitous that it is easy to forget how recent they are. In the last three decades, technological developments have created a new infrastructure, which has transformed the entire economic landscape. Far from merely allowing old business to be done differently, computers, communications networks, and new financial instruments and procedures enter into a coevolutionary process that continues to accelerate. These complex dynamics shaped the critical intersection of technological change and economic policy that occurred in 1973. The same year Bretton Woods completely dissolved, Reuters introduced the first system for automated electronic currency trading. With the end of the gold standard, the creation of NASDAQ, and the beginning of electronic trading systems, the necessary pieces are in place for the unprecedented expansion of the global economy. Commentators and critics frequently describe these changes in terms of the transition from an industrial to a postindustrial economy or from a manufacturing to an information economy. For reasons that will become clear in the course of the analysis, this new situation is better understood in terms of an *emerging network economy.*

Economic and technological transformations never take place in a vacuum but are closely related to broad cultural changes. The shift from an industrial to a network economy coincides with the transition from modernism to postmodernism in the arts, architecture, literature, philosophy, and religion. This is not to suggest that culture is merely the superficial effect of deeper economic and technological transformations. On the contrary, in a network economy where information is the currency of the realm, it is no longer possible to separate infrastructure and superstructure in a way that allows reductive analysis. Cultural and economic processes are tangled in negative and positive feedback loops of mutual determination. The recognition of the interplay between economics and culture is not, of course, new. Max Weber and R. H. Tawney, for example, long ago stressed the importance of Protestantism for the rise of capitalism. More recently, cultural critics like Fredric Jameson, Antonio Negri, and Michael Hardt have argued that postmodernism is a symptom of so-called late capitalism.[12] Though differing in subtle ways, these contemporary critics share a Marxist perspective in which cultural processes can always be reduced to a supposedly material economic base. This approach has been very influential but suffers from two fatal flaws. First, while claiming that economic factors determine cultural production, these critics do not analyze the distinctive characteristics of the new network economy. Indeed, they offer surprisingly little discussion of anything having to do with actual economic processes. Their theoretical perspective rests on industrial models that are as outdated as the neo-Marxist ideology they promote. Second, these critics do not adequately explore the ways in which culture—art, philosophy, and especially religion—shapes economic realities. This is a crippling oversight when investigating a situation they admit is postindustrial. In today's network economy, infrastructure and superstructure both consist of recodable bits circulating through distributed networks. To understand how the network economy operates, it is as important to probe the ways in which cultural symbols and practices influence economic activity as it is to consider how economic policies and procedures condition culture.

If, as I have argued, there is a quasi-dialectical relation among religion, art, and economics, then grasping the dynamics of the new network economy presupposes an appreciation of the role of both religion and art in contemporary life. In chapters 2 and 3, I will examine the ways in which theological ideas have shaped the development of capitalism as well as some of the most influential theories of money and markets.[13] I will return to the issue of religion in the final chapter where I consider different forms of faith in contemporary network culture. As we begin this investigation, it is important to recall that the 1960s was the era of the so-called death of God and the secular city.[14] For theologians as well as psychologists, sociologists, and anthropologists, secularization appeared to be an inescapable by-product of modernization. Furthermore, these analysts argued that the interrelated processes of modernization and secularization are irreversible. Religion appeared to be a primitive vestige that modern people and societies inevitably would leave behind. It is now obvious that this line of analysis is completely wrong: religion *never* disappears. When seemingly absent, religion actually takes different forms, which often are unrecognizable to traditionalists. Since proponents of the secularization theory had a limited understanding of religion, they were not able to understand emerging alternative forms of spirituality and could not appreciate the complicated ways in which religion indirectly informs all culture and society.

By the late 1970s, the religious landscape, like the political and economic climate, had changed significantly. For the past two decades, the social and political power of religion has been growing so fast in many traditions throughout the world that it is no exaggeration to insist that what is occurring is a *global religious revival.* The timing of this revival is hardly accidental. In this country, the resurgence of religion begins at the precise moment when the economic reforms that prepared the way for the explosive growth of global capitalism were enacted. Global capitalism, in other words, is inseparable from a global religious revival. It is important to note that the religion that appears in the late 1970s differs significantly from the liberal Christianity that inspired the civil rights and antiwar movements in the 1960s. For the past twenty-five years, the fastest growing religions in the United States as well as other countries have been conservative if not fundamentalist. There is, however, a critical difference in the relation of religion, politics, and economics within and beyond U.S. borders. For many people living outside the United States and Europe, Westernization and modernization pose threats to personal, national, and cultural identity. In this situation, conservative or even fundamentalist religion often becomes a strategy to resist global capitalism and all it represents. In the United States, by contrast, conservative religion is commonly used to promote the spread of global capitalism. As we will see, the economic developments of the 1980s and 1990s would not have been possible without a shift to a neoconservative political agenda and neoliberal economic policies. To the conservatives of the 1980s, the liberalism of the 1960s entailed a relativism and nihilism whose lingering vestiges had to be purged. This conflict of values led to culture wars pitting self-proclaimed defenders of the Western tradition against proponents of one or another version of postmodernism. In the heat of the debate, neither side recognized the contradictions in its own position. On the one hand, postmodernists did not understand the ways in which their theories and practices grew out of and actually promoted the very economic system they so strongly resisted. On the other hand, religious and political conservatives did not grasp how their economic policies undercut their cultural agenda and advanced the cause of the postmodernism they so abhorred. After tracing the displacement of religion by art and then the displacement of art by economics, I will return to religion. Religion, like money and markets, we will discover, is an artful confidence game.

CURRENCY OF ART)   In 1978, Joseph Beuys, the most Hegelian artist of the twentieth century, wrote an essay entitled "What Is Capital?" in which he comments: "But what is capital? I deduce that it can only be a question of human abilities. The expanded concept of 'art' is the concrete concept of 'capital': art = capital"[15] (figure 1).

From Duchamp's *Tzanck Check* to Boggs's bills, artists have struggled to figure the relation between art and money. The more one examines this tangled interplay, the clearer it becomes that art and capital are caught in a thoroughly ambivalent relationship throughout the modern era. The very notion of fine or high art does not emerge until the end of the eighteenth century. With the collapse of the patronage system, artists had to support themselves by producing works for the newly emerging art market. But art created for profit was not regarded as true art. Far from being useful, genuine art, many believed, was produced primarily for the enjoyment of other artists and had to remain "untainted" by market forces. This view of art was given its classical formulation in Kant's account of beauty in his *Critique of Judgment* (1790). The structure of the beautiful work of art, as Kant defines it, informs the influential doctrine of *l'art pour l'art,* which guides the theories of many critics and practices of many artists throughout the twentieth century. There are, however, other currents circulating in Kant's ideas that complicate the relation between art and capital. As we will see in chapter 3, Marx reads Kant's notion of the beautiful through Hegel's account of spirit to formulate an interpretation of money and capital in which religion, art, and economics intersect in unexpected ways.

Figure 1
Joseph Beuys, *Art = Capital (Kunst = Kapital).* © 2004 Artists Rights Society (ARS), New York / VG Bild-Kunst, Bonn.

What Marx anticipates becomes an economic and cultural reality a century later.

By the middle of the twentieth century, consumer culture and art had
become thoroughly entangled. With characteristic insight and wit, Andy
Warhol declared, "All department stores will become museums and all
museums will become department stores."[16] William Leach's survey of
shopping suggests that Warhol's comment is actually more of a historical
observation than a prediction: "it was in department stores, not museums
that modern art and American art found their first true patrons."

> The Gimbel brothers, inspired by the Armory Show of 1913, became
> among the most ardent supporters of modern art, buying up Cezannes,
> Picassos, and Braques, and displaying them in the store galleries in
> Cincinnati, New York, Cleveland, and Philadelphia. . . . John Wanamaker,
> the man most apt to advertise his stores as "public institutions," was, not
> surprisingly, also the most innovative merchant of all in his display of
> art. He deplored the way museums jumbled pictures together "on walls,
> destroying the effects of the finest things," and month after month, to
> sustain customer interest, rotated his personal collection for the "studio"
> in Philadelphia—a Constable here, a Reynolds there, to say nothing of a
> Titian or a Turner, a Wanamaker favorite—to his New York store and
> back again.[17]

The association between art and department stores dates back to the nineteenth century. The transformation of separate shops, enclosed by the
iron-and-glass architecture of the arcades, into department stores created
what Walter Benjamin, following Louis Philippe, labeled "temples of commodity capital."[18] The Paris opening of Bon Marché, designed by L. C.
Boileu and Gustav Eiffel in 1852, marked a new chapter in the economic
history of the West. Five years later, Macy's opened in the United States.
These stores and their new marketing strategies were the result of the need
for mass production to create mass consumption.

In addition to print media, department stores used the latest technology to fashion elaborate display windows for experimental designs.
Though windows filled with commodities began to appear in the United
States as early as the 1840s, it was not until after the turn of the century
that window display became an art. From 1897 to 1902, L. Frank Baum,
who published *The Wizard of Oz* in 1900, edited a highly influential
monthly journal entitled *The Show Window,* whose primary purpose was
to advance the "arts of decoration and display." Using mechanical devices

and electrical technology, Baum sought to create spectacular displays that, in his own words, would "arouse in the observer the cupidity and longing to possess the goods."[19]

As window dressers developed their art, they often entered into collaborative relations with museums and employed artists to create enticing displays. There is, of course, a long history of cooperation among modern art, industry, and commerce. During both its European and its American phases, the Bauhaus was dedicated to fostering collaboration between art and industry. Russian Constructivism, as well as the Werkbund and de Stijl, also sought to bridge the worlds of art and business. In the United States, John Dewey promoted an "arts-in-industry" movement, which contributed to the establishment of the Pratt Institute and the New York School of Fine and Applied Arts, later the Parsons School, where commercial art was taught after 1900.[20] Such alliances were not limited to applied and commercial arts. Many of the great modern museums were created by successful capitalists: the Brooklyn Museum, the Newark Museum, the Metropolitan Museum of Art, the Museum of Modern Art, and the Guggenheim were all established and endowed by wealthy businesspeople. Without denying patrons' interest in art, it is clear that in many cases, supporting museums was good business. The prestigious Metropolitan Museum of Art, for example, exercised considerable influence in industrial design. In 1914, the Met hired Richard Bach to fill the newly created position of associate in industrial arts. Under Bach's leadership, the Met established a design service and created workshops and laboratories for the development of commercial products. In 1927, the Met cosponsored the first Macy's Exposition devoted to a consideration of the impact of modern art on industrial design.

The collaboration between art and commerce extended from institutional arrangements to individual artists and commissions. In addition to exhibiting art created in the studio, stores also employed artists to develop new work for their windows. While in most cases window designers remained anonymous, it was not uncommon for established artists to do store windows. In her insightful and beautifully illustrated study, *Windows: The Art of Retail Design,* Mary Portas claims that "it was Salvador Dalí who really made shop windows respectable."[21] As window designs became more sophisticated, the line separating high and low, fine art and commercial art, artist and artisan, and art and business became more obscure. The two most important twentieth-century window designers in the United States were Gene Moore, who is best known for his work at Tiffany's, and Simon Doonan, who transformed Barneys in the 1980s and

1990s. The careers of some of the most important artists of the last half of the twentieth century were launched in Moore's windows. The first exhibitions of the paintings of Warhol and Johns as well as works by Rauschenberg and Rosenquist were in Moore's windows at Bonwit Teller (figure 2). Tiffany's, however, is where Moore really made a name for himself. Well into the 1950s, Tiffany's remained a paragon of "good taste" and conservative design. When Walter Hoving took control of Tiffany's in 1955, the store's approach to advertising and marketing changed dramatically. Hoving was the father of Thomas Hoving, who, as the director of the Met, would revolutionize the museum world in the 1970s with commercial marketing practices first developed at Tiffany's. One of Walter Hoving's first moves was to hire Gene Moore to create window designs that would transform Tiffany's and in the process change retail practices throughout the commercial world.

Faced with a daunting challenge, Moore turned to artists with whom he had worked in the past. Warhol, Johns, Rauschenberg, and Rosenquist followed Moore to Tiffany's. With their help and contributions from many lesser-known designers and artists, Moore made store windows integral to the Tiffany's brand. Though Warhol drew no distinction between his commercial and fine art, Johns and Rauschenberg always did window displays under the shared pseudonym of Matson Jones. Moore's collaboration with

Figure 2
Andy Warhol, window display at Bonwit Teller, New York, 1961. © 2003 Andy Warhol Foundation for the Visual Arts / Artists Rights Society (ARS), New York.

artists confirmed Warhol's view of the relation between department stores and museums. While Warhol transformed the store window into a museum, Thomas Hoving converted the museum into a store window. After taking over the Met, Hoving invited his father's famous window designer to create displays for the museum.

The only window designer who comes close to Moore's commercial importance and artistic influence is Simon Doonan. Doonan left the Metropolitan Museum of Art's Costume Institute to join Barneys in 1986. Throughout the 1980s Barneys literally provided a window on the relationship between business and the postmodern art world. During this era of recycled images, fashionable art, and celebrity designers, the stock market and the art market followed the same curve. Art became a profitable investment for people with excessive money made in the market. Riding the wave of the 1980s art boom, Doonan created unrivaled display windows that in many cases were more creative and provocative than the art in downtown galleries and uptown museums. In addition to his experience at the Met, Doonan brought with him a history of West-coast design, which drew on the dark side of LA life, as well as a fascination with the excesses of punk culture.

Barneys was founded by Barney Pressman in the 1930s as a men's and boy's discount clothing store in New York's Hell's Kitchen. With each succeeding generation of Pressmans, Barneys became more upscale. Barney's son, Fred, introduced American men to designer clothing: Givenchy, Chardin, and, most important, Giorgio Armani. Joshua Levine, who chronicles the store's history in *The Rise and Fall of the House of Barneys,* claims that Fred Pressman "discovered Giorgio Armani." Though the relationship eventually dissolved in contentious litigation, Barneys and Armani never would have become what they did without each other. When Gene Pressman took over from his father, Fred, his ambition was nothing less than to transform Barneys into a new Bauhaus.

Outdoing postmodern artists, Barneys' designers borrowed the strategy of appropriation to create windows, which quickly became indistinguishable from the work displayed in nearby galleries. Eagerly promoting business as art and art as business, Doonan explains:

> I became an enthusiastic proponent of this entente cordiale between art and commerce and regularly invited artists either to create their own installations or to loan individual pieces for window-display purposes. Sandy Skogland, Josh Gosfield, Annette Lemieux, Duane Michaels, Candyass, David Seidner, Konstantin Kakanias, and Michael Byron all de-

signed entire installations from scratch. Countless others loaned art or participated in group installations, into which clothing was thrown.[22]

Even more important than the cooperation between business and art was the buzz generated by Doonan's ability to make Barneys part of the downtown art scene and the celebrity culture surrounding it (figure 3). His calculated strategy was enormously successful: "It was not just the physical plant that made Barneys groovy. The downtown location of the original store gave Barneys an art world alliance not shared by any of the snooty uptown competition; Ross Bleckner and Jean-Michel Basquiat were not shopping at Lord & Taylor. Given the proximity to arty SoHo, it was inevitable that downtown Barneys would become the eighties art boom headquarters for artists who were starting to make money and wanted to look spiffy."[23]

As the economy soared and the art market boomed, artists were caught up in a culture of celebrity greater than anything Warhol ever imagined. Artists became media stars whose personae created the market value of their work. The aura spread from person to artwork; bad art by big names brought excessive prices. As the stakes of the game escalated, even collectors became celebrities courted by the media and featured in glossy magazines. With the market expanding faster than the capacity for production,

Figure 3
Window display at Barneys. From Simon Doonan, *Confessions of a Window Dresser* (New York: Penguin, 1998). Courtesy of Barneys New York.

artists scrambled to meet consumer demand. When originals could not be produced fast enough, many artists followed the lead of architects like Frank Gehry and Michael Graves and began to create a variety of reproducible products that could be marketed in high-end stores and retail outlets. Though highly prized and priced at the time, these works proved to be the junk bonds of the art world. Yet such outlandish excesses only seemed to increase the aura of Barneys, and the enterprise continued to grow (figure 4).

Expansion, like the fashionable art fueling it, had become an end in itself. In 1993, Barney Pressman's discount clothing store moved from Hell's Kitchen to Madison Avenue and Fifty-seventh Street, which at the time was about the most expensive real estate in the world. A year later, Barneys, having also become a leader in women's fashion, invaded the west coast by opening a luxurious store in Beverly Hills. Expressing supreme confidence in this moment of triumph, Doonan summed up the Barneys revolution with words as over-the-top as his window designs: "The unapologetically hip luxe of the Barneys image has redefined high-end retailing without precedent. . . .The cognoscenti grooviness of the original Barneys store has become an axiom for hip consumerism; if a character in a movie needs to look upscale and trendy, they dress him from Barneys, and then shove a Barneys bag into his hand."[24] Less than two years later, the house of Barneys collapsed: on January 11, 1996, the owners filed for bankruptcy. Like companies financed by junk bonds and Internet companies that produced nothing, Barneys proved to be a speculative house of cards without a secure foundation.

Doonan concludes his revealing memoir with an homage to the person he dubs "the patron saint of window dressing"—Andy Warhol. Whether or not he deliberately followed Warhol's script, Doonan surely subscribed to his gospel: "Being good in business is the most fascinating kind of art."[25] Throughout the late 1980s and early 1990s, Barneys and artists formed an alliance that was mutually profitable. In 1989, two years after Warhol's death, the Andy Warhol Museum organized an exhibition, "The Warhol Look," which included an extensive section devoted to his work as a window dresser. When this exhibition traveled to the Whitney Museum, on Madison Avenue a few blocks north of Barneys, the acceptance of the alliance between art and business seemed complete.

Not everyone, of course, agreed with Warhol's promotion of the art market. In the years following the end of the Second World War, the center of the art world, like the center of the financial universe, shifted to New York City. During the war, many leading European artists fled to the United

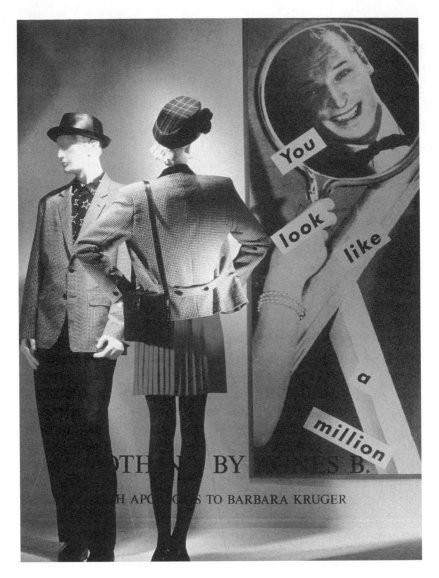

Figure 4
Window display at Barneys. From Simon Doonan, *Confessions of a Window Dresser* (New York: Penguin, 1998). Courtesy of Barneys New York.

States. As American artists mingled with European masters, they gradually overcame the anxiety of influence and began to stake out a distinctively American art, whose guiding principle was a deep commitment to human freedom and individual expression. The search for artistic identity and cultural autonomy received unexpected support from the federal government. Concerned about the spread of communism, the United States Information Service enlisted the support of artists by subsidizing their work and sponsoring exhibitions. In ways that rarely were obvious, art and culture promoted "the American way of life" at home and abroad.

The critic most closely associated with the quest for a uniquely American art is Clement Greenberg. Paradoxically, Greenberg turned to Europe for his definition of modernism. Citing Kant, Greenberg declared, "The essence of Modernism lies, as I see it, in the use of characteristic methods of a discipline to criticize the discipline itself, not in order to subvert it but in order to entrench it more firmly in its area of competence."[26] From this point of view, modern art is self-critical and thus reflexive or self-referential. Art, in other words, is about art. Instead of representing the world or anything else, art, in the strict sense of the term, refers to other art. Armed with this understanding of art, Greenberg proceeded to construct a teleological narrative of the history of art. From its earliest beginnings, art steadily moves toward ever greater formalism and increasing abstraction, which culminates in midcentury American art—particularly Abstract Expressionism. In his highly informative study of American art and Cold War politics, Serge Guilbaut effectively summarizes Greenberg's conclusion.

> American art was described as the logical culmination of a long-standing and inexorable tendency toward abstraction. Once American culture was raised to the status of an international model, the significance of what was specifically American had to change: what had been characteristically American now became representative of "Western Culture" as a whole. In this way American art was transformed from regional to international art and then to universal art.[27]

At this point, art history and criticism become indistinguishable from the government's expansionist cultural policy. Art not only reflects but actually promotes America's global power.

Greenberg's critical position harbors contradictions that, though not immediately recognized, largely determined the course of artistic developments during the middle decades of the twentieth century. In the late

1940s and 1950s, his campaign on behalf of American artists combined with the rapid expansion of the New York gallery system to draw so-called high art into the very market system from which Greenberg had sought to protect it. The postwar economic boom quickly raised the standard of living for the American middle class. With social distinctions becoming harder to draw, intellectuals and leftists formed an unexpected alliance with the so-called upper class by turning to the works of the artistic avant-garde for cultural markers that would set them apart from the supposedly unsophisticated masses. Advertisements in fashionable publications like *Partisan Review* transformed high art into an unmistakable sign of a particular life style. Commenting on an ad for engravings by Pollock and Gottlieb, Guilbaut writes:

> The text was directed at wealthy, modern-minded clients interested in luxury living and hence in the work of the avant-garde, in what was unusual and out of the ordinary. The avant-garde was used in this case as a marketing asset, a mark of difference. In the eyes of the public and the company that paid for the ads, the unusual stood for escape, for access to a higher rung of the social hierarchy. For example, the Pollock engraving became identified with the social position of the people for whom the homes being advertised were intended. These were exclusive homes for those who sought to distinguish themselves from the mass of "housing developments" . . . then burgeoning in the suburbs to accommodate the growing middle class.[28]

Though intended to confer social status, the purchase and display of "advanced" art is but another example of the conspicuous consumption characteristic of postwar consumer culture. Works dubbed high art are not free from market forces but are merely one more commodity to be consumed.

As might be expected, many artists saw the commodification of the work of art as the betrayal of modernism's mission. Attempting to free themselves from market forces, some of the most important artists in the 1960s and 1970s struggled to produce works of art that resisted commodification. In their early stages, performance art, video, and earthworks all represented, among other things, efforts to create art that could not be marketed and sold. More effective challenges to market forces, however, grew out of radicalizations of Greenberg's doctrine of abstraction. In Minimalism and Conceptualism, the work of art progressively dematerializes until it becomes nothing more than an idea. When pushed to the limit, abstract art denies representational and symbolic content and stresses formal structures and procedures. Leo Steinberg correctly identifies the logical conclusion of Greenberg's doctrine of abstraction when he points out that recent Abstract American painting is frequently "defined and described almost exclusively in terms of internal problem-solving." "The dominant formalist critics today," he explains, "tend to treat modern painting as an evolving technology wherein at any one moment specific tasks require solution. . . . The artist as engineer and research technician becomes important insofar as he comes up with solutions to the right problems."[29]

While the Abstract Expressionists, having been influenced by Surrealism, were convinced that genuine art is the product of the spontaneous expression of the creative individual, the succeeding generation of artists sought to erase both the immediacy and the individuality of the work of art. No artist understood the far-reaching implications of abstraction better than Frank Stella. For Stella, Greenberg's claims about the self-referentiality and flatness of the painted surface as a circumscribed plane posed a problem to be systematically solved. In his most famous dictum about painting Stella quipped, "What you see is what you see."[30] Stella implicitly repeats Kant's insight: true art is about art. If art does not refer beyond itself, the work becomes an object whose point is nothing other than its "objectness." In contrast to the trancelike gestures of a Pollock, Stella deliberately plans his work before he begins and methodically executes his program. "The painting," he explains, "never changes once I've started to paint on it. I work things out before-hand in the sketches."[31] For Stella, the true act of creation is the formulation of the *idea* of the work rather than its material production.

There is an implicit tension in Stella's position that, when explicitly formulated, clears the way for Minimalism and, more important for our purposes, Conceptualism. On the one hand, if the work of art is a nonreferential object in which "what you see is what you see," then it would seem that the representation and what it represents implode and become identical. On the other hand, Stella claims, "I do think that a good pictorial idea is worth more than a lot of manual dexterity."[32] From the latter point of view, the painting appears to re-present the idea in a way that presupposes oppositions between concept/work, creation/production, conception/execution, and form/matter. Throughout the history of Western metaphysics, such binary oppositions are always hierarchical. Stella, like his philosophical and theological precursors, privileges the first term in each dyad over the second: the concept is essential, its appearance accidental.

In the 1960s, Conceptual artists extended this argument to push abstraction to its *logical* conclusion. "I wasn't really that interested in ob-

jects," Sol LeWitt confesses. "I was interested in ideas."[33] The separation of
the conception and production of the work of art is not, of course, new. For
centuries, students and assistants of painters and sculptors have produced
works bearing their master's name. What *is* new is the justification of Conceptual Art's subordination of object to idea. LeWitt's 1967 comment has
proven even more seminal than he could have imagined: "In Conceptual
Art the idea or concept is the most important aspect of the work. When an
artist uses a conceptual form of art, it means that all the planning and decisions are made beforehand and the execution is a perfunctory affair. The
idea becomes a machine that makes the art."[34] As if to appropriate Walter
Benjamin's account of the work of art in the age of mechanical production,
LeWitt not only destroys the aura of the work, but also attempts to efface
the hand of the artist. In direct opposition to Abstract Expressionism, in
which the work of art is the *free* creation of the *individual,* Minimalism
and Conceptualism suppress originality in works that are produced mechanically and anonymously if not autonomously. This strategy points to
unexpected similarities between the abstractions of Minimalism and Conceptualism and the richly figured works of Pop artists. If art is about art, it
is a play of signs in which any reference to an independent reality seems
to disappear. In semiotic terms, signifier and signified collapse into each
other to create signs that are not grounded in anything beyond themselves.
Warhol and his fellow Pop artists appropriated signs of consumer culture
—Coke bottles, Brillo boxes, Campbell's soup cans—while Le Witt and his
fellow Minimalists produced works whose straight lines and right angles
are as precise as the assembly lines they mimic. Rather than pursuing the
romantic dream of originality, artists recycle images while longing to become productive machines. At one point Warhol goes so far as to declare,
"I think everybody should be a machine. I think everybody should be like
everybody."[35] In Warhol's Factory, artworks roll off the assembly line with
minimal human intervention. "In my art work," he explains, "hand painting would take much too long and anyway that's not the age we're living in. Mechanical means are today."[36] Such mechanically produced works
of art enact the disappearance or even the death of the artist. In retrospect
it is clear that Pop and Minimalism not only prepare the way for postmodern art and architecture but also anticipate the transition from industrial and consumer capitalism to digital capitalism and the network economy. By the late 1960s, money, like art, was becoming a "matter" of floating
signs and circulating information.

   During the late 1950s and early 1960s, the machines artists imagined
were industrial. By the end of the decade, however, information processing

machines were beginning to appear. Though still working with industrial metaphors, Warhol's fellow Pop artist Roy Lichstein pointed toward the technological, social, and economic transformation that was already under way: "I want my painting to look as if it had been programmed. I want to hide the record of my hand."[37] This comment is, in effect, a gloss on LeWitt's claim that "the idea becomes a machine that makes the art." When the idea producing the work becomes a program, art enters the information age. As the industrial age gives way to the information age, Greenberg's notion of the artist as engineer must be changed to the artist as information processor and game player. The history of art becomes something like a circumscribed game with a finite set of moves. Just as the work of art is programmed before production starts, so the history of art is programmed from its beginning. When all the programmed moves have been made, the game is over. This does not mean that art ends, but its creative possibilities have been exhausted. Or so it seems.[38]

GAMES AND PLAY) Nothing would seem farther from Warhol's acceptance of the commodification of art and promotion of consumer capitalism than the machinations of Conceptual Art. Upon closer examination, however, it becomes clear that more than any other form of art, Conceptualism accurately represents and even prefigures the direction of finance capitalism and the network economy during the last four decades of the twentieth century. With the invention of digital technologies, the currency of exchange effectively dematerializes into bits of information registered in flickering light. Concurrent with these technological innovations there arose new interpretations of the economy in terms of information processes and game theory. Similar developments unfolding simultaneously in postmodern and poststructural theory point to previously unnoticed interconnections between economics and culture.

Three works published in the 1940s had a significant impact on economic theory, transformed economic markets, and decisively shaped the social sciences, arts, and humanities in the 1960s and 1970s: John von Neumann and Oskar Morgenstern, *Theory of Games and Economic Behavior* (1944); Claude Shannon, "The Mathematical Theory of Communication" (1948); and Norbert Wiener, *Cybernetics; or, Control and Communication in the Animal and Machine* (1948). The intersection of information theory, cybernetics, and game theory created new ways of understanding human behavior. Von Neumann's role in the early history of the computer is well known. His most important contribution was "the idea that the logical conception of a calculating machine [is] *separable* from the design of its circuitry."[39] This fundamental insight eventually led to the distinction between hardware and software, on which all subsequent computing depends. An uncommonly gifted thinker, von Neumann made important contributions to a wide range of disciplines and played a crucial role in the American war effort throughout the 1940s. In addition to inventing cellular automata, von Neumann was also an early leader in the fields of neurobiology and complexity studies. He first advanced his ideas on game theory in a 1928 paper entitled "Zur Theorie der Gesellschaftsspiel," in which he proposed a mathematical account of the way in which competing players can best determine the *rational* course of action in a given situation. In *Theory of Games and Economic Behavior,* he and Morgenstern extended this analysis by attempting to find the "way in which this theory of games can be brought into relationship with economic theory." In contrast to the use of mathematical theory in the natural sciences, where the inquiring subject is active and the object of investigation is passive, the mathematical analysis of "games of strategy" must calculate the interaction of agents who not only act upon but deliberately anticipate each other's actions. While stressing that their analysis is "dominated by illustrations from Chess, 'Matching Pennies,' Poker, Bridge, etc., and not from the structure of cartels, markets, oligopolies, etc.," von Neumann and Morgenstern insisted that the intersubjectivity of the game in no way undercuts the possibility of expressing its rules mathematically.[40] Their definition of a game is both simple and inclusive: "the *game* is simply the totality of the rules which describe it."

> We have described . . . what we expect a solution—i.e. a characterization of "rational behavior"—to consist of. This amounted to a complete set of rules of behavior in all conceivable situations. This holds equivalently for a social economy and for games. The entire result in the above sense is thus a combinatorial enumeration of enormous complexity. But we have accepted a simplified concept of utility according to which all the individual strives for is fully described by one numerical datum. Thus the complicated combinatorial catalogue—which we expect for a solution—permits a very brief and significant summarization: the statement of how much the participant under consideration can get if he behaves "rationally."[41]

Rationality in this context is defined as the maximization of utility. Players are rational when they can "(i) assess outcomes; (ii) calculate paths to outcomes; and (iii) choose actions that yield their most-preferred out-comes, given the actions of other players."[42]

For many economists, the binary structure and rational presuppositions of the game reinforce their preference for equilibrium models derived from Newtonian mechanics.[43] Von Neumann's use of game theory not only provides a way to describe the behavior of individuals and markets, but also suggests how to develop mathematical models for economic policy and investment strategy. In his monumental work, *The Theory of Money and Financial Institutions,* Martin Shubik uses game theory to formulate a comprehensive account of money and financial institutions. "Money," Shubik avers, "is what money does." And what money does is inseparable from the rules of the game that enable it to circulate: "'Moneyness,' whatever that is, is a systematic property that depends upon the rules of the game."[44] According to a paradoxical logic that appears to be circular, money creates the game that creates moneyness. When money is so understood, *there is nothing outside the game in the art of finance.*

The full force of von Neumann's extension of game theory to economics did not become apparent until it was joined to information theory and cybernetics. From 1943 to 1954, the Macy Foundation brought together a group of extraordinary individuals in different disciplines with the aim of developing a theory of communication that could be used to govern or control mechanical, natural, and social systems. At one time or another Norbert Wiener, Claude Shannon, Warren McCulloch, Margaret Mead, Gregory Bateson, and Talcott Parsons participated in these conferences. Von Neumann was an active contributor to the debates that led to the emergence of the field of cybernetics. The title of the first Macy conference, held in New York in 1946, suggests the overall direction of the project: "Feedback Mechanisms and Circular Causal Systems in Biological and Social Systems." The combination of Shannon's information theory and Wiener's cybernetics led to a view of human beings and social systems as information-processing machines that could be controlled by feedback devices. In a related conference held at Cal Tech in 1948, von Neumann presented his historic paper, "The General and Logical Theory of Automata," in which he attempted to demonstrate "how a reliable automaton can be made out of unreliable components, and what principles of organization are sufficient to give an automaton the capacity for self-reproduction."[45] The implications of his argument are staggering and have taken decades to emerge. In addition to anticipating both artificial intelligence and artificial or digital life, von Neumann's theory of automata also forms the foundation of recent theories of the origin of life as well as the relation between mind and brain. In this context, it is important to note that the theory of cellular automata contributed significantly to the emergence of the interpretation of markets as information-processing machines.

Von Neumann was not alone in discerning a relationship between cybernetic systems and markets. F. A. Hayek, a leading figure in the influential Austrian school of economics whose work we will return to in later chapters, credits Adam Smith with discovering cybernetics.

> Though in Hume, and also in the works of Bernard Mandeville, we can watch the gradual emergence of the twin concepts of the formations of spontaneous orders and selective evolution, it was Adam Smith and Adam Ferguson who first made systematic use of this approach. Smith's work marks the breakthrough of an evolutionary approach which has progressively displaced the stationary Aristotelian view.... While Smith has been recognized by several writers as the originator of cybernetics, recent examinations of Charles Darwin's notebooks suggest that his reading of Adam Smith in the crucial year 1838 led Darwin to his decisive breakthrough.[46]

This observation becomes even richer when one considers Hayek's claim that markets are actually distributed information-processing systems. The model, which resulted from the integration of game theory, information theory, and cybernetics, was widely applied to areas of inquiry far beyond economic theory.

At the same time as the Macy conferences were being held in the U.S., structuralism was emerging in France. Drawing on the linguistic theory presented in Ferdinand de Saussure's *Course in General Linguistics* (1916), structuralists developed accounts of psychological, social, artistic, and economic processes in terms of universal structures, which function like rules in a game, computer programs, or algorithms. This influential French movement invaded the United States in the fall of 1966, when Johns Hopkins University sponsored a symposium, "The Languages of Criticism and the Sciences of Man." The proceedings were published four years later in a volume entitled *The Structuralist Controversy*. The papers presented at this conference launched both structuralism and poststructuralism in the United States and, by so doing, set the terms for cultural debate for the next twenty-five years. In rarely noted opening remarks, Richard Macksey points to the importance of von Neumann's game theory for issues considered by many of the contributors to the symposium. His comments deserve to be quoted at length because they suggest the important yet over-

looked relationship between cultural criticism on the one hand and economic theory and practice on the other.

> If one reflects for a moment on the pervasive role which the "game meta-
> phor" has played when extended to recent model-building in the human
> sciences, the full force and mixed consequences of such a comparison
> to our present undertaking can be briefly assayed.... By far the most fa-
> mous of recent applications of games to human behavior is ... the work
> of John von Neumann and his colleagues on formal decision theory in
> economics and strategic conflict situations.... The "game" is conceived
> as involving two or more players, a succession of choices or moves by
> certain rules of play, which result in successive "situations"; the choices
> by each player may or may not be known to others, though most board
> games are classified as "games of perfect information"; play is governed
> by a termination rule, which results in the adjudication of certain "pay-
> offs." So far, the basic description would seem to apply to the properties
> of our symposium game, which could further be analyzed in terms of
> its "zero-sum" (but negotiable) character, its "saddle-points" (which im-
> ply optimal pure strategy), the application of "mini-max" or "maximin"
> and so on. If the "moves" could, hypothetically, be reduced to sufficient
> simplicity, we could even take the first step toward analysis—reduction
> from the *extensive* (or diachronic) *form* of the "game-tree" to its *normal
> form* as a synchronic matrix.[47]

The appropriation of game theory, cybernetics, and economic models in
the social sciences and humanities, however, was not direct but was mediated by modern continental philosophy.

Paul Ricoeur once described structuralism as "Kantianism without the
transcendental subject." This remark is both analytically correct and historically suggestive. Philosophy's preoccupation with formal structures
through which our knowledge of the world is constituted goes back at least
to Plato. In the modern era, Kant in effect rewrites classical ontology as
epistemology by translating Plato's transcendent forms into forms of intuition and categories of understanding. The mind, according to Kant, has
a universal structure or, in a more contemporary idiom, is hardwired. In
structuralism, Kant's formal categories of consciousness become infra-
structures of the mind and society. Structuralism, then, is an inverted Platonism. What attracted so many philosophers and critics to structuralism
was the prospect of making the human sciences "genuinely scientific" by
mimicking the ideas and methods of the natural sciences. The mathemat-

ical rigor of game theory and cybernetics seemed ideally suited to meet this challenge.

The tendency to extend scientific modes of explanation to human behavior was reinforced by a profound shift in philosophical anthropology. During the years immediately following the Second World War, French intellectual life was dominated by existentialism. The fundamental tenets of French existentialism were the radical freedom and responsibility of the individual in a world where God was distant or dead and ethical norms were obscure or absent. Just as Abstract Expressionists saw art as the free creation of the individual, so existentialists viewed life as the expression of the individual's free decisions. To reinforce this freedom, thinkers like Sartre drew a sharp opposition between the human and the nonhuman: the human is free and the nonhuman, however it is conceived, is determined. In a particularly revealing remark, Sartre quipped: "The inhuman is merely . . . the mechanical."[48] While Sartre and other existentialists sought to protect human agents from heteronomous determination, structuralists not only argued that human being is machinic but, like Warhol, saw a strange liberation in the identification with the machine. In a manner strictly parallel to Conceptual Art's displacement of Abstract Expressionism, Lévi-Strauss (anthropology), Lacan (psychology), Barthes (literature), and Althusser (economics) turn away from a focus on the free individual to develop analyses of human behavior in terms of fixed structures, which function like the rules of a game or quasi-cybernetic systems. Instead of starting with individual players who freely enter into a game, structuralists begin with the game and argue that individual players are constituted by their positions and moves.

In 1955, Lacan presented an important lecture entitled "Psychoanalysis and Cybernetics, or On the Nature of Language," in which he underscored the close relation between cybernetic and linguistic systems. He elaborates three distinctions borrowed from Saussure.[49] First, he argues, linguistic systems are made up of arbitrary signs, which are composed of a signifier and a signified. The signified, or referent, is not an object but a concept or idea, which can be expressed with an oral or written signifier. The specificity of any sign is a function of its relation to other signs. In Derrida's prescient formulation, "There can be arbitrariness only because the system of signs is constituted solely by differences in terms, and not by their plenitude. The elements of signification function due not to the compact force of their nuclei but rather to the *network* of oppositions that distinguishes them, and then relates them one to another."[50] From this point of view, language is something like a *difference engine,* which forms a complex *net-*

work of signifiers. Second, every linguistic system includes what Saussure describes as "language" (*la langue*) and "speech" (*la parole*). Communication presupposes shared—if not universal—linguistic structures as well as individual speech events. *La langue* is the underlying structure, which is the condition of the possibility of every speech act (*la parole*). The foundational structure functions like a coded program or language game that plots in advance what individuals can say. In this way, language, operating like an information-processing machine to decenter consciousness, speaks through the individual. This decentering of the subject lies behind the much-celebrated "death of the author" and "end of man." From this point of view, language games play speaking subjects more than individual subjects play language games. Third, structuralists stress synchronic forms, which like Platonic forms are unchanging, more than diachronic or temporal developments. Structuralists' foundational structures, like Plato's transcendent forms, are unchanging. Unlike Plato, however, structuralists argue that the forms themselves are organized according to the metastructure of binary opposition. Each form is constituted by its relation to and difference from other forms. Once established, this linguistic model is extended to create a generalized system of exchange that, in turn, is applied to kinship systems, literary texts, psychological drives, and economic processes.

Though not immediately evident, structuralism involves several important insights that both reflect broader cultural currents and anticipate critical developments in cultural theory and economic practice. The most significant change structuralism proposes is a shift from a referential to a relational notion of value. As we will see in chapter 3, the dialectical analyses of Hegel and Simmel anticipate this insight. If, as Saussure insists, the meaning of any element in a linguistic system is a function of its difference from other elements rather than its reference to a nonlinguistic thing or object, the signified itself is a signifier. Signifiers, in other words, are always signifiers of signifiers. Within the game of language, nonlinguistic referents disappear in an endless play of signs. Inasmuch as structuralism seeks to elaborate a *generalized theory of exchange*, structural analysis can be applied to all socioeconomic systems. A persistent theme running through the work of many structuralists is the close relationship between language and money. In *Symbolic Exchange and Death* (1976), Baudrillard traces this seminal insight back to Saussure.

> Saussure located two dimensions to the exchange of terms of *la langue*, which he assimilated to money. A given coin must be exchangeable

against a real good of some value, while on the other hand, it must be possible to relate it to all the other terms in the monetary system. More and more, Saussure reserves the term *value* for this second aspect of the system: every term can be related to every other, their *relativity,* internal to the system and constituted by binary opposition. This definition is opposed to the other possible definition of value: the relation of every term to what it designates, of each signifier to its signified, like the relation of every coin to what it can be exchanged against. . . . This revolution consists in the dislocation of the two aspects of the law of value, which were thought to be coherent and eternally bound as if by a natural law. *Referential value is annihilated, giving the structural play of value the upper hand.* The structural dimension becomes autonomous by excluding the referential dimension, and is instituted upon the death of reference.[51]

This "structural play of value" emerges in a relational network of signifiers, which is not grounded by any independent or transcendent signified. The implosion of signifier and signified appears to mark the death of the referent, which restages the death of God. When the coin of the realm is a sign, money becomes little more than a mask signifying naught. If currency is an empty cipher, the economy must be a confidence game.

Baudrillard frames his argument largely in terms of media and consumer culture in the 1960s and early 1970s. To appreciate the far-reaching implications of the shift from the referential to relational theory of value, it is necessary to extend the analysis from image to information. Linguistic and economic activity obviously presuppose the differentiation of tokens of exchange. Echoing Saussure's claim that in language "there are only differences," Gregory Bateson, a leading figure in postwar discussions of cybernetics, defined information as "a difference that makes a difference."[52] Though there can be differences that communicate no information, there can be no information without differences. With the invention of electronic computation, structuralism's binary opposites can be reconceived as the 0/1 of digital codes. If, as is becoming increasingly apparent, biological, social, cultural, and economic systems are in some sense information systems, then they are constituted by the differential play of signs, which forms operational programs. In some cases, these programs can be rewritten to change the organization and function of the system on which they operate.

When the principles of structuralism are extended to economic systems, markets can be understood as information processing machines.

If these machines are interpreted in terms of cybernetics, they appear to be self-governing and, like the systems defined by structuralists, closed. Systems as such do not evolve but regulate themselves through negative feedback mechanisms, which maintain a condition near equilibrium. While many social scientists drew on work being done in game theory and cybernetics, most economists remained unaware of concurrent developments in the arts and humanities. During the 1950s and 1960s, people working in the rapidly developing field of financial economics were defining theories that are completely consistent with the analytic models structuralists were creating at the same time. These economic theories eventually coalesced into the efficient market hypothesis, which, we will see in chapter 7, was enormously influential in the 1980s and 1990s.

For critics like Baudrillard, the transformation of society into the culture of simulacra, where referents disappear in an endless recycling of signs, harbors devastating social and economic consequences. When media networks and information systems become increasingly programmed, individual differences appear to be leveled as society and culture become more homogeneous. Baudrillard attributes this process to what he describes as "the terrorism of the code."[53] As codes become more sophisticated and pervasive, multinational media and corporations program consumers to be even more passive. According to this point of view, the game of global capitalism is inevitably hegemonic.

But this is not the only way to understand games and play. The Hopkins conference where structuralism was introduced to America also launched the movement that eventually would displace it—poststructuralism. The most influential figure in this countermovement was Jacques Derrida, whose contribution to the conference, published a year later in *Writing and Difference,* was titled "Structure, Sign, and Play in the Discourse of the Human Sciences." Drawing on the work of Nietzsche, Derrida presents a thoroughgoing critique of the metaphysical presuppositions and social implications of Lévi-Strauss's structuralism. His criticism turns on alternative accounts of play and, correlatively, a different reading of the structure and operation of systems. The notion of system, as Lévi-Strauss defines it, is a centered structure that remains closed. Far from a radical departure, structuralism, Derrida argues, is really the latest version of a fundamentalism or foundationalism running through the Western theological and philosophical tradition.

> The concept of centered structure is in fact the concept of a play based on a fundamental ground, a play constituted on the basis of a funda-

mental immobility and a reassuring certitude, which itself is beyond the reach of play. And on the basis of this certitude anxiety can be mastered, for anxiety is invariably the result of a certain mode of being implicated in the game, of being caught by the game, of being as it were at stake in the game from the outset.[54]

Derrida realizes that a closed binary system tending toward equilibrium reinscribes precisely the kind of transcendental ground that a relativistic or differential notion of meaning and value undercuts. The persistence of this foundational structure is symptomatic of the desire to avoid uncertainty and hedge risk in a world that is increasingly volatile. Paradoxically, this volatility is created by a condition that structuralists themselves identify. When signs—be they religious, artistic, linguistic, or economic—are signs of other signs, they are grounded in nothing beyond themselves. In other words, signs have no anchor to secure their meaning and value. In the absence of a stable foundation, signs float freely in complex networks and worldwide webs where currents tend to be turbulent. The operational logic of these networks conforms to neither the principles of structuralism nor the equilibrium theories of economists. The *play* of signs disrupts the stability of systems. Instead of being closed and programmed, systems of exchange are complex adaptive networks that are emergent and have gaps where the aleatory erupts. The play of chance ceaselessly transforms these networks, thereby lending them a history that takes shape far from equilibrium.

In the past two decades, advances in computer technology have made it possible to create models of complex adaptive systems that can be used to explore biological, social, and economic systems.[55] In the following pages, I will argue that new models of complex adaptive systems provide a better way to understand the network economy than the intrinsically stable systems of structuralism and the efficient market hypothesis. These theoretical issues are not without practical significance; indeed, much of the economic, social, and cultural turbulence of the 1980s and 1990s has been the result of the persistence of policies and practices that presuppose stable equilibrium systems in a world that operates according to the principles of complex systems.

If, as I have suggested, religion, art, and economics are bound in a dialectic without synthesis in which each displaces but does not replace the other, then to appreciate these developments, it is necessary to understand the interplay between culture and markets. Before turning to a consideration of trends in economics and their impact on culture during the past forty years, I will trace the roots of our current understanding of markets, money, and capital to theological and aesthetic theories developed in the eighteenth and nineteenth centuries. These theological and aesthetic ideas become the economic realities of the twentieth and twenty-first centuries. Then, at the very moment when the market seems to triumph, the real, figured in religion, returns to disrupt what seemed to have displaced it.

2

MARKETING PROVIDENCE

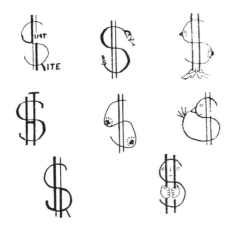

Figure 5
From William Gaddis, *JR* (New York: Penguin, 1993). Copyright
© 2004 by Sarah Gaddis and Matthew Gaddis, reprinted with the
permission of The Wylie Agency, Inc.

"HOLY SHIT!"[1]) Money is mysterious and is getting more so. The mystery of money is at least in part the result of the oppositions it embodies: valuable/worthless, material/immaterial, rational/irrational, useful/useless . . . (figure 5). These contradictions create an irreducible ambiguity, which renders money simultaneously attractive and repulsive. As a result of the ambivalence money provokes, it has repeatedly been associated with both God and the Devil. In his monumental work, *The Philosophy of Money*, Georg Simmel maintains that it is precisely money's paradoxical character that suggests its relation to God.

> In reality, money in its psychological form, as the absolute means and thus as the unifying point of innumerable sequences of purposes, possesses a significant relationship to the notion of God—a relationship that only psychology, which has the privilege of being unable to commit blasphemy, may disclose. The essence of the notion of God is that all diversities and contradictions in the world achieve a unity in him, that he is—according to a beautiful formulation of Nicholas de Cusa—the *coincidentia oppositorum*. Out of this idea, that in him all estrangements and irreconcilables of existence find their unity and equalization, there arises the peace, the security, the all-embracing wealth of feeling that reverberate with the notion of God that we hold.[2]

The relation between God and money is ancient and often obscure; as we will see, money *is* God in more than a trivial sense. But the God who becomes money is no traditional God—nor is money simply what it traditionally appears to be.

The history of money is, of course, extremely complex. In different times and places money has assumed a seemingly endless variety of forms.

In the West, Aristotle first identified what have come to be the distinguishing characteristics of money.

> Then the things that they [two traders] have to exchange must be made comparable. That is why money was invented. Money is a sort of medium or mean; for it measures everything and consequently measures excess and defect, for instance, the number of shoes equivalent to a house or meal. As a builder then is to a shoemaker, so must so many shoes be to a house; otherwise there would be no exchange and no intermingling. And the calculation will be impossible, unless the goods are somehow equalized. Hence the necessity of a single universal standard of measurement.[3]

Implicit in Aristotle's definition are four essential functions of money. Money is:

1. a medium of exchange.
2. a unit of account.
3. a store of value.
4. a standard of deferred payment.

Money is first and foremost a *medium* of exchange. Aristotle formulates what becomes the traditional view of money as originating in the exigencies of trade. In its most primitive phase, the argument goes, exchange takes the form of barter in which goods are directly traded (figure 6).

The structure of this basic relationship informs all subsequent economic models. Barter, for example, involves a *binary* relationship in which trading partners enter into *reciprocal* exchange, which seeks a balance or

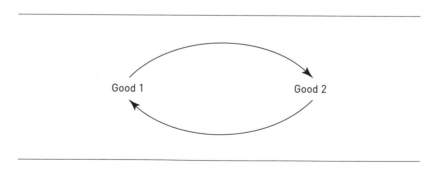

Figure 6

equilibrium. It is important to note that barter presupposes no supplement beyond the items traded; good is directly exchanged for good without any intermediate good or third party. The relation, in other words, is immediate rather than mediated.

Barter, however, is limited by what economists call the "double coincidence of wants." Each partner must want what the other has for the deal to be consummated. If exchange is to occur in the absence of the double coincidence of wants, there must be a mediating third, which facilitates *indirect* or *mediated* exchange. This is the role money plays (figure 7).

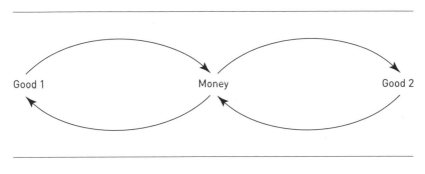

Figure 7

The earliest forms of money were particular commodities: shells, cattle, salt, etc., and eventually precious metals—especially gold and silver, though sometimes copper and bronze. Traces of commodity money persist in the English words *pecuniary,* which derives from the Latin *pecunia* (wealth in cattle) and *salary,* which comes from the Latin *sal* (salt). To serve as the "universal equivalent," which Aristotle identifies, money "must be *acceptable* to (that is, usable by) most traders, of *standardized quality,* so that any two units are identical, and be *durable,* so that value is not lost by spoilage."[4] These characteristics enable a medium of exchange to fulfill the necessary functions of money. Standardization allows money to be a unit of account and durability creates the possibility of storing value. If money is an acceptable medium of exchange, which serves as a unit of account and store of value, it can be a standard of deferred payment.

As a medium of exchange, money establishes a structure of mediation, which interrupts the immediacy of barter both spatially and temporally. As money emerges and develops, the face-to-face of the local market gives way to anonymous relations mediated by increasingly abstract media and distributed over ever-expanding geographical areas. Insofar as money is a standard of deferred payment, time is introduced into the economic system. Rather than having to be consummated in the present moment, the circuit of exchange can be completed at an indefinite future date. Not only is time money but, as we will see in more detail, money is time.

Whatever its form, money's intermediate status is what lends it an ambiguity that provokes ambivalence. In his creative application of game theory and complexity studies to money and finance, Shubik observes that other than money, "financial instruments are always created in pairs that net to zero."[5] This insight has implications that extend far beyond economic relations as they are traditionally understood. Since financial instruments and the relations they establish are always created in pairs, they form a structure characterized by binary opposition. As the exception to this rule, money falls *between* these opposites and thus can serve as the medium of exchange. Money, therefore, is *liminal;* always betwixt 'n' between, it is the condition of the possibility of a structure that cannot incorporate it. To be an effective *medium* of exchange determining different values, money must retain a certain neutrality that, in Shimmel's terms, is "completely adaptable to any use."[6] As a result of this neutrality, money can take many forms; it is, in other words, polymorphous, polyvalent, and, some would insist, perverse.[7]

The history of money follows a consistent trajectory from the material to the immaterial. As form becomes function, the currency of exchange changes from physical things to nothing but electricity and light: commodities, precious metals, coins, paper, coded information. Every transformation of money depends on new technologies: precious metals require mining, metallurgy, and accurate weights and measures; coins are impossible apart from engraving and imprinting techniques; paper currency needs the printing press; and electronic and digital currencies presuppose computers and networks. As money becomes more abstract and uniform it creates the possibility of quantification and calculation, which some historians argue are necessary conditions for analytical reason and the rise of modern science. This is one of the reasons classical economic theorists tend to associate money with rationalization. Norman O. Brown points out that "many analysts have assumed that economic activity was always and everywhere essentially the same in the fundamental motivation; economic activities were governed by economic motives—that is, by economizing calculation."[8] However, the very processes of abstraction that make such calculation possible can also subvert rationality. With the dematerialization and virtualization of tokens of exchange, money, like floating signifiers, is no longer secured by any anchor that can check its free play. When this occurs, speculation can become excessive; the proliferation of dangerous monetary and financial supplements can threaten the stability of the economic system. Money is, among other things, currency whose turbulent flows often operate far from equilibrium in ways that can destabilize binary structures and reciprocal exchanges. Sometimes these currents, which are not always rational, spin out of control.

Medium, liminal, surplus, supplement, fluid, irrational, excessive, polymorphous, polyvalent, perverse: money appears to be dangerous; and this danger is precisely what makes it so attractive—as well as repulsive. The reason money seems fraught with danger is that it cannot be captured or contained in the clear and precise binary oppositions of closed systems that seem to pattern thought and organize experience. Uncategorizable and uncontrollable, excess can be identified with the lowest as well as the highest. Throughout history, money has been related to the profane as well as the sacred—the Devil as well as God. It is common to describe money as filthy lucre, which threatens to contaminate all it touches and pollute all who touch it. From a psychoanalytic perspective, money is shit and the obsession with it a mark of an anal personality. Excrement contaminates because it is marginal, liminal, or interstitial. Julia Kristeva's description of abjection illuminates the danger filthy lucre poses: "It is . . . not lack of cleanliness or health that causes abjection but what disturbs identity, system, order. What does not respect borders, positions, rules. The in-between, the ambiguous, the composite."[9] As an inside that is outside, excrement is a fuzzy trace of the paradoxical intersection of purity and impurity, which threatens to foul clear distinctions. Efforts to the contrary notwithstanding, the impure can never be completely separated from the pure. According to Freud, the pure, no matter how it is figured, is *always* tainted by impurity. In the economy of the psyche, low can become high through the process of sublimation. While this psychic process is commonly acknowledged, its ancient lineage is rarely noted. The notion of sublimation originated with the practice of alchemists who attempted to transform dirty base metals mined in the bowels of Mother Earth into pure gold. Sublimation, in other words, is the process by which the useless becomes the priceless. In Freud's theory, this metallurgical technique reappears as the psychological process in which base instincts that have been repressed return in disguise as images, ideas, and ideals. Through sublimation, shit assumes a mask of gold, which serves as the token of God. Shit, it seems, can indeed be holy.

High and low meet in money, which now appears to be worthless (shit) and priceless (gold) as well as useless and useful. The coincidence of uselessness and usefulness marks the point at which religion, art, and economics intersect. Paradoxes associated with money entail alternative logics that harbor contrasting economies. Georges Bataille labels these two economies "restricted and general."[10] The restricted economy is a closed system in which reciprocal exchange seeks to maintain a productive equilibrium. Here the highest value is utility, which presupposes reasonable expenditures and profitable returns on all investments. The general economy, by contrast, is open and operates far from equilibrium, where relations are never reciprocal and the highest good is excessive expenditure with no expectation of profitable returns. These two economies are not so much opposed as intertwined in such a way that each corrects but never balances the other. The difference between these economies is strictly parallel to the distinction between games (closed, restricted) and play (open, general), which we noted in the first chapter.[11]

The easiest way to grasp the importance of the difference between a restricted and a general economy for religion and art is through the contrast between an economy based on accumulation and an economy based on expenditure. A restricted economy places a high premium on the accumulation of wealth. From this point of view, power and prestige come from possessions; any expenditure that holds little or no prospect of increasing wealth is deemed irrational. Many interpreters associate the discipline and parsimony necessary for such accumulation with the Protestant ethic. Capitalism, of course, would not have been possible without the accumulation of reserves, which were prudently invested with the expectation of profitable returns. But capitalism requires spending as much as saving. Indeed, without excessive expenditure and consumption, the capitalist system grinds to a halt.

The roots of the prodigal spending necessary to fuel the capitalist economy can be traced to so-called primitive gift economies in which power and prestige come from spending and giving rather than saving and possessing. Bataille explains this important distinction:

> Human activity is not entirely reducible to processes of production and conservation, and consumption must be divided into two distinct parts. The first, reducible part is represented by the use of the minimum necessary for the conservation of life and the continuation of individuals' productive activity in a given society. . . . The second part is represented by so-called unproductive expenditures: luxury, mourning, war, cults, the construction of sumptuary monuments, games, spectacles, arts, perverse sexual activity (i.e., deflected from genital finality)—all these rep-

resent activities which, at least in primitive circumstances, have no end beyond themselves. Now it is necessary to reserve the use of the word *expenditure* for the designation of these unproductive forms, and not for the designation of all the modes of consumption that serve as a means to the end of production. Even though it is always possible to set the various forms of expenditure in opposition to each other, they constitute a group characterized by the fact that in each case the accent is placed on a loss that must be as great as possible in order for that activity to take on its true meaning.

This principle of loss or "unconditional expenditure" stands in marked contrast to "the principle of balanced accounts."[12] Elaborating examples of such expenditure, Bataille cites "beautiful and dazzling" jewels for which "one sacrifices a fortune." "In the unconscious," he proceeds to explain, "jewels, like excrement, arc cursed matter that flows from a wound: they are part of oneself destined for open sacrifice (they serve, in fact, as sumptuous gifts charged with sexual love)." It is the association of jewels with liminality ("cursed matter that flows from a wound") that connects them with excrement and lends them their ambiguity. The mention of sacrifice points to broader sacrificial practices to which I will return. In addition to jewels and sacrifices, Bataille describes competitive games like horseracing, football, and gambling, which all require considerable sums of money and provide the occasion for "the ostentatious display of the latest luxurious fashions." Finally, he argues, some forms of art entail unconditional expenditure and thus fall within a general economy:

> In their major form, literature and theater . . . provoke dread and horror through symbolic representations of tragic loss (degradation or death); in their minor form, they provoke laughter through representations which, though analogously structured, exclude certain seductive elements. The term poetry, applied to the least degraded and least intellectualized forms of the expression of a state of loss, can be considered synonymous with expenditure; it in fact signifies, in the most precise way, creation by means of loss. Its meaning is therefore close to that of sacrifice.[13]

What unites these otherwise disparate phenomena is their uselessness within a restricted economy. It is, of course, possible to create art for the market, just as one can play games for profit. But for Bataille, the business of art no more involves true art than the sports industry allows real play.

Certain religious practices and works of art fault the rationality and closure of restricted economies by remaining insistently nonutilitarian. In a general economy, jewels, games, and art serve no practical purpose.

Just as the restricted and general economies are inseparably interrelated, so the line separating the useful from the useless is never secure. The useless tends to become useful and the useful often turns out to be useless. The interplay between usefulness and uselessness can be seen most clearly in the way the restricted and general economies are braided together in capitalism. As I have noted, capitalism requires the disciplined accumulation of wealth, which can be invested with the expectation of profit. Surplus capital must not remain idle but should be put to work. Insofar as capital underwrites production, it is undeniably useful. When production is profitable, capital reproduces itself and multiplies. Such self-reproduction is necessary because the law of capital is ceaseless expansion. Capital increases through geographic extension and temporal acceleration. As markets reach their spatial limits, products must turn over even faster. If people buy and consume only what they need, the economy stagnates. The growth of capitalism, therefore, presupposes both waste and excessive expenditure. The trick upon which the success of market economies turns is the creation of desire where there is no need. Capitalism works its magic through planned obsolescence, which turns waste to profit, thereby rendering the useless useful.

Restricted economies entail a further contradiction, which threatens the foundational principle of utility: accumulation itself can become excessive. Beyond miserly obsessions, the accumulation of wealth often becomes an end in itself. There is a common impulse to make money for money's sake. While economic motives vary considerably, there seem to be three stages in the accumulation of wealth: First, people struggle to make money so they can meet their needs and fulfill their desires. Second, the amassing of a fortune becomes a way of keeping score in the competitive struggle for recognition. In different ways, both of these practices remain bound by utilitarianism. Third, wealth becomes an end in itself. In some cases, people become so rich that money no longer serves useful purposes. Strangely, however, the extremely wealthy often seem compelled to increase their fortunes long after it has become practically pointless to do so. When this occurs, the self-replication of capital becomes pleasurable play and what participants most fear is being left out or forced to the sidelines. It is, of course, always possible for the principle of accumulation to reverse itself and become unbounded generosity. As money generates money, a surplus develops. This excess wealth can be reinvested yet again or given away. Gift giving can conform to either the principles of a restricted or a general economy. On the one hand, gifts and charitable donations can be investments calculated to win praise and gain prestige or, on the other hand, they can be freely given with no expectation of any kind of return. In the latter instance, giving is disinterested and gifts bear no interest.

These alternative forms of gift giving point to different understandings of sacrifice. In a general economy, sacrifice must be absolute; that is to say, it must be done without any anticipation of personal benefit. Such giving is, in Freud's terms, beyond the pleasure principle, which is always restricted by the search for equilibrium. Within this psychological economy, there can be no investment or cathexis that does not expect to profit from a reduction of psychosocial tensions. Beyond the pleasure principle lies the domain of Thanatos, which is the field of play for uncalculating sacrifice. The sacrificial victim is a substitute in which the sacrificing subject sees itself reflected. If sacrifice is radical, it becomes self-sacrifice—incalculable generosity even unto death. In a haunting passage describing ancient religious rituals, Bataille indirectly sheds strange light on the principle of creative destruction at the heart of the consumer economy:

> Everything that exists destroying itself, consuming itself and dying, each instant producing itself only in the annihilation of the preceding one, and itself existing only as mortally wounded.
> Ceaselessly destroying and consuming myself in myself in a great festival of blood.[14]

The blood of the sacrificial festival is sacred, and as such, is pure and impure, clean and dirty, attractive and repulsive.

Sacrificial blood, however, can circulate in restricted economies. Upon reflection, it is clear that all economic relations are in some sense sacrificial. At the most basic level, both parties in an exchange give up something but—and this is the important point—expect something in return. For the transaction to be reasonable, the expected return must be equal to or greater than the value of what is sacrificed. Though rarely noted, there is considerable evidence to suggest that money actually originated in sacrificial economies between gods and humans. From ancient times, money has been associated with the gods. "All Greek money," Simmel points out, "was once sacred; it emanated from the priesthood, as did other generally valid concepts of measure referring to weight, size and time. This priesthood represented at the same time the unity of various regions. . . . The shrines had a nonparticularistic centralizing significance, and money expressed this by bearing the symbol of the common God. The religiosocial unity, crystallized in the temple, became active again through the money that was put into circulation, and money acquired a basis and function far beyond the significance of the metal content of the individual coin."[15] A similar pattern can be observed in the ancient Roman world. The word *money* derives from the epithet for Jupiter's sister and wife—Juno Moneta.[16] As the warning goddess, Juno Moneta was best known for three "monitory tales: (1) she advised the Romans to sacrifice a pregnant sow to Cybele, to avert an earthquake; (2) she told them, when they feared for finances in the war against Pyrrhus, that money would never fail those whose cause was just; and (3) the geese that were crated for sacrifice in her temple at the city wall cackled and thus alerted the Romans to the intended surprise attack by the Gauls in 390 B.C.E. Roman coins were first minted in the Temple of Juno Moneta," thereby initiating the ancient practice of associating mints with temples. "The oldest altar to Juno Moneta was located on Mons Albanus, where a bull sacrifice, the central ritual of the Latin confederacy, was annually held."[17]

Other etymological clues suggest a link between money and ritual sacrifice. The German word *Geld* (money), Horst Kurnitzky points out, "means more or less 'sacrifice' [*Opfer*]. *Geld ist Geld, weil es gilt* [Money is money, because it is valid]. But in the eighth century, this verb *gelten* [to be valid] meant 'to sacrifice.'"[18] The Greek word *drachma,* which is the name of a common coin, once was used to designate a handful of sacrificial meat (*oblos*). In Latin *pecunia,* which, I have noted, is the root of the English *pecuniary,* derives from *pecus* (cattle). The association of money with sacrificial animals—especially cattle and bulls—is particularly suggestive. As is well known, the bull was commonly used in ancient ritual sacrifices. In Rome, the Mithraic cult, which at one time posed a serious threat to early Christianity, centered on the sacrifice of the bull, and in Greece, the god Dionysus was traditionally represented as a bull. In many of its forms, religion involves an economy of sacrifice in which the relationship between the believer and the god is established by the currency they share.

Within this sacrificial economy, the current flows in two directions: from worshipper to god and from god to worshipper. Ritual practices establish a system of exchange in which devotees offer sacrifices to secure protection and benefits from the gods. In the early stages of religious development, these offerings tended to be either human or animal sacrifices. In time, however, substitutions were introduced. At first, small figures of the sacrificial animals that usually were made out of precious metals and later coins bearing the images of the animals were offered to the gods. As the rituals were formalized, priests and other religious and political leaders prescribed the terms of exchange. Within this scheme, an established offering "purchased" certain benefits.[19]

A second equally important aspect of this economy of sacrifice is the communal meal. Anthropologists have long recognized the important role that sharing and eating the flesh of the sacrificial animal plays in the constitution of the religious community. The animal is not only an offering *to* God but is also an embodiment *of* the deity. Sacrifice, therefore, involves the death—or more precisely the murder—of God. As Freud maintains in his myth of social origins in *Totem and Taboo,* participants in ritual sacrifice attempt to share guilt and identify with the god by consuming the body of the deity. From this point of view, all culture is consumer culture. The portion of the animal's flesh the communicants received was determined by each person's social status. An inscription in Attica from 330 BCE defines the rules for distributing the flesh of the sacred bull.

> Five pieces each to the presidents.
> Five pieces each to the nine archons.
> One piece each to the treasurers of the goddess.
> One piece to each of the managers of the feast.
> The customary portions to others.

The practice of sharing sacrificial flesh explains why Moneta is also the name of the goddess Aequitas, who "represents the *equity* or fair apportionment which the state grants to its citizens."[20] It was not uncommon for the share of the bull's flesh to serve as a legal means of payment. At this point, the practice of substitution again intervened. Tokens, which often took the form of coins made of precious metal with the imprint of the sacred animal, replaced animal flesh. Within such a restricted sacrificial economy, all money is blood money. The religious community is constituted by an act of "originary" violence in which the god who dies on the sacrificial altar is reborn or quite literally becomes incarnate in the social body.[21] The token of divine presence in the community is the coin of the realm that bears the *imago dei.*

During the Middle Ages, the communion wafer often took the form of a stamped coin, which was something like fiat money backed by the priest, whose word magically transformed worthless bread into the priceless body of Christ. By the eighteenth century, the wafer had changed into an actual token, which was used in Protestant churches for admission to communion (figures 8 and 9).[22] Though such communion tokens are no longer used, today's currency continues to bear the stamp of its religious origin. The dollar sign—$—is derived from the insignia *in hoc signo* (by this sign) inscribed on Christian coins (figure 10).[23]

It is impossible to comprehend the complexity of money without understanding how religion and art inform its historical and psychological origins. While necessary, this is not sufficient. If form is function, we must proceed to see how money works in broader economic structures and systems. As Shubik points out, "It is extremely difficult and of dubious value to define money *in vacuo* without specifying the rules of the monetary system and the market and financial institutions."[24] From money, then, we must proceed to markets and their makers.[25]

MARKET MAKERS) In Greek mythology, Hermes is the god of trade and commerce. Messenger of the gods and guide to the underworld, Hermes is a polymorphous trickster whose multiple guises anticipate the elusive confidence man. In one of his roles, Hermes is a thief; neither this nor that, he is as liminal as the space he occupies.

In its initial phase, the market was a place as much as a process. The word *economy* derives from the Greek word *oikonomos,* which means

manager of a household (*oikos,* house + *nomos,* managing). The earliest economy was domestic and involved neither barter nor trade. In Greece, Jean-Christophe Agnew explains, "early trade developed at the outskirts of the household economy. Embryonic markets first materialized at the periphery of settlement, in neutral zones or marches lying between villages, tribes, and societies. Their neutrality was secured by a variety of magical or reli-

Figure 8

Communion token, 1613. *American Journal of Numismatics and Bulletin of American Numismatic and Archaeological Studies* 22, no. 1 (1887). American Numismatic Society, New York.

gious rights associated with the crossing of boundaries."[26] The space of exchange was marked by a boundary stone or *herm* to identify the liminal territory as sacred. "Situated within a domestic mode of production, where the redistribution of goods was structured largely within and among households, such inland exchange as occurred among early Greek communities frequently took the form of a mutually sanctioned theft—a 'silent trade'—between persons who never saw one another but merely left and retrieved their goods at a sacred boundary stone."[27] These networks of exchange with invisible strangers were fraught with mystery and

Figure 9
Communion token, Ballingry Church, Scotland, 1864. Photograph © Copyright The British Museum.

provoked many superstitions. With the rise of the Greek city-state, the periphery migrated to the center and the *agora* became both the central market and primary gathering place for the community. The shift from margin to center did not erase the mystery and religious aura of the surrounding market; to the contrary, the marketplace became the site of regular festivals and admission to it required one "to perform a rite of purification." Transactions in the marketplace could not be completed without "oaths, witnesses, and/or visible tokens, or *symbola*." Though central markets and coinage were widespread throughout Greece by the sixth century BCE, suspicions of market exchange first expressed by Aristotle ran deep through-

Figure 10
Crucifix, 1750–75.

out the ancient world. Anticipating the tension between restricted and general economies, Aristotle argued that "exchange for exchange's sake," which he labeled "'chrematistic exchange,' threatened to transform the *nomos* of *oikonomos* from the householder's obligation of hospitality and liberality into a narrow calculus of cost and benefit; it diverted goods from their natural uses and limits to a sphere of intermediaries, where circulation and accumulation could accelerate and expand without purpose and, more important, without limit."[28]

Aristotle's aversion to market activity continues through the Middle Ages and is not finally overcome until the emergence of Calvinism. For a variety of reasons, the market economy developed slowly in Europe. With the collapse of the Roman Empire, Europe was plunged into the Dark Ages when the extensive market structure and monetary system that the Romans had developed vanished. By the ninth century, "the West was a closed domestic economy more or less without markets. The empire of Charlemagne was essentially agricultural, and the merchant classes had disappeared from it." The feudal system rested on social and economic obligations between lord and vassal, which created an immobile workforce bound to the land and laboring in a largely nonmonetary agricultural economy. Markets did not cease to exist but tended to be regulated by bishops, whose power increased in the political vacuum of the era. Ecclesiastical officials "began to control taxation, general administration, and through their granaries and storehouses, even the food supply. There were annual fairs and almost always weekly markets for produce. Taxes were levied in kind and in labor."[29] The stability of feudalism was shaken in the fourteenth century by a series of natural disasters and social upheavals. During this period, France suffered a succession of severe droughts that bred famine, economic insecurity, and social unrest. In the 1340s the Black Death swept through much of France, Britain, and Italy. In many areas from one-fourth to one-half of the population perished. This human tragedy had a significant impact on feudalism. Widespread death and illness prompted a labor shortage, and manor lords had to compete for surviving workers. Such bargaining gave common laborers greater mobility and hastened the spread of a monetary economy. The eventual result of these developments was the abolition of serfdom and with it the collapse of feudalism. Freed from lord and land many sought a better life in cities only to have their hopes frequently crushed by growing urban ills.

There is considerable dispute about exactly what a market is and precisely when markets emerge in Europe. The word *market* first appears in the English language in the fourteenth century. "In its earliest usage," Agnew explains, "the word referred alternately to the area, the occasion, or the gathering of buyers and sellers assembled within a specified time and place."[30] In Europe, as in ancient Greece, markets and fairs initially were held on the outskirts of towns, usually at or near a crossroads. In his monumental study, *Civilization and Capitalism: 15th–18th Century*, Fernand Braudel points out that these markets were "a sort of itinerant village, as the fair was a sort of traveling town." The decisive step "was taken when the *town* appropriated these hitherto modest little markets." For Braudel, a market is a process rather than merely a place: "Historically one can speak of a market economy" he argues, "when prices in the markets of a given area fluctuate in unison, a phenomenon the more characteristic since it may occur over a number of different jurisdictions or sovereignties."[31] According to this definition, markets clearly existed in Europe by the twelfth century. It is important to stress, however, that during the Middle Ages, markets did not include the entire economy or all social classes. The monetary economy reflected the social stratification of the period: upper classes used money, lower classes did not. In his influential and controversial book, *The Great Transformation: The Political and Economic Origins of Our Time*, Karl Polanyi maintains that, contrary to conventional wisdom, markets did not develop endogenously through an evolution from barter to local, national, and finally international trade but were exogenous. In other words, foreign trade gave rise to domestic markets rather than the reverse. In early Europe, foreign and domestic markets tended to be separate and were governed by different rules. While local markets handled retail goods and were noncompetitive as well as carefully regulated, foreign trade was competitive and remained largely unregulated. "Spices, salted fish, or wine had to be transported from a long distance and were thus the domain of the foreign merchant and his capitalistic wholesale trade methods. This type of trade escaped local regulation and all that could be done was to exclude it as far as possible from the local market. The complete prohibition of retail sale by foreign merchants was designed to achieve this end. The more the volume of capitalistic wholesale trade grew, the more strictly was its exclusion from local markets enforced as far as imports were concerned." The regulation of foreign trade reflected the fear that "mobile capital" would disrupt or even subvert the domestic economy and local institutions.[32] In addition to entering into relations with anonymous strangers, people who engaged in foreign trade were drawn into an impersonal exchange process where the immediacy of the face-to-face re-

lation in the domestic economy was displaced by the machinations of abstract structures of mediation. In retrospect, it is clear that what many
people most feared—and indeed continue to fear—about the market was
its abstract mediation and the accompanying loss of an idealized immediacy. Even if such immediacy were possible, it would be unavoidably fragile and always slipping away. As towns and cities appropriate peripheral
markets, the "outside" becomes an unassimilable "inside" that disrupts the
domestic economy as if from within.

Strictures on markets and commerce were imposed not only by secular
authorities; the Catholic Church also exercised its considerable power to
regulate expanding markets. While the church eagerly entered the business of agriculture, it was considerably more suspicious of merchants and
mercantilism. The primary hurdle to involvement with commerce was the
church's insistent prohibition of usury. Sanctions against usury date from
ancient and biblical times. In his *Politics,* Aristotle condemns usury as "unnatural exchange."

> The trade of the petty usurer is hated most, and with most reason: it
> makes a profit from currency itself instead of making it from the pro-
> cess, which currency was meant to serve. Currency came into existence
> merely as a means of exchange; usury tries to make it increase [as
> though it were an end in itself]. This is the reason why usury is called
> by the word we commonly use [the word *tokos,* which in Greek also
> means breed or offspring]; for as the offspring resembles its parent, so
> the interest bred by money is like the principal that breeds it, and it may
> be called "currency the son of currency." Hence we can understand why,
> of all modes of acquisition, usury is the most unnatural.[33]

There are five biblical texts on usury, four of which are in the Hebrew
Bible and one in the New Testament. Exodus 22:24, for example, states, "If
you lend money to one of your poor neighbors among my people, you shall
not act like an extortioner to him by demanding interest from him." Luke
6:34–35 extends this prohibition in a passage that was critical for the
Middle Ages: "If you lend to those from whom you expect repayment,
what merit is there in it for you? Even sinners lend to sinners, expecting
to be paid in full. Love your enemy and do good; lend, without expecting
to be paid in full."[34] During the medieval period, the term *usury* was used
only for monetary interest on monetary loans. In Scholastic theology,
usury designates any loan that yields a profit, and not only excessive in-

terest rates. The Second Lateran Council (1139) decreed that unrepentant usurers could not receive the sacraments and could not be buried in consecrated ground. In spite of these restrictions, the practice of usury persisted and actually spread.

The Catholic Church's prohibition of usury discouraged many Christians from entering business. This situation created an opportunity for enterprising Jewish people. Since Jews were legally excluded from numerous occupations and professions, it was not uncommon for them to become merchants and financiers. Many of the prejudices against Jews can be traced to the emergence of mercantile capitalism in the Middle Ages. Jacques Le Goff points out that "historically the image of the usurer has been closely tied to the image of the Jew. Until the twelfth century, Jews negotiated most interest bearing loans. These loans did not involve large sums and were carried on solely within the barter economy. That is they loaned grain, clothing, raw materials, or objects, and received a greater amount of these items than they had originally loaned."[35] European anti-Semitism is inseparable from the identification of Jews with usurers. The filth of lucre is transferred to the person of the Jew to create a figure of abjection, which had to be contained and controlled by structures and strategies of repression and exclusion. The Fourth Lateran Council confirmed a pattern that continues in one way or another down to the present day: "Wishing on this matter to prevent Christians from being treated inhumanly by Jews, we have decided . . . that if, for any pretext whatsoever, Jews have extracted heavy and excessive interest from Christians, all Christian commerce with them will be forbidden until they have atoned."[36] History has shown the policies of exclusion extended far beyond economic sanction.

The reasons for the condemnation of usury are multiple and complex. The theological justification for the sanction is that the usurer sells time, which properly belongs to God. Like Hermes, the usurer is a thief who steals not only from his fellow man but, more important, from God.[37] This theological explanation, however, is inadequate for it is obviously overdetermined in many ways. The deeper reason for the fear of usury is its association with illegitimate excess and unlawful surplus. Far from avoiding money's perversity, the usurer freely traffics in supplements whose danger is not merely economic but is, more insidiously, sexual. The censure of usury rests on a dread of perverse sexuality. This is already evident in Aristotle's claim that usury is "unnatural" because money gives birth to money. The generation of money by money seems to be a process of autoinsemination that breeds illegitimate offspring. By the Middle Ages, the association of usury with sexual perversity led to its condemnation as a form of bestiality.

Practice, of course, did not always conform to theory. As the medieval economy slowly revived, credit and interest became economic and social necessities. The prospect of economic profit prompted many Christians to ignore church dictates and openly practice usury. The development of the doctrine of purgatory had the unexpected consequence of encouraging usury by making the results of earthly sin less than final. Through the intercession of survivors and the purchase of indulgences, even usurers could be saved. The rejection of usury was not limited to Catholicism but extended to early Protestantism. In his *Long Sermon on Usury* (1520), Luther vehemently condemned the practice. As we will see below, Luther believed that mercantilism and capitalism are quite literally the work of the Devil. Not until Calvin was interest accepted and commercial enterprise warmly embraced rather than reluctantly tolerated.

A final hurdle had to be cleared before the market economy could expand throughout Europe. We have seen that, while foreign trade was unregulated and competitive, domestic trade was regulated and noncompetitive. The primary means of regulation was through the doctrine of the just price. "The practical application of this conception," Tawney explains, "is the attempt to try every transaction by a rule of right, which is largely, though not wholly, independent of the fortuitous combinations of economic circumstances. No man must ask more than the price fixed, either by public authorities, or, failing that, by common estimation." Accordingly, the price of goods should not exceed what is required to enable each person "to have the necessaries of life suitable for his station."[38] Accelerating economic activity in the High Middle Ages made it more and more difficult to enforce just price legislation. When the practice finally collapsed under the weight of economic pressure, competitive markets grew rapidly.

The expansion of cities and increase of trade went hand in hand. By the twelfth century, a significant merchant class had emerged in and around European urban centers. The needs of cities generated the demand for more foreign trade. The extension of markets would have been impossible without new financial procedures and institutions. The most basic yet critical innovation was double-entry bookkeeping. By the 1340s, merchants and civil authorities in Genoa were keeping their accounts in double-entry format. The German economic historian Werner Sombart has gone so far as to claim: "Double-entry book-keeping was born from the same spirit that gave rise to the systems of Galileo and Newton and the teachings of

modern physics and chemistry. It uses the same methods as they to organize phenomena into an artificial system: indeed, it is the first cosmol-
ogy on the basis of mechanical thought." This remark suggests that the
implications of double-entry bookkeeping extend far beyond a particular
accounting practice. As a result of this method of accounting, economic
calculations are made in terms of binary oppositions, economic systems
are believed to tend toward equilibrium, and financial instruments, with
the exception of money, always occur in pairs. It is not too much to suggest that double-entry accounting is "a machine for calculating the world"
that is, in effect, a proto–information-processing program.[39]

In addition to new methods for keeping records, mercantile capitalism
required a sophisticated banking system and new monetary instruments.
There were, of course, banks in the ancient world, but they mostly disappeared with the Roman Empire. According to Braudel, the first bankers in
Europe were "the exchange dealers, whether itinerant, traveling from fair
to fair, or settled in places like Barcelona, Genoa or Venice." Over the years,
the center of banking shifted from Florence (c. 1300) to Genoa (late sixteenth to early seventeenth century) and, by the eighteenth century, to
Amsterdam, London, Paris, and Geneva. While the history of banking is
enormously complex, for our purposes, it is necessary to concentrate on
several financial instruments that were important for emerging financial
institutions. Though the first banknotes were issued by the Bank of Stock-
holm in 1661 (the Bank of England followed in 1694), paper currency and
deposit banking can be traced to much older practices of goldsmiths. In
Genoa and Venice, receipts for gold deposits began to circulate and, when
signed, functioned as currency. Realizing very early that it was highly unlikely that all deposits would be collected at the same time, goldsmiths
began making interest-bearing loans that exceeded their gold reserves.
Though credit and money are not the same, the line separating them is not
always easy to draw. From its earliest days, capitalism would have been impossible without credit. Around the turn of the fourteenth century, there
was an explosive expansion of banking and credit in Florence. According to Braudel, "credit was something central not only to the entire history
of the city, but to that of her rivals among the Italian towns, not to say the
whole Mediterranean or the Western world. It is in the context of the revival of the European economy from at least the twelfth century that we
must view the establishment of the great merchant banking houses of
Florence."[40] Backed by a banking system far more sophisticated than elsewhere in Europe, Florentine power extended from Spain and Portugal to
England and Scotland. This financial empire eventually collapsed in 1345,

when Edward III's default on his enormous debt combined with the devastation of the Black Death to create an international financial crisis.

As the power of Florence declined, the power of Genoa grew. The Genoese extended Florentine innovations by developing a system of credit "based on negotiable bills of exchange, which were passed from fair to fair or exchange to exchange. Bills of exchange were already known and made use of in Antwerp, Lyons, and Augsburg, in Medina del Campo and elsewhere, and these money markets did not become deserted overnight. But under the Genoese, paper acquired a new importance. Indeed the Fuggers are supposed to have said that doing business with the Genoese meant playing with pieces of paper . . . whereas they themselves operated with real money, *Baargeld*—the typical reaction of traditional financiers failing to understand a new technique." The use of bills of exchange involved a series of transactions on increasingly integrated international markets. Later chapters will make it clear that medieval bills of exchange anticipate today's futures and options. In the most elementary transaction, a merchant might buy a farmer's crop before it is harvested and then sell the bill of exchange to another merchant on a different market. The seller, like the farmer, would get his money immediately and the buyer would receive payment for the produce at its market value when the contract came due. As European markets and fairs grew and became centralized, bills of exchange facilitated international financial payments. Genoese merchant banks were the major clearinghouses for these transactions. By the end of the sixteenth century, Europe—especially Spain, which was deeply indebted to Genoa—was flooded with silver from America. With this increase in the supply of specie, the Genoese paper empire crumbled.[41]

By the seventeenth and eighteenth centuries, Amsterdam was playing the role Florence and Genoa had played earlier. Mercantile capitalism was thriving and, more important for our purposes, the Amsterdam Stock Exchange had opened. Amsterdam quickly became the capital of speculative finance whose markets governed trade throughout Europe by means of something approximating remote control or action at a distance. Braudel points out that the complexity of the instruments and transactions on the Amsterdam exchange far surpassed anything that had gone before and anticipated financial instruments and practices three hundred years later.

> Speculation on the Amsterdam Stock Exchange had reached a degree of
> sophistication and abstraction which made it for many years a very special trading center of Europe, a place where people were not content
> simply to buy and sell shares, speculating on their possible rise or fall,

but where one could by means of various ingenious combinations speculate without having any money or shares at all. This was where the brokers came into their own. They were divided into two coteries—known as *rotteries*. If one group pushed up the price, another, the "underminers" (or "bears" as they would be known in London) would try to bring it down. . . . All shares were however nominal, and the Dutch East India Company held the certificates; a buyer could only acquire a share by having his name entered in a special register kept for the purpose. The company had initially thought in this way to prevent speculation . . . but speculation could operate without ownership. The speculator was in fact selling something he did not possess and buying something he never would: it was what was known as "blank" buying. The operation would be resolved by a loss or a gain. The difference would be settled by a payment one way or the other and the game would go on.

With the spread of mercantile capitalism and the emergence of speculative financial markets, the market economy reached a remarkable level of complexity. Not only was it easier to borrow money in Holland in the 1750s than it was in New York in the 1980s, but the Amsterdam exchange of the 1700s is remarkably similar to the financial markets of the 1980s and 1990s.[42] The question that remains is how this astonishing speculative market grew out of Calvinism.

INVISIBLE HAND) Hayek not only credits Adam Smith with the creation of cybernetics but also maintains that Scottish philosophers anticipated the theories underlying the most sophisticated contemporary interpretations of money and markets: "Thus from the Scottish moral philosophers of the eighteenth century stem the chief impulses towards a theory of evolution, the variety of disciplines known as cybernetics, general systems theory, synergetics, autopoiesis, as well as the understanding of the superior self-ordering power of the market system, and of the evolution also of language, morals and law."[43] In spite of this remarkable insight Hayek, like most other commentators, fails to note that both Scottish moral philosophy and Smith's understanding of the market are ultimately rooted in theology and aesthetics. The close relationship between capitalism and Protestantism has, of course, long been recognized. As Max Weber famously argues, the Protestant emphasis on individual responsibility and the disciplined exercise of the will on the one hand, and on the other the aversion to idleness and luxury led to an "inner worldly asceticism" whose values coincide with the needs of early capitalism. The virtues of prudence and frugality led to disciplined saving, which created reserves for profitable investment in emerging mercantile ventures and speculative markets.[44]

When considering the importance of Protestantism for capitalism, it is essential to distinguish Lutheranism from Calvinism. Although the Reformation is an extraordinarily complex social, economic, political, and religious phenomenon, it was sparked by controversy over a relatively simple theological issue. The cornerstone of Reformation theology is Luther's appropriation and radicalization of Paul's doctrine of justification by faith alone, which he opposed to the medieval Catholic belief that man becomes acceptable to God by accumulating merit through doing good works or the purchase of indulgences. For Luther, redemption occurs by means of a completely personal relation between the individual and God. This doctrine had devastating consequences for the power and authority of the Catholic Church. Since the relation between self and God is a private transaction, salvation need not be mediated by the church but can occur in whatever way God ordains. Far from the extension of the Kingdom of God on earth, the Catholic Church, Luther declares, is part of the corrupt kingdom of the world, which is ruled by the Devil. The ostentatious wealth of the church offended Luther's peasant values and became the target of his most vehement criticism. He actually went so far as to declare, "The pope is the Devil incarnate." Luther associated the excesses of the Catholic Church with nascent capitalism. "Under the papacy," he argues, "the Devil has established a market for souls."[45] For Luther, the greatest sin of the Catholic Church was the commodification of religion. In his highly informative yet underappreciated *Religion and the Rise of Capitalism*, R. H. Tawney maintains that Luther

> hated the economic individualism of the age not less than its spiritual laxity. . . . His attitude to the conquest of society by the merchant and financier is the same as his attitude towards the commercialization of religion. When he looks at the Church in Germany, he sees it sucked dry by the tribute, which flows to the new Babylon. When he looks at the German social life, he finds it ridden by a conscienceless money-power, which incidentally ministers, like the banking business of the Fuggers, to the avarice and corruption of Rome. The exploitation of the Church by the Papacy, and the exploitation of the peasant and the craftsman by the capitalist, are thus two horns of the beast which sits on the seven hills.[46]

Luther expressed his utter disdain for worldly corruption by consistently associating the Devil with the anus and filthy lucre with excrement or shit. In his classic account of the Protestant era, Norman O. Brown explores the psychoanalytic implications of Luther's language and imagery.

> To see the Devil as lord of this world is to see the world as a manure heap, to see universal filth: "*Scatet totus orbis,*" Luther says. The avarice in Leipzig is the Devil's work and by the same token "filth." And since in Luther's historical eschatology the world was going to get worse before it got better, he sees the approaching end of the world as taking the form of a "rain of filth." The Second Coming will reduce sublimations to the anality out of which they are constructed. The Devil turns cow dung into a crown, but "Christ, Who will shortly come in His glory, will quiet them, not indeed with gold, but with brimstone." And in this world in line with Luther's new *theologia crucis,* though grace may keep the inward spirit clean, the Christian must surrender his flesh to the extremest assaults of anality.[47]

But no matter how deep the shit gets, the Second Coming is always deferred. In order to survive, the church had to find ways to accommodate itself to a fallen world. By the time Calvin arrived on the scene, both Protestantism and capitalism had changed significantly.

The problems Calvin confronted as a second-generation reformer differed from those Luther had encountered. Luther's temperament and the exigencies of his struggle with the Catholic Church left him little time to develop a coherent statement of his theological principles. Calvin faced the task of working out the systematic implications of the Protestant doctrine of salvation. The result was his monumental *Institutes of the Christian Religion* (1536), which still forms the foundation of the Reformed tradition. In the years between Luther's break with Rome and Calvin's rise to power, Protestantism expanded from the country to cities in Northern Europe. A gifted politician, Calvin managed to move beyond the agrarianism of Luther's peasant roots by working out an accommodation between the new religion and the rapidly expanding urban commercial bourgeoisie. In order to accomplish this end, Calvin modified some of Luther's basic theological principles.

One of Calvin's most important departures for the history of Protestantism and capitalism was his acceptance of loans and interest. "What reason is there," he asks, "why income from business should not be larger than that from land-owing? Whence do the merchant's profits come, except from his own diligence and industry."[48] With this change in attitude, the major obstacle preventing Christians from entering business and commerce was removed and the wedding of Protestantism and capitalism could be consummated. Far from the kingdom of darkness, the commercial world now appears to be an important part of God's created order.

Calvinism not only underwrote the expansion of capitalism in the sixteenth and seventeenth centuries but also inspired the most sophisticated and influential theoretical analysis of money and markets in the eighteenth century. When Adam Smith published *The Wealth of Nations* in 1776, it marked the culmination of developments that had been unfolding in Scottish moral philosophy through the eighteenth century. It is no accident that classical political economy emerged in Scotland. The version of Calvinism characteristic of Scottish Presbyterianism combined with the moral philosophy promoted at the University of Glasgow to form an interpretation of markets that is deeply indebted to theology and aesthetics. In the work of Smith and his Scottish precursors, God, art, and economics intersect in an account of capitalism whose implications do not become clear for two centuries.

To understand the distinctive form of Calvinism that shaped the intellectual climate during Smith's formative years, it is necessary to return to the seminal work of the thinker whose insights were decisive for the eruption of Protestantism—William of Ockham (born between 1290 and 1300). Every theology prior to postmodernism falls into one of two categories: those that give priority to word (reason) over deed (will), or those that give priority to deed over word. The choice is between the Gospel of John—"In the beginning was the word"—and Goethe's *Faust* or Freud's *Totem and Taboo*—"In the beginning was the deed." In a theistic model of God, if reason always guides will, human beings are reasonable and the world is both orderly and intelligible. If, however, God's will is antecedent to reason, the world as well as reason is radically contingent and human life is wrapped in mystery and haunted by uncertainty. During the High Middle Ages, Scholastic theologians elaborated a view of the world as hierarchically ordered and transparently rational. The most comprehensive formulation of this position was developed in Thomas Aquinas's extensive theological treatises. By comparison with the turmoil of the Dark Ages, Aquinas's time was an era of revival; confusion and anxiety gradually were replaced by a sense of order and confidence. For Aquinas, the rational order of the world derives from God's creative power and intelligent government. God is always reasonable and never arbitrary; in Aquinas's own terms, "There is will in God, just as there is intellect: since will follows upon intellect." After creating the world, God established the rational laws through which He manages His creation. *"Providence,"* Aquinas insists, *"is the divine reason itself, which, seated in the Supreme Ruler, disposes all things."* [49] The order of the world and rationale for life reflect God's rational will.

By the late Middle Ages, the world did not seem so orderly and God did not seem so reasonable. The social calamities during the first half of the fourteenth century brought radical change throughout much of Western Europe. The human tragedy wrought by the Black Death weakened the hierarchical structure of feudalism and hastened the spread of the use of cash and the market economy. Freed from lord and land, individuals were thrown back on their own resources both in daily economic matters and in their quest for religious assurance in a world that seemed enigmatic, mysterious, and often cruel. William of Ockham's revolutionary theology reflected this strange new world. In contrast to Aquinas, for whom God's will is always guided by His reason, Ockham gives absolute priority to God's omnipotent will. God is bound by absolutely nothing—not even His own reason—and thus is free to act in ways that sometimes seem arbitrary and often are incomprehensible. From this theological perspective, the ground of the universe is the productive will of God, which is the condition of the possibility of reason and unreason and therefore is neither precisely rational nor irrational. Since the divine will is unknowable, faith cannot be a matter of knowledge; one believes *in spite of* not because of reason. Though not immediately evident, Ockham's theological reversal of Scholasticism harbors cosmological, anthropological, and linguistic implications that play a critical role in the emergence of Protestantism and the development of capitalism.

If the universe is the product of God's productive will, unguided by the divine Logos, the order of things is contingent or even arbitrary, rather than necessary. As a result of the constant activity of the divine will, there can be no certainty about the continuation or stability of the cosmic order. What God institutes He can always undo. To blunt the far-reaching implications of this argument, Ockham distinguished God's *potentia absoluta* (absolute power) from his *potentia ordinata* (ordained power). While God has the absolute power to do anything that is not self-contradictory, He freely chooses to limit Himself by ordaining a particular systematic order for the world. It is crucial to note that this system is constituted from without and even when seeming to be stable is always subject to unanticipated disruptions. If understood in this way, Ockham's criticism of Scholasticism's rational systems anticipates the poststructural deconstruction of structuralism's closed systems, which we considered in chapter 1.[50] In subsequent chapters, it will become clear that the alternative theological visions developed by medieval Scholastics and their heirs on the one hand and by Ockham and his Protestant followers on the other indirectly inform the contrasting models of systems (i.e., intrinsically stable systems vs. complex adaptive systems), which play a critical role in economic developments during the last half of the twentieth century.

Ockham's anthropology is a mirror image of his theology and accordingly has two fundamental tenets: the anteriority and priority of the singular individual over the social group, and human freedom and responsibility. His position on these issues led to his most devastating critique of medieval theology and ecclesiology. The issue over which Ockham split with his predecessors is the seemingly inconsequential status of universal terms. For Scholastic theology, the universal term, idea, or essence is ontologically more real than the individual and epistemologically truer than empirical experience. This doctrine was known as Realism. For the realist, humanity, for example, is essential, and individual human beings exist only by virtue of their participation in the antecedent universal. Exercising his fabled razor, Ockham rejects Realism and insists that universal terms are merely names, which might serve as useful heuristic fictions to order the world and organize experience but are not real in any ontological sense. This position eventually came to be known as Nominalism (from *nom,* which means name). For the nominalist, only individuals are real. In the case of human beings, individuals are not defined by any universal idea or atemporal essence but constitute themselves historically through their own free decisions. The defining characteristics of human selfhood are individuality, freedom, and responsibility. For the nominalist, the whole, up to and including the human race, is nothing more than the sum of all the individuals that make it up.

Finally, Ockham's Nominalism entails a new understanding of language and, most important, of the relation between words and things. Translating Ockham's theology and anthropology into semiotic terms, Meyrick Carré explains:

> Universals are signs, standing for a set of qualities or objects; they are universal by meaning. Thus the historic controversy over the nature of universals becomes pointless. For to discuss whether a universal is related to an individual is like discussing whether the name or sign "table" is part of the table. Some signs stand for one thing, others stand for many things, and these are universals; but everything which actually ex-

ists is a single thing. All the difficulties about universals spring from the attempt to make them both singular and plural at the same time. Species and genus do not name substances, but signs.[51]

Insofar as language is general, if not universal, and subjects as well as objects are singular, existing entities cannot as such be represented linguistically. As linguistic beings, we traffic in signs, which do not refer to things but are signs of other signs. While appearing to represent the world, language is nothing more than a play of signs unanchored by knowable referents.

The implications of Ockham's theology are nothing less than revolutionary; indeed, it is no exaggeration to claim that Ockham is the first modernist. His empiricism prepares the way for modern science; his voluntarism points to nineteenth-century romanticism as well as Nietzsche's will to power and Freud's unconscious; and his linguistic theories anticipate both British analytic philosophy and recent Continental semiology. In this context, however, it is the *theological* impact of Ockham's ideas that is of interest. Luther's reformation would have been impossible without Ockham's account of both God's omnipotent will and the freedom and responsibility of the individual person. As I have already suggested, Calvin elaborates Luther's soteriology to form the first systematic Protestant theology. According to Calvin, belief in salvation by grace rather than works presupposes an all-powerful Creator God who is radically free and completely unconstrained by external circumstances. Rather than a one-time event, creation is an ongoing process in which God constantly governs the universe. The doctrine of creation, therefore, necessarily entails the doctrine of providence.

> To make God a momentary Creator, who once for all finished his work, would be cold and barren, and we must differ from profane men especially in that we see the presence of divine power shining as much in the continuing state of the universe as in its inception. . . . For unless we pass on to his providence—however we may seem both to comprehend with the mind and to confess with the tongue—we do not yet properly know what it means to say: "God is Creator."[52]

According to Calvin, providence is not merely general but extends to each event and every individual. From the beginning of time, the course of the world is predestined. Within this theological framework, there is no such thing as fortune or chance because everything "is directed by God's ever-present hand." God's hand is not, of course, always visible; on the contrary, since God's plan is "secret," "the true causes of events are hidden to us."[53] The hand of providence, in other words, is *invisible*. Calvin, then, is the first to suggest the image of the invisible hand, which Smith makes famous.

Calvin's doctrine of providence leads to an understanding of the world and life in it that differs significantly from Lutheranism. In contrast to Luther, for whom the world, sunk in sin, is irredeemably corrupt and capitalism is a pact with the Devil, which draws people away from God, Calvin sees the world as the theater of God's glory, where "divine power shines brightly." The world and our activity in it reveal the power and grandeur of the Lord. Contrary to the usual view of Puritanism as austerely antiaesthetic, Calvin maintains that the *beauty* of creation reveals the glory of the Creator.

> Has the Lord clothed the flowers with the great beauty that greets our eyes, the sweetness of smell that is wafted upon our nostrils, and yet will it be unlawful for our eyes to be affected by that beauty, or our sense of smell by the sweetness of that odor? What? Did he not so distinguish colors as to make some more lovely than others? What? Did he not endow gold and silver, ivory and marble, with a loveliness that renders them more precious than other metals or stones? Did he not, in short, render many things attractive to us, apart from their necessary use?[54]

This often-overlooked intersection of theology and aesthetics is very important in Scottish Calvinism.

Rejecting Lutheranism's identification of mercantilism and capitalism with the work of the Devil, Calvinism views economic success as a sign, though never the cause, of redemption. Worldly vocation is not only religiously validated but actually extends God's providential governance. This point must be carefully understood because it implies a dialectical reversal of the divine-human relation with far-reaching consequences. By emphasizing God's omnipotence so strongly, Calvin inadvertently collapses transcendence into immanence. If all acts and events are ultimately the result of God's providence, divine and human wills are finally indistinguishable even if they are not precisely identical. No longer imposed from without, divine purpose now emerges within the play of worldly events. With this aestheticization of creation and the immanentization of purpose, the way is prepared for Scottish moral philosophy and the birth of modern political economy.

In his introduction to *The Wealth of Nations,* Robert Reich notes that the invisible hand is "perhaps the most famous, or infamous, bodily metaphor in all of social science."[55] What Reich and others do not realize is that before it is a social scientific metaphor, the invisible hand is first a theological and then an aesthetic metaphor. Nor do most commentators know that seventeen years before he described the market through the operation of the invisible hand, Smith used the image in *The Theory of Moral Sentiments* (1759). The passage in which the invisible hand appears falls under the heading, "Of the beauty which the appearance of UTILITY bestows upon all productions of art, and the extensive influence of this species of Beauty."[56] Explaining the unintended consequences of the actions of the wealthy, Smith writes:

> They are led by an invisible hand to make nearly the same distribution of the necessaries of life, which would have been made, had the earth been divided into equal portions among all its inhabitants, and thus without intending it, without knowing it, advance the interest of the society, and afford the means to the multiplication of the species. When Providence divided the earth among a few lordly masters, it neither forgot nor abandoned those who seemed to have been left out in the partition. . . . The same principle, the love of system, the same regard to beauty of order, of art and contrivance, frequently serves to recommend those institutions which tend to promote the public welfare.[57]

Recasting the theological doctrine of providence in terms of aesthetic sensibility, Smith describes the "beauty of order" in which individuals are harmoniously related even when their intentions seem to be conflicting. This vision shapes Smith's understanding of the economic order.

The Scottish moral philosophy on which Smith was nourished is marked by its consistent effort to interpret morality through aesthetics. Within this framework, the good is beautiful and the beautiful is good. During the first half of the eighteenth century, leading Scottish philosophers developed a critical response to Hobbes's philosophy in which they proposed an alternative to his egoistic anthropology and authoritarian morality. Far from completely self-centered, they argued, human beings are also *social* creatures. This sociality gives them a natural moral sense, which frees them from the necessity of external moral dictates promulgated by priests and princes. The two most important figures in this philosophical movement were Anthony Ashley, third earl of Shaftesbury (1671–1713), and Francis Hutcheson (1694–1746). Returning to the Greek ideal of balance and harmony, as the romantics would a century later, Shaftesbury maintained that human beings are part of an intricate order in which individual good must be balanced and harmonized with the social whole. Self-interest and the interests of the group do not necessarily clash but can actually be mutually reinforcing. The guiding principle of harmony is grasped through the sense of beauty. "My inclinations," Shaftesbury confessed, "lead me strongly this way, for I am ready enough to yield that there is no real good besides the enjoyment of beauty."[58] At this point, moral sense and aesthetic sensibility become one and the same.

It was left for Hutcheson to organize and elaborate Shaftesbury's insights. Smith attended Hutcheson's lectures and after his death assumed his chair in moral philosophy at the University of Glasgow. In *An Inquiry into the Original of Our Ideas of Beauty and Virtue* (1725), Hutcheson defined beauty as "uniformity amidst variety."[59] In classical philosophical terms, beauty is unity-in-multiplicity. When this aesthetic sensibility is translated into moral sense, the primary virtue becomes benevolence, which is the apprehension of and responsiveness to the harmonious order of things. If generalized to form a moral maxim, the principle of benevolence promotes the greatest good for the greatest number. Once again, self-love and altruism are not necessarily antithetical, for, as Hume would argue some years later, "'tis evident that the passion is much better satisfy'd by its restraint, than by its liberty, and that in preserving society, we make much greater advances in acquiring of possessions, than in the solitary and forlorn condition."[60] The reason Smith maintained that beauty is "the appearance of utility" here becomes clear. The greatest good for the greatest number is an expression of benevolence, which reflects and promotes "uniformity amidst variety." As we will see in the next chapter, by the end of the century, beauty and utility are opposed.

At first glance, it might appear that a significant shift occurs between *The Theory of Moral Sentiments* and *The Wealth of Nations*. In one of the best-known passages in the history of economic theory, Smith writes, "It is not from the benevolence of the butcher, the brewer, or the baker that we expect our dinner, but from their regard to their own interest. We address ourselves, not to their humanity but to their self-love."[61] It is, however, a mistake to set up a simple opposition between benevolence and self-love. To see why this is so, it is necessary to examine more closely the precise meaning of moral *sense*. From Shaftesbury and Hutcheson to Hume and Smith, Scottish philosophers assume that reason alone cannot govern the passions. If social order is to be maintained without authoritarian control, the passions must control themselves. In his influential study, *The Passions and the Interests: Political Arguments for Capitalism before Its Triumph,* Albert Hirschman argues that for eighteenth-century moral philosophy, the passion of self-interest could be checked only by a "countervailing passion." Though he had been introduced to this idea in lectures and readings, Smith encountered a powerful formulation of it in his conversations with the Physiocrat Helvétius during his sojourn in France (1764–66). In *De l'esprit,* Helvétius argues:

> There are few moralists who know how to arm our passions against one another . . . for the purpose of having their counsel adopted. Most of the time their advice would inflict too much injury if followed. Yet they should realize that this sort of injury cannot win out over feeling; that *only a passion can triumph over a passion.* . . . The moralist might succeed in having their maxims observed if they substituted in this manner the language of interest for that of injury.[62]

Before proceeding to a consideration of the distinction between passion and interest, it is important to note that the Physiocrats extend the notion of countervailing passions to form a laissez-faire economic policy, which rests upon a "harmony-of-interests doctrine according to which the public good is the outcome of the free pursuit by everyone of his own self-interest." Unable to leave Hobbes completely behind, however, they "advocate both freedom from governmental interference with the market and the enforcement of this freedom by an all-powerful ruler whose self-interest is tied up with the 'right' economic system."[63]

In the writings of Scottish moral philosophers, the distinction between passions and interests is equivalent to the difference between private concerns (passions) and public good (interests). Initially framed in terms of moral aestheticism, the analysis of the interplay between passions and interests was quickly extended to economic relations. Shaftesbury already moved in this direction when he wrote, "If the regard toward [acquisition of wealth] be moderate, and in a reasonable degree; if it occasions no passionate pursuit—there is nothing in this case which is not compatible with virtue, and even suitable and beneficial to society."[64] Later thinkers moved beyond Shaftesbury when they not only argued that private gain can be beneficial to society but contended that self-interest is in effect a virtue. As Mandeville had said in *The Fable of the Bees: or, Private Vices, Publick Benefits,*

> Thus every part was full of Vice,
> Yet the whole Mass a Paradise.[65]

This position has a further consequence. Instead of fueling the war of all against all, the pursuit of economic self-interests can actually check destructive selfish passions. Extending this argument, some analysts have maintained that the market in general and capitalism in particular can actually civilize society. As economic interests become more integrated, the likelihood of personal and political conflict decreases.

According to the notion of countervailing passions, human beings are not merely selfish but are inwardly divided between private and public concerns. Social control, therefore, need not be imposed from without but can also arise from within. Though not immediately apparent, this account of passions and interests involves a subtle yet important shift. Alexander Pope glimpsed this insight when he wrote,

> Thus God and Nature formed the general frame
> And bade self-love and social be the same.[66]

If "self-love and social be the same," passion and interest are inseparably interrelated and inherently dialectical. In other words, each implicitly includes the other within itself and, through its own expression or self-development, turns into what appears to be its opposite. This dialectical reversal, which is fraught with theological significance, becomes vital to the classical theory of markets: the sin of avarice becomes virtually indistinguishable from the virtue of benevolence. This point is, of course, thoroughly Protestant. For both Luther and Calvin, sin and redemption are dialectically related—redemption can only occur *in and through* sin. Within the overall economy of salvation, therefore, sin and the fall, though painful, are always fortunate.

With one final insight, we are in a position to understand why Hayek credits Scottish moral philosophy with creating cybernetics as well as anticipating evolution, general systems theory, synergetics, and autopoiesis. A few pages before introducing the notion of the invisible hand in his moral theory, Smith offers a remarkably rich comment.

> We are then charmed with the beauty of that accommodation, which reigns in the palaces and economy of the great; and admire how every thing is adapted to promote their ease, to prevent their wants, to gratify their wishes, and to amuse and entertain their most frivolous desires. If we consider the real satisfaction which all these things are capable of affording, by itself and separated from the beauty of that arrangement which is fitted to promote it, it will always appear in the highest degree

contemptible and trifling. But we rarely view it in this abstract and philosophical light. We naturally confound it in our imagination with the order, the regular and harmonious movement of the system, the machine or economy by means of which it is produced.[67]

In this passage, Smith expands his understanding of beauty and utility to argue that the economy is a well-oiled machine that effectively regulates private conflicts to maintain a balanced and harmonious system. The metaphor of the world as a machine was, of course, very popular throughout the eighteenth century. Attempting to preserve a role for God in a Newtonian universe, Deists imagined the world as a giant clock, which God creates and then allows to run according to laws He establishes. Smith modifies this metaphor in two important ways. First, by interpreting the machine in terms of beauty, he obscures the line that usually separates machines and organisms. As if anticipating artificial intelligence and digital life, Smith implies that machines are organic and organisms are in some sense machines. Second, purpose in the economic system is internal rather than external. The machine of the economy and the beautiful system it generates are characterized by what Kant will describe fourteen years later as "inner teleology." It is therefore self-regulating and thus is autotelic, autopoietic, or autoaffective. Rather than imposed from without, the invisible hand emerges in and through the free interplay of individual agents. Insofar as God is what God does, we might go so far as to say that the market *is* God and the activity of the market is always a hand job. The market, in other words, is a *theological* notion and as such is a matter of faith.

3

FIGURING CAPITAL

—No wait hey I mean holy shit I don't mean where everybody's crazy about us and all, see good will that means the excess of the purchase price over the value of these net tangible assets where they really screwed us on that Endo deal see so ouch!

—That's not what it means! That's what I'm trying to, listen all I want you to do to take your mind off these nickel deductions these net tangible assets for a minute and listen to a piece of great music, it's a cantata by Bach cantata number twenty-one by Johann Sebastian Bach damn it JR can't you understand what I'm trying to, to show you there's such a thing as as as intangible assets? what I was trying to tell you that night the sky do you remember it? walking back from that rehearsal that whole sense of, of sheer wonder in the Rhinegold you remember it?

William Gaddis, *JR*

ARTISTIC ABSOLUTE) In his richly suggestive *At Home in the Universe: The Search for the Laws of Self-Organization and Complexity,* biologist Stuart Kauffman points out:

> Immanuel Kant, writing more than two centuries ago, saw organisms as wholes. The whole existed by means of the parts; the parts existed both because of and in order to sustain the whole. This holism has been stripped of a natural role in biology, replaced with the image of the genome as the central directing agency that commands the molecular dance. Yet an autocatalytic set of molecules is perhaps the simplest image one can have of Kant's holism. Catalytic closure ensures that the whole exists by means of the parts, and they are present both because of and in order to sustain the whole. Autocatalytic sets exhibit the emergent property of holism.[1]

What makes Kauffman's remark so intriguing is the link he establishes between the rapidly growing field of complexity studies and late eighteenth-century philosophy. Complexity theorists bring together the fields of information theory, evolutionary biology, and digital life to form an analysis of complex adaptive systems, which, they argue, can be found in physical, biological, social, and cognitive structures. As we will see in chapter 8, in recent years some economists have been using the insights of complexity studies to develop new models for markets.[2] Their conclusions both confirm many of Smith's arguments and extend his insights in unexpected directions. Before proceeding to a consideration of economic developments during the past four decades, we must attempt to understand in greater detail precisely how current systems theories are related to post-Kantian theology, aesthetics, and philosophy.

While Smith, as Hayek has suggested, might well have anticipated cybernetics, general systems theory, autopoiesis, and self-ordering processes, the roots of his theories, we have discovered, lie in Scottish moral philosophy and Calvinism. By the end of the eighteenth century, however, the bond between beauty and utility, which inspired Smith's view of the market, had been decisively broken. Far from serving useful purposes, beauty came to be defined as nonutilitarian: the beautiful is both purposeless and useless. As our consideration of Bataille's restricted and general economies has led us to suspect, however, the useful and the useless are not simply opposites but are braided together in complicated ways. In the progression from Kant through Schleiermacher, Hegel, and Marx to Simmel, religion, art, and economics are interwoven, unwoven, and rewoven to form an interpretation of culture, money, and markets that helps to explain much of what happened during the last half of the twentieth century.

No period is more decisive for subsequent social and cultural developments than the last decade of the eighteenth century. During the 1790s, a group of remarkably creative theologians, artists, and philosophers gathered in the small German duchy of Jena to forge a vision of the world that continues to shape experience in subtle yet crucial ways. The world as we know it would not exist without the work of these seminal thinkers. The cultural developments during this pivotal era were inseparably bound to changes in the so-called "real" economy. Most important for our purposes was the emergence of an unprecedented art market. This market grew out of economic changes that created both new consumers and new producers of art. With the spread of industrialization, members of the growing urban bourgeoisie accumulated considerable wealth and began to search for cultural markers that would distinguish them from the working class. The purchase and display of art became one of the primary ways in which this need was met. At the same time that this art market was emerging, structures of support on which artists had relied for centuries were disappearing. By the latter part of the eighteenth century, the patronage system had eroded to the point of collapse and artists had to find ways to support themselves and their work. No longer able to rely on the church or the aristocracy, artists were driven to produce art to meet the demand of the burgeoning middle class. The result was the commodification of works of art and the emergence of a culture industry, which often deployed the same industrial methods of mass production that had created the bourgeoisie's excess wealth. The aesthetic tastes of these new consumers of culture were decidedly conservative; they preferred their art decorative, realistic, and representational. In this commercial market, artists attempted to meet "pre-existing demands" in "pre-established forms." For artists themselves, such art is thoroughly utilitarian and conforms to traditional economic principles. In the newly emerging market, Pierre Bourdieu explains, "there is the 'economic' logic of the literary and artistic industries, which, since they make the trade in cultural goods just another trade, confer priority on distribution, on immediate and temporary success, measured, for example, by the print run, and which are content to adjust themselves to the preexisting demand of a clientele."[3] Many artists were so ambivalent about these developments that they refused to admit that works produced for the market were "true" art. This assessment of commercial art led to the distinction between high and low art or fine art and craft, which emerged for the first time at the end of the eighteenth century.

In contrast to low art, which is created for consumers who are not producers, high art is created for other artists and is supposed to remain free from market forces. Rather than seeking popular acceptance by meeting preexisting demands with preexisting forms, true art challenges convention by creating art that frustrates or even shatters expectations. Through a curious reversal, rejection becomes a sign of success. In contrast to decorative, realistic, and representational bourgeois art, so-called advanced art tends to be abstract, nonreferential, and transgressive. For the avant-garde, it is not only art that is supposed to be transgressive; the life of the artist should also challenge bourgeois values. Always positioning themselves at the edge of the social economy on which they nonetheless depend, artists become liminal figures whose marginality provokes fascination as well as suspicion.

While low art is calculated to be profitable and thus useful, high art is nonutilitarian and hence follows an "inverse economic logic." "These fields are the site of the antagonistic coexistence of two modes of production and circulation obeying inverse logics. At one pole, there is the anti-'economic' economy of pure art. Founded on the obligatory recognition of the values of disinterestedness and on the denegation of the 'economy' (of the 'commercial') and of the 'economic' profit (in the short term), it privileges production and its specific necessities, the outcome of an autonomous history."[4] According to Bourdieu, fine art operates within a "restricted economy whose distinguishing characteristic is its autonomy, i.e., its independence from the outside influence of either patrons or the market." According to the rules by which this game is played, art has no other purpose than itself; art, in other words, is always for the sake of art. In the inverted world of the restricted economy, commercial success is artistic failure.

> The symbolic revolution through which artists free themselves from bourgeois demand by refusing to recognize any master except their art produces the effect of making the market disappear. In fact they could not triumph over the "bourgeois" in the struggle for control of the meaning and function of artistic activity without at the same time eliminating the bourgeois as a potential customer. At the moment when they argue, with Flaubert, that "a work of art . . . is beyond appraisal, has no commercial value, cannot be paid for," that it is *without price,* that is to say, foreign to the ordinary logic of the ordinary economy, they discover that it is effectively *without commercial value,* that it has no market.[5]

The market, however, always finds a way to incorporate whatever is designed to elude it. As the bourgeoisie sought to mark their social status by consuming traditional art, upper social classes started buying avant-garde art to secure their distinction from those they deemed their social inferiors.

It should be clear that Bourdieu's restricted economy is the functional equivalent of Bataille's general economy. Not limited by the necessity of making calculations for profitable returns, such inverted economies value the useless more than the useful. Bourdieu enriches Bataille's analysis by lending it historical depth. What neither Bourdieu nor Bataille adequately acknowledges, however, is that post-Kantian philosophers and writers developed the doctrine of *l'art pour l'art* in ways that were decisive for twentieth-century art, culture, and economics.

Kant translated the economic realities of the late eighteenth century into the language of philosophical aesthetics. The nineteenth century effectively begins with the publication of Kant's Third Critique in 1790. By attempting to mediate *Critique of Pure Reason* (1781) and *Critique of Practical Reason* (1788), *Critique of Judgment* marks the completion of Kant's critical philosophy. Each part of this philosophical project is devoted to one of the three classical philosophical problems: truth (First Critique), goodness (Second Critique), and beauty (Third Critique). By considering beauty in the Third Critique, Kant attempts to demonstrate how art and aesthetic sensibility mediate the conflicts and resolve the tensions created by the antitheses and antimonies of our cognitive and volitional faculties. What unites the three critiques is Kant's interpretation of the principle of autonomy. Autonomy (*auto,* self + *nomos,* law) means self-government or self-regulation. Autonomy functions differently in each of our three faculties: reason is autonomous when it determines itself through a priori forms of intuition and categories of understanding; the will is autonomous when it freely gives itself the universal moral law; and aesthetic sensibility is autonomous when it is free of external influence and thus remains disinterested. In the Third Critique, Kant articulates the structure of the principle of autonomy in terms of what he describes as "inner teleology" or "purposiveness without purpose" (*Zweckmässigkeit ohne Zweck*). In contrast to external teleology, in which ends are imposed from without or lie beyond the means, in inner teleology, end and means are reciprocally related in such a way that each arises in and through the other. Kant repeatedly describes the contrast between external and internal teleology in terms of the opposition between mechanisms and organisms. Between the publication of Smith's *The Theory of Moral Sentiments* and Kant's *Critique of Judgment,* the image of the machine changed from being the source of the harmony reconciling beauty and utility to being blamed for ugly social divisions and disruptive personal fragmentation. Schiller captured the importance of this shift in his *Letters on the Aesthetic Education of Man* (1795). "*Utility,*" he declared, "is the great idol of the age." Devotion to this idol is dehumanizing: "Eternally chained to only one single little fragment of the whole, man himself grew to be only a fragment; with the monotonous noise of the wheel he drives everlastingly in his ears, he never develops the harmony of his being, and instead of imprinting humanity upon his nature he becomes merely the imprint of his occupation, of his science."[6] This change in attitude was largely the result of the devastation wrought by the spread industrialization. Driven by oppressive forces fueled by servitude to machines, people became inwardly and outwardly divided. For Kant and his followers, the task of philosophy as well as art was to find a way to overcome this personal and social fragmentation, division and opposition by reconciling opposites that too long had been sundered. In the Third Critique, Kant argues that while biological organisms are the natural embodiment of this synthetic reintegration, beautiful works of art are its ideal expression.

The beautiful work of art, like the organism, is a "*self-organized being.*" In both the *l'oeuvre d'art* and the organism, order is not imposed from without but *emerges* within through a complex interplay of parts that, in the final analysis, constitute the activity of the whole. According to the principle of inner teleology or "*intrinsic finality,*" "*an organized natural product is one in which every part is reciprocally both end and means.*" This is the self-organizing structure in which Kauffman correctly sees the anticipation of contemporary theories of autopoietic systems and autocatalytic sets. In Kant's terms:

> The parts of the thing combine of themselves into the unity of a whole by being reciprocally cause and effect of their form. For this is the only way in which it is possible that the idea of the whole may conversely, or reciprocally, determine, in its turn the form and combination of all the parts, not as cause—for that would make it an art product—but as the epistemological basis upon which the systematic unity of the form and combination of all the manifold contained in the given matter become cognizable for the person estimating it.[7]

In a utilitarian relation, the purpose of the means is to realize an end other than itself. If, by contrast, means and end are internally related, their relation is nonutilitarian; the purpose of the means does not lie beyond but is intrinsic. The reciprocal relation of means and end constitutes a self-reflexive structure, which points to nothing beyond itself and is therefore self-referential. Neither determined by nor directed toward anything other than itself, this autonomous structure defines the high art that emerged at the end of the eighteenth century and continues down to our own day. Advanced or true art, the argument goes, is about nothing other than art and thus refers only to itself. Though others might appropriate avant-garde art for their own ends, its value to the artist as well as the genuine connoisseur is completely independent of its market value.

As I have already noted, during the 1790s, art displaced religion as an expression and inspiration of spiritual values. This change occurred in two seemingly opposite ways, which led to the same result: on the one hand, art turns into religion and, on the other hand, religion is aestheticized and turns into art. The stress on the autonomy can make art appear so transcendent as to be otherworldly. Influenced by nothing other than itself, *l'oeuvre d'art* seems to be the image of the Unmoved Mover lying beyond every worldly economy. Eschewing the temptations of Mammon, the artist becomes a high priest dedicated to preserving the purity of art. This transcendent work of art can only be appreciated through a disinterested contemplation that remains free of earthly concerns.

The self-reflexivity or self-referentiality of the work of art, however, can be understood differently. Extending Kant's analysis, Schiller called for a reversal of the transcendence of art in a radical immanence that would reconcile art and world. For Schiller, the true work of art is not a sacred object placed on a pedestal or hung on a wall but is a sociopolitical community in which individuals are vital members of an organic whole. Convinced that outward change presupposes inward transformation, he concludes that "it is through beauty that we arrive at freedom": "If the principles I have laid down are correct, and if experience confirms my portrayal of the present age, then we must continue to regard every attempt at political reform as untimely and every hope based upon it as chimerical, as long as the split within man is not healed, and his nature so restored to wholeness that it can itself become the artificer of taste, and guarantee the reality of this political creation of reason." The artist is the prophet whose "aesthetic education" will create the inward change necessary to transform the world into a work of art. The aesthetic utopia toward which we are progressing is the worldly embodiment of what once was known as the Kingdom of God. When this utopia is completely realized, its purpose will be nothing other than itself. In this kingdom, humanity finds fulfillment in play, which, we have already discovered, must be purposeless. "Man plays," Schiller concludes, "only when he is, in the full sense of the word, a man, and *he is only wholly a man when he is playing.*"[8] By transforming religious vision into artistic mission, Schiller defined what eventually became the task of the twentieth-century avant-garde.

Friedrich Schleiermacher, the founder of modern theology, reached the same conclusion from the opposite direction. The only avowed theologian in the Jena group, Schleiermacher wrote what remains the classic romantic interpretation of religion, *On Religion: Speeches to Its Cultured Despisers* (1799). Religion, he argues, essentially involves neither thinking nor willing but is a matter of feeling. As such, religion is an aesthetic (*aisthetikos,* pertaining to sense perception) sensibility or, in Schleiermacher's characteristically poetic terms, "true religion is sense and taste for the Infinite." The distinguishing trait of religious affection is the ability to experience "the unity of the original source of life." Inasmuch as thinking and willing presuppose the division between subject and object, they are incapable of apprehending this unity. In Schleiermacher's theology, the "self-organized being," definitive of Kant's beautiful work of art, becomes the Infinite, which unites the divine with the entire sphere of finitude.

The contemplation of the pious is the immediate consciousness of the universal existence of all finite things, in and through the Eternal. Religion is to seek this and find it in all that lives and moves, in all growth and change, in all doing and suffering. It is to have life and to know life in immediate feeling, only as such an existence in the Infinite and the Eternal. . . . Wherefore it is a life in the infinite nature of the Whole, in the One and in the All, in God, having and possessing all things in God, and God in all. . . . In itself it is an affection, a revelation of the Infinite in the finite, God being seen in it and it in God.[9]

In a pattern that repeats itself throughout the modern era, the transcendent divine dies and is reborn to sacralize what otherwise would remain profane. Schleiermacher's Infinite is a beautiful whole in which the oppositions separating God, self, and world are overcome. In a manner reminiscent of Scottish Calvinists and moral philosophers, Schleiermacher envisions an artistic absolute in which the invisible hand of providence appears as the immanent principle of unity operating throughout the cosmos. What Schleiermacher, along with Kant and Schiller, as well as nineteenth-century romantics, cannot imagine is the aestheticization of money and markets. The bridge between the artistic and economic absolutes is Hegel's speculative philosophy.

ECONOMIC ABSOLUTE) During the early decades of the nineteenth century, Schleiermacher and Hegel were bitter rivals at the University of Berlin. While Schleiermacher insisted that rational reflection could not grasp the Infinite, Hegel argued that reliance on feeling rather than reason prevented the full realization of human being. In Hegel's comprehensive system, the real is rational and the rational is real; nothing falls outside the realm of reason, and thus everything is rationally comprehensible. In spite of their obvious differences, Hegel and Schleiermacher are closer than they admit. The all-encompassing Infinite that Schleiermacher experiences in feeling, Hegel grasps through dialectical reason, which reconciles all opposites. With two important qualifications, Hegel's Absolute Idea is the conceptual articulation of Schleiermacher's artistic Infinite: first, the harmony of the whole in Hegel's system develops in and through the conflict of the parts; second, the unity of this whole includes rather than represses differences. More inclusive than Schleiermacher's religious vision, Hegel's system, when fully developed, includes *all* reality. In ways that will become increasingly apparent, Hegel's speculative reason lays bare the structure of what eventually become speculative markets.

In Hegel's system, philosophy brings the truth expressed in religious representations and artistic images to conceptual clarity. Kant's notion of inner teleology implicitly articulates the truth revealed in the Christian doctrine of the trinity and, in retrospect, anticipates Hegel's Absolute Idea. This Idea is thoroughly logical and therefore can be grasped through the exercise of reason. For Hegel, however, logic is not merely subjective but defines the rational structure of all reality—objective as well as subjective. Far from static or fixed, this structure is dynamic and unfolds through a dialectical process, which Hegel charts in his monumental *Science of Logic* (1812–16). *"The Notion is everything,"* he argues, "and its movement is the *universal absolute activity,* the self-determining and self-realizing movement." When taken as a whole, the moments in the *Logic* define the rational order of a self-organizing process whose goal is its own self-perpetuation. The end or purpose that orders the whole is *"immanent"* in the parts, which form the content of the Idea. "In teleology," Hegel explains, "content becomes important, for teleology presupposes a Notion, something *absolutely determined* and therefore self-determining, and so has made a distinction between the *relation* of differences and their reciprocal determinedness, that is the *form,* and the *unity that is reflected into itself, a unity that is determined in and for itself* and therefore *a content."* [10] Within the logical structure of the whole, parts assume determinate specificity through reciprocal interrelations. Anticipating the insight that lies at the base of Saussure's linguistic theory a century later, Hegel maintains that identity *is* difference. The Logos of thought is the interplay of differences where everything becomes itself in and through its own other. Conceived synchronically, this Logos is the rational foundation of subjectivity and objectivity; considered diachronically, the Logos forms the rationale for historical development. The Absolute Idea is nothing above or beyond the moments through which knowledge becomes aware *of itself* as knowledge in *sensu strictissimo.* When knowledge knows itself as such, it turns back on itself to close the circle of its own becoming. In this self-reflexive structure, subject and object are united *in their differences.*

In contrast to Schleiermacher and many other romantics, for whom unity excludes differences and harmony denies conflict, Hegel consistently maintains that the unity of the whole is inseparable from the conflict of the parts. More precisely, unity emerges *through* conflict and thus is impossible without it; just as there can be no redemption without sin, so there can be no harmony without strife. Hegel's Absolute is neither transcendent nor eternal but is the restless pulse of temporal change and historical becoming. Since the Absolute is what it is by becoming other than itself, the ceaseless unrest of becoming renders everything finite unstable. The activity through which all things are created and destroyed is a process of *negation,* which simultaneously posits particular differences and overcomes their simple opposition: "The negative appears as the *mediating* element, since it includes within it itself and the immediate whose

negation it is. So far as these two determinations are taken in some relationship or other as externally related, the negative is only the *formal* mediating element; but as absolute negativity the negative moment of absolute mediation is the unity, which is subjectivity and soul."[11] Absolute
negativity is double negation in which negation itself is negated and opposites are reconciled as reciprocal differences. In the first moment of
negation, for example, A constitutes itself by the negation of non-A.
Through the very effort to sustain itself by negating its opposite, however,
A discovers that it cannot be itself without non-A. Since non-A is a constitutive moment in its own being, A *is* non-non-A. This negation of its own
negation is the unity-in-difference of A and non-A, which overcomes the
indifference of isolated individuality and establishes identity as thoroughly relational difference. Inasmuch as the Hegelian universal is the
global network of relations in which all individuals become themselves,
the individual *is* the universal and the universal *is* the individual.

In the *Phenomenology of Spirit* (1807), Hegel describes the movement
from isolated individuality to concrete universality as the transition from
substance to subject. The subject, which is the active embodiment of the
logical Idea or Logos, is "the movement of positing itself . . . the mediation
of its self-othering with itself." This process is

> pure, *simple negativity,* and is for this very reason the bifurcation of the
> simple; it is the doubling which sets up opposition, and then again the
> negation of this indifferent diversity and of its opposition. Only this
> self-restoring identity, or this reflection in otherness within itself—not
> an *original* or *immediate* unity as such—is the True. It is the process of
> its own becoming; the circle that presupposes its end as goal, having its
> end also as its beginning; and only by being worked out to its end, is it
> actual.

As the alpha and omega of becoming, this end is the *"purposive activity,"*
which Hegel identifies as reason.[12] Rational purpose is not imposed from
without by a transcendent God or autonomous agents but, like the inner
teleology of Kant's beautiful work of art, is immanent in becoming as its
internal logic. For Hegel, this purpose, working itself out through the
conflict of natural forces and historical actors, unaware of the end coming
to realization through their activities, is "the cunning of reason."

The cunning of reason is, among other things, a speculative rendering
of Calvin and Smith's invisible hand. The structure of double negation,
which transforms oppositions into reciprocal differences, is not limited to

the abstractions of logic but constitutes the foundation of concrete reality and actual relations. In the realm of history, the cunning of reason turns the violence of competitive struggle against itself to weave a web of mutual interests out of the clash of selfish pursuits. If interpreted in this way, Hegel's Absolute Idea reveals the logical structure of Smith's market.

In his voluminous writings, Hegel devotes very little explicit attention to the writings of Adam Smith. His three-volume *History of Philosophy* includes only four pages on Scottish philosophy and but one sentence on Smith. He identifies Smith as a member of a group, which also included Dugald Stewart, Edward Search (a.k.a. Abraham Tucker), Ferguson, and Hutcheson. The distinguishing characteristic of this school of thought, according to Hegel, is an emphasis on the subjective constitution of consciousness and the insistence on the immanence of norms of judgment: "It is a popular philosophy, which . . . has the great merit of seeking in man, and in his consciousness, for the source of all that could be held by him as true, the immanence of what should be esteemed by him."[13] The real influence of Smith on Hegel's mature philosophy, however, becomes evident only in his *Philosophy of Right*. Though mentioned merely parenthetically in an explanatory note, Smith's analysis of the political economy shapes Hegel's influential interpretation of civil society. As the second moment in a characteristic three-stage analysis of "ethical life," civil society marks the transition between the substantial unity of the family in which members are not yet separate individuals and the integrated whole of the state in which individuals achieve self-realization through participation in the social group.

> The family disintegrates (both essentially, through the working of the principle of personality, and also in the course of nature) into a plurality of families, each of which conducts itself as in principle a self-subsistent concrete persona and therefore as externally related to its neighbors. In other words, the moments bound together in the unity of the family, since the family is the ethical Idea still in its concept, must be released from the concept to self-subsistent objective reality. This is the stage of difference.[14]

The differences among self-subsistent individuals are initially constituted and sustained through conflicts motivated by selfish interests. Considered in logical terms, this is the moment in which the individual attempts to assert himself through the negation of others. In Hegel's dialectical vision, however, nothing is ever merely itself for, as we have seen, everything includes its other as a condition of its own possibility. Self-assertion through the negation of others, therefore, inevitably negates itself because competitors and opponents need each other in order to be themselves. Far from antithetical, selfishness and cooperation are inseparable. To seek one's own ends is unknowingly to pursue the ends of others one appears to oppose: "In the course of the actual attainment of selfish ends—an attainment conditioned in this way by universality—there is formed a system of complete interdependence, wherein the livelihood, happiness, and legal status of one man is interwoven with the livelihood, happiness, and rights of all. On this system, individual happiness, etc. depend, and only in this connected system are they actualized and secured." Instead of removing competition and conflict, the unity arising through the pursuit of self-interest presupposes tensions and instabilities, which keep everything unsettled and in motion. Hegel's analysis of the dynamics of self-interest is completely consistent with Smith's interpretation of the market. For Hegel, as for Smith and his fellow Scottish moral philosophers, order emerges internally through checks and balances that transform opposition into cooperation. "A selfish purpose directed towards its particular self-interest," Hegel argues, "apprehends and evinces itself at the same time as universal."[15] This realization of the universal through self-interested individuals is, of course, the cunning of reason, which is the invisible hand of both providence and the operation of the market.

Just as conventional philosophical wisdom maintains a clear opposition between Continental rationalism and both British empiricism and analytic philosophy, so conventional economic wisdom sets up an opposition between market and Marxist models. Our analysis of the genealogy of the market suggests, however, that things are not so simple. The shared theological and aesthetic background from which Smith's market economics and Hegel's speculative philosophy emerge lead to remarkable similarities between their understandings of economic and social process. Moreover, Hegel's consideration of civil society issues in a further conclusion, which points to an unexpected link between Smith's view of the market and Marx's analysis of capital. In one of its guises, Hegel argues, the Absolute manifests itself as *capital.*

> When men are thus dependent on one another and reciprocally related to one another in their work and the satisfaction of their needs, subjective self-seeking turns into a contribution to the satisfaction of the needs of everyone. That is to say, by a dialectical advance, subjective self-seeking turns into the mediation of the particular through the universal,

with the result that each man in earning, producing, and enjoying on his own account is *eo ipso* producing and earning for the enjoyment of everyone else. The compulsion that brings this about is rooted in the complex interdependence of each and all, and it now presents itself to each as the universal permanent capital, which gives each the opportunity, by the exercise of his education and skill, to draw a share from it and so be assured of his livelihood, while what he thus earns by means of his work maintains and increases the general capital.[16]

Having morphed from religion to art, the Hegelian Idea becomes incarnate in capital to form the Economic Absolute. While claiming to overturn Hegel, Marx's seminal reading of money and capital reveals surprising implications of Hegel's philosophical speculation.

Marx famously claimed that he had turned Hegel's dialectical philosophy on its head to form his dialectical materialism. Marx's debt to Hegel, however, remains profound. In his *Philosophical Notebooks,* V. I. Lenin goes so far as to claim: "It is impossible completely to understand Marx's *Capital* . . . without having thoroughly studied the *whole* of Hegel's *Logic.*"[17] Though never explicitly acknowledging his strategy, Marx appropriates Hegel's interpretation of the Absolute to develop his account of money and capital. The genesis of Marx's mature philosophy can be traced to his tentative reflections recorded in his notebooks entitled *Grundrisse: Foundations of the Critique of Political Economy* (written in 1857–58 but not published until 1953) and his early musings on religion. In *Grundrisse,* Marx concisely formulates the insight that guides his argument in *Capital* a decade later: "Everything that has been said here about money holds even more for capital, in which money actually develops in its completed character for the first time. The only use value, i.e., usefulness, which can stand opposite capital as such is that which increases, multiplies and hence preserves capital."[18] In elaborating this insight, Marx combines Hegel's philosophical rendering of religious and aesthetic representations with the inner teleology of Kant's aesthetics to forge an account of the self-reflexivity of capital.

In ways that are not immediately obvious, money and its development in capital on the one hand and God on the other are mirror images of each other. As early as 1843, Marx claims: "The god of the Jews has been secularized and has become the god of this world. The bill of exchange is the real god of the Jew. His god is only an illusory bill of exchange."[19] In the *Grundrisse,* Marx extends his argument to include the entire economic realm: "Money is therefore the god among commodities. . . . From its servile role, in which it appears as mere medium of circulation, it suddenly changes into the lord and god of the world of commodities. It represents the divine existence of commodities, while they represent its earthly form." This theological interpretation of money or, conversely, economic interpretation of theology, suggests the source of what Marx describes as "the seemingly transcendental power of money."[20] Money is the creative-destructive medium in which economic value arises and passes away.

This argument turns on the well-known distinction between use value and exchange value. In its two most basic functions, money is a measure of value and a medium of exchange. It is clear, however, that money can be a measure of value only if it is a medium of exchange. For Marx, as for Hegel and later Saussure, value is differential and hence is measured by the *relative* worth of exchanged items. Insofar as commodities meet needs or fulfill desires, they have a use value. Though they are sometimes commodities, media of exchange are more effective if they *are not* useful and thus are not themselves commodities that can be traded. Marx's distinction between use and exchange value is strictly parallel to the aesthetic distinction between usefulness and uselessness as a commodity. What makes money useful as a medium of exchange is its uselessness. In ways we have already discerned, money is a surplus or supplement remaining "outside" the binary relation of exchange, which it nevertheless makes possible. In attempting to explain the paradoxes of this medium, Marx repeatedly invokes theological or, more precisely, Christological language to make his point. Money, he suggests, is the "*mediator*" that "becomes an *actual god*," or elsewhere, "money is the incarnation of exchange value." As the mediator between God and man, Christ not only reconciles the divine and the human but also overcomes the oppositions dividing sinful individuals. In a similar way, money, as the incarnation of exchange value, mediates the conflicts of individuals who are pursing their own self-interests: "Christ is God *externalized,* externalized *man.* God has value only insofar as he represents Christ; man has value only insofar as he represents Christ. It is the same with money."[21]

While Marx does not, of course, limit himself to theological language in his mature theory, its traces nonetheless remain. Citing words of Faust we have already encountered ("*Im Angang war die That*"), he elaborates the notion of the general equivalent, which, we have seen, dates back at least to Aristotle. In a circle that appears to be vicious, exchange presupposes a common measure of value, which presupposes the act of exchange. Parties in an exchange "cannot bring their commodities into relation as values and therefore as commodities, except by comparing them with some one or another commodity as the universal equivalent." Marx expresses this relation formulaically (figure 11):

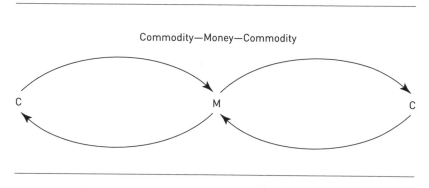

Commodity—Money—Commodity

Figure 11

Money is the *common* measure by which the value of *different* commodities is assessed. Though the universal equivalent is embodied in a particular material, the "money-form" is "quite distinct from" any "palpable form: it is, therefore, a purely ideal or mental form."[22] *Money,* in other words, *is more mental than metal.* This is a remarkable confession by a dialectical materialist, who claims to turn Hegel upside-down. Far from materiality being essential, money is "only a *symbol* whose material is irrelevant."[23]

Marx's interpretation of money anticipates Saussure's semiology and the linguistic theory of representation it entails (figure 12).

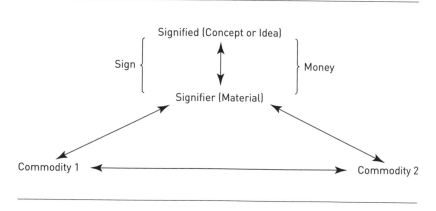

Figure 12

In money, as in language, the signified is a concept or idea embodied in a material signifier. This immaterial-material sign is the medium that establishes and maintains the differential identity and determinate value of everything within the system of exchange. Since the signified is always already encoded, the sign is always the sign of a sign.

> Commodities as use-values now stand opposed to money as exchange-value. On the other hand, both opposing sides are commodities, unities of use-value and value. But this unity of differences manifests itself at two opposite poles, and at each poll in an opposite way. Being poles they are as necessarily opposite as they are connected. On the one side of the equation we have an ordinary commodity, which is in reality a use-value. Its value is expressed only ideally in its price, by which it is equated to its opponent, the gold, as to the real embodiment of its value. On the other hand, the gold, in its metallic reality, ranks as the embodiment of value, as money. Gold as gold, is exchange-value itself. . . . These antagonistic forms of commodities are the real forms in which the process of their exchange takes place.

The two phases or poles of exchange are expressed in the following formula:

$$C - M - C: M - C \text{ (purchase)} + C - M \text{ (sale)}$$

Within this circuit of exchange, money, like Hegel's Absolute, secures the unity-in-difference that transforms opposition into reciprocity. Accordingly, the circulation of money repeats the circular rhythm of the absolute Idea. "The two phases, each the inverse to the other, that make up the metamorphosis of a commodity," Marx explains, "constitute together a circular movement, a circuit."[24] With the closure of this circuit, exchange becomes a self-reflexive process: "While, originally, the act of social production appeared as the positing of exchange values and this, in its later development, as circulation—as completely developed reciprocal movement of exchange values—now, circulation itself returns back into the activity which posits or produces exchange values. It returns into it as into its ground." This account of the circulation is a *direct* application of the structure of Hegel's logical Idea to the flow of capital. In this self-reflexive loop, which repeatedly turns back on itself, exchange value gives rise to circulation, which in turn is the condition of the possibility of exchange.

The complete realization of money is capital. "*Money as capital* is an as-

pect of money that goes beyond its simple character as money." In his rich-
est and most suggestive description of capital, Marx implicitly draws on
Kant's aesthetics and Hegel's philosophy.

> Only with *capital* is exchange value posited as exchange value in such a
> way that it preserves itself in circulation; i.e., it neither becomes sub-
> stanceless, nor constantly realizes itself in other substances or a totality
> of them; nor loses its specific form, but rather preserves its identity with
> itself in each of the different substances. It therefore always remains
> money and always commodity. It is in every moment both of the mo-
> ments that disappear into one another in circulation. But it is this
> only because it itself is a constantly self-renewing circular course of
> exchanges.[25]

This constantly self-renewing circular exchange is nothing other than a
reinscription of Hegel's Absolute in which substance becomes an "endless
process" where everything solid dissolves in perpetual circulation. In the
"circle of exchange," the self-reflexivity of the Absolute Idea appears in
capital as the "self-reproducing exchange of value." In contrast to exchange
value whose purpose is external, i.e., the acquisition of useful commodities, capital has no end beyond itself, and thus its purpose is internal. The
purpose of capital, in other words, is to generate more capital in a process
that approximates autoinsemination. "The first quality of capital," Marx
argues, "is, then, this: that exchange value deriving from the circulation
and presupposing circulation preserves itself within it and by means of it;
does not lose itself by entering into it; that circulation is not the movement
of its disappearance, but rather the movement of its real self-positing as exchange value, its self-realization as exchange value." As "the process of its
own becoming, the circle that presupposes its end as its goal, having its
end also as its beginning," capital, like Hegel's Absolute is, for Marx, "im-
mortal." From this point of view, capital is in effect the unmoved mover
that keeps everything in motion. "The circulation of capital," Marx maintains, "constantly ignites itself anew, divides into its different moments,
and is a *perpetuum mobile.*" "The restless currency of money," engenders
the infinite unrest of becoming.[26] The Economic Absolute also moves
through a process of negation, which Joseph Schumpeter eventually labels
"creative destruction." Never simply a stabilizing force, capital flows far
from equilibrium in distributed currents that keep everything in perpetual motion. Like ancient gods, this restless Economic Absolute makes finitude tremble.

ART OF FINANCE) Lenin once suggested that Hegel is the most idealist and the most materialist philosopher who ever lived. Though Marx intended to invert Hegel's idealism to create his own materialism, we have found that his understanding of money and capital remains haunted by the idealism he struggles to escape. While acknowledging the latent idealism of his analysis, Marx never developed an adequate theory of culture, which would have enabled him to elaborate the far-reaching implications of his recognition of the symbolic dimensions of capital. This task was left to Georg Simmel.

The twentieth century begins with the publication of Freud's well-known *The Interpretation of Dreams* and Simmel's no less important though consistently overlooked *The Philosophy of Money* (1900). Deeply steeped in modern psychology, philosophy, aesthetics, and economic theory, Simmel extends the avant-garde project of transforming the world into a work of art by developing a philosophical account of the aestheticization of reality. S. Hübner-Funk observes that "Simmel not only *consciously* concerned himself with art but also *transposed* its specific structural qualities onto social phenomena."[27] Simmel's interest in money grew out of his conviction that money is the key that unlocks the mystery of the modern age. The restlessness playing in Hegel's Absolute and Marx's capital is, for Simmel, the distinctive mark of modernity. Drawing together many of the themes we have been exploring in a remarkable passage that deserves to be quoted at length, he writes:

> I believe that this secret restlessness, this helpless urgency that lies below the threshold of consciousness, that drives modern man from socialism to Nietzsche, from Böklin to impressionism, from Hegel to Schopenhauer and back again, not only originates in the bustle and excitement of modern life, but that, conversely, this phenomenon is frequently the expression, symptom and eruption of this innermost condition. The lack of something definite at the center of the soul impels us to search for momentary satisfaction in ever-new stimulations, sensations and external activities. Thus it is that we become entangled in the instability and helplessness that manifests itself as the tumult of the metropolis, as the mania for traveling, as the wild pursuit of competition and as the typically modern disloyalty with regard to taste, style, opinions and personal relationships. The significance of money for this kind of life follows quite logically from the premises that all the discussions in this book have identified. It is only necessary to mention here the dual role of money. Money stands in a series with all the means and

tools of culture, which slide in front of the inner and final ends and ultimately cover them up and displace them. . . . Money interweaves this sequence as the means of means, as the most general technique of practical life, without which specific techniques of culture could not have been developed. Indeed, even in this respect, money exhibits the duality of its functions through whose unification it repeats the form of the greatest and the deepest potentialities of life: on the one hand, it is an equal member or even the first among equals *in* the series of human existence, and, on the other, it stands *above* them as an integrating force that supports and permeates every single element. In the same way, religion is a force in life, one interest among others and often opposed to them. It is one of those factors that are constituents of life and yet, on the other hand, it expresses the unity and the basis of our whole existence—on the one hand it is a link in life's organism, and on the other it stands opposed to that organism by expressing life through the self-sufficiency of *its* summit and inwardness.[28]

The infinite restlessness that Simmel associates with money is for Freud the symptom of insatiable desire. The "lack at the center of the soul" creates ceaseless striving for a fulfillment that never arrives. Simmel shares Freud's insistence that social and cultural phenomena are in some sense rooted in psychological processes. Indeed, he goes so far as to assert that economic value is the "objectification of subjective values" and drives (65). Simmel does not, however, commit the mistake of simple reductionism to which orthodox Freudianism as well as Marxism falls prey. "Subject and object," he argues, "are born in the same act" (65). Paradoxically stated, "the concept of 'two' exists prior to the concept 'one'"; in order for one to be one, there must be at least two (92). Translated into Hegel's dialectical terms, the specificity of one presupposes relation to a second, which, therefore, is not secondary. Once again, identity appears to be differential—there can be no subjectivity without objectivity, and vice versa. Inasmuch as subject and object are born together, they are co-originary and always coevolve. Thus, neither can be reduced to the other; by extension, nature and culture as well as world and mind are braided together in such a way that one is a necessary condition of the possibility of the other.

The mind creates the world—the only world that we can discuss and that is real for us—according to its receptivity and its ability to construct forms. But on the other hand, this world is also the original source of the mind. . . . Considered historically, the mind with all its forms and con-

tents is a product of the world—of the same world, which is in turn a
product of the mind because it is a world of representations. (112–13)

If mind creates world as much as world creates mind, the traditional opposition between—be it psychological, social, or economic—infrastructure and mental and cultural superstructure collapses; neither materialism
nor idealism provides an adequate interpretive framework. Natural, social,
and cultural processes form complex feedback and feedforward loops,
which are reciprocally determinative.

Though he rejects all forms of reductionism, Simmel is convinced that
money and its history play a crucial role in the modern world. In developing an account of money, he brings together insights from post-Kantian
idealism with a sophisticated aesthetic theory to form an understanding
of the co-origination and coevolution of money and culture. The history
of money, Simmel maintains, follows a clear trajectory "from substance to
function."

> The broad cultural ramifications of the nature and significance of money
> are to be seen in the movements that lead money towards its pure con-
> cept and away from its attachment to particular substances. Thus,
> money is involved in the general development in every domain of life
> and in every sense strives to dissolve substance into free-floating pro-
> cesses. On the one hand, money forms part of this comprehensive de-
> velopment; on the other, it has a special relationship with concrete val-
> ues, as that which symbolizes them. Furthermore, money is influenced
> by the broad cultural trends, and it is at the same time an independent
> cause of these trends. (168)

In this text and many others, Simmel not only illuminates the dynamics
of modernity and modernism but also presents an astonishing anticipation of postmodernity.

While Simmel makes few explicit references to Marx's work, his interpretation of money bears many similarities to arguments developed in
Grundrisse and *Capital*. Rereading Marx through idealistic philosophy and
aesthetics, Simmel presents a theory better suited to the modern and
postmodern worlds. As we have seen, Marx's mature work is filled with
analogies and comparisons between economics on the one hand and theology and art on the other. Though these connections are quite suggestive,
they remain peripheral to Marx's overall argument. In Simmel's work, the

peripheral becomes central. Echoing Marx, Simmel presents a "concept of money as the incarnation and purest expression of economic value" (101). As substance dissolves into function to create "free-floating processes," the regime of representation implodes.

> Function is universal in relation to the purpose that it serves. Religious sentiment is a universal by contrast with the content of a particular creed; cognition is universal as against any one of its particular objects; power is universal by contrast with the specific and varied problems to which it is always applied in the same way. All of these are forms and frameworks that comprehend a great variety of material. Money seems to participate in this trend when valuation becomes independent of the material of money and is transferred to its function, which is universal and yet not abstract. . . . The form in which money exists for us is that of mediating exchanges and measuring values. . . . The decisive point, however, is that its value no longer resides in what it represents; on the contrary, the latter is quite secondary, and its nature has no importance except on technical grounds, which have nothing to do with the sense of value. (202–3)

Value, in other words, no longer is a function or representing an independent referent but is determined by reciprocal relations among entities and forms. Simmel's analysis of economic value anticipates the structuralist revolution, in which meaning and value shift from referentiality to relationality. With the eclipse of representation, value becomes, in Simmel's terms, *relative:* "The economic value of objects is constituted by their mutual relationship and exchangeability" (120). Money, he concludes, "is not only the absolutely interchangeable object . . . it is, so to speak, interchangeability personified" (124).

To grasp the importance of Simmel's argument, it is essential to understand that relativity *is not* subjectivity. To the contrary, he argues, "the relativity of valuation signifies its objectivity" (79). In lines that might well have been written by Hegel, Simmel extends his account of money to form a universal ontological principle.

> *Money is a reification of the general form of existence according to which things derive their significance from their relationship to each other.*
>
> The philosophical significance of money is that it represents within the practical world the most certain image and the clearest embodiment

of the formula of all being, according to which things receive their meaning through each other, and have their being determined by their mutual relations. (128–29)

Relativity, in other words, is relationality. Instead of separating isolated subjects and/or objects, relativity draws everyone and everything out of self-enclosure and into a field of reciprocal relations. As the incarnation of interchangeability, "money is nothing but the symbol of . . . relativity" (126). The value of a specific entity shifts with the field within which it forms. Simmel makes this point by drawing an analogy between the physical and the economic cosmos.

> The position of a body is not a quality of the body itself, but is a relationship to other bodies; and in every change of position, these others, as well as the body itself, may be regarded as the active or passive subject. In the same way, since the value of A consists of its relation to the economic cosmos, it would be equally justified and only less convenient to interpret any change in the value of A as a change in the value of B, C, D, and E. (120)

And, of course, vice versa.

The more deeply Simmel probes the economic cosmos, the more contradictory money becomes. Money, he concludes, is a *coincidentia oppositorum,* which brings together "proximity and distance," "the equal and the non-equal," and "absolute means and absolute end" (128, 93, 232). The most interesting paradox Simmel observes is even more important than he realized: money, he suggests, involves something like the liar's paradox.

> Money is . . . one of those normative ideas that obeys the norms that they themselves represent. All such cases result in first-order complications and circular movements of thought, although these can be resolved: the Cretan who declares that all Cretans are liars, falling under his own axiom condemns his own statement as a lie. . . . Thus money stands as the measure and means of exchange above valuable objects; and because its services initially require a valuable representative and give value to their representative, money is ranked with those objects and is subsumed under the norms that are themselves derived from money. (122)

As we have already discovered, money is *simultaneously* inside and outside the system of exchange. In terms of our previous discussion of the relation between general and restricted economies, money is an excess or surplus that is "inside" the economic system as an "outside" that cannot be incorporated in binary relations or reciprocal exchange. Every system of exchange presupposes as a condition of its own possibility something it cannot include and yet does not precisely exclude. If read through Kant's notion of inner teleology and the logical structure of the Hegelian idea, it becomes clear that the paradox Simmel recognizes is a function of the self-reflexivity of money. What Simmel discerns in the economic system, Gödel eventually identified as a characteristic of all systems that are supposed to be complete. While his "On Formally Undecidable Propositions in *Principia Mathematica* and Related Systems" (1931) is directed against logical arguments advanced by Russell and Whitehead, its implications are considerably farther reaching. Gödel demonstrates that axiomatic systems of sufficient complexity necessarily include propositions that are consistent inside the system but whose truth or falsity is not ascertainable in terms of the system itself. Therefore, it is impossible for a system to be both *consistent* (i.e., free of contradictions) and *complete.* "The proof of Gödel's Incompleteness Theorem," Douglas Hofstadter explains, "hinges upon the writing of a self-referential mathematical statement, in the same way as the Epimenides paradox is a self-referential statement of language."[29] The paradox of self-reference is that systems necessarily include what they cannot include. Turning back on itself, the structure of self-referentiality leaves a gap that cannot be closed. In economic systems, money flows in this gap. With this insight, we simultaneously move beyond, while remaining within, the closure of the Hegelian system and begin to approach complex systems, which do not necessarily tend toward equilibrium.

Though his work points toward a theory of complex adaptive systems and all the uncertainty and volatility they entail, Simmel remains committed to the metaphysical principle of unity. As our discussion of the relativity of being shows, for Simmel, as for Hegel, unity and difference are internally related and thus mutually constitutive. Nevertheless, Simmel, like Hegel, tends to privilege unity over difference metaphysically as well as economically: "Yet money is the most all-embracing instance of the fact that even the most radical differences and antagonisms in the human world always leave room for similarities and community of interests. But money is more than this. . . . Money is the symbol in the empirical world of the inconceivable unity of being, out of which the world, in all its breadth, diversity, energy and reality, flows" (497). When money is understood in this way, it takes on spiritual significance. Though ostensibly different from religious and spiritual phenomena, the "inconceivable unity of being" incarnate in money is actually indistinguishable from "the spiritual essence and the absolute—which creates and manifests itself in all phenomena—as a spiritual substance." "This absolute," Simmel explains, "must at the same time be recognized as something relative" (496). Stressing that the interplay between the absolute and the relative constitutes the Infinite, he summarizes the conclusion toward which his argument as well as our own has been steadily progressing.

> The interdependence of things, which relativism establishes as their essence, excludes the notion of infinity only on a superficial view, or if relativism is not conceived in a sufficiently radical way. The contrary is indeed true: a concrete infinite seems to me conceivable only in two ways. First, as a rising or falling series, where every link depends upon another, and a third one is dependent upon it—as may be the case with spatial distribution, causal transmission of energy, chronological sequences or logical derivation. Secondly, what this series presents in an extended form is provided in a succinct circular form by interaction. If the effect that one element produces upon another then becomes a cause that reflects back as an effect upon the former, which in turn repeats the process by becoming a cause of retroaction, then we have a model of genuine infinity in activity. Here is an immanent Infinite comparable to that of the circle. . . . Since the basic characteristic of all knowable existence, the interdependence and interaction of everything, also refers to economic value and conveys this principle of life to economic material, the essential quality of money now becomes comprehensible. For the value of things, interpreted as their economic interaction, has its purest expression and embodiment in money. (118–19)

The Infinite embodied in money is the *economic absolute*. It is crucial to understand precisely what is at stake in the notion of this "immanent Infinite" or relative Absolute. This Infinite or Absolute is not above or beyond the finite and relative but is *in their midst*. If being is relative, there can no more be an Absolute without the relative than there can be a relative without the Absolute. The Absolute is nothing other than the structure of relation that mediates the relativities constituting life. In different terms, the Infinite is the immanent play of finite differences. In a *coincidentia oppositorum* worthy of Nicholas of Cusa, Simmel claims that money is the "unmoved mover," which is at the same time the "*actus purus*" that keeps the world in motion (171, 511). Insofar as this unmoved mover is embodied in the restless currents of the economy, money and its extension in capital form is the divine milieu in which modernity and postmodernity arise and pass away.

In Simmel's aestheticization of reality, economics returns to art and religion, which, though repressed, never disappear. In the dialectic without synthesis whose rhythms we have been tracing, development is neither simply linear nor progressive. Religion, art, and economics are caught in interwoven webs that can never be unraveled. It is no more possible to understand economics without religion and art than it is to understand religion and art apart from economics. Different cultural formations entail different forms of currency and, correlatively, contrasting economic systems—and vice versa. As one moves from exchanging goods through exchange mediated by representational money (e.g., metal and paper) to spectral currencies (figure 13), which are completely immaterial, there is

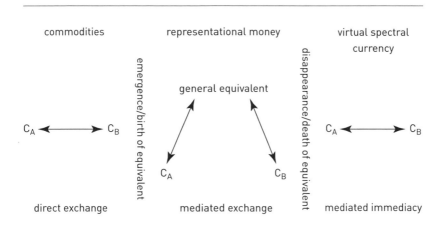

Figure 13
Three forms of currency.

a shift from immanence (actual things) through transcendence (referential signs) to relational signifiers traded on virtual networks, which are neither immanent nor transcendent. (The reason for designating these currencies *spectral* will become clear in the next chapter.) This trajectory initially seems to be characterized by progressive abstraction and dematerialization. Industrial and information technologies transform life by creating abstract economic processes and dematerializing financial instruments. Throughout much of the twentieth century, art follows a parallel course: as art becomes more abstract and progressively dematerializes, it becomes further and further removed from the everyday world. The aesthetic equivalent of religious transcendence is the autonomy of the work of art. This autonomy, we have seen, is expressed in the self-referentiality of *l'oeuvre d'art,* which mirrors the self-reflexivity of capital. At the moment when abstraction seems complete, however, everything changes. Just as the transcendence of God reaches a tipping point at which it inverts itself and becomes radical immanence, so artistic abstraction eventually reverses itself and reengages the world. Simmel correctly argues: "The slogan *'l'art pour l'art'* characterizes perfectly the self-sufficiency of the purely artistic tendency. But from the standpoint of a cultural ideal, the situation is different. Here it is essential that the independent values of aesthetic, scientific, ethical, eudaemonistic and even religious achievements are transcended in order to integrate them all as elements in the development of human nature beyond its natural state" (447). To reverse abstraction and invert dematerialization by bringing art to life is effectively to transform the world into a work of art. This is the dream of the avantgarde, which we have traced to Schiller's refiguring of the kingdom of God as an earthly artistic utopia made possible by "the aesthetic education of man." What the nineteenth century dreamed, the twentieth century realized. But the dream did not come to life where artists and philosophers expected it. From the Bauhaus to museums and galleries, from department stores to Tiffany's and Barneys, from Wall Street to cyberspace, art and economics are woven ever more closely together until the worldwide webs in which they are caught seem seamless. Warhol's words return with greater force than ever: "Business art is the step that comes after Art. . . . Being good in business is the most fascinating kind of art."[30] At this point, the art of finance is the only way capital can be figured.

4

MONEY MATTERS

Okay but just a second . . . the doors closed,—Look I'm in a hurry but Nonny I mean don't you ever say I told you to do something illegal I mean what do you think I got you for! I mean if I want to do something illegal what do I want with a lawyer I mean holy shit where do you think we are over at Russia? where they don't let you do anything? These laws are these laws why should we want to do something illegal if some law lets us do it anyway like selling those looms in the US aid program at South America that's this US money coming back here like did we invent this tax break we get with it? I mean if we put a hundred thousand like a million dollars in this here drilling exploration did we invent we get to take off eighty percent for these intangible drilling costs? If we found oil or gas or something we're supposed to just leave it there if they give us this here twenty-two percent depletion allowance to go ahead and deplete it? I mean these are these laws which you're supposed to find out exactly the letter of them and that's what we do exactly the letter! Okay?

William Gaddis, *JR*

LOSING WEIGHT)   In 1843—eight years before *Moby-Dick* and fourteen years before *The Confidence-Man*—Edgar Allan Poe published a fascinating story entitled "The Gold-Bug." Poe, like Melville, realized that debates about the value of different kinds of currency then raging raised
theological and artistic as well as economic issues. When understood from
the perspective of subsequent developments, Poe's story of ambiguity and
uncertainty becomes a parable of our era.

The tale revolves around an amateur entomologist, William Legrand,
and his faithful Negro servant, Jupiter, who have recently moved from New
Orleans to Sullivan's Island near Charleston, South Carolina. Roaming the
beach, Legrand finds a strange gold bug. Jupiter interrupts his master's description of his discovery and, in his distinctive dialect, unknowingly ut-
ters the word upon which Poe's tale turns.

> "It is of a brilliant gold color—about the size of a large hickory-nut—
> with two jet black spots near one extremity of the back, and another,
> somewhat large, at the other. The *antennae* are—"
>
> "Dey aint *no* tin in him, Massa Will, I keep tellin' on you," here inter-
> rupted Jupiter; "dey bug is a goole-bug, solid, ebery bit of him, inside
> and all, sep him wing—neber feel half so hebby a bug in my life."[1]

"No tin." These words can be read in two opposite ways: the gold bug is
pure because it has no tin in it; or the pure gold of the gold bug is specious
because it is really *notin*—nothing. No tin or notin? Infinitely valuable or
useless? Or perhaps infinitely valuable *and* useless? For the true gold bug,
money is a sign whose value is secured by the substance it embodies or the
material to which it refers. But what backs the value of gold?

.   .   .

As he approached the camp, Moses saw the bull-calf and the dancing, and he was angry; he flung the tablets down, and they were shattered to pieces at the foot of the mountain. Then he took the calf they had made and burnt it; he ground it to powder, sprinkled it on water, and made the Israelites drink it. (Exodus 32:20)

In their long and tangled histories, it is often impossible to know whether money represents God or God represents money. It is also difficult to be sure whether God and money represent something or "notin." Both religion and financial markets are, after all, confidence games. As we have seen, the origin of money is inseparable from certain ancient religious rituals and sacrificial economies. Fears of idolatry notwithstanding, gold harbors a sacred aura in many religious traditions. Beyond tokens offered to the gods in ancient Greek and Roman temples, in Western and especially Eastern Orthodox Christianity, Christ and the saints are often represented in golden images. In ancient India, the Satapatha Brahmana identifies immortality and gold; in ancient China, gold represented heaven. From Egypt to Peru, mummies are wrapped in gold, which, it once was believed, would be useful in the afterlife.[2] It is not uncommon for different mythologies to represent solar gods and lunar goddesses with gold and silver respectively. In *Heiliges Geld: Eine historische Untersuchung über den sakralen Ursprung des Geldes,* Bernhard Laum goes so far as to suggest that the relative value of gold to silver $(1:13\frac{1}{2})$ from ancient to modern times was determined by the astrological ratio between the sun and moon.[3]

Various explanations for the value of gold have been repeatedly advanced. One of the most common and obvious sources of gold's worth is its scarcity. Peter Bernstein points out that if all the gold ever mined were piled "in one solid cube, you could fit it aboard any of today's great oil tankers; its total weight would amount to approximately 125,000 tons."[4] Other analysts associate gold's exceptional worth with its natural and aesthetic qualities. In the former case, the value of gold is taken to be a function of its usefulness; in the latter, it is seen as the result of its uselessness. "In terms of its natural qualities, as a physical substance, gold is quite literally incorruptible: it is highly resistant to chemical reactions and is immune to the corrosion that affects baser metals."[5] In addition to this, gold can also be precisely divided and distributed. All of these qualities make gold a useful medium of exchange. Once purified, gold's luminosity becomes the source of its aesthetic attraction. In his *Principles of Psychology,* William James argues that the appeal of "glittering, hard, metallic, odd pretty things," is an innate "aesthetic sense."[6] So understood, the value of gold, like the value of art, is *intrinsic* rather than extrinsic or utilitarian.

Some of gold's natural qualities, however, are not well suited for economic transactions. It is heavy and difficult to transport and store securely. Coinage was created as an initial solution to such problems. The use of precious metals as money can be found in Mesopotamia as early as the twentieth-fourth century BCE, when the king and religious authorities determined standard weights and established the value of commodities in silver.[7] In Egypt, where a similar system of standard weights was established, gold was more common than silver. Records of trade between Mesopotamia and Egypt give evidence of a common monetary standard. The scarcity of these metals, however, eventually led to the search for other materials that could be used as their substitutes. The invention of coinage can be traced to the Lydian empire in Asia Minor, which came to an end around 547 BCE. The Lydians forged coins from a natural alloy of gold and silver known as electrum found in the Pactolus River. King Croesus, who ruled ca. 560–546 BCE, established a bimetallic standard and issued the first known coins with various signs and insignias. Once the technique of coinage was established, it spread slowly but steadily. By 250 BCE, the use of gold, silver, and bronze coins was common around the Mediterranean and throughout the Near East as well as India. In retrospect, it is clear that the practice of inscribing tokens of exchange with marks establishing their worth began a long process in which value gradually shifts first from substance to the sign it bears and then to substanceless signs that become unbearably light.

The allure of gold extends from ancient times down to the modern period and even continues today. Many, from Marx and Nietzsche to Jack Kemp and Ronald Reagan, believe that gold provides a "secure anchor" that can serve as the foundation of a stable economy. Marx always feared that the disappearance of gold and money's loss of weight could have a destabilizing effect on the economy. He observes that "the natural tendency of circulation to convert coins into a mere semblance of what they profess to be, into a symbol of the weight of metal they are officially supposed to contain, is recognized by modern legislation, which fixes the loss of weight sufficient to demonetize a gold coin, or to make it no longer legal tender." The separation of nominal value and real weight creates a distinction between coins "as mere pieces of metal on the one hand, and as coins with a definite function on the other." This development, Marx cautions, "implies the possibility of replacing metallic coins by tokens of some other material, by symbols serving the same purpose as coins."[8] When gold gives way to symbols, there is nothing to prevent monetary authorities from freely printing money until it becomes as worthless as the paper it is printed on. Nietzsche shares Marx's concern about money's loss of weight but realizes that insubstantial signs have consequences extending far beyond the economic realm. Nothing less than truth itself is at stake in the currency of exchange. "What, then, is truth?" Nietzsche asks. "A mobile army of metaphors, metonyms, and anthropomorphism—in short, a sum of human relations, which have been enhanced, transposed, and embellished poetically and rhetorically . . . ; truths are illusions about which one has forgotten that this is what they are; metaphors, which are worn out and without sensuous power; coins, which have lost their pictures and now matter only as metal, no longer as coins."[9] When truth, like money, loses its substance, it is revealed as the illusion it always has been. The death of truth, Nietzsche believes, is the death of God, and vice versa. Gold, God, and truth are related illusions constructed to provide certainty and security in a world from which they have fled. In semiotic terms, God and gold are signs constructed to deny their status as signs and thereby ground the meaning and value of all other signs. These foundations, however, are specious because they are grounded in nothing other than acts of faith; gold and God are valuable only because of our ungrounded confidence in them. In matters of economics as well as religion: *In the beginning is faith.*

Whether real or illusory, gold, like God, has important economic effects. The function of gold, Shubik explains, is to provide "automatic discipline" for the economic system. "The appeal of the gold standard to libertarian and peasant alike is that faith was to be placed in gold not politicians or the state."[10] Lawrence White summarizes the principal utilitarian reasons for the gold standard.

1. To provide a reliable unit of account that lowers the risk of long-term nominal contracts and long-term bonds, thereby encouraging long-term investment.
2. To serve as an automatic mechanism for determining the quantity of money.
3. To protect against the possibility of an effective governmental tax imposed by the unexpected and arbitrary monetary expansion or debasement.[11]

Contrasting positions on the gold standard reflect not only economic interests and political persuasions but also social class, geographical region, and even national allegiance. For most of the nineteenth century, the United States and much of Europe adhered to the gold standard. Throughout history, however, gold convertibility often has been suspended to allow the monetary expansion necessary to fund wars. During the Civil War, convertibility was revoked and irredeemable fiat money, known as greenbacks, was issued for the first time. The years after the war were marked by heated controversies between backers of gold (gold bugs) and backers of silver (silverites). This dispute, which came to a head in the 1896 presidential election pitting William Jennings Bryan against William McKinley, was not settled until the 1900 Gold Standard Act, which decided the issue in favor of the backers of gold.[12]

Though the gold standard established in 1900 did not completely collapse until 1973, the beginning of the end can be traced to World War I. The United States remained committed to the gold standard until the 1930s but financial exigencies created by the war forced most participating countries to suspend it much earlier. During the first half of the decade, exchange rates were allowed to float but by the late 1920s, most countries returned to the gold standard for a brief period. In 1931, The Bank of England did not have sufficient gold reserves to maintain convertibility and was forced to let the pound float. In the wake of these developments, the fledging international monetary system unraveled and global markets were thrown into turmoil. By 1933, President Roosevelt was finally forced to suspend the gold standard.

Questions raised by the fate of the gold standard were theoretical as well as practical. Kevin Dowd points out that "in the 1920s, Keynes and his followers had put forth a series of policy proposals—of which the main planks were opposition to the official policy on gold, and public works to help reduce unemployment—but their influence on policy in those years was somewhat limited."[13] When England gave up the gold standard, however, Keynesian views gained new respectability. The economic principles that would govern much of Western Europe and the United States from the end of World War II to the late 1960s were developed most fully in Keynes's *The General Theory of Employment, Interest, and Money* (1936). I will consider certain aspects of Keynes's position in the next section, but at this point it is important to note his consistent opposition to the gold standard. Invoking ancient mythologies, Keynes writes: "Thus gold, originally stationed in heaven with his consort silver, as Sun and Moon, having first doffed his sacred attributes and come to earth as an autocrat, may next descend to the sober status of a constitutional king with a cabinet of Banks; and it may never be necessary to proclaim a Republic." In *A Trea-*

tise on Money, however, Keynes insists that this victory would be short-lived, because gold is destined to vanish into nothing.

> The little household gods, who dwelt in purses and stockings and tin boxes, have been swallowed up by a single golden image in each country, which lives underground and is not seen. Gold is out of sight—gone back again into the soil. But when gods are no longer seen in a yellow panoply walking the earth, we begin to rationalize them; and it is not long before nothing is left. . . . It is not a far step from this to the beginning of arrangements between Central Banks by which, without ever formally renouncing the rule of gold, the quantity of metal actually buried in their vaults may come to stand, by a modern alchemy, for what they please, and its value for what they choose.[14]

For Keynes, latter-day alchemy and the traces of gods can do little to solve modern economic problems.

Even before the end of the Second World War, it was clear that the international monetary system was in hopeless disarray and something drastic had to be done. From 1941 to 1944, the Allies held meetings to develop a plan for postwar economic reconstruction. These discussions culminated in the 1944 Bretton Woods agreement. The two most influential participants in these discussions were Keynes and the American assistant secretary of the treasury, Harry Dexter White. The ambitious aim of the accord was to reestablish order in the world economy after the devastation wrought by years of war. Toward this end, participating countries created two new multilateral institutions that have been critical for the world economy ever since: the International Monetary Fund and the World Bank. The IMF was charged with overseeing a system of fixed but adjustable exchange rates and "was given the resources to help countries in balance of payments disequilibria, so they would not have to resort to potentially damaging restrictions on trade and payments or competitive devaluations to cope with shortfalls in their foreign exchange reserves." The International Bank for Reconstruction and Development, or World Bank, was responsible for financing the reconstruction of Europe and Asia as well as providing support for developing countries.[15] In addition to creating these institutions, participants in the Bretton Woods discussions devised plans to establish an International Trade Organization (ITO) but did not approve the accords. This agreement outlined the rules to liberalize trade policies and settle trade disputes that later formed the basis of the General Agreement on Tariffs and Trade (GATT) approved in the late 1940s. These accords have played a critical role in the IMF's imposition of liberalized economic policies on developing countries during the last three decades. In addition to these new institutions and policies, the Bretton Woods agreement reestablished a limited form of the gold standard based upon the U.S. dollar. The agreement committed countries to accept exchange rates set at an agreed-upon ratio against the dollar, whose value was determined in terms of gold ($35 per ounce). The United States assumed the responsibility of exchanging dollars for gold at this fixed rate whenever any foreign country wanted to do so.

The Bretton Woods accord maintained relative stability in global markets for almost three decades. But by the late 1960s, domestic economic and political problems in the United States combined with a changing international situation to make the dollar an unreliable anchor. Once again the international monetary system began to unravel. To a certain extent, these problems were the result of the *success* of postwar U.S. economic policies. By the 1960s, the project of rebuilding Europe and Japan had created robust industrial economies able to compete with the United States. As these economies strengthened, pressures on the American economy increased. These problems were compounded by domestic developments. To fund the growing cost of Great Society programs and the expanding war in Vietnam, President Johnson and Congress ran deficits, which were inflationary because the Fed allowed the quantity of money to rise. As the economic situation worsened, foreign governments and financiers became less likely to invest in U.S. markets. Billions of dollars—called Eurodollars—accumulated offshore and quickly became an alternative source of investment capital on global markets. By 1971, foreign institutions held dollars worth more than twice the gold reserves the United States had available. At this point, international gold convertibility, which had been the foundation of the international economy established at Bretton Woods, was effectively dead.

Events came to a head on August 15, 1971, when President Nixon suspended the gold standard. The architects of this new economic policy were Secretary of the Treasury John Connally and Paul Volcker, the treasury undersecretary for monetary policy. In addition to ending gold convertibility, Nixon imposed a temporary 10 percent surcharge on imports. Foreign exchange markets closed for a week; when they reopened, currencies were allowed to float. In an effort to cope with this crisis, an international conference was held on December 17–18 at the Smithsonian Institution in Washington. Participants reluctantly agreed to a devaluation of the dollar in exchange for the lifting of the 10 percent import surcharge, and fluctuation bands of 2.25 percent were established for all currencies. This effort to manage exchange rates—albeit loosely—did not last long. In 1972, when England was forced to allow the pound to float downward, international currency speculators drove the dollar down. By February 1973, the United States had to devalue the dollar again, and one month later the effort to salvage the postwar economic order established at Bretton Woods completely broke down. The United States' gold convertibility guarantee ended, fixed exchange rates were abandoned, and currencies were allowed to float freely. For the first time in history, all the currencies in the world were fiat money. While everyone realized that this marked the end of an era, for some devoted believers in gold the collapse of Bretton Woods was symptomatic of a broader religious crisis that grew out of the social turmoil of the 1960s. Bill Dannemeyer, a conservative Republican congressman from southern California, wrote to his constituents: "It is not an accident that the American experiment with a paper dollar standard, a variable standard, has been going on at the same time that our culture has been questioning whether American civilization is based on the Judeo-Christian ethic or Secular Humanism. The former involves formal rules from God through the vehicle of the Bible. The latter involves variable rules adopted by man and adjusted as deemed appropriate."[16]

Whether a religious offense or not, the effect of floating exchange rates was immediate and far-reaching. Floating signifiers unmoored from any stable referent had neither secure nor predictable value. This new situation created the conditions for an era of speculation in which money and capital became *spectral*. Erstwhile economist and former German chancellor Helmut Schmidt dubbed the new world disorder a "floating non-system."[17] Nixon's action resulted in a precipitous drop in the value of the dollar, which had a major impact on the world economy. For the governments, businesses, and investors who held $300 billion in foreign banks, the dollar's drop meant a significant loss in purchasing power. As the value of the dollar decreased, inflation increased, beginning a pattern that persisted throughout the 1970s. In times of financial uncertainty, there is often a flight to U.S. Treasury bills, bonds, and notes. With the end of fixed exchange rates, new speculative markets for treasuries as well as futures contracts on currencies erupted. Since the accepted currency of the oil market then, as now, was the U.S. dollar, Nixon's decision had an important impact on the price of oil. The decline in the value of the dollar contributed to a significant drop in the purchasing power of revenues of oil-producing countries. This unexpected turn of events influenced the decision of the recently formed Organization of Petroleum Exporting Countries to increase the price of oil from $1.90 to $9.76 per barrel six months after Nixon's action. By 1979, the price of oil had risen to $29.76 per barrel.

Escalating oil prices had a major impact on the world economy. With rapidly rising prices, speculation on all kinds of commodities—especially oil—increased. Higher prices rippled through the economy, creating difficulties for both industrial and developing economies. Poorer nations were forced to borrow to pay for more expensive oil. At the same time, oil-producing countries were accumulating vast dollar reserves, known as petrodollars. In a circle that quickly became vicious, these dollars were recycled through loans to developing countries, which, in turn, used the money to purchase more oil. By 1974, many industrial economies were in recession and economies in underdeveloped countries were plunging into a debt crisis from which many still have not recovered.

In retrospect, it is clear that the end of the gold standard was a major factor in the eventual emergence of the postmodern economy of the 1980s and 1990s. Much of the volatility and uncertainty that have characterized financial markets for the past two decades can be traced to August 15, 1971. But the 80s and 90s would have turned out differently without another pivotal event. On October 6, 1979, the United States shifted the course of its monetary policy, and once again Paul Volcker was at the eye of the storm, this time as the chairman of the Federal Reserve Board.

GOING PRIVATE) With the end of the gold standard and fixed exchange rates, money and markets had to be managed as never before. This responsibility fell largely to the Federal Reserve Bank. Though central banks had long played an important role in European economies, American suspicion of centralized authority and support of states' rights delayed the establishment of the Fed until 1913. In addition to this, conflicting interests among different political parties and social groups further complicated the deliberations that eventually led to the Fed. The most divisive issue was the question of how to balance the concerns of bankers and Wall Street with the interests of the country as a whole. As early as 1910, a group of Wall Street moguls met secretly to devise a plan to solve the banking problem. Their proposal favored private finance and gave bankers enormous power over the national economy. In order to provide a more equitable balance of power, President Wilson insisted on a Federal Reserve Board, appointed by the president and located in Washington, which included among its members the secretary of the treasury and the comptroller of the currency. There would be twelve regional Federal Reserve

Banks, with New York playing the leading role. Representatives of these banks would serve on the Federal Advisory Council and would meet regularly with the Federal Reserve Board. Though many bankers balked at the prospect of governmental interference in financial affairs, Wilson's compromise actually gave commercial banks significant power. This basic structure remained intact from 1913 until 1935, when the acknowledgment of the impact of the Fed's money supply policy on the whole economy led to important changes. Roosevelt further consolidated the power of the board of governors over regional banks while at the same time taking steps intended to depoliticize monetary policy by removing the secretary of the treasury and the comptroller of the currency from the board. Control of monetary policy was taken over by the new Federal Open Market Committee, made up of seven governors and five bankers.[18]

In its present form, the Fed has five primary functions:

1. To serve as a bankers' bank.
2. To control note issue.
3. To act as a lender of last resort.
4. To regulate commercial banks.
5. To conduct monetary policy.[19]

Since the end of the gold standard, the Fed's responsibility for managing the economy has become greater than ever. The Fed attempts to regulate liquidity and manage often-turbulent economic flows through the discount rate, the federal funds rate, and reserve requirements. The discount rate, which is set by Fed policy, is the rate a Federal Reserve Bank charges commercial banks for loans made to them. While the discount rate is not a very important instrument of monetary policy, it does signal the Fed's position and, more important, can be significant in adjusting reserves at some commercial banks. Federal funds are commercial banks' deposits in Federal Reserve Banks. Commercial banks lend these funds to each other typically, but not always, overnight in a competitive market. The Fed targets the federal funds rate in setting monetary policy and seeks to accomplish this by open market operations. The federal funds rate target set by the Fed is a benchmark but, since the market is competitive, the rate tends to be slightly different from the target. Finally, when the Fed wants to increase bank reserves by buying securities on the open market, it simply credits the reserve account of the bank that sells the securities or the reserve account of the bank whose customer buys the securities. When the

Fed wants to decrease bank reserves by selling securities, it charges the account of the bank that buys them, or the account of the bank whose customer buys them. (Paper currency is printed by the Bureau of Printing and Engraving on orders from the Fed. The Fed pays the bureau's printing costs and not the face value of the currency. The currency notes are then issued by different Federal Reserve Banks and are made available to commercial banks when they are needed.)

Throughout the 1970s, the role of the Fed in managing the economy was hotly debated. The two major poles in these discussions were the Keynesians, who had dominated economic theory and practice from the end of the war through the 1960s, and the neoliberals, led by Martin Friedman and his supply-side colleagues at the University of Chicago, whose influence grew steadily throughout the 1970s.[20] The critical issue on which debate about the role of the Fed turned was the strategy for controlling inflation. During the Second World War, America's industrial capacity expanded rapidly and income rose steadily. By the end of the war, per capita income was 40 percent higher than it had been in 1939. When wage and price controls were lifted and a thriving consumer economy emerged alongside a still strong military-industrial complex, pent-up demand was released and prices began to rise. Increased spending on social programs and the war in Vietnam helped to fuel inflation well into the 1970s.

Keynes and Friedman represented characteristically European and American perspectives on the world and its economy. Though he suffered through the travails of wartime Europe, Keynes's view of life was shaped as much by his participation in the influential Bloomsbury group as by economic theory. His involvement in London bohemian culture did nothing to dampen his enthusiasm for capitalism. Indeed, he was convinced that if appropriate policies were enacted, capitalism stood on the brink of an important revival. In the wake of two world wars and a global depression, it seemed impossible to believe in the efficacy of self-regulating free markets. For Keynes, persistent financial instability and especially unemployment were proof of the failure of the invisible hand. The only way to avoid further disaster was for governments to take a more active role in managing the economy. With the economy in deep depression and interest rates close to zero, Keynes argued that the best instruments for accomplishing this end were taxes and spending.

For Keynes and his followers, economic problems are best addressed by effectively managing demand. To stimulate demand, Keynes supported policies that encourage consumer spending. As consumers spend more, companies produce more, unemployment drops, and a self-reinforcing circuit of exchange is completed. To spend money people must, obviously, have money; employment, therefore, is a critical variable in the economic equation. Unemployment and inflation are inversely related: when employment is high, wages are high and there is inflationary pressure; conversely, when unemployment is high, wages are lower and prices drift downward or at least do not rise with decreasing demand. Faced with high unemployment, Keynes favored lower interest rates, which should help to stimulate the economy. The quickest and most efficient way to increase consumer demand, however, is through government spending. When the government spends money to finance various programs, it pumps money into the system, which leads to an increase in national income that exceeds the original expenditure. When the injected money circulates through the system, it multiplies as it is spent and respent. During the Kennedy and Johnson administrations, this fiscal policy funded social programs as well as the war in Vietnam. For most of the decade, this approach worked well; there was a steady economic expansion and a very strong stock market. By the end of the 60s, however, the economy was beginning to falter; spending was out of control and inflation was rising. There was a growing sense among many people that alternative policies were necessary.

One of Keynes's most persistent critics was Milton Friedman, who won the Nobel Prize in 1976. Friedman grounded his critique in theory as well as careful historical analysis. In 1963 he and Anna Schwartz published the influential *Monetary History of the United States, 1867–1960*. One of the most important parts of Friedman's controversial analysis for his assessment of Keynesianism is his interpretation of the causes of the Depression. For Friedman, the Depression was triggered by a liquidity crisis exacerbated by the Fed's failure to take timely corrective action. As he studied the crisis of the 1920s and 1930s, he concluded that the critical variable in the economy is the money supply rather than interest rates. Against Keynes, he argues that what is most important is monetary rather than fiscal policy. In his well-known dictum, *money matters*. While certainly not ignoring the problem of unemployment, Friedman sees controlling inflation as the key to an orderly economy. Departing from a fundamental tenet of Keynesianism, he contends that this is best accomplished by regulating the money supply instead of manipulating interest rates. As the supply of money increases, the economy expands and as it decreases, the economy contracts. It is important to stress that when economists talk about money, their understanding of the term differs from common usage. In calculating the money supply, they organize financial instruments into three categories labeled M-1, M-2, and M-3 (figure 14).[21] The money supply is determined by M-1, i.e., the money that is immediately available for purchases. As we will see, new financial instruments created questions about whether M-1 is the right definition of an aggregate for purposes of monetary policy.

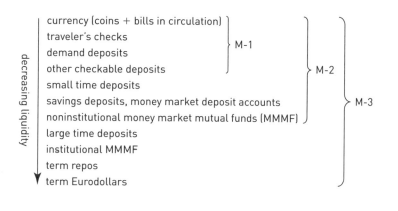

Figure 14

The differences between Friedman and Keynes are as much philosophical as economic. Reflecting a general commitment to state-sponsored social welfare programs, Keynes allows the government greater control in running the economy. Friedman, by contrast, believes in the freedom and autonomy of individuals and thus resists centralized authority and governmental interference in social and economic matters. Standing in a long tradition dating back to Hume, Smith, and Hayek, and less obviously but no less importantly to Ockham, Luther, and Calvin, Friedman argues that economic matters are better left to market forces. When politicized and popularized, this economic vision was translated into the now familiar mantra: less government, lower taxes. As Friedman's views gained wider acceptance, they became allied with what Herbert Stein in 1976 labeled "supply-side economics." While the first expression of what becomes supply-side economics was formulated in a 1971 paper by Robert Mundell, its roots can be traced to Irving Fisher's quantitative theory of money supply, published in 1911. By the 1970s, Mundell and Arthur Laffer, who were Friedman's colleagues at the University of Chicago, were countering Keynes's claim that consumer spending creates demand for more production by arguing that it is supply that creates demand. If there were sufficient incentives for investment, production would increase and demand would follow. According to supply-siders, the best way to boost investment is to lower taxes. Until the early 1960s, the marginal tax rate was as high as 91 percent, which Mundell and Laffer insisted was not only punitive but actually discouraged investment and thus slowed the economy. While claiming to benefit the economy as a whole, supply-side policies obviously favored the wealthy individuals and corporations with substantial financial assets.

In the mid to late 70s, supply-side tax policy combined with Friedman's monetary theory to create a new orthodoxy. According to Friedman, the Fed's policies had been ineffective and actually had caused the very volatility they were intended to control. By first increasing and then decreasing the money supply, the Fed created unpredictable and unnecessary cycles. Friedman's solution to this dilemma is to give up managing interest rates and to focus on controlling the money supply through a fixed rule that insures the slow, steady, and predictable growth of M-1. When this policy is faithfully followed, he argues, the monetary "authority is bound to a formula that dictates the growth rate of some measure of the money stock, and, thus, dictates the inflation rate (absent shocks to real demand for that measure of money), without reference to the values of the unemployment rate or other real variables."[22] Reminiscent of something like William of Ockham's *potentia ordinata,* this self-imposed rule is designed to protect the economic system from interference on the part of fallible mortals.

In spring of 1979, world events conspired to propel monetarism from the realm of economic theory to the center of governmental practice. In response to the Iranian revolution, OPEC doubled oil prices and inflation rose sharply. Responding to spreading political and economic uncertainty, President Carter addressed the nation on July 15. The topic was supposed to be energy policy but turned into his famous "malaise" speech in which he blamed himself and the American people for the country's social and economic woes. Once again, religion—more specifically Protestantism— turns out to be central to economic concerns.

> In a nation that was proud of hard work, strong families, close-knit communities and our faith in God, too many of us now tend to worship self-indulgence and consumption. Human identity is no longer defined by what one does, but by what one owns. But we have discovered that owning things and consuming things does not satisfy our longing for meaning. We have learned that piling up material goods cannot fill the emptiness of lives which have no confidence or purpose.[23]

Sounding a familiar populist note, Carter set Main Street against Wall Street, while at the same time telling people to turn down their thermostats and wear more sweaters. This was not a message many wanted to hear. Two days later, things seemed to be spinning out of control: Carter asked for the resignation of his entire cabinet and top White House officials. The markets were rattled; the dollar dropped, and gold soared to over $300 an ounce. To make matters worse, G. William Miller, who was highly regarded by Wall Street, resigned as chairman of the Federal Reserve Board to replace W. Michael Blumenthal as secretary of the treasury. After considerable debate within the administration, Paul Volcker was appointed to replace Miller.

As we have seen, Volcker had served in the Nixon administration and was instrumental in dismantling the Bretton Woods accord. Assuming his new position in the Carter administration, it seemed as though Volcker had been preparing for the post for his entire life. As an undergraduate at Princeton, he had written an honors thesis entitled *Fed: The Problems of the Federal Reserve Policy since World War II.* The young Volcker concluded that the fundamental problem facing the Fed was that it no longer was able to control either money or inflation.[24] When Volcker took over the chairmanship of the Fed, inflation had been so high for so long that the expectation of it had become a self-fulfilling prophecy; the expectation kept driving up wages and spending. Faced with a rapidly deteriorating economy, Volcker made a critical decision that significantly altered the economic landscape: he made controlling inflation his highest priority. This decision, combined with the end of the gold standard, created the climate for a new economy in the 1980s and 1990s and prepared the way for the longest bull market in history.

To see why Volcker's decision was so important, it is necessary to understand how the policies he enacted tilted in favor of the financial economy at the expense of the productive or what some describe as the "real" economy. Inflation tends to have a more negative impact on people and organizations with financial assets than on people who are wage-earners or have real assets like real estate, gold, art, jewelry, etc. Since increasing inflation erodes the value of financial assets, it functions as something like a progressive tax on the wealthy. Some analysts argue that people with no financial assets who must borrow money can actually benefit from inflation by repaying their loans with cheaper dollars. From this point of view, high inflation favors debtors and low inflation favors creditors. While additional factors were surely involved, the explosive growth of the financial economy relative to the productive economy during the past two decades would have been impossible without the policies Volcker engineered at the Fed.

Having settled on his course of action, Volcker had to decide whether to use interest rates or the money supply as the instrument to control inflation. Suspicious of what he took to be the monetarists' propensity to oversimplify complex economic issues, Volcker initially followed a strategy of incremental increases in interest rates. Accordingly, on August 10, 1979, the Fed raised the discount rate from 10 percent to 10.5 percent, which at the time was the highest in the history of the Federal Reserve System.[25] The impact on the economy was negligible; inflation continued unabated and bank credit was rising at an alarming rate. It quickly became clear to Volcker but not to all the members of the Board of Governors that a gradualist approach would not work. Consumers and investors were not yet convinced that the Fed was really serious about defeating inflation. This situation created a difficult dilemma for Volcker: he knew rates had to rise significantly very quickly but realized he did not have the votes on the board to implement this policy. So on October 6, 1979, he changed course: the Fed, he announced, would no longer manipulate interest rates but would manage the money supply, allowing M-1 to grow at an annual rate of 5 percent. In this new regime, the market would determine interest rates. Volcker's decision was historic because it broke with postwar economic orthodoxy and adopted the use of monetary policy close to what Friedman and his followers had been promoting. With the 1980 presidential election looming on the horizon, Carter and members of the administration were both shocked and dismayed by the decision. Whether Volcker's move was a matter of conviction or convenience, its impact was immediate: the Dow Jones Industrial Average dropped and the federal funds rate quickly rose to 14 percent. For Volcker, the unpredictability of interest rates had the beneficial effect of curtailing bank loans and thus cooling speculative banking practices. The impact of rapidly rising interest rates was unevenly distributed across the economy. While much of the financial economy benefited, the productive economy suffered.

By the time Ronald Reagan took office in 1981, the prime rate stood at 21 percent, unemployment was 8.4 percent, and double-digit inflation stubbornly persisted. Unlike Carter, who blamed himself and the American people, Reagan blamed the government from which he tried to distance himself. Reagan's economic platform consisted of three basic planks. First, he supported a monetarist policy similar to the one championed by Friedman. Second, following his predisposition to promote the principles of supply-side economics, he called for significant tax cuts. According to supply-side theory, the money freed up by tax reductions would be invested and eventually would stimulate production. The magnitude of the tax cuts, however, created the prospect of significant budget deficits for years to come. Never a person to worry about consistency, Reagan made the third plank in his economic program a balanced budget. At the same time that he was trying to stimulate the economy with major tax cuts, which would lead to significant deficits, he called for a balanced budget in which deficits would be eliminated. It is unclear whether Reagan understood the economic principles he claimed to support well enough to realize that his tax policy made a balanced budget impossible, but his advisors surely were fully aware of the confidence game they were playing. Their disingenuousness put Volcker in an impossible situation: Reagan was pursuing expansionary policies through tax cuts while at the same time calling on the Fed to restrain the economy through tight money and high interest rates. Where Reagan's and Volcker's policies were in agreement was in the advantage they gave to people, institutions, and companies that had money. Reagan's tax cuts consistently favored business interests and wealthy individuals with significant financial assets. Though Reagan's rhetoric of austerity was often worthy of Calvinism, the pain his policies inflicted was unevenly distributed across the economic spectrum. The more money one had, the less one suffered.

Under the Reagan administration, the policy of deregulation was not limited to interest rates but extended to other sectors of the economy. Changes in the banking industry triggered by the Fed's actions had major effects on financial markets for the next two decades. The Monetary Control Act of 1980 was the most significant banking reform since the 1933 Glass-Steagall Act. The perceived need for new legislation arose largely from difficulties the Fed faced. The 1913 statute establishing the Fed made membership in the system voluntary. By the 1970s, banks were dropping out of the Federal Reserve System because the Fed did not pay interest on the reserves participating banks were required to maintain. Since this flight threatened the Fed's ability to manage the economy, then-chairman William Miller approved interest payments on reserve deposits in 1978. While not disagreeing with this move, Congress understandably preferred a legislative solution and two years later passed the Monetary Control Act. In exchange for making participation in the Federal Reserve System mandatory, the Fed agreed to reduce reserve requirements. The final version of the bill, however, went far beyond the issues of interest payments and reserve requirements.

The Glass-Steagall Act originally had been designed to avoid the problems that led to the Depression. The most important provision of the bill was the effort to minimize instability in the banking industry by separating the commercial banks and investment banks. The 1980 legislation overturned this critical part of the Glass-Steagall Act. Throughout the 1980s, the walls between banking and investment banking eroded until in 1997 banks were actually permitted to acquire securities firms. This enabled them both to lend money and to underwrite securities. The conflict of interests resulting from this change led to many of the recent financial and accounting scandals.[26] In addition to commercial and investment banks, the thrift industry was drawn into the fray. Prior to 1980, there were two kinds of thrifts: savings and loan associations and savings banks, both of which committed most of their assets to residential mortgages. Since federal regulations held interest rates for mortgages artificially low, sky-rocketing rates in the early 1980s created a crisis for S&Ls. With most of their funds committed to long-term loans paying no more than 3 to 4 percent, S&Ls could no longer attract deposits while other banks and money markets were offering rates as high as 18 to 21 percent. The only solution seemed to be to lift the ceiling on interest rates and allow all banks to compete with each other. As regulations fell and banks struggled to gain a competitive advantage, differences among financial institutions became obscure. Thrifts competed directly with banks for short-term financing and moved into areas of real estate investment in which they had little experience.[27] A final regulatory revision enacted in the early 1980s contributed to changes in banking practices and played a significant role in subsequent developments. Congress approved legislation permitting all banks to pay interest on checking accounts in what were called NOW (negotiable order of withdrawal) accounts. Though not immediately apparent, this policy had significant implications for the Fed's new monetary policy. While the range of the Fed's power increased with mandatory participation, its ability to control credit decreased with the deregulation of interest rates and the banking system.

The Fed's policies under Volcker and the deregulatory program of the Reagan administration combined to create an era of financial entrepreneurship, which former secretary of labor Robert Reich has labeled "paper entrepreneurialism." The way had been prepared for this burgeoning paper empire in 1975 with the end of fixed stock brokerage commissions. The cumulative effect of these changes was the emergence of fee-based banking, which, according to Ken Auletta, involved a shift from practices based on long-established relations between bankers and clients to a system based on the competitive financial advantage of individual transactions. In this new banking world, Peter Peterson, former head of Lehman Brothers, explains, "traditionally high-margin products [are] reduced to commodities, where price and distribution are more important in selecting a banker than historic and social relationships."[28] As banking became more competitive, it grew more speculative until there seemed to be little difference between bankers and traders. New financial instruments, like Michael Milken's junk bonds, fueled a surge in mergers and acquisitions and created the overheated climate so memorably recorded in films like Glenn Jordan's *Barbarians at the Gate* and Oliver Stone's *Wall Street*. In the short term, investment banks and other financial intermediaries reaped huge profits. Commenting on banking practices at the time, investment banker Herbert Allen identifies some of the most troubling problems plaguing business and financial markets: "The fees paid today are outrageous. . . . It's a terrible system! Investment bankers are like ambulance-chasing lawyers who sue on every deal on the basis of getting fees. It's a bribe. Directors of many corporations are derelict in their responsibility and are paying investment bankers huge fees for long reports, which only serve as protective padding for their own rear ends."[29] By the beginning of the twenty-first century, Allen's words proved not only historically accurate but also prophetic of difficulties that became even worse in the 1990s.

The short-term advantage of these changes for many large banks could not hide deeper problems that were brewing. The financial economy was roaring but the productive economy was sagging. When the economy entered recession in 1981–82, it became apparent that the very policies that were creating record profits in the banking industry were also sowing the seeds of a crisis that began with S&Ls and quickly spread throughout the entire system. In 1980, there were 4002 S&Ls; three years later, 962 had failed. Multiple factors contributed to this collapse. A drop in real estate values in the Southwest created problems for savings and loan associations, which had recently ventured into unfamiliar investment territory. In addition to this, the policies of many lending institutions during boom times returned to haunt them when the economy slowed. With inflation and interest rates rising rapidly, banks encouraged many property owners—especially farmers—to borrow more money to cover operating expenses. The logic was as familiar as it was flawed: borrow now at lower interest rates, pay back later with cheaper money. The only way people could do this was to leverage their land. But as the economy fell into recession and interest rates did not adjust quickly enough, property owners could not meet their debt obligations and defaulted on their loans. At the same time, the value of their land was declining, thereby decreasing the value of their collateral. As matters worsened, debtors' problems quickly became creditors' problems.

Further turbulence was generated by new financial instruments created in the wake of the deregulation of the banking and financial industries. As we will see in the next chapter, the securitization of mortgages transformed both lending and investing practices. This development, along with others, increased the power of large banks like Chase Manhattan and Citibank. As competition among major institutions increased, smaller players were forced to become more aggressive. Repeating the mistake of many small property owners, banks became highly leveraged. (I will consider this problem in more detail in the next chapter.) When the impact of the United States' policies spread to the global economy, the situation of many banks became precarious. As rising interest rates had proved disastrous for Midwestern farmers and Southwestern real estate interests, so they created enormous problems for developing countries. With the debt burden growing, countries with large loans faced the increased likelihood of default. The first episode in a world debt crisis, which continues today, occurred in Mexico in 1982. Since the nine largest banks in the U.S. had 44 percent of their capital tied up in Mexican loans at the time, the Mexican crisis threatened the entire United States banking system. The Fed now faced an intractable dilemma and the way it responded set a pattern that would be repeated over the next two decades. The primary responsibility of the Fed from the time of its founding in 1913 was to protect the banks from failing. But the policies it enacted in the late 1970s and early 1980s led to critical difficulties for the very industry the Fed was created to support. The scope of the crisis and the possible consequences of failure left the Fed little choice but to intervene and in effect bail out the banks whose own aggressive pursuit of profits had gotten them into the mess in the first place. What became the unannounced doctrine of too-big-to-fail not only rewarded financial irresponsibility but also encouraged other bankers and investors to repeat the mistakes made in Mexico by giving them assurances that the federal government would always be there to save them from themselves.

The domestic and international banking crisis both grew out of and contributed to the recession in the early 1980s. As problems spread at home and abroad, it was becoming clear that monetarism was not working. In addition to the obvious reasons for this changing situation, less obvious economic issues were involved. As we have seen, monetarism attempts to stabilize the economy by holding the money supply to a slow and steady rate of growth. Monetarists use M-1, which includes assets with the greatest liquidity like checking accounts, demand deposits, and currency, to determine the money supply. Savings accounts and money market accounts are less liquid and thus were classified as M-2. After the deregulation of the banking industry, however, it became less clear how to define money—especially the critical M-1 variable. With the introduction of NOW accounts, the line separating M-1 and M-2 broke down. The proliferation of new financial instruments in the next few years further complicated this already difficult situation. Two additional factors contributed to the Fed's growing dilemma during the 1981–82 recession. First, the velocity of money slowed down, creating further uncertainty about M-1. While Friedman certainly recognized the importance of the velocity of money, his theoretical position was that velocity changes more slowly and more predictably than the quantity of money. Thus, he argued, it makes more sense to focus on the quantity of money in analyzing short-term fluctuations in the economy. In addition to uncertainties created by changes in the velocity of money, the Fed's restriction of the money supply forced banks and other lending institutions to devise new strategies to raise capital. When the two most obvious courses of action—selling government securities and borrowing at the discount window—proved inadequate, financiers, hungry for funds to loan at high rates of return, turned to the international Eurodollar market, which was growing even more rapidly as the U.S. economy faltered. What seemed to be an advantage to borrowers was a major problem for the Fed because there were no reserve requirements on capital raised on the Eurodollar market. This meant that banks and other financial intermediaries could borrow freely and lend more aggressively than ever. As lenders became more venturesome, banks became dangerously leveraged. To make matters worse, there was little the Fed could do to correct the situation; the Fed, in fact, was losing control of the economy.

Faced with recession at home and spreading debt crises abroad, Volcker once again changed course. On July 1, 1982, the Fed abandoned its experiment with monetarism; interest rates were relaxed to increase liquidity throughout the economic system. In the following five months, there were seven rate reductions, which was good news for the stock market. During the next six months, the market rose dramatically, triggering what would become the longest bull market in history. This is not to imply that the course from August 1982 to March 2000 was without its ups and downs; indeed, the 1987 crash was the largest drop in the market since 1929. But financial markets recovered surprisingly quickly and continued an upward trajectory that did not end for more than a decade. By the time Volcker left the chairmanship of the Fed and Alan Greenspan took over in 1987, inflation had dropped from 13 percent to 4 percent, but the cost had been high.

The implications of the changes in the economy during the 1970s and early 1980s extend far beyond the economic realm and the United States borders. What was occurring in the economy both reflected and influenced broader social and cultural changes. The displacement of the industrial, productive, or real economy by the financial economy involved a shift from privileging material to immaterial assets. Like postmodern art and architecture recycling images and literary texts folding words into words, the economy became a play of floating signifiers whose relations to "real" referents grew ever more tenuous. As the real became a shadow of what it once seemed to have been, the economy became more spectral. When the program of deregulation spreads from banking and finance to computers and telecommunications, new technologies emerge, which lead to the invention of financial instruments that further change the economy and transform culture.

During the 1970s and early 1980s, the globalization of the economy also proceeded at an accelerated rate. From Nixon's decision to abandon the gold standard to Volcker's experiment with monetarism, actions originating in Washington rippled across the world and returned to influence the U.S. economy in unexpected ways. When the global economy expanded, countries, financial institutions, and individuals became increasingly entangled in worldwide webs from which there is no escape. With ever faster proliferation of new information and telematic technologies, the specter of a global network economy becomes unavoidable.

5

SPECTERS OF CAPITAL

—OK boy but if this here bank finds out the class put money
in some account where you take it out to piss away on this
debunture crap and they find out you kept this here clock boy
you're in . . .

—We got a clock! We already got a clock right up by the door in
the classroom and I mean holy shit who said I'm taking any
money that's not what you do! I mean didn't you ever see these
things where they say come right down and borrow up to a hundred percent of your passbook balance, while it goes right on
earning these top dividends and all? So whose business is it if
I just start this other account and loan against this here first
one where they have my signature so they know it's me, I mean
it's just different electric numbers on these checks and all which
this computer reads them it doesn't give a shit if you're three
years old just if the money's there, I mean that's all Mary Lou
honey that's all this Mister Wall that's all these here folks that's
all any of it is don't tell me I did something against the law
boy, that's just what you do! I mean this here class account I just
loan against it and get through this here forks deal I never even
touched it right?

William Gaddis, *JR*

Marx begins *Manifesto of the Communist Party* on a ghostly note: "A specter is haunting Europe—the specter of Communism. All the Powers of old Europe have entered into a holy alliance to exorcise this specter: Pope and Czar, Metternich and Guizot, French Radical and German police-spies." Declaring opposition to be a mark of growing strength, Marx claims that communism is destined to conquer the entire world. This belief rests upon what can only be described as a *theology* of history. Tucked away in a footnote on the first page of the manifesto, Marx suggests that the social and personal fragmentation plaguing modernity do not represent the original condition of the human race. Before the emergence of capitalism, there was a primitive form of communism: "The inner organization of this primitive Communistic society was laid bare, in its typical form, by Morgan's crowning discovery of the true nature of the *gens* and its relation to the *tribe*. With the dissolution of these primeval communities, society begins to be differentiated into separate and finally antagonistic classes."[1] The trajectory Marx describes is identical to the familiar nineteenth-century romantic version of the traditional Judaeo-Christian theology of history as beginning with unity (Garden), falling into opposition (Fall), and finally moving toward a richer harmony (Kingdom). In Marx's three-part story, primitive communism gives way to the sin of capitalism, which will be overcome with the arrival of communist redemption.

As Marx's vision struggled to become a reality in the early twentieth century, artists played as important a role as politicians. Echoing Schiller's call for the redemptive education of man, the Russian avant-garde sought to transform the world into a work of art. To accomplish this lofty goal, art had to move from pedestal to street and from gallery to factory. On the occasion of the famous $5 \times 5 = 25$ exhibition, sponsored by Moscow's Institute for Artistic Culture in September 1921, Alexander Rodchenko echoed Nietzsche's declaration of the death of God: "Art is dead! . . . Art is as dangerous as religion as an escapist activity. . . . Let us cease our speculative activity and take over the healthy bases of art—color, line, materials, and forms—into the field of reality, of practical construction."[2] For Rodchenko and his fellow Constructivists, the move from "speculative activity" to "practical construction" entails a commitment to create socially useful products. As "pure art" becomes "production art," Rodchenko turns his attention to graphic design—advertising posters, books, and magazines—furniture design, information centers (i.e., kiosks), interior design, theater sets, and eventually film. The course of his career both illustrates and illuminates broader social and artistic currents circulating in Russia during the decisive decade of the 1920s. The movement from studio and gallery to street and factory spread as the effort to implement the communist vision accelerated. What inspired this attempt to integrate modernism and modernization was the conviction that social equality, economic justice, and political freedom could be realized only when artistic vision becomes practically effective by directing the forces of mass production and mass media.

The communist project, of course, fails. This failure is the result of another specter that, for Marx, is far more dangerous than communism: the specter of money in its most developed form—capital. In his subtle study, *Specters of Marx,* Derrida writes:

> Marx always described money, and more precisely the monetary sign, in the figure of appearance or simulacrum, more exactly of the ghost. He not only described them, he also defined them, but the figural presentation of the concept seemed to describe some spectral "thing," which is to say, "someone" . . . . *The Critique of Political Economy* explains to us how the existence (*Dasein*) of money, metallic *Dasein,* gold or silver, produces a *remainder.* This remainder is—it remains, precisely—but the shadow of a great name: ". . . The body of money is but a shadow. . . ." The whole movement of idealization . . . that Marx then describes, whether it is a question of money or of ideologems, is a production of ghosts, illusions, simulacra, appearances, or apparitions.[3]

History has shown that Marx was right to worry about the specter of capital. By the end of the twentieth century, the dream of communism had collapsed and the world had been taken over by specters—ghosts, illusions, simulacra, appearances, and apparitions—whose realm extends far beyond the economy.

NETWORKING THE ECONOMY) In a world of docudramas, infotainment, and reality TV, it is often difficult to know whether art imitates life or life imitates art. It often seems that for many people, something is not real until it appears on TV. With networks competing for viewers 24/7, TV makes news as much as it reports it. Events are transformed into media spectacles as fast as they occur. It took only one year for the collapse of Enron to appear as a made-for-TV movie. By January 2003, Dallas's infamous JR Ewing had been recast as Houston's calculating Ken Lay. While JR's real oil had been transformed into Enron's energy reserves, which proved to be virtual, the wheeling and dealing of Texas tycoons was no less intriguing for viewers. CBS's *The Crooked E: The Unshredded Truth about Enron* was based on Brian Cruver's book, *Anatomy of Greed: The Unshredded Truth from an Enron Insider,* which had already been published the previous September. The CBS Web site promoting the movie boasts, "The insightful movie is based on facts—some well-known, others not at all—and will be an insider's view at one of the biggest scandals of the decade." In the opening scene, we learn the unshredded truth: "At Enron perception is everything." The conversation in which this truth is revealed to impressionable newcomers takes place at a lavish Texas barbecue where employees swap tales about huge profits on new deals investors have never before seen. A company veteran boasts to a newcomer: "Reagan is in the White House; deregulation is the law of the land. There's only one rule and that's that there are no rules!"

The world that made Enron possible began two decades earlier, when new technologies and changing political attitudes overhauled both the economic landscape and transformed financial markets. Since the dawn of trading, technological innovation has always transformed markets. When what is being exchanged is stuff, new transportation networks create new markets, which require different investment strategies. As bits become more valuable than stuff, communication networks become more important than railroads, highways, seaways, and airways. In recent decades media, information, and network technologies have both created new products and markets and changed the way material as well as immaterial commodities are produced, marketed, and distributed. While much has been written about the shift from an industrial or manufacturing to an information economy, the most important development has been overlooked: the distinctive character of our age is not simply the spread of computers but the impact of connecting them. When computers are networked, *everything* changes. The constantly changing networks that increasingly govern our lives have a distinct logic, which we are only beginning to understand. The new territory opening in our midst will remain incomprehensible until the complex interrelation of technology, politics, economic theory, and markets is mapped.

On November 9, 1989, almost exactly a decade after Paul Volcker's decision to change the direction of United States economic policy and only two years after Alan Greenspan took over the chairmanship of the Fed and Andy Warhol died, the Berlin Wall fell. Two years later, the Soviet Union collapsed, the World Wide Web was launched, and the Internet was opened to commercial use. If the 1980s began in 1979, the 1990s began in 1989. When the end of communism actually came, it was as much the result of economic as military factors. New media and communications technologies rendered walls obsolete and made the attractions of consumer culture irresistible. More was at stake, however, than the desire for commodities and the appeal of American pop culture. The collapse of the Berlin Wall and dissolution of the Soviet Union signaled the failure of a centralized, hierarchical economic system and the triumph of a more decentralized, nonhierarchical system. One of the first to detect in the market dynamics of capitalism a different principle of organization, Hayek had long argued that the triumph over socialism was all but inevitable because of capitalism's "superior capacity to use dispersed knowledge." Writing in *The Fatal Conceit: The Errors of Socialism,* he observes:

> This is true not only of economics, but in a wide area, and is well known today in the biological sciences. This insight was only the first of a growing family of theories that account for the formation of complex structures in terms of processes transcending our capacity to observe all the several circumstances operating in the determination of their particular manifestations. When I began my work I felt that I was nearly alone in working on the evolutionary formation of such highly complex self-maintaining orders. Meanwhile, researches on this kind of problem— under various names, such as autopoiesis, cybernetics, homeostasis, spontaneous order, self-organization, synergetics, systems theory, and so on—have become so numerous that I have been able to study closely no more than a few of them.[4]

Communism and the version of capitalism emerging in the latter half of the twentieth century embody two contrasting logics, which represent the organizational structures of industrial and information societies respectively. The authoritarian communist political system bred suspicion of the disruptive effects of new information technologies. With the world changing around it, the Soviet Union remained committed to a form of industrialism whose time had passed. In the United States, by contrast, a neoconservative political agenda and neoliberal economic policies joined in a symbiotic relation with information technologies, which proved to be mutually reinforcing. During the past three decades, what has unified politics, economics, and technology has been the principle of decentralization originally formulated in Smith's analysis of markets. With positive feedbacks accelerating the social and economic rate of change, new organizational structures have emerged that are thoroughly transforming society and culture. This new system is best described as the *network economy*.

The network economy is characterized by the increasing interrelation, complexity, and dematerialization of items and channels of exchange. Describing the transition from an industrial to an information economy, Walter Wriston, former chairman of Citicorp, claims, "In 1971 we switched from the gold standard to the information standard."[5] When currency becomes information and information is the coin of the realm, money, as Shubik points out, becomes "a network phenomenon" and is therefore subject to the network effect.[6] A network derives its value from the number of agents or nodes it includes. When new participants act in ways similar to early joiners, each additional node increases the value of the network by a factor > 1. Let n be the number of nodes; then the value of a network with n nodes is $v(n) = n^2 - n$. According to this formula, the value of a network of 1 [or $v(1)$] obviously is 0; as nodes are added, value increases: $v(2) = 2$, $v(3) = 6$, $v(4) = 12$, $v(5) = 20$, $v(6) = 30$, etc. This pattern leads to the tendency of networks to expand exponentially. The first American Web site, for example, appeared in 1991; five years later there were over 100,000 Web sites. By 1993, traffic on the World Wide Web was increasing at an annual rate of 341,631 percent. In 1998, 1.5 million Web pages were being added every day. With this pattern of growth, it quickly becomes apparent that networking the economy creates the possibility of an exponential increase in the value of being connected (see figure 15).

While many other factors were involved, the emergence of a genuine global economy in the past three decades would have been impossible without the network effect. Globalization, of course, is not new, but its current form is different. George Soros, head of Soros Fund Management and founder of a global network of foundations supporting "open societies," defines the globalization now occurring as "the free movement of capital and increasing domination of national economies by global financial markets and multinational corporations."[7] With globalization steadily extending its reach as a result of the growing network economy, people, institu-

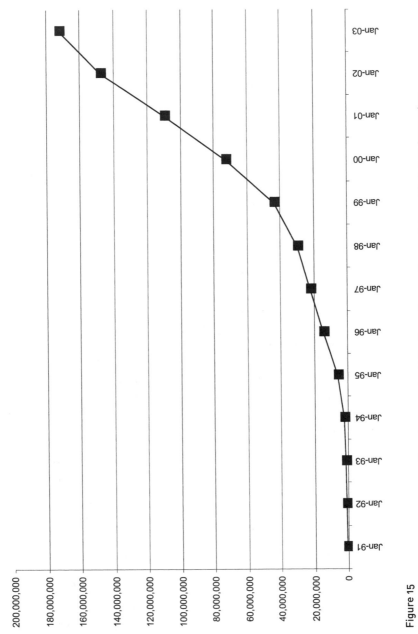

Figure 15

Internet domain survey host count. Based on a graph at http://www.isc.org. Source: Internet Software Consortium.

tions, and countries are bound in ever more complex webs of interrelation. The complexity of these networks and worldwide webs is not only the result of greater connectivity but also a function of the increasing dematerialization of items and systems of exchange. The shift from the gold to the information standard prepares the way for the transition from trading stuff to exchanging bits at a distance. In emerging network economies, all marketing is rapidly becoming telemarketing (the Greek *tele* means at a distance). As we have seen, the tendency toward dematerialization began with the tilt from the productive or real to the financial or spectral economy in the 1970s. During the 1980s and 1990s, new political and economic policies combined with new information and telematic technologies to create the demand for new currencies, financial instruments, and exchange networks (figure 16).

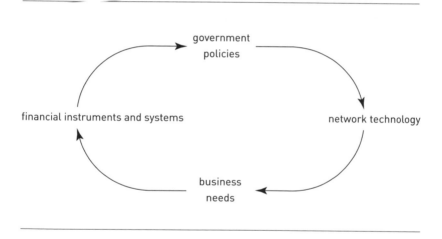

Figure 16

In ways that are not immediately apparent, the structural complexity of economic systems is directly related to the dematerialization of instruments and media of exchange. In *Economic Evolution and Structure: The Impact of Complexity on the U.S. Economic System,* Frederic Pryor argues that it is possible

to measure the structural complexity of the financial system either in terms of the ratio of financial to physical wealth or in terms of the rela-

tive importance of financial intermediaries, whose activities are reflected in the financial instruments. For the financial system, therefore,
the measure of complexity corresponds to what is commonly known as
leverage and, as a result, we can draw upon a vast literature on the topic.
Given this approach, two possible indicators are available to measure the
complexity of the financial superstructure:

- The first is the ratio of total financial assets to total physical assets.
  This is sometimes called the *financial interrelations ratio*.
- The second is the ratio of assets of financial institutions to all U.S.
  financial assets. This measure of the relative importance of financial
  institutions (banks, insurance companies, and private pension funds)
  is sometimes designated as the *financial intermediation ratio*.[8]

From the period from 1974 to 1990, the financial interrelations ratio (i.e.,
"the ratio of total financial assets of the private sector to total tangible assets of the private sector") increased from 129 percent to 152 percent, and
the financial intermediation ratio (i.e., "the ratio of financial assets held by
the private financial sector to the total financial assets held in the economy") increased from 34.9 to 38.1. This shift from tangible to financial assets as well as the growth of financial intermediaries resulted in the increasing complexity of the economy.

With the growing dematerialization, interrelation, and complexity of
the economy, the speed of economic activity rapidly accelerates. More information is exchanged by more machines and agents across more networks at greater speeds than ever before. These developments lead to an
increase in instability and volatility, which episodically drive the economy
far from equilibrium. With greater volatility comes greater risk. Financial
markets have an ambivalent relation to risk: they cannot make a profit
without risk and yet they cannot bear too much of it. When it becomes
clear that in the network economy volatility is the rule rather than the exception, economic theorists, investors, and money managers become pre-
occupied with devising strategies to manage risk by redistributing it from
people who cannot tolerate it to people who can. Contrary to expectation,
the strategies and new financial instruments designed to avoid risk often
end up creating greater volatility and thus actually *increase* risk.

Sometimes it is difficult to remember just how recent are the technological innovations that have led to this economic revolution.[9] With the
decline of financial markets, the collapse of the dot-coms and telecoms,
and the corporate scandals at the end of the millennium, many analysts

have argued that far from passing away, the "old" economy is actually more reliable than the "new." The distinction between the old (i.e., industrial) and new (i.e., information) economy, however, has always been specious. Information and networking technologies are changing manufacturing, production, and marketing processes as much as the financial economy. In the last forty years, something fundamental has occurred: new technologies have transformed the very infrastructure of the economy and in the process have profoundly altered society and culture in ways that have yet to be appreciated. To begin to understand these changes, it is necessary to get a better grasp of the complex interplay of politics, economics, and technology.

It is a mistake to see the collapse of the Berlin Wall as signifying simply the victory of a laissez-faire system, which resists government interference and regulation, over a centralized system with a tightly managed economy. The policies of deregulation and privatization behind the market ideology of the 1980s and 1990s involve significant and sustained government action. Analyzing what he aptly describes as "the neoliberal networking drive," Dan Schiller writes:

> The architects of digital capitalism have pursued one major objective: to develop an economywide network that can support an ever-growing range of intracorporate and intercorporate business processes. . . . Only a network capable of flinging signals—including voices, images, videos, and data—to the far ends of the earth would be adequate to sustain this open-ended migration into electronic commerce.
>
> To create such a system meant that the foundations of the world's electronic information infrastructure had to be recast. The new network system, within which the Internet loomed largest by the mid-1990s, required a sweeping metamorphosis of the structure and policy of existing telecommunications.[10]

One of the many paradoxes of policies that have led to the new network economy is that getting the government off the backs of individuals and businesses has required extensive government intervention. From the end of World War II through the mid-1970s, government regulations, many of which dated back to the Depression, played a major role in the economy. The continuing weakness of the economy finally led to significant policy shifts that favored deregulation. Once again, the trajectory was from the real to the virtual. During the Carter administration, deregulation began with the airline, trucking, and railroad industries. The effect was quick and dramatic; as more players entered the game, competition increased and prices fell. With the long-term problems created by these changes still in the future, enthusiasm for deregulation grew. As we have already seen, the 1980s saw the deregulation of the banking and financial industries. By the 1990s, policies of deregulation were extended to telecommunications, computers, and networks. As has often been noted, the information revolution grew out of the military-industrial complex during and after the Second World War. With the advent of the Cold War, the federal government entered into new alliances with private industries and universities to conduct research in, among other things, computers and telematic technologies. As the postwar education boom spread, computers began to play an important role in university education. Not until the early 1960s, however, were commercial and business applications developed, which led to the personal computer revolution in the early 1980s. By this time, there was a consensus on both sides of the political aisle that the growth of information technologies was impossible without further deregulation and privatization. The rapid increase in people investing in the stock market, triggered by the approval of 401Ks and Individual Retirement Accounts (IRAs), created widespread popular support for these neoconservative and neoliberal policies. While these changes began in the United States and the United Kingdom, they quickly spread across the globe.

During the 1980s, the telecommunications industry underwent a complete transformation as the result of new technologies and regulatory policies. Even before the exponential growth of the Internet, it was clear that the future of the telecommunications industry would be with data more than voice. The Internet was such a threat to the telecoms because it involves a different technology, which requires a different infrastructure. The Internet grew out of decentralized packet-switching technology originally developed for military purposes in the Arpanet program. In contrast to traditional circuit switching, which directly links communicating parties and tends to be more centralized, packet switching breaks the message into segments and routes it across different circuits through a decentralized network. The Internet is really nothing more than codes and protocols that enable computers to communicate. "Although it was developed within the U.S. military-industrial complex, this foundational technology lies in the public domain. The rights to use it were made freely available, at first to a select group of cooperating universities and other military contractors and then more widely. The result, as Robert H. Reid declares, was that 'nobody owned the network. Virtually nobody made money from it directly. And almost every piece of software that governed or accesses it was free.'"[11] By the early 1980s, the National Science Foundation had established NSFNET, which enabled universities to communicate for purposes of research. At the same time commercial networks were beginning to emerge: CompuServe (1979), Prodigy (1982), and AOL, originally Quantum Computer Services (1985). Not until 1994 did the NSF announce that control of the network structure on which the Internet depends would be turned over to commercial carriers. Digital technologies can, of course, transmit both data and voice. Since Internet technology is superimposed upon telecommunications networks, telecoms suddenly found themselves supporting a new technology that posed a major competitive threat. It was obvious that for the telecoms to survive, they had to change the way they did business.

As computers and networks spread beyond government and education, their commercial potential quickly became evident. With the shift from industrial to informational modes of production and reproduction, business and financial institutions needed dependable and cost-effective technologies for data transmission. Corporations discovered that the decentralized network structure originally developed by the military was more robust and reliable than the systems that were publicly available. Instead of adapting to existing technologies, many businesses began to create proprietary systems known as Local Area Networks (LANs). As spending increased, the influence of corporations on the direction of computers and network technology grew until it eventually extended from LANs to the Internet itself. These changes were facilitated by developments extending back to the 1960s. During this pivotal decade, corporate interests pressured the Federal Communications Commission to require telecommunications companies to grant businesses special rates and privileges. They also mounted a successful campaign to "prevent any extension of regulatory oversight to computer services involving the use of communications facilities—that is, networks." These efforts culminated in a critical policy decision that, Schiller explains, carried far-reaching implications.

> Regulators embraced the fiction that computer networks—which in fact made *increasing* use of the existing telecommunications infrastructure—could be treated as if they existed independent of that infrastructure. Proliferating network systems were therefore freed by regulators to be configured and reconfigured as needed in support of business users' objectives. The unregulated suppliers of these systems, chiefly computer companies, were effectively licensed to metamorphose from vendors of electromechanical business instrumentation, tabulators, type-

writers, cash registers, calculators, and like machinery into pioneers of next-generation network equipment and services.[12]

Throughout the post–World War II era, most developed countries remained committed to a policy of universal access to telecommunications services. While in many countries this policy led to state-owned utilities, in the United States, AT&T was the primary provider of long-distance service until the early 1970s. The FCC's decision to separate the computer and networking industries from regulations governing telecommunications effectively exempted computer-mediated communications from the requirement of universal access and prepared the way for telecoms to enter new and unregulated markets.

By the 1980s, new players like MCI and Sprint as well as new technologies like cable and communications satellites were creating pressure to open all parts of the telecommunications industry to competition. The neoliberal policies favored by the Reagan administration led to the breakup of AT&T between 1982 and 1984. At the same time, Margaret Thatcher was dissolving the state monopoly of the communications industry by privatizing British Telecom. Thirteen years later there were over 120 telecommunications companies in the United Kingdom. The alliance between Reagan and Thatcher created conditions favoring the American domination of global telecommunications and networks. The privatization of British Telecom gave the United States entry to European markets, while England got a head start over the rest of Europe in this rapidly changing industry. In the next few years, deregulation and privatization spread rapidly. Before 1989, only nine countries, most of which were in the developing world, had privatized telecommunications. Between 1984 and 1996, forty-four countries, including all major industrial nations, privatized their telecommunications industries. The spread of free market principles in Europe led to new international alliances designed to gain competitive advantage in the global marketplace. Deutsche Telekom and France Telecom, for example, joined to form Global One. In 1994, the European Union opened all voice communication, which previously had been controlled by national companies, to free competition. Meanwhile in the United States, deregulation and privatization had become the new orthodoxy of both political parties. The 1996 Telecommunications Act went so far as to mandate that "local telephone companies that chose to modernize their networks in hopes of supplying customers with broadband Internet access had to make these new facilities available to would-be rivals at cut-rate wholesale prices."[13]

The privatization of telecommunications was not limited to developed countries but quickly extended throughout the so-called developing world. Indeed, corporate interests in developed countries saw the possibility of highly profitable markets in developing countries. The primary accomplices of U.S. corporations in these developments were the International Monetary Fund, the World Bank, and the World Trade Organization. With the unraveling of the Bretton Woods accord and the recovery of Western Europe, the IMF and World Bank moved from providing short-term support and backing postwar reconstruction to intervening in economies in crisis in ways that led to longer and more sustained involvement. As its power continued to grow, the United States became the major influence in world financial institutions. The wave of foreign debt crises rippling through the developing world in the 1980s and 1990s presented the opportunity for U.S. corporations to expand their interests through the policies of the IMF. In order to receive support from the IMF to service their foreign debt obligations, many countries were required to enact liberal reforms, which often led to increased economic hardship.[14] In addition to exercising fiscal discipline by cutting taxes and curtailing spending, countries were required to open their financial markets to foreign investment and to privatize and deregulate their telecommunications industries. Once these reforms were enacted, global corporations and telecoms quickly moved in and took over what previously had been national enterprises.

By the mid-1990s, the WTO had assumed a pivotal role in the global computer and telecommunications industries. In late 1996, the Ministerial Declaration on Information Technology called for eliminating tariffs on computer and software products worth $500 billion. Two months later, the WTO "agreed to open basic telecommunications markets within some seventy countries accounting for 94% of world telecommunications markets—around $600 billion in overall annual revenue—and just over half of the world population. . . . Transnational telecommunications carriers obtained commitments allowing foreign investment—at levels that varied but often ran as high as 100%—in existing national service providers that had long been sheltered from outside control."[15]

Two additional governmental actions in 1997 had a significant impact on the development of the Internet and networking technologies. The first was the Supreme Court decision in *Reno* v. *American Civil Liberties Union*, which determined that important provisions of the Communications Decency Act are not applicable to the Internet. Extending the principle of freedom of speech to computer-mediated communication, this decision extended greater protection from government regulation to networking technologies than to any other public communications system. At about the same time as this court decision, the Clinton administration released its *Framework for Global Electronic Commerce.* Noting that what once was a resource for education and research had become a major force in the global economy, the report stressed that the primary challenge was to protect the Global Information Infrastructure from regulations that would have a negative economic impact.

> As the use of the Internet expands, many companies and Internet users are concerned that some governments will impose extensive regulations on the Internet and electronic commerce. Potential areas of problematic regulation include taxes and duties, restrictions on the type of information transmitted, control over standards of development, licensing requirements and rate regulation of service providers. Indeed, signs of these types of commerce-inhibiting actions already are appearing in many nations. Preempting these harmful actions before they take root is a strong motivation for the strategy outlined in this paper.

The report identifies five basic principles that should guide the development of the Internet:

1. The private sector should lead.
2. Government should avoid undue restrictions on electronic commerce.
3. Where governmental involvement is needed, it should aim to support and enforce a predictable, minimalist, consistent and simple legal environment for commerce.
4. Governments should recognize the unique qualities of the Internet.
5. Electronic commerce over the Internet should be facilitated on a global basis.[16]

When President Clinton endorsed this report, the course for the future development of the Internet was set. Instead of establishing new operational principles, *Framework for Global Electronic Commerce* made explicit how far-reaching the results of two decades of deregulation and privatization policies had become.

The intersection of government policy, business interests, and technological innovation in the 1980s and 1990s created what is sometimes described as digital capitalism.[17] This form of capitalism, it is argued, constitutes the stage after industrial capitalism and is characteristic of so-called information society. While digital technologies are, of course, critical to the changing economic landscape, the transformative effects of *network* technologies are even more important. What has proven so revolutionary is not only new machines but *how they are connected.* The changes brought by networking have profound consequences for all of life. If, as we have come to suspect, to be is to be related, then to be related differently is to *be different.* As worldwide webs continue to grow, it seems as if the Hegelian Idea is becoming embodied in space and time. To recognize the economic significance of what is occurring, it is necessary to understand how networking technologies change *every* part of the economy—production, retail, banking, finance, investing, and trading—and by extension transform all aspects of life.

As I have noted, the misleading opposition between the old and new economies obscures the extent to which networking technologies alter processes of production as well as retail strategies and practices. With the advent of intranets and the Internet, corporations extended their global reach as never before and many companies involved in more or less traditional manufacturing began to decentralize and globalize their operations. As companies downsized at home, they outsourced production to less developed countries, where labor was cheaper. While companies were, of course, outsourcing production before the 1990s, new digital and network technologies greatly increased the speed, efficiency, and extent of the practice. These changes led to the rapid growth of multinational and transnational corporations. There were seven thousand transnational corporations in 1973; by 1993 their number had grown to twenty-six thousand. "By the mid-1990s, transnational companies generated some two-thirds of total world exports of goods and services."[18]

The impact on retail operations has been no less significant. New information technologies have made it possible to track sales and monitor inventories in real time. Cash registers have become computer terminals that feed information to data banks where it is processed and directed to production facilities. Accurate real-time information makes it possible to reduce inventories and to shift to just-in-time production. As early as 1976 the Universal Product Code, i.e., barcode, enabled retailers to track products directly at the point of sale. Commenting on the importance of the barcode, Hiromi Hosoya and Markus Schaefer explain that bit structures "make it possible to manage diversity, distribute identity, and disembody territories. Bit structures establish the laws of the 'network economy,' which state that by connecting dumb and cheap parts, networked systems will, in an exponential manner, rise from obscurity to dominance."[19] As if this were not enough, information technologies are also transforming credit cards from a payment mechanism to a marketing resource. Data collected from customers is analyzed and used for niche advertising and marketing. In some cases, marketing specialists go so far as to feed this information into data banks that store information gathered from computer-based geographic information systems (GIS) to create virtual maps intended to direct the attention and influence the conduct of consumers. "Instead of a physical description of a city's composition, GIS—now the dominant tool of retail site analysis and selection—is a matrix of information layers, 'an organized collection of computer hardware, software, geographic data and personnel designed to efficiently capture, store, update, manipulate, analyze and display all forms of geographically referenced information.'"[20] With the commercialization of the Internet, retail sales gained another important outlet. Though many entrepreneurs initially thought e-commerce would be more bits than stuff, the Internet is proving to be an unexpectedly robust environment for selling traditional products ranging from cars and refrigerators to books and prescription drugs.

In addition to manufacturing and retail, digital and networking technologies are radically altering money and how it is both exchanged and managed. The shift from paper—cash and checks—to electronic currencies actually began in the late 1950s with the introduction of plastic charge cards. Having started with fee-based cards like Diners Club, American Express, and Carte Blanche, the credit card industry quickly became national. By 1970, there were two major cards: National BankAmericard (later Visa) and Master Charge/Interbank (later MasterCard). Not until the 1980 Monetary Control Act and 1982 Garne St. Germaine Acts extended deregulation did plastic become ubiquitous. Thrifts as well as banks could issue credit cards and consumer debt became an important revenue stream. Even though private credit card companies posed a competitive threat to banks, the structure of the industry still preserved a place for financial intermediaries. But this situation changed with the introduction of smart cards or stored-value cards (SVCs). These cards use a technology in which money is downloaded into a memory chip and can be transferred directly to another SVC or deposit account. As Elinor Harris Solomon points out, "here the Gordian knot is severed. We can now spend the stored value without directly accessing a bank account—the value on the card is prepaid. Once in hand, the money can pass from card to card (in some systems such as Mondex), just as cash can travel from hand to hand without direct bank intervention. The value can also move from card to card to a special 'reader' at the merchant's vending machine or store when you want to buy something."[21]

It is a short step from SVCs to cybermoney or e-money. In a 1996 issue entitled "The Future of Money," *Business Week* confidently declared, "In many ways, E-cash, which can be backed by any currency or other asset, represents the biggest revolution in currency since gold replaced cowry shells."[22] In contrast to credit cards and smart cards, e-money is actually computer money stored somewhere on a hard drive. It can be issued by either banks or other companies or institutions. E-money is "not co-mingled with other deposits on a bank balance sheet, nor is it a generally measured part of the money supply. E-money represents a liability (or IOU) of some nonbank firm, or a segregated special account of a bank. Given its newness, the use of this money is as yet not circumscribed in any way by law." Widespread acceptance of e-money depends on the development of reliable encryption software. With companies like DigiCash, CyberCash, Visa, Microsoft, Xerox, and Citicorp competing for the e-money market, there is little doubt that cybermoney soon will become an increasingly important medium of exchange. What makes e-money different from other currencies and potentially so revolutionary is the fact that it circulates through networks *outside* the banking system and can be privately created and backed by anything users will accept. E-money, in other words, harbors the prospect of private currencies, which are neither regulated nor backed by the federal government.[23] In addition to the problems and possibilities this poses, extensive use of e-money would further compound the difficulties of calculating M-1, which, we have seen, is essential to controlling the money supply and managing the economy.

The impact of new technologies is not limited to commerce and the private sector but has had an equally important influence on banking and finance. As early as 1918, the Fed introduced the first direct funds transfer network using Morse code, telegraph operators, and dedicated lines. By the 1970s, the Fed was using a prototype of Internet packet switching to transfer funds to member banks. At the same time, the automated Clearing House Interbank Payment Systems (CHIPS), which is owned and privately operated by banks, was handling the major part of international currency exchanges.[24] Just as corporations developed LANs, so banks entered into agreements with computer, satellite, and telecommunications companies to create local and global networks. As a result of these developments, banking became as transnational as business.

The final area in which networking has changed the way business is done is investing and trading. One of the most important symptoms of this change was the introduction of an automated quotation system by the National Association of Securities Dealers in 1971. NASDAQ, which was one of the first real-time computer networks and actually anticipated the Internet, was destined to transform Wall Street and thereby influence the entire global financial system. Though NASDAQ developed during the 1970s and 1980s, its real impact was not felt until the dot-com mania of the 1990s. I will therefore defer consideration of NASDAQ until chapter 6.

The new technologies that created new forms of currency and business practices also generated the demand for different financial products. Technological and financial innovation are bound in positive feedback loops that lead to accelerating change. Before proceeding to a consideration of these circuits, it is necessary to consider a final feature of e-money and electronic exchange networks. As we have seen, one of the most important consequences of digital and networking technologies is the increasing speed of circulation and thus reduction of transaction time. As currency changes from metal and paper to bits and light, time becomes money in surprising ways. With checks and traditional credit cards, the float, i.e., the delay between payment and settlement, creates the possibility of one party in the exchange making money. For example, if I write a check using my NOW account, I continue to earn interest until the check is cashed. With SVCs, immediate transfer almost erases the float, thereby eliminating the advantage to the payer and the disadvantage to the payee. Though transfers appear to be immediate, there is nonetheless a slight delay between payment and settlement. As Solomon points out, "the electronic money transfer message moves very fast. The legal and institutional mechanisms don't always work that fast, especially when many currencies, languages and laws enter in. The result is fast-as-light money flow but not quite so fast balance sheet transfers through a string of banks and wires." Interest income lost by the reduction in transfer time is more than made up for by the increase in the volume of transactions. As global banking and financial networks expand exponentially and international currency traffic increases, the implications of this float become more significant.

Consider the huge flows on CHIPS and Fedwire and their foreign counterparts. They overhang as many multiples of the underlying money base. As the speed ratchets up, and money turns over faster and faster, we have a form of money mass that isn't quite there, money that never becomes a permanent balance sheet entry, never really gets to be counted, money that self destructs. In short, injected into the staid money business we have virtual money, unaccounted for and unmeasured except sporadically as gross transactions values.

This money that "isn't quite there" is very important for the global economy. Solomon labels this strange money "phantom"; I would call it spectral. She writes:

> Stephen Hawking defines a virtual particle in modern quantum mechanics . . . as "a particle that can never be directly detected, but whose existence does have measurable effects." From such a definition, I derive the virtual money concept. Often our phantom money can't be directly detected either, but its effects are real enough—volatility of foreign exchange on capital markets prices. The tangible effects can thwart the stabilizing activities of central banks as they defend their own currencies and markets. A real effect from the global stir of all virtual brief-lived money particles doubtless does exist. It includes unusual heavy spurts of traders' flows and the engineered derivative models that capture the possibilities of rapid money turnaround.[25]

Playing with such phantoms and specters, traders in the 1980s and 1990s turn the art of finance into the magic of creation *ex nihilo.*

CREATION *EX NIHILO*)   In 1987, the same year the market crashed, hedge fund manager George Soros published a criticism of the principle of equilibrium underlying most modern economic theory in *The Alchemy of Finance: Reading the Mind of the Market.* Alchemy, we have discovered, originated in ancient mining rituals and metallurgical techniques intended to turn base matter into precious gold. As the process of sublimation continues from metal to paper, and then from plastic to electrons, the alchemy of finance actually seems to succeed in turning something (metal) into virtually nothing (bits). But just when this process seems to be complete, it unexpectedly reverses itself. The financial innovations of the late twentieth century seem to achieve the even more ancient dream of creation *ex nihilo* by making something (money, capital) out of nothing (bits or even mere ideas, concepts, fictions, and consensual hallucinations).

As currencies dematerialize and financial currents accelerate, they become more turbulent. Volatility, I have stressed, breeds risk, which financial markets need yet cannot bear. During the 1950s, a new area of financial economics emerged, which was primarily devoted to developing ways to manage risk. Over the next two decades, new financial products changed the investment world. In 1952, Harry Markowitz proposed a different way of understanding risk with his portfolio theory. The language of portfolios has become so common that it is difficult to appreciate what a change in thinking Markowitz's theory represented. Markowitz's most important contribution was his proposal to shift from figuring the risk of *individual* stocks to measuring the *relative* risk of a diversified portfolio of stocks. It is impossible to make money without risk since all investments have some risk (even investing in a safe U.S. Treasury bond cannot offer protection from unexpected inflation). Therefore, the aim of investing is not to avoid risk completely but to spread risk among investments in order to minimize the risk of the portfolio for any given rate of return. Quadratic programming yields a menu of possibilities, each with a different rate of return and risk. This enables investors to calculate the relative risk of the portfolio as a whole. Before turning to a consideration of the changes in investment strategies that grow out of Markowitz's portfolio theory, it is important to understand the new financial products that were created largely to hedge risk.

One of the reasons managing risk became such an urgent necessity was that banking deregulation had transformed the bond markets. Bonds are loans, typically made to federal, state, and municipal governments but sometimes also to businesses and corporations. The most common bonds are U.S. Treasuries, which are classified according to their maturity periods (bills, from a few months to one year; notes, up to five years; and bonds proper, longer term). Interest rates paid on bonds are related to risk. Above the risk-free rate (i.e., free of default risk), the interest rate differential is a positive function of risk. While for U.S. Treasuries, rates are relatively low and the default risk is almost nil, corporate bonds pay higher rates depending on the stability of the company.[26] The less stable the company, the greater the risk and therefore the higher the rate of return. The mergers and acquisitions frenzy of the 1980s was largely fueled by very high-risk junk bonds, which paid extremely high interest rates. Prior to this development, as long as the government remained primarily committed to holding down unemployment, if yields began to creep upward, the Fed would take measures to hold interest rates constant. The price and yield of bonds are inversely related; if interest rates go up, bond prices go down and vice versa. The bond market is also related to the stock market in complicated ways. When stock prices change mostly because of recession, bond and stock prices move in opposite directions because recession reduces profits, which in turn reduces stock prices. If efforts to counter recession lead to a reduction in interest rates, the price of bonds rises. When stock prices change mostly as the result of changes in interest rates, bond and stock prices move together.

Volcker's experiment with monetary policy in 1979 created fluctuations of interest rates, which introduced unusual volatility in the bond market. For those seeking a safer haven than securities, bonds no longer were a reliable investment. In addition to this, the U.S. Treasury sought to raise additional revenues by creating a broad array of new bonds with different coupons and maturities. The increasing diversity and volatility of the bond market created the opportunity for venturesome bond arbitrage. As we will see in chapter 8, in 1998 this new area of investment came perilously close to causing a meltdown in the global economy.

One of the most important changes in the bond market was the acceleration of the securitization of mortgages, which occurred in the wake of the deregulation of the S&Ls. On September 30, 1981, Congress passed legislation intended to help S&Ls by allowing them to sell their low-rate long-term mortgage loans and to use the income from the sales to invest or loan at higher rates. These mortgages were bundled and sold as bonds known as Ginnie Maes through the Government National Mortgage Association (GNMA). The GNMA buys mortgages guaranteed by the Federal Housing Administration, the Department of Veterans Affairs, and Farmers Home Administration and sells them as securities. The Federal National Mortgage Association (FNMA) also purchases mortgages from lenders and resells them to investors as securities called Fannie Maes. These pools of mortgages, known as Mortgage Backed Securities were then "split into several classes (or 'tranches') of securities, each of which entitles investors to different seniority and rates of return—or split into securities entitling investors to only the interest payments or only the principal payments."[27] Some, though not all, of these innovations made the bond market more speculative and thus more volatile.

In response to these changes, both financial engineering and hedge funds grew rapidly in the 1980s. Concentrating largely but not exclusively on fixed income investments, financial engineers create customized products for their clients. Many of these products are later standardized and sold off the shelf on specialized markets. Financial engineers, who work in what is known as structured finance, understand the economy as a game made up of a set of agreed-upon rules. The challenge for financial engineers is to manipulate these rules to create new products, which are designed to increase income, decrease taxes, and redistribute risk.

In contrast to financial engineering, hedge funds date back to the 1920s. Alfred Winslow Jones created the first postwar hedge fund in 1949.[28] Whereas mutual funds are regulated and open to all investors, hedge funds are private, unregulated, and usually restricted to a limited number of large institutional or very wealthy investors. Between the late 1960s and early 1990s, hedge funds grew significantly: in 1968 $300 billion was invested in hedge funds and by 1990 the amount had grown to $3.2 trillion. The practice of hedging, like portfolio investing, is based upon the relativity of risk. In structured finance, the economy appears to be a quasi-equilibrium system similar to Hegel's dialectical system or structuralists' binary systems. When hedging, investments are understood as offsetting pairs that are supposed to be reciprocally or perhaps even dialectically related. An investor hedges by placing bets and counterbets. Such wagers need not be one-for-one but can involve a complex series of interrelated bets. What is important is the *relative* movement of the investments. The trick of the trade is to place bets balanced enough to be safe but risky enough to offer potential profits.

While it is possible to hedge with established products like commodities, stocks, and bonds, the growing complexity and volatility of markets created the demand for more sophisticated financial instruments, which computers and networks make possible. As the 1980s unfolded, derivatives became the primary instrument for managing risk. Derivatives provide a way to shift risk from people who do not want it to people who are willing to bear risk for the possibility of a profitable return. There are three basic types of derivatives—futures, options, and swaps—each of which can involve commodities, stocks, bonds, interest rates, or currencies. With the continuing demand for new products, there has been an increasing range of derivatives, which have become more and more abstract. In *The Handbook of Financial Engineering* (1990), Clifford Smith and Charles Smithson list more than one hundred derivative products and note that more appear every day. Establishing the value of many of these derivatives requires complex mathematical calculations and significant computing power. The effectiveness of derivative transactions depends on extensive information from global markets readily available in real time. Derivative investments are not only highly speculative but are also off-book, i.e., they do not show up on balance sheets. Moreover, derivatives are highly leveraged; in some cases, they require little or sometimes even no capital up front. Throughout the 1990s, the derivatives market continued to grow until, in 1998, it had a nominal value of $70 trillion, *eight times* the annual Gross National Product of the United States.[29]

Options and futures, of course, are not new. Indeed, there is evidence of an instrument resembling an option in the 3,800-year-old Babylonian Code of Hammurabi. Twelve hundred years later, the Greek philosopher Thales invented an option contract that enabled him to purchase crops before they were planted.[30] In today's markets, an option is "*a right without an obligation.* More precisely, the holder of an option has a right without an obligation but the writer (or seller) of the option has an absolute obligation. For the right that the option provides, the option purchaser pays the option writer an up-front one-time fee called the option premium." There are two basic kinds of options, which have countless variations: puts and calls. A call gives its holder the right "to *purchase* the underlying asset from the option holder on or before the option's expiration date. If the option holder chooses to exercise the option, he or she must pay the option writer the options strike price."[31] A put option involves the same kind of agreement for selling underlying assets. While an option grants a right without an obligation, a futures contract "obligates its owner to purchase a specified asset at a specified exercise price on the contract maturity date."[32] In addition to providing opportunities to hedge investments, options and futures make it possible to manage volatility in commodities and currencies as well as stocks and bonds by limiting downside risk while not necessarily losing upside possibilities. It is important to note that the seller does not necessarily have to own the security or commodity when the option or future is sold. One can sell these contracts while owning *nothing* and gamble that the direction of the market will make it profitable. If it becomes necessary to close the deal, one can purchase the security or commodity at the time the option is exercised or the futures contract matures.

In many cases, hedging encounters the same problem we have seen in barter—the double coincidence of wants. In order to complete a hedge, one must find someone willing to take the other side of the bet. The solution to this problem is the same as it was with barter: the development of new markets for new products. On April 27, 1973, the Chicago Board of Trade Options Exchange opened and other exchanges quickly followed. The Chicago Board of Trade (CBOT) had been founded in 1848 as a commodities market. Located in the heart of the Midwest at the intersection of land and water transportation routes, the CBOT soon became the biggest center for trading agricultural products in the country. Options, futures, and forward contracts for commodities were already used extensively in the nineteenth century. One of the important contributions of Chicago traders was to standardize options and futures contracts, thereby making them much easier to use and hence more popular. In 1934, Congress, worried about the reliability of the nation's food supply, passed a law banning all options except on stocks. Since futures were obligatory rather than optional, they did not pose the same threat to the food supply and thus still were permitted.[33] By the 1970s, traders were buying and selling options and futures on all kinds of commodities on markets throughout the world. In Chicago, however, major exchanges had become more involved with trading money than commodities.[34] As trading things or options on things increasingly gave way to exchanging money and buying and selling intangible options and futures on currencies, the nature of the game changed. Exchanges began to resemble high-stakes casinos more than agricultural markets. According to Thomas Bass, Las Vegas actually provided the model for the Chicago Board of Trade's new venture: "Borrowing the idea from Las Vegas, where the game was first played, the Chicago Board of Trade opened a pit in the early 1970s for betting on the price of individual stocks, like IBM and Texaco. Then it opened another pit for betting on the aggregate value of America's five hundred leading stocks. . . . [In these pits,] the action is a fast-ball series of round-robin plays in which brokers buy options on stocks and sell futures contracts on the stock index."[35] With the shift from betting on stuff to first betting on stocks and then on indexes, options, and futures, gambling turns back on itself and investing becomes the postmodern game of betting on bets.

At this point, volatility once again increases and the search for yet more sophisticated hedging strategies begins all over again. It was not long before financial engineers figured out how to hedge options and other derivatives. Dunbar argues that "the great leap in finance theory was that options could be hedged dynamically. By buying and selling a certain amount of stock at each up or down fork in the price, the seller of an option could replicate it and be almost perfectly immunized against risk."[36] As the incentive to hedge increased, new hybrid products began to appear almost daily: "In addition to options on shares and options on physical commodities, *options on futures contracts* made their appearance in 1982." Options on futures are, in effect, a bet on a bet. By the late 1980s, there were even options on swaps, called swaptions. "In early 1989, the market for swaptions was particularly active as bond issuers were using swaptions to sell the interest rate option embedded in the call provision of a bond."[37] At the same time, new funds were created that allowed investors to spread their bets across a range of securities as well as derivative products. The stock index fund had appeared as early as 1971. In index funds, one bets on the overall direction of the market rather than on a particular stock or related financial product. As derivative markets expanded, there was an even quicker migration from customized instruments to off-the-shelf products, and betting on bets became the fastest growing game in town. It is important to note that the value of options and related derivatives increases when volatility is high. Though initially designed to redistribute risk, these new products often ended up selling the volatility they are created to avoid.

Swaps are one of the most interesting and important derivatives. The first modern swap deal was between IBM and the World Bank in 1981. By the end of the decade, billions of dollars were streaming into the swap market. John Marshall and Kenneth Kapner explain the principle of a generic swap: "A swap is a contractual agreement evidenced by a single document in which two parties, called counterparties, agree to make periodic payments to each other. Contained in the swap agreement is a specification of the currencies to be exchanged (which may or may not be the same), the rate of interest applicable to each (which may be fixed or floating), the timetable by which the payments are to be made, and any other provisions bearing on the relationship between the two parties."[38] The emergence of swaps was directly related to the federal government's regulatory policies. Before deregulation, U.S. commercial banks were not allowed to trade equities. In order to avoid what they took to be confining restrictions, major banks opened operations abroad—especially in London—where such regulations were not a problem. As these banks began trading in the Eurodollar market, which was growing rapidly at the time as the result of the influx of petrodollars, bankers and money managers noticed minor but nonetheless significant variations in interest rates in different countries. This gap resulted from the British policy of imposing taxes on foreign-exchange transactions to keep capital in the country during the 1970s. For financial engineers, government regulations are little more than rules to be manipulated in a game whose primary end is its own perpetuation. Recognizing an opportunity to make money in these gaps, they developed the tactic of parallel loans, whose interest payments are then exchanged or swapped. Suppose company A needs to borrow $100 million to build a new plant in the country of company B, and company B needs to borrow $100 million to build a new plant in the country of company A. Since both companies can get a better interest rate by borrowing in their own country, they borrow the money and then swap the interest obligations. Swaps are "a natural extension of parallel and back-to-back loans that originated in the United Kingdom as a means of circumventing foreign-exchange control."[39] Figure 17 illustrates the basic structure of a swap using the example of a fixed-for-floating interest trade

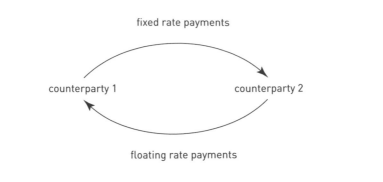

fixed rate payments

counterparty 1   counterparty 2

floating rate payments

Figure 17
From John Marshall and Kevin Kapner, *Understanding Swaps* (New York: Wiley, 1993), 4.

exchange. This kind of swap became much more popular with the volatility of interest rates, which developed after the end of Bretton Woods and Volcker's decision to let the market determine rates.

The most important and, for our purposes, most interesting part of swap deals is what is called *notional principle* or simply *notionals*. The basis of swaps is *fictive* or *imaginary* capital rather than *real* capital. The use of fictive money and capital is not new. As early as the Middle Ages, *la monnaie de compte* and *la monnaie scriptuaire* were used for banking and accounting purposes. What is distinctive about the recent use of fictive money is the role it plays in *speculative* investments. In a fixed-for-floating rate swap, for example,

> the first counterparty agrees to make fixed-rate payments to the second counterparty. In return, the second counterparty agrees to make floating-rate payments to the first counterparty. These two payments are called the legs or sides of the swap. The fixed rate is called the swap coupon. The payments are calculated on the basis of hypothetical quantities of underlying assets called notionals. When notionals take the form of sums of money, they are called notional principals. Notional principals are ordinarily not exchanged. Further, if the counterparties' payments to each other are to be made at the same time and in the same currency, then only the interest differential between the two counterparties' respective payments needs to be exchanged.[40]

In other words, the underlying asset upon which such transactions are based is nothing more than a fictive construct created to calculate the relative value of interest rates.

As products were standardized and the swap market grew, a new financial intermediary emerged—the swap dealer. This leads to a modification of the structure of swaps (figure 18). Since swaps often involve multiple

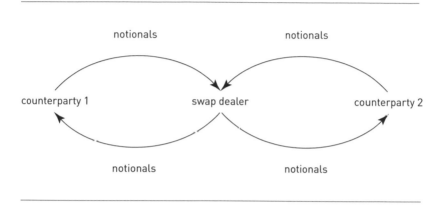

Figure 18

parties and sometimes cross markets, they usually are much more complex than this simple structure. For example, a swap may be of a fixed payment for a fluctuating payment, with the two payments also being in different currencies. As parties multiply, the number of intermediaries grows, thereby further complicating transactions. In the early stage of these developments, "the emphasis was on the intermediary arranging the transaction rather than accepting risk from the transaction; thus investment banks were the natural intermediaries. But, as the swaps became more standardized, it became essential for the intermediary to be willing and able to accept part or all of a potential transaction into its books. Hence commercial banks, with greater capitalization, became a more significant factor."[41] With growing involvement in swap markets, banks became exposed to more risk. Banks, other financial institutions, and investors were not, however, deterred from playing the swaps game. Figure 19 indicates the growth in interest rate swaps from 1981 to 1986.[42] There is a similar pattern for other kinds of swaps.

A final instrument that was popular in the 1980s further illustrates the trajectory we have been tracing in options, futures, and swaps—repur-

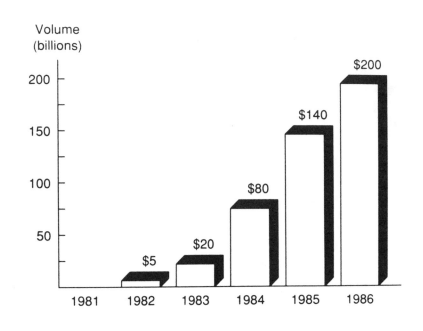

Figure 19
Interest rate swaps.

chase agreements or *repos.* Repos, according to Dunbar, provide "an ingenious way of owning bonds without physically purchasing them."[43] A
repo involves a purchase (or sale) of a security with a *firm* commitment to
sell (or buy) back the same security some time later (often a very short time
later). These bonds, in effect, have more than one owner. Traders often use
repos to play the bond market when they are unwilling to commit funds
long term. In some ways, repos are even stranger than notionals because
they allow traders to invest without any cash and therefore greatly increase leverage. The bundling of repos and swaps in new hybrid products
greatly accelerated the relative shrinkage of collateral.

By the mid-1990s, derivative markets were spinning out of control. According to Bass, "the notional value of derivative contracts in the world was
fifty-five trillion dollars. This is greater than the total value of global trading in stocks and bonds, which in 1995 was thirty-five trillion dollars, far
greater than the annual gross national product of the United States, which
was seven trillion dollars."[44] Deals involving these derivatives were based

on *virtually nothing*. With the development of these financial products the ancient theological dream of creation out of nothing seems to become a reality. But such legerdemains are always illusions.

COLLATERAL DAMAGE) The best place to understand Wall Street during the 1970s and 1980s is Las Vegas. Vegas is, of course, the birthplace of postmodern architecture. In 1968, Robert Venturi, Denise Scott Brown, and Steven Izenour conducted a studio on Las Vegas at Yale University, which four years later issued in their influential book, *Learning from Las Vegas*. This groundbreaking work not only launched the movement that came to be known as postmodern architecture but also set the direction of what would become the distinctively American version of postmodernism. Though their fundamental insight is architectural, its implications extend far beyond building and buildings. Surveying the Vegas Strip, they observe: "Symbol dominates space. Architecture is not enough. Because the spatial relationships are made by symbols more than by forms, architecture in this landscape becomes symbol in space rather than form in space. Architecture defines very little: The big sign and the little building is the rule along Route 66. The sign is more important than the architecture."[45] While modernism had labeled ornament a crime and developed an architecture of seemingly pure form, Venturi and his colleagues called for an architecture of signs in which decorative surface absorbs structural foundations. The signs that are important to postmodernists are not original but are recycled; they are, in other words, signs of other signs. In the postmodern world beginning to emerge in the early 1970s, there seemed to be no escape from recycling signs.

Though not immediately apparent, the argument in *Learning from Las Vegas* rests on a broader insight into what was occurring at the time: by the late twentieth century, image had to a large extent become reality and reality had become image. During the 1950s and 1960s, Venturi, Brown, and Izenour argue, the shift from substance to surface reflected the spread of automobile culture and everything accompanying it. Roads brought with them signs and, as engines grew more powerful, cars increased their speed on highways that had become more complex.

A driver 30 years ago could maintain a sense of orientation in space. At the simple crossroad a little sign with an arrow confirmed what was obvious. One knew where one was. When the crossroads becomes a cloverleaf, one must turn right to turn left. . . . But the driver has no time to ponder paradoxical subtleties within a dangerous, sinuous maze. He or she relies on signs for guidance—enormous signs in vast spaces at high speeds.[46]

As industrial technologies morphed into information, telematic, and virtual technologies, speed continued to accelerate until signs eventually burst free of referents and floated in electronic currents that no longer appeared to be anchored in what once was called "real." To walk down the Strip in the 1980s was to roam through virtual space where floating signs were constantly shifting and thus were no longer able to provide orientation. It is no exaggeration to say that *you cannot understand Wall Street in the 1970s and 1980s if you do not understand Las Vegas.*

By the 1980s, the combination of deregulation and privatization as well as new technologies, financial instruments, and markets had turned Wall Street into a casino. Computer scientist and hedge fund manager Edward Thorpe declared, "Wall Street is like a big gambling casino. The game is much bigger and much more interesting to me than casino gambling."[47] Thorpe should know because he had long been interested in gambling. As a graduate student at MIT in 1960, he sought out Claude Shannon, the creator of modern information theory, who had also developed the mathematical equations for switching electrical networks, to help him with a paper on card counting. Two years later Thorpe published *Beat the Dealer,* a best-selling book about how to win by counting cards. At the same time, he was also working on a system for beating roulette wheels. Shannon was so intrigued by Thorpe's ideas that he collaborated on the project and actually accompanied him on a visit to Vegas to test the system they developed. For Thorpe, Wall Street was nothing more than an extension of the Strip. In 1967 he published *Beat the Market: A Scientific Stock Market System,* and in the 1980s he put his ideas into practice by founding a hedge fund, Princeton/Newport Partners, which managed as much as $300 million until his partner, Jay Regan, was charged with racketeering, conspiracy, and insider trading in 1989. Thorpe escaped unscathed and continued to push his theories.

With the pace of financial activity continuing to accelerate and the stakes of the game still growing, the atmosphere on Wall Street became even more frenzied. In *Liar's Poker,* a memorable account of bond traders in the 1990s, Michael Lewis writes:

The American bond market was shooting through the roof. Imagine how crowds would overwhelm a casino in which everyone who plays wins big, and you'll have some idea what our unit was like in those days. The attraction of options and futures . . . was that they offered both liquidity and fantastic leverage. They were a mechanism for gambling in bond markets, like superchips in a casino that represent a thousand dollars but cost only three. In fact, there are no superchips in casinos; options and futures have no equivalent in the world of professional gambling because real casinos would consider the leverage they afford imprudent. For a tiny down payment, a buyer of a futures contract takes the same risk as in owning a large number of bonds; in a heartbeat he can double or lose his money.[48]

Casinos, it seems, were more fiscally responsible than many banks and brokerage houses. What kept this casino economy afloat was, as Lewis suggests, leverage. By the latter part of the 1990s, Wall Street was leveraged at a rate of 25:1. This explosion of leverage created a *collateral crisis*. As leverage grew, there was an exponential expansion of speculative finance capital on a relatively shrinking base of collateral. Eventually, a significant part of the financial system became a complex pyramid scheme teetering on a vanishing foundation. The possibility of collapse carried the threat of extensive collateral damage whose repercussions would reverberate far beyond the economy.

These developments would not have been possible without a significant change in attitudes toward debt. For the generation that had lived through the Depression, debt was as much a moral or even religious issue as it was an economic matter. Debt, many thought, was wrong—perhaps even a sin. Though they were not wealthy, many middle-class families never borrowed money—not even to buy a house. As economic practices and policies adapted to the postwar era, it was not only the federal government that increased deficit spending. Debt became such an important engine for individuals and businesses as well as governments that the 1980s are sometimes labeled "the decade of debt." Traders as well as mergers and acquisitions specialists not only declared "Greed is good!" but preached "Debt is good!"[49] As this gospel spread, it often became difficult to distinguish debt and equity. To understand what this change meant, it is important to recognize the way the role of debt in the economy changed. Whereas in the past debt usually was incurred when a person or company wanted to buy goods or services, during the past two decades there has been a growing tendency to borrow money to speculate in ever more volatile financial markets. For example, between October 1999 and March 2000, the month the bull market that began in 1982 finally ended, investors borrowed over

$100 billion to invest in stocks.[50] With the attitudinal shifts about borrowing and debt and new government policies encouraging the creation of the new financial products computers and networks make possible, a collateral crisis became unavoidable.

When viewed from an economywide perspective, this collateral crisis can be seen as a symptom of the shift from the real to the spectral economy. In addition to the burgeoning financial economy, growing traces of the spectral economy can also be detected in the invention and dissemination of new currencies and systems of exchange. With the progression from plastic and electronic funds transfer to stored value cards and e-money, more and more currency was put into circulation on the basis of fewer and fewer reserves. The result was an inverted pyramid that became ever less stable (figure 20). The situation was made even more precarious by a significant increase in margin purchases of stocks, bonds, and securities that was occurring at the same time. With Wall Street leveraged at

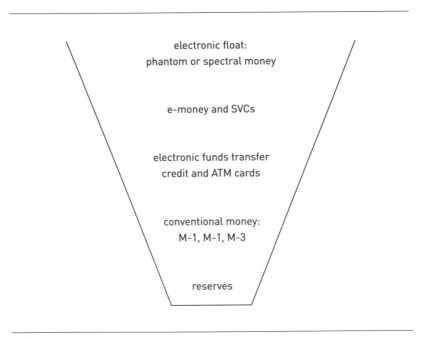

Figure 20
Based on Elinor Harris Solomon, *Virtual Money: Understanding the Power and Risks of Money's High-Speed Journey into Electronic Space* (New York: Oxford University Press, 1997), 91.

25 : 1 it might have seemed reasonable at least to extend margin rules to derivatives. But policies tended in the opposite direction. In his testimony before Congress in 1995, Alan Greenspan actually proposed completely *eliminating* all margin requirements: "Removal of these financing constraints would promote the safety and soundness of broker-dealers by permitting more financing alternatives and hence more effective liquidity management. . . . In the case of broker-dealers, the Federal Reserve Board sees no public purpose in being involved in overseeing their securities credit."[51] In the absence of regulation, options, futures, swaps, and repos provided sources for almost unlimited leverage with minimal capital.

Not only was collateral shrinking if not disappearing, but its nature was changing. As we have seen in our consideration of repos, it had become possible to borrow money to buy securities and then use the very securities purchased as collateral for the loan. Since such deals are always highly leveraged, if the price of the security declines, the value of the collateral deceases and sometimes margins have to be called. If other sources of capital are not available, the borrower must sell the security purchased and used for collateral to meet the margin call. These deals are often so big that the number of shares that have to be sold to meet a margin call is high enough to drive the price farther down, thereby starting a positive feedback loop that can lead to a precipitous drop in value. As we will see in chapter 7, this is precisely what happened to Long-Term Capital Management in 1998.

With all of these new financial instruments and investment strategies, the days of S&L loans backed by real assets in the form of real estate seem but a distant memory. Indeed, even the mortgage market changed in the 1990s. In their ongoing effort to make something out of nothing, financial engineers ended up transforming something into nothing; the ground virtually disappeared from beneath the real estate market. The securitization of mortgages through the creation of Mortgage Backed Securities and Collateralized Mortgage Obligations led to pyramiding schemes in markets that once seemed secure. John Geanakoplos explains how this pyramiding leads to a relative shrinkage of collateral.

> Wall Street took the whole operation a step further by buying big mortgage pools and then splitting them into different pieces or "tranches," which summed up to the whole. These derivative pieces are called collateralized mortgage obligations (CMOs) because they are promises secured by pools of individual promises, each of which is backed by a physical house. As the following diagram [figure 21] makes clear, there

is a pyramiding of promises in which the CMO promises are backed by pools of promises which are backed by individual promises which are backed by physical homes. The streams of promises sometimes come together when many promises are pooled to back other promises, and sometimes split apart when one (derivative) promise is tranched into many smaller promises.

Promises compound faster than interest, leaving the principle of investment considerably diminished. "More recently," Geanakoplos continues,

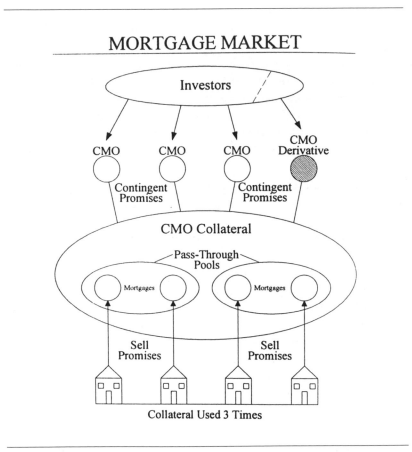

MORTGAGE MARKET

Collateral Used 3 Times

Figure 21

From *The Economy as an Evolving Complex System, II*, ed. W. Brian Arthur et alia. Copyright © 1997. Reprinted by permission of Perseus Books PLC, a member of Perseus Books, L.L.C.

the complexity of collateral has taken several more giant steps forward. Pyramiding occurs when an agent A puts up collateral for his promise to B, and then B in turn uses A's promise to him, and hence in effect the same collateral for a promise he makes to C, who, in turn reuses the same collateral for a promise to D. Mortgage pass through securities offer a classical example of pyramiding. Pyramiding naturally gives rise to chain reactions, as a default by Mr. A ripples through, often all the way to D.[52]

At this point it becomes difficult to deny that the confidence game has become not only a casino but is actually a house of cards.

As collateral damage spreads, it gradually becomes clear that the entire economy is a pyramid scheme resting on a disappearing foundation. Throughout the 1980s and 1990s, financial markets differentiate themselves into four distinct but interrelated levels.[53] Moving from the bottom to the top of this inverted pyramid (figure 22), financial instruments and networks of exchange become more abstract and more complex. As money and capital become more abstract, they become more liquid and circulate faster and faster. At the most basic level, a company sells stock to raise capital to invest in its operation. In many cases, this money is used for facilities, materials, and personnel to improve productive capacity. The securities resulting from these transactions can then be traded on local, national, and global stock exchanges. These transactions result in profits and losses

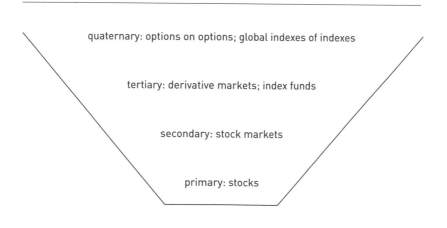

quaternary: options on options; global indexes of indexes

tertiary: derivative markets; index funds

secondary: stock markets

primary: stocks

Figure 22

for investors and influences the ability of companies to access capital markets. At a higher level of abstraction yet further removed from the productive economy, there are derivative markets and index funds. While stocks and stock markets are bets on different companies, derivative markets, index futures, and index options are bets on bets. Money invested in these tertiary markets does not trickle down to lower markets or the productive economy but remains caught in recursive loops of self-replication. Finally, at least for the moment, quaternary markets emerge in which options on options can be purchased and resold. These markets are bets on bets on bets, which seem to have little or nothing to do with the value of the underlying assets on which they are based. Bass correctly points out that when taken together, these markets form a complex emergent self-organizing system.

> Driving this process is the invisible hand of Adam Smith. The fundamental force—which today is called a complex adaptive system—somehow manages to transform private greed into public good. Since the markets are always busily filling up the mathematical space available to them, this fundamental force is already engaged in creating the quaternary markets, which are options on options and doubly derived derivative bets on global indexes of indexes.[54]

As the economy evolves from level to level, it becomes increasingly spectral until it is virtually nothing but the play of floating signifiers endlessly recycling in recursive loops that are unmoored from what once was called the "real" economy. The real, however, does not simply disappear but is temporarily repressed and eventually returns to disrupt what had seemed to replace it. The spectral economy continues to be haunted by the real economy, which hides but does not vanish. When the repressed finally returns, collateral damage is difficult to contain. The full range of this damage did not become evident until the end of the dot-com craze at the turn of the millennium. It should now be clear that in the spectral economy of the 1980s and 1990s assets are more liquid and move at an accelerating rate and thus are subject to new dynamics. The growing volatility of markets creates turbulence that defies the mechanics of systems operating at or near equilibrium. Many of the problems that surfaced in the late 1990s were the result of policies and investment strategies based on models of systems that are at odds with the dynamics and complexities of a network economy.

6

YAHOO NATION

I mean these funny hours my mother's always working how do I know when she's going to walk in, like I mean this here bond and stock stuff you don't see anybody you don't know anybody only in the mail and the telephone because that's how they do it nobody has to see anybody, you can be this here funny lookingest person that lives in a toilet someplace how do they know, I mean like all those guys at the Stock Exchange when they're selling all this stock to each other? They don't give a shit whose it is they're just selling it back and forth for some voice that told them on the phone why should they give a shit if you're a hundred and fifty all they . . .

William Gaddis, *JR*

FROM LAS VEGAS TO TIMES SQUARE) On May 5, 2001, the New York-New York Hotel and Casino in Las Vegas issued a press release bearing the title "The Greatest City in Las Vegas."[1] When it opened on January 3, 1997, New York-New York featured a simulacrum of the New York skyline featuring a forty-seven-story knockoff of the Empire State Building and replicas of the Brooklyn Bridge and Soldiers and Sailors Monument, as well as a Coney Island–style roller coaster called the Manhattan Express. Material issued by the resort's public relations office suggests that the copy is actually better than the original: it is safer, cleaner, and above all *faster.* Noting that more than ten million visitors have crossed New York-New York's Brooklyn Bridge, while only 940,000 people cross the real thing each year, the news release observes: "It will take visitors to the property only two minutes to traverse New York-New York's Brooklyn Bridge. In 1876, however, mechanic E. F. Farrington was the first to cross the Brooklyn Bridge, while its development was in progress. It took him 22 minutes to cross the bridge using a steam-driven rope." All of the amusements, restaurants, and entertainment are, of course, nothing more than a lure to attract gamblers.

> The uncanny realism of the New York theme provides pizzazz, color and energy to the property's larger-than-life 84,000 square foot casino, which includes 80 gaming tables and more than 2,000 state-of-the-art slot machines. Set against a backdrop of famous New York landmarks and icons that bring to life the charm of Greenwich Village and the excitement and bustling Times Square, this unique casino puts gamers right in the middle of the action.

One of the most popular slot games in the casino is the New York-New York Slot Exchange, "which allows guests to earn points each time they play multi-coin nickel, as well as quarter and above slot and video poker machines."

By the time New York-New York opened for business, the dot-com frenzy was heating up. While it was always clear that the Vegas casino-resort was a copy of New York, by the mid-1990s, it was beginning to appear as if New York itself were a copy of the copy of New York on display along the Strip. While you cannot understand the Wall Street of the 1970s and 1980s if you do not understand Las Vegas, you cannot understand Wall Street of the 1990s if you do not also understand Times Square (figure 23). In Vegas you learn that the real is fake and in Times Square you discover that the fake has become real. As Gordon Gekko, played by Michael Douglas, put it so memorably in Oliver Stone's classic film *Wall Street,* "It's not a question of enough, pal. It's a zero-sum game. Somebody wins, somebody loses. Money itself isn't lost or made, it's simply transferred from one perception to another. Like magic. This painting here, I bought it ten years ago for $60,000; I could sell it today for $600,000. The illusion has become real and the more real it becomes, the more desperately they want it. Capitalism at its finest." In today's Times Square, one can see that the signs of the time illuminate what can best be described as the finance-entertainment complex, which flourished during the last decade of the millennium.

Figure 23
"Times Square." Photograph by Alan Thomas.

The transformation of Times Square began in the early 1980s with an effort to clean it up by getting rid of the porno shops and XXX-rated movie theaters as well as the "undesirables" who patronized them. While some protested the loss of the distinctive character of the old Times Square, the commercial interests of real estate developers easily prevailed. The first urban renewal plan, developed by Philip Johnson and John Burgee, featured four massive towers with granite facades. The proposal was quintessentially postmodern and was, in fact, an extension of Johnson's AT&T building (now owned by Sony), which was then under construction on Madison Avenue between 56th and 57th Streets.[2] A collapse in the real estate market in New York led to a delay of the Times Square renewal project and a scrapping of Johnson's original design. By the time the economy had recovered and development began in the late 1980s and early 1990s, the architecture of signs had become all-consuming. In addition to broader cultural currents, this change had been brought about by a 1987 zoning law *requiring* buildings on Times Square to have extensive signage. The aim of this legislation was to ensure that the glitz and glitter would not fade even though outdoor advertising was no longer as necessary as it once had been.

During the 1980s, the interests of architecture and nature of buildings changed significantly. In a *New York Times* article entitled "The Sign Makers Turn Up the Wattage," published on June 29, 1997, David Dunlap observed: "In the Spectacolor projects, buildings are retrofitted to accommodate signs. New towers like Four Times Square incorporate signs into their very architectural fabric. 'Signage is built *into* the building,' said Robert Fox, one of the architects. 'It's not applied. If you took it off, the building would look very funny. It wouldn't look right.'" Architecture, like everything else, virtually disappears in signs. The building at the very heart of Times Square, where the ball drops every New Year, is almost nothing but signs. Above the first floor, the most original and provocative design for this site was not built. In 1997, Frank Gehry proposed locating the Warner Brothers store below ground, exposing the skeleton of the structure and wrapping it in a convoluted wire mesh (figure 24). On the surface of the building, Warner Brothers animated cartoon characters would be displayed each hour.

Preprogrammed by computer to perform several different scenarios highlighted with the use of lasers, smoke machines, and other advanced technologies, the characters interact with the building's exposed structural skeleton and with the translucent metallic fabric, creating an

Figure 24
Frank Gehry, "One Times Square."

hourly urban spectacle on Times Square that solidifies the significance
of the building as the area's most important entertainment destination.[3]

What is not generally known is that Gehry also intended to bring art into
this wired world of entertainment. One of the huge video screens on the
front of the building was planned to connect directly to the SoHo Guggenheim and would have displayed exhibitions continuously in real time.

As Gehry's ingenious design suggests, the signs of today's Times Square
are not the same as the signs of Las Vegas. The shift from passive to interactive and from neon to pixels is symptomatic of the technological, social,
cultural, and economic changes that were occurring throughout the 1990s.
Paul Goldberger, architecture critic for *The New Yorker,* shrewdly observes:

> The new towers in Times Square show us, unambiguously, that the
> idea of the skyscraper as a pure object is dead. The new buildings have
> a fluid identity, and it is tempting to think of their dematerialization as
> neatly paralleling the shift toward cyberspace—from mechanization to
> electronics to pixels. This notion is especially appealing as an explana-
> tion of why so many of the new skyscrapers have gone up in a place
> where media headquarters converge and the latest technologies enliven
> the signs. What better architectural expression of the new world could
> there be?[4]

Neon does not completely disappear, but the technology, aesthetics, and
economics that it represents are definitely displaced. In 1991, the Coke
sign, which has been at Two Times Square for more than seventy-five
years, was given a $3.5 million facelift. While it still has one mile of neon
tubing, it now also has sixty miles of fiber optic cable weighing fifty-
five tons. On the north as well as the south, Times Square is bounded
by major financial institutions whose buildings have high-tech signs as
their distinctive mark. At 745 Seventh Avenue, between 49th and 50th
Streets, Lehman Brothers' granite curtain wall is wrapped in three stories
of spandrel panels with light-emitting diodes displaying highly animated
signage projecting brightly colored videos running at least eighteen hours
a day. Above this video wall is a five-story-high map of the world with the
time, the date, and the firm's name. The video art shown on the building
surpasses much of what can be seen in downtown galleries. A few blocks
away on Broadway between 47th and 48th Streets, the Morgan Stanley
building has five screens with multi-time-zone clocks. On the east side of
the building, stock prices and financial news circulate in ten-foot letters on

a simulated stock ticker. At the south end of Times Square an impressive sign, which is 290 feet tall and cost $20 million, went into operation on the Reuters: Instinet building in January 2002. "Its chief function . . . is as a 'big window into the building,' said the designer, Edwin Schlossberg. 'I wanted to create a metaphor for the sign: information coming from the top, from the ether and sliding into the building,'" A news thermometer registers the importance of the day's events on a scale ranging from red hot to cool blue. "It is programmed automatically to draw news, pictures, videos, financial data and graphics from 27 sources; standardize the information; store it in a database; and schedule its display, coordinating images so they move seamlessly across the face of the signs and the voids between them." Elsewhere around Times Square signs range from the World Wrestling Federation's $7.5 million re-creation of the 1927 Paramount marquee to Toys "R" Us's spectacular forty-eight-foot-long scrolls suspended between mechanical rollers. "The scrolls, changed monthly, are imprinted with seven different images and also have one clear panel, so that the entire façade can be made transparent."[5]

New York Times architecture critic Herbert Muschamp understands the significance of these signs as well as others. In an article on Stephen Wilkes's photographs of what lies behind the signs on Times Square, Muschamp asks, "Could it be that New York's most exciting architecture is not its buildings but its high-tech signs—and all the stuff that lurks behind them?" "As expressions of contemporaneity," Muschamp insists, "this covert architecture far outshines the new skyscrapers in Times Square."[6] Drawing on Guy Debord's *Society of the Spectacle,* he argues, "the spectacle is the material reconstruction of the religious illusion. Spectacular technology has not dispelled the religious clouds where men had placed their own powers detached from themselves; it has only tied them to an earthly base." The society of the spectacle, according to Debord, issues in false consciousness created by media and advertising's projection of a consumer utopia that is unattainable for most working people. This distortion forms an inverted world where being is reduced to having. In one of his most prescient insights, Debord declares "the spectacle is *capital* to such a degree of accumulation that it becomes an image." Echoing Marx's account of the self-reflexivity of capital, Debord concludes, "The spectacle aims at nothing other than itself."[7]

Muschamp's appropriation of this notion of spectacle translates Debord's analysis of postwar consumer capitalism and the military-industrial complex into terms relevant for the finance-entertainment complex. When understood in this way, the spectacle is integral rather than supplemental to the economic process. As we have come to realize, by the 1990s, important sectors of the economy had become a spectacular play of signs. Many of the most important fibers constituting this complex emerging network economy intersect in Times Square. All three major television networks have a presence in Times Square: ABC, which is owned by the Disney Corporation, has a studio and televises from the middle of Times Square; the headquarters of the media conglomerate Viacom, which owns CBS, is located at Broadway and 44th Street; and Tom Brokaw regularly signs off NBC's *Nightly News* with a live shot from the top of One Times Square. Under the direction of Robert Pittman, who later became AOL's chief pitchman and remained so until his ouster in the aftermath of the Time Warner debacle, MTV was launched in 1981 and quickly transformed both the music business and television. Today the network's major studio is in Times Square. With a second-floor stage exposed to the street, the television screen becomes a two-way interface where viewers in Times Square become part of the show. With MTV, ABC, and ESPN all encouraging audience participation, the stage of the surrounding theater district becomes an interactive performance space projected for the whole world to watch. Perched atop the Doubletree Hotel are six Earthcams, which transmit real-time images of New York on the Internet 24/7. And just below the pole for the New Year's Eve ball and above the Discover Card screen where Brokaw appears nightly, there is a small space projecting live videos of people on the street. The Joe Boxer company, which sells offbeat underwear, has even gone so far as to create a sign to display personal e-mails sent from around the world.

While Times Square has become a critical node within the global network economy, the most important node within this node is located in the Condé Nast building across from Reuters: Instinet on Broadway between 42nd and 43rd Streets. This global news and entertainment conglomerate owns print and a rich array of electronic publications: *Vogue, The New Yorker, Architectural Digest, Traveler Magazine, Swoon, Investors Business Daily, Technical Analysis of Stocks and Commodities,* and, of course, *Wired.* At the corner of this building, which, like the Reuters: Instinet building, was designed by Fox and Fowle, stands the headquarters of NASDAQ. Though several years older than its competitors, the NASDAQ sign remains the most spectacular show on the Square. An eight-story cylindrical structure with a ten-thousand-square-foot screen, the sign consists of 8,200 panels capable of displaying *16.7 million* distinct colors. Eight simultaneously operated screens with eighteen million light-emitting diodes are attached to microcircuits. Each screen, according to confidence man Jayson

Blair, is made up of "one-foot square panels, which have 256 pixels each. Behind each panel is a logic board that takes signals from a distributor that translates data into code for the pixels."[8] This technology, designed by Smartvision, makes it possible to project true colors around an unprecedented 170 degree arch. This show-stopping sign both surrounds and hovers above a semblance of the only headquarters that NASDAQ has.

The choice of the site and design of the building and sign reflect the recognition that the town square of New York City has become the world square of the global economy. In contrast to Wall Street's solid classical architecture and dark canyons so memorably portrayed in Melville's short story "Bartleby the Scrivener," the NASDAQ sign suggests a world where everything solid is vaporized in ether(nets). At street level, a television and Internet studio displays activity on NASDAQ in real time on a video wall worthy of Naim June Paik. On the massive sign outside the building, stock prices are displayed along with the brilliant colors of company logos instead of the staid letters and numbers of the classical stock ticker running along the Morgan Stanley building. With video walls inside and outside, more than architecture has become signs all the way down. The Web site for NASDAQ's MarketSite Broadcast Studio describes the purpose of the facility:

> The MarketSite houses a state-of-the-art digital broadcast studio that transmits 175 live market updates by a host of networks including CNBC, CNN Headline News, CNNfn, Bloomberg, BBC, Reuters and other financial networks to reach millions of viewers around the world with up-to-the-second market news. Dedicated NASDAQ technical and production staff provide real-time trading information 14 hours a day. CNBC broadcasts its morning show, 'Wake-Up Call with Liz Claman and Carl Quintanilla' live from the MarketSite studio. The show, which is part of CNBC's Business Day line-up, airs Monday through Friday from 5:00–7:00 am E.T.

Intended to signal a New Age extending beyond the world of markets and finance, the opening of the NASDAQ studio in Times Square was scheduled for what company officials hoped would be an auspicious occasion: the turn of the millennium in January 2000. When NASDAQ soared above four thousand for the first time in January, worries about Y2K quickly faded and preparations for the celebration began. Though few suspected it at the time, when the director of NASDAQ threw the switch and turned on the lights, shadows were gathering, which only three months later would cloud the horizon and expose New Age economics as a cruel confidence game.

FINANCE-ENTERTAINMENT COMPLEX]   It took almost two decades for the world William Gaddis imagined in *JR* to become a "reality." This remarkable novel is as much a theoretical treatise mixing philosophy, theology, literary criticism, and financial economics as a fictional narrative. Filled with references to figures like Marx, Engels, Weber, Simmel, and Gibbs as well as—though this seems completely unbelievable in the early 1970s—Milken and Greenspan, *JR* probes issues that by now should be familiar: the loss of the real, counterfeiting, recycling images, and disembodiment. The work is composed entirely of dialogue, and speakers often remain so uncertain that their identities become as fluid as the "realities" with which they deal.

JR is an eleven-year-old who lives in Massapequa, Long Island, and sometimes commutes to New York City. His name or nickname suggests, among other things, that we live in a world kids understand better than adults.[9] The story opens with Edward Bast, whose name (Bast[ard]), when associated with the moniker JR, raises questions about legitimacy, holding a rehearsal for Wagner's *Ring* in, of all places, the local Jewish temple. Wagner's monumental work is the fullest expression of the composer's profound commitment to the modernist doctrine of the *Gasamtkunstwerk*, which, in the hands of leading avant-garde artists, led to the program of transforming the world into a work of art. For Gaddis, the intersection of art and money in the 1960s and 1970s represents a devastating parody of the dreams of modernism. While the world was becoming a matter (or nonmatter) of image, art was becoming a matter of money driven by market interests.

Bast and his students have to rehearse in the temple because of deep cuts in the school budget for the arts. While Bast struggles to maintain his faith in the redemptive power of art, most of the teachers and administrators at the local public school are more concerned with business than education or art. For educators, the latest media and technology hold the tempting prospect of profitable new businesses in education and art. An administrator prepping his staff for a visit by representatives of a wealthy foundation comments, "I don't hardly need to say that the point in this is to show them how we're using, utilizing this new media to motivate the cultural drive in these youngsters should give things a nice boost right up their. . . ."[10] Grammar, obviously, is not a high priority for these educators, politicians, and businesspeople eager to commercialize courses to be televised in "remote classrooms" (91). The pilot for the TV show/class is being developed by Mrs. Flesch (flesh), who has been designated as the school's first "real video personality" (24). School officials are seeking financial backing to produce Wagner's *Ring,* and Bast is helping Mrs. Flesch stage the production. With lights glaring and cameras rolling, the kids are rehearsing *Das Rheingold.* Administrators and politicians, who are supposed to be watching but are intently discussing budget cuts and money-making schemes, are startled when the children suddenly scream: "Rhein . . . G O L D."

> A joyful cry! Bast thumped out the theme again on the piano, missed a note, winced, repeated it.—Can't you sound joyful, Rhinemaidens? Look, look around you. The river is glittering with golden light. Your's swimming around the rock where the Rheingold is. The Rheingold! You love the Rheingold Rhinemaidens, you . . . (32)

It quickly becomes apparent that the issue is more money than art. An interested politician offers to have his wife, a former Miss Rheingold, who advertised "a golden beer named Rheingold," introduce the film. In this play within a play, Rhinegold is no longer *rein* (pure) gold but has become a debased currency watering down educational and artistic standards.

At a critical juncture, the issue of money directly intrudes into the rehearsal. Mrs. Flesch was using a bag of money as a prop. The money had been collected from students by another teacher named Mrs. Joubert (pronounced Jew-bert), who, when asked about it, explains:

> — . . . It's what they've saved to buy a share in America. We're taking a field trip to the Stock Exchange to buy a share of stock. The boys and girls will follow its ups and downs and learn how our system works, that's why we call it our share . . .
> —In what.
> —In America, yes, because it's actually owning it themselves they'll feel . . .
> —No, I mean what stock.
> —That's our studio lesson today deciding which one, if you want to look in on our channel. We have a resource film from the Exchange itself, too. (18)

The rehearsal is thrown into confusion when someone notices that the bag of money has disappeared. As the story unfolds, it gradually becomes clear that JR stole the money and is using it to create a "paper empire," which eventually threatens the stability of global financial markets.

On the class trip to the New York Stock Exchange, JR shows that he has picked up the lingo of investors, traders, and LBO experts. Grilling the class's host about options, warrants, and futures, he demonstrates that he knows more about new financial instruments and emerging markets than the adults running the exchange. Most important, JR recognizes the ways in which new technologies—especially phones, faxes, computers, and innovative credit markets—are changing the game of finance. When he returns home, JR develops a scheme to make money by recycling military surplus. Leafing through spot-bid catalogues, which for no apparent reason are delivered to his home, he discovers that it is possible to buy hundreds of thousands of plastic picnic forks from the Navy and to sell them to the Army for a significant profit. Puzzled that the Army does not purchase the forks directly from the Navy, JR becomes a middleman and negotiates a series of profitable arbitrage transactions. To play this role, he explains to his girlfriend, he must conceal his age by creating a virtual identity.

> What like with this here Mary Lou honey you're suppose to be twenty-one and over? I mean how does she know any more than this dumb bank at Nevada all she knows she gets this five dollars off you for her jumbo set so you're twenty-one and over, what's the difference of her and this here bank someplace. I mean where Glancy gave us about modern banking would be impossible without the wonders of the computer see all these electric numbers down here? I mean like this here Mary Lou gets you five dollars why should they give a shit if you're a hundred wait give me that, boy I been looking for that. (168)

With the money from these initial deals in plastic, JR builds an extensive financial empire, which steadily expands until it includes factories in the United States and abroad, stock transactions, banking interests, and even a cemetery and funeral home franchise. While he draws some of his friends and teachers into the operation, his parents have absolutely no idea what he is doing. The key to the whole venture is JR's *invisibility*.

> I mean these funny hours my mother's always working how do I know when she's going to walk in, like I mean this here bond and stock stuff

you don't see anybody you don't know anybody only in the mail and the telephone because that's how they do it nobody has to see anybody, you can be this here funny lookingest person that lives in a toilet someplace how do they know, I mean like all those guys at the Stock Exchange where they're selling this stock to each other? They don't give a shit whose it is they're just selling it back and forth for some voice that told them on the phone why should they give a shit if you're a hundred and fifty all they . . . (172)

The operation finally becomes so large that he has to set up the JR Corporation. With phones, faxes, and computers, JR uses his offshore corporate headquarters to negotiate a string of major mergers and acquisitions as well as a series of LBOs. Once he grasps the magic of leverage, the game shifts to another whole level.

> — . . . I mean holy shit who said I'm taking any money that's not what you do! I mean didn't you ever see these things where they say come right in and borrow up to a hundred percent of your passbook balance while it goes right on earning these top dividends and all? So whose business is it if I just start this other account and loan against this here first one where they already have my signature so they know it's me, I mean it's just different electric numbers on these checks and all which this computer reads them it doesn't give a shit if you're three years old Mister Wall that's all these here forks that's all any of it is don't tell me I did something against the law boy, that's just what you do! I mean this here class account I just loan against it and get through this here forks deal I never even touched it right? (172–73)

Inevitably, the house of cards JR so ingeniously constructs collapses. With the leverage spinning out of control, the JR Corporation is "threatened by a credit squeeze whose dramatic repercussions could be felt throughout the corporate and financial world" (649–50). When the SEC undertakes an investigation, government officials find what initially appears to be incriminating evidence stuffed in JR's school locker.

> Not worth the damn trouble no, marshals sealed some off uptown picked some up at the Waldorf heard Zona's half-baked detectives found some hid in a school locker someplace but . . . He called who . . . ? Well by God can you . . . just says it looks like they followed the damn letter of the damn law damn it Monty IRS says his social security number's

same one on a million sample cards in dime store wallets, filed under
that don't constitute massive fraud does it? (701)

JR remains unfazed throughout the investigation, insisting that it's "just
numbers on paper half the time you don't even know where the dot goes
you don't even . . ." (639). When all promising leads dry up, the SEC drops
criminal charges and initiates a civil suit barring JR from running any publicly traded company. The novel ends with JR on the phone negotiating a
deal to find a ghostwriter to do a book about his experiences.

                              •   •   •

On September 21, 2000, the U.S. Securities and Exchange Commission
settled its case against Jonathan Lebed. The SEC's press release explained that the fifteen-year-old Jonathan—the first minor ever charged
with stock market fraud—had used the Internet to promote stocks from
his bedroom in Cedar Grove, New Jersey. Armed only with accounts at
AOL and E-Trade, the kid had bought stock, then using "multiple fictitious names," posted hundreds of messages on Yahoo Finance message
boards recommending that stock to others. He'd done this eleven times
between September 1999 and February 2000, the SEC said, each time
triggering chaos in the stock market. In advance of the chaos he'd left
sell orders in the marketplace, in case shares rose in price. . . . Between
September 1999 and February 2000 his smallest one-day gain was
$12,000. His biggest was $74,000. Now the kid had agreed to hand over
his illicit gains, plus interest, which came to $285,000.[11]

The case of Jonathan Lebed (JL) bears an uncanny resemblance to the
story of JR. JL attracted the attention of the SEC when he made $800,000
trading online during a six-month period. As Michael Lewis narrates his
story with characteristic wit and style, it quickly becomes clear that the
youngster understands the network economy not only better than his parents but also better than the SEC officials prosecuting his case. Indeed, the
much heralded SEC chairman Arthur Levitt looks like a fool who has very
little understanding of the new world he is supposed to be managing.

JL got his first AOL account when he was eleven years old—precisely
the age JR started trading stocks. Listening to his parents occasionally discuss their modest investments in blue chip companies, JL became interested in the market and started to watch CNBC religiously. On his twelfth
birthday, a savings bond his parents had bought for him came due and JL

persuaded his father to let him invest the $8,000 in stocks. Though his father insisted it was a "stupid" investment, JL convinced him to buy AOL at $25 a share. A few weeks later, the stock rose five points and JL sold it. As Lewis points out, JL learned three lessons from this experience: "(a) you can make money quickly in the stock market, (b) his dad didn't know what he was talking about, and (c) it paid him to exercise his own judgment on these matters" (39). Just as JL was beginning to play the market, CNBC started a stock-picking contest for kids. JR formed a team with friends from school and soon became one of the leading contestants on the show. When TV cameras showed up in Cedar Grove, friends of JL's parents started hounding him for investment advice.

As he became more and more successful at CNBC's game, JL decided it was foolish not to play with *real* money. Within a year, he turned his $8,000 into $28,000. A devotee of the Internet, JL set up a Web site named Stock-Dogs.com where he facilitated discussions of the small market cap stocks he found interesting. All the information upon which he based his analysis and investments was gathered from material available online. The posts JL issued on his Web site are remarkably sophisticated; indeed, in many cases, it is impossible to distinguish his analysis of companies from the reports and recommendations of analysts with Harvard and Stanford MBAs who are working for major Wall Street brokerage houses. Nevertheless, the SEC was convinced that JL was engaged in improper if not illegal activity and summoned the twelve-year-old and his mother to appear at the World Trade Center for what turned out to be an eight-hour interrogation. An exchange between JL and the SEC investigator cited by Lewis suggests the sophistication of the youngster's understanding of markets and his appreciation for the importance of media.

SEC: It appears, Jonathan, that you bought and sold Keytel, you bought it twice and you sold it twice on that day and the sales were at a loss. Can you explain your trading in this stock for us?
JONATHAN: I was trying to day trade it for a profit with the momentum that it was having that day.
SEC: What do you mean when you say "momentum"?
JONATHAN: It was moving up very, very fast that day. I think it doubled that day or something because they announced that they would be selling their music on the Internet and stuff. So I just tried to buy it and sell it throughout the day to make money with it.
SEC: Is there any possibility that you were trying to contribute to some of that momentum by day trading?

JONATHAN: No, the volume was like real high. My trading wouldn't contribute at all.

SEC: What do you mean it wouldn't contribute at all?

JONATHAN: My trading—it was just like 1,000 shares and the volume for the day was in the millions. It was trading a lot, so it was not like it would contribute . . .

SEC: Where did you learn your technique for day trading?

JONATHAN: Just on TV, internet.

SEC: What TV shows?

JONATHAN: CNBC mostly—basically CNBC is what I watch all the time. (46–47)

This remarkable exchange reveals not only how much the twelve-year-old JL understands but also how little the SEC knows about the implications of computers, networks, and the new media. Expressing concern about his age, the SEC representative asks JL if the people frequenting Stock-Dogs.com knew his age. When pressed about why he had not discussed a particular stock deal, JL's response indicates that he, like JR, realized that invisibility and virtual identities are essential to his enterprise: "Because if I talked about it on the Internet people would just know that I'm fourteen and would just ignore me." (50).

When JL refused to stop peddling advice and trading online, Levitt became obsessed with prosecuting him for providing unreliable information and advice to investors and manipulating stock prices. While claiming to be protecting small investors, the chairman was actually defending the interests of the Wall Street elite. After all, if a twelve-year-old kid is as successful as many of the leading professional analysts and traders, what kind of a confidence game is Wall Street playing? During an interview, Lewis asks Levitt what it means to manipulate the market. The chairman of the SEC draws a blank and has to turn to his director of enforcement, Richard Walker, who explains: "It's when you promote a stock for the purpose of artificially raising its price" (67). The question, of course, is what "artificially" means in this context. For the SEC, prices that are not "artificial" are determined by "ordinary market forces." But what are "ordinary market forces" in a network economy? An exchange between Levitt and Lewis makes it clear that the SEC chairman has no doubt about what is artificial and what is real.

"Can you explain how you distinguished the illegal trades from the legal ones," I asked.

"I'm not going to go through the case point by point," he said.

"Why not?"

"It wouldn't be appropriate."

At which point Arthur Levitt, who had been attempting to stare into my eyes as intently as a man can stare, said, in his deep voice, "This kid had no basis for making these predictions."

"But how do you *know* that?"

And the chairman of the SEC, the embodiment of investor confidence, the keeper of the notion that the numbers gyrating at the bottom of the CNBC screen are "real," draws himself up and says, "I *worked* on Wall Street . . . "

"So did I," I said.

"I worked there longer than you." (70)

What more needs to be said? The emperor has no clothes; the chairman of the SEC turns out to be a confidence man in more ways than he realized. But why trust grown-ups when twelve-year-olds understand the market better than people who think they are still running the show? By 2000, the art of finance had become a video game where quick thumbs turn big profits. More important, JL realizes that what once was called reality has virtually disappeared. In an email to his lawyer about an Internet play made by CNN Moneyline's host Lou Dobbs, JL writes: "The comments about turning profitable sooner and diversifying beyond the Web just prove that the entire business and financial world revolves around perception and nothing else" (55).

The world JR anticipates and we along with JL inhabit would not be possible without NASDAQ. Located in the heart of Times Square, NASDAQ is the prism through which the tangled webs of the finance-entertainment complex become comprehensible. NASDAQ and new tech companies are bound in mutually reinforcing feedback loops: NASDAQ depends on the technologies produced by many of the companies it lists, and the exchange provides need capital for these companies. Because the cost and requirements of listing there are considerably lower than on the NYSE, many start-ups open on NASDAQ and in most cases remain there. As we have seen, in 1971, the National Association of Securities Dealers introduced the first computer network that was able to give investors access to quotes for stocks traded over-the-counter (OTC) in real time. Twenty years later, another innovation transformed the way securities are traded: NASDAQ created a system that allows individuals as well as professional traders, brokerage houses, and financial institutions to trade online without going through a financial intermediary. Automation had been a part of trading since the introduction of the stock ticker in 1867. There were, of course, early systems of exchange using telegraph and telephones, but for decades technological limitations restricted the use of such systems to regional exchanges. Indeed, before 1933, there was not even a direct telephone line between Hartford and New York City. As telecommunications technology became more sophisticated, securities exchanges became more wired. The use of real-time systems for tracking prices and executing trades during the past three decades marked a quantum leap in the speed and complexity of transactions. Only at this point does the prospect of genuinely global exchanges become realistic. Commenting on the anticipated merger between NASDAQ and the London Stock Exchange in 2002, *The Economist* suggested that the first global exchange probably will combine network technology and the financial instruments that have been created to take advantage of it. "The first truly global exchange is more likely to trade derivatives than equities. Derivative contracts for bonds, commodities and even equities are less tied than shares to their country of issue. For example, trading in options on shares of Nokia, Finland's telecoms giant, is bigger in Frankfurt than Helsinki."[12] Having become more-or-less unlinked from the real economy, derivatives are free to circulate across the globe on virtual exchanges that know no national boundaries.

Like so many other financial institutions and policies, the roots of NASDAQ go back to the Depression era. In the wake of the turmoil of the 1920s and 1930s, the National Association of Securities Dealers was created to bring order and stability to over-the-counter markets. The term *over-the-counter* dates back to the 1800s and refers to the countertops on which dealers transacted trades in securities for smaller, less established companies. OTC markets were much more volatile and trading was considerably more speculative than on established exchanges. In the 1920s and 1930s, OTC trading was largely unregulated and took place through informal arrangements on local or regional exchanges. In the absence of any method for collecting and distributing stock quotes, brokers resorted to phones and telegrams among themselves to determine prices and execute trades. During the roaring twenties, this system created the opportunity for widespread fraud. As Mark Ingebretsen points out, flagrant abuses led to reforms in the 1930s.

> As one of the first steps, Roosevelt and Congress set about sifting through the carnage of the markets, trying to find out what went wrong and where to lay the blame. The result of the hearing were two land-

mark laws that would put the securities markets under government scrutiny more than ever before. In 1933, the Glass Steagall Act prohibited banks from speculating using depositors' money. The Securities Act of 1933 and the Securities Exchange Act of 1934 required that companies tell investors the truth about their financial situation and that those selling securities put the interest of their customers—that is, individual investors—first.[13]

An addition to the 1934 Securities Exchange Act, known as the Maloney Act (after Francis Maloney, the chairman of the Senate Banking Committee), eventually proved decisive for the emergence of NASDAQ. This provision gave established associations registered with the SEC the responsibility and authority to regulate the industry. The need for such self-regulation led to the founding of the National Association of Securities Dealers. In addition to creating a regulatory mechanism, the Maloney Act added a financial incentive for OTC traders to participate in NASD. By 1945, the number of securities dealers participating in NASD had risen to 25,000.[14]

One of the primary ways NASD initially sought to bring order to chaotic OTC markets was by gathering and publishing price information for both investors and traders. Prior to this, there was no way for buyers or sellers to verify the actual price of a security. Early efforts to collect accurate market information and distribute it in a timely matter were largely unsuccessful. As markets grew rapidly after the Second World War, the need for better information became urgent until the market turbulence in the 1960s finally drove the SEC to take action. In 1963, the SEC presented to Congress a report entitled *Special Study of the Securities Markets,* which not only developed an insightful analysis of the current situation but also outlined what proved to be an unusually prescient account of future developments.

> Automation has only slightly touched the over-the-counter markets, present uses being largely concentrated in servicing back office operations. Recent rapid advances in technology now offer the prospect of major new applications in the over-the-counter markets in the handling of quotations and otherwise.
>
> It appears to be technically feasible to use a central computer to record and report interdealer quotations for some or all over-the-counter securities on a continuous basis. In addition to providing a method for instantaneously determining best quotations, such a system might pro-

vide wholly new means of matching buy and sell orders and even accomplishing their executions in some circumstances. The same system
might be used for reporting and storing actual transaction information,
thus for the first time making price and volume data available on a current and continuous basis.[15]

It took almost three decades for these recommendations and predictions
to become a reality. By 1971, computer and networking technologies were
able to gather and distribute accurate real-time information about OTC securities. Though the technology for universal online trading was in place
by the 1980s, political wrangling and conflicting economic interests delayed its introduction until the early 1990s.

During the years when NASDAQ was emerging, other trading networks
were also being developed. As early as the late 1960s, some major brokerage houses were establishing Electronic Communications Networks
(ECNs), which enabled them to trade with each other directly, eliminating
all third parties or other financial intermediaries. One of the most successful ECNs was Instinet, founded in 1969. In addition to displaying bids
and offers, Instinet enabled member institutions but not individuals to execute transactions electronically. The initial attraction of ECNs was that
they allowed major institutional investors to trade large blocks of stock
when the markets were closed. After-hours trading had what initially
seemed to be several advantages. One of their most appealing features was
that ECNs gave "participants total anonymity. As a rule, trades did not even
register on the Nasdaq network. They were invisible to the public eye. In
fact, few retail investors even knew that this vast behind-the-scenes trading arena existed. . . . [T]he anonymity afforded by ECNs helped professional traders move stocks among themselves without causing short-term
price fluctuations that cut into profits."[16] There were, however, also some
disadvantages to ECNs. During the day, non-ECN trades pass through a
market maker, who could adjust bids and offers to close a deal. ECN trading, by contrast, was completely automated or programmed and therefore
required a perfect match for the trade to be consummated. For the most
part, major institutional investors found the advantages of ECNs far out-
weighed the disadvantages. By the late 1980s, however, it was becoming
clear that this fast-growing trading technique was subject to abuse and required regulatory statutes and procedures.

Recognizing the increasing significance of automated trading, the British media conglomerate Reuters purchased Instinet in 1987. In spite of
the market crash that year and a price-fixing scandal in the early 1990s, In-

stinet continued to grow; by the middle of the 1990s, five thousand brokers were subscribers. As the most successful ECN, Instinet was handling 20 percent of NASDAQ trades in stocks and was also linked to fifteen other markets. Reuters's bet paid off: in 1996, Instinet generated a profit of $588 million and by 1998, 350,000 terminals were generating an annual revenue of almost $2.5 billion.[17] In 2002, the NASDAQ market executed 31 percent of the trades in NASDAQ stocks and Instinet completed 26 percent of the trades.

To appreciate the reasons for this growth and see why new regulations were required, it is necessary to understand how trading on NASDAQ differed from trading on the New York Stock Exchange in the 1990s. The function of any market is, of course, to match buyers and sellers. When an individual, institution, or corporation wants to buy or sell a security, the trade usually goes through a financial intermediary. There are two ways to place a buy or sell order: first, one can place a market order in which the trade is executed at the best available price; or second, one can place a limit order in which a particular price for the transaction is specified. On NASDAQ, trading always goes through a market maker, who is a licensed broker and is responsible for maintaining an orderly market in a specific security "by standing ready to buy or sell round lots at publicly quoted prices." On the NYSE, the actual trade is executed on the floor of the exchange by a specialist, who represents the member firm responsible for a specific security. "Only one specialist can be designated for a given stock, but dealers may be specialists in several stocks." The primary responsibilities of specialists "include executing limit orders on behalf of other exchange members for a portion of the floor brokers' commission, and buying or selling from his own account to counteract temporary imbalances in supply and demand and thus prevent wide swings in stock prices."[18] While market makers and specialists make money by taking a cut of the brokers' commissions, their real advantage is privileged access to information. On the NYSE, they are the only ones who know the actual bid-ask spread and depth of the market at any given time. Since here, as in all transactions, money is made in the gap created by the spread, this information is extremely valuable.

NASDAQ trading practices differ from those on the NYSE and other exchanges in several important ways. These differences are, in large part, a function of a different technological infrastructure. By the 1990s, NASDAQ had become a fully operational electronic trading network. In contrast to the stately temple-like building housing the NYSE on Wall Street, NASDAQ has no real trading floor. This exchange is nothing more than a computer network whose hub, located in Trumbull, Connecticut, links more than three hundred thousand computers as well as individual investors trading on the Internet. The exchange as such, like the currencies and instruments traded on it, disappears into the virtual time-space of the network. At the NYSE, the specialist is a real person who actually stands on the trading floor and regulates the transactions among member brokers. In NASDAQ's virtual exchange, market makers are not physically present but mediate transactions electronically at a distance. In other words, all trading is teletrading. A second important difference is that unlike the NYSE, NASDAQ market makers do not have a monopoly on the stocks they handle. Rather, "several market makers might compete with one another to buy and sell a particular security. Usually they do this by broadcasting their best bid and ask prices over the Nasdaq." [19] In this way, competition among market makers leads to greater access to price information. As a result of this difference, NASDAQ eventually developed a system with greater transparency and wider access to information.

From its earliest years, NASDAQ has provided three levels of information at different price points. Level I, intended for brokers who deal with retail customers, gives quotes but not in real time. Level II, targeted for market makers, who represent large institutional investors like mutual and pension funds, gives extensive real-time information indicating the depth of the market and suggests its short-term direction. Finally, Level III, which originally was open only to market makers, makes it possible to enter and cancel orders directly. The growth in the use of personal computers during the 1980s made it possible for more people to access more information quickly and easily. Acknowledging the importance of this development, NASDAQ introduced its Workstation I in 1986. This was a software program that enabled users to track up to thirty stocks without a dedicated terminal. [20]

While these changes introduced greater transparency and distributed information to those who were willing to pay for it, online trading was not available to individuals until the early 1990s. The 1987 market crash made it clear that reforms were necessary to ensure more equal access to information and to enable investors to execute trades when they wanted to do so. In 1982, the exchange had introduced a small-order execution system (SOES), which completed transactions at listed prices automatically, but market makers were not required to participate in it. When the market plummeted in 1987, many market makers ducked their responsibility to serve as the buyer of last resort by simply not answering their phones. At the same time, the computers and networks used in programmed trading became overloaded and many SOES orders were not executed. Less than a year later, NASDAQ, with backing from the SEC, mandated that all market makers participate in SOES. With this requirement and the upgrading of the technology necessary for online and programmed trading, the execution of trades on lots of all sizes became much more reliable.

This policy change, however, had unexpected consequences that became very important in the 1990s. As is so often the case, creativity emerged at the edge of the system.

> What Nasdaq planners apparently failed to realize following the crash of 1987 was that SOES brokerages would make access to the market directly available to their customers. That is, they would allow their customers to route their orders by themselves. And that is exactly what a few SOES brokerages set themselves up to do. They offered self-service trading. What SOES traders received at these brokerages was a fast computer terminal, armed with trading software and hardwired to the Nasdaq via a dedicated network connection (this is in the pre-Internet era). As stock quotes fielded by Nasdaq market makers changed in something close to real time, the SOES bandits hovered over them like raptors.[21]

The ability to execute trades directly in real time with instant access to reliable information made it possible to turn a profit on small directional shifts in the price of a security. These new developments, in effect, mark the birth of day trading.

The explosive growth of day trading did not occur, however, for another decade. Among the most important factors triggering this development was the action taken by the SEC on June 20, 1997, to remedy trading improprieties that had developed on NASDAQ. By the mid-1990s, NASDAQ traders had added a second proprietary network—SelectNet—to Instinet. These networks, which were closed to individuals and small traders, not only gave large institutional traders unfair advantages but actually distorted the markets. Ingebretsen cites the Financial Economists Roundtable's "Statement on the Structure of the Nasdaq Stock Market," which concisely summarizes the implications of ECNs.

> Alternative interdeal markets for Nasdaq listed stocks may reduce the incentive for dealers to post quotes that will narrow the displayed spread. An example is SelectNet, which is an interdealer trading system that allows dealers to trade among themselves at prices different from

those available to the general public. Such parallel markets permit dealers to adjust their inventory without the need to offer better quotes over
Nasdaq.[22]

When understood in this way, ECNs facilitate something like a variation on insider trading. After a two-year investigation, the SEC took two
major actions: first, all investors were given access to prices and order
sizes, which previously had been restricted to market makers, specialists,
and select institutional investors; and second, ECNs—even Instinet and
SelectNet—were opened to all investors. It was not long before new private trading networks for individual traders like Archipelago, BRUT, and
REDIbook sprang up and began to spread. Unlike Instinet, these new
ECNs did not require a dedicated terminal but operated on regular PCs. In
1996, Datek Online introduced an ECN called Island, which enabled individuals to make direct bids and offers on NASDAQ-listed stocks. A year
later, Island "gave individuals the ability to access markets the same way
that market makers do without incurring the cost and without having to
fulfill the rigorous requirements of becoming a member of Nasdaq and/
or being a market maker."[23] Once again anticipating the implications of
the changes that were occurring, Reuters purchased Island. In the fall of
2001, Island's market share of NASDAQ's trades was actually greater than
Instinet.

By the late 1990s, NASDAQ's growth had become exponential and the
era of day trading was at hand. The number of shares traded on NASDAQ
grew to 1.7 billion per day, more than twice the volume of the NYSE. At
the same time, NASDAQ listed 4,800 companies, which was also double
the companies on the NYSE. Between 1995 and 1999, the market capitalization of NASDAQ companies grew 257 percent to $5 trillion. In addition
to this, NASDAQ became the primary market for initial public offerings
(IPOs) throughout the 1990s Internet boom.[24] From 1990 to 1999, the
NASDAQ composite index rose from 500 to 3,500. With plans to expand
to Europe and Japan, NASDAQ firmly established itself as the most important web portal for online trading, linking 5,400 brokerage firms, 88,000
trading offices, 670,000 brokers, and about 10,000,000 individual online
investors. The United States had become the most wired nation in the
world and was steadily extending the global reach of its worldwide webs.

During the 1990s, new technologies and regulatory policies transformed the investment habits of millions of individuals. Backed by new requirements to make more information available to nonprofessionals, the
SOES and ECNs assumed great importance for individuals. Suddenly in-

dividual investors were able to trade directly online and had access to the information necessary to do so intelligently. Marc Friedfertig and George West, who are leading members of Broadway Trading, a brokerage firm specializing in online trading, explain the significance of these changes.

> The new order handling rules accomplished two critical steps toward ensuring a fair and orderly market, which allows customers to ultimately get the best price. The first step required market makers to fill or display any customer's limit order that improves on the inside price. . . . The second step forbade market makers to display prices better than the Nasdaq's market in private markets such as Instinet unless those quotes were displayed and accessible to the public. This step opened the way for ECNs, such as Instinet, Island, Spear, Leeds and Kellog, Teranova, and Bloomberg to be represented on the Nasdaq system, effectively creating one market with the best price. These changes have led to narrower spreads and fairer treatment for customer orders. Most importantly, these changes opened the way for Nasdaq to pair up customer orders where customers could trade with each other rather than solely with market makers.[25]

Needless to say, financial firms and brokers resisted these changes because they resulted in what came to be known in the Internet world as "disintermediation." When individuals can trade directly with each other, there is no need for an intermediary like a broker, market maker, or specialist. Where some saw threat, others saw opportunity: online trading companies like E*Trade and Datek Online as well as several major investment firms quickly realized they had to enter this emerging market to remain competitive. By early 1999, there were sixty day-trading firms with three hundred offices throughout the country. While there were only about 5,800 to 6,800 full-time day traders, they received disproportionate media attention. Day trading, however, was an extreme form of what was becoming a widespread practice. In the early 1990s, approximately five million people had online accounts and America was rapidly becoming what John Cassidy aptly describes as a "trading nation." Between 1989 and 1998, the percentage of Americans owning stock rose from 31.6 percent to 48.8 percent: "By the middle of the 1990s, there were about 130 million mutual funds accounts. . . . At the end of 2000, mutual funds contained more money than the banking system—about $7 trillion, of which more than $4 trillion was in stock funds." As markets boomed, the nature of the game changed; playing the market became a recreational activity. In 1992 there were 7,200 investment clubs in the United States and by 1999 the number had swollen to 37,000.[26]

Day traders trade differently from traditional investors. For years, the conventional wisdom promulgated by investment counselors was "buy and hold." It did not take long for day traders to learn the lesson JL had discovered: you can make money quickly in a wired stock market. Rather than buy and hold, the new mantra was buy often and sell quickly. Network technologies, which both delivered news and price information and permitted trading in real time, made this strategy possible. In addition to this, online trading firms drastically cut commissions, thereby reducing transaction costs significantly. What JL described as "momentum trading" became a preferred strategy for day traders. This way of playing the market significantly changes how and why people invest. Day trading is more like a video game than traditional stock investing and, as with video games, almost all the players are male. Just as JL had started Stock-Dogs .com, so sites promoting day trading like Motley Fool (Fool.com), Raging-Bull.com, and TheStreet.com quickly sprang up. These Web sites distributed information, gave advice, and, most important, hosted wildly popular discussions about technology, investing, and markets.

The Internet was not, of course, solely responsible for creating the buzz about dot-coms; traditional print, radio, and television media also played significant roles in fueling the mania of the late 1990s. As markets and media were joined in positive feedback loops, playing the market became a new form of mass entertainment. With more people invested in the game, markets received greater media coverage and as media coverage increased, more people played. Having become undeniably cool, the stock market was as fashionable as the art market and Barneys' latest styles. The fascination with the market and new technologies was not, however, limited to the uptown crowd. William Gibson's 1984 novel *Neuromancer* created the genre of cyberpunk, which made technology sexy by associating it with the edgy counterculture that can be traced back to the 1960s. With the appearance of the first issue of the Berkeley-based magazine *Mondo 2000* in 1989, the seemingly incongruous association of technology with drugs, sex, and New Age spirituality became explicit. Though rarely noted, the distance between Haight Ashbury and Silicon Valley is not as great as it often appears. The 1960s technophobia always harbored a technophilia. Eventually computers replaced drugs as the consciousness-altering agent of choice. Stewart Brand, one-time member of Ken Kesey's Merry Pranksters (whose band was the Grateful Dead), founder of the *Whole Earth Catalogue,* and author of *The Media Lab: Inventing the Future at M.I.T.,* makes this telling point clearly and concisely: "This generation swallowed computers whole, just like dope."[27] One of the primary places where the counterculture morphed into cyberculture was the early popular Web site known as the WELL (Whole Earth Lectronic Link). In addition to members from San Francisco's Homebrew Computer Club, without whom the personal computer as we now know it never would have been invented, writers, artists, and countless freaks joined in debates about the transformative effective of the so-called digital revolution. One of the most influential products to emerge from the world of the WELL was *Wired* magazine. One year after its launch in January 1993, Wired had 30,000 subscribers and two years later it had a monthly circulation of over 200,000. In form it was 1960s hippie, with psychedelic colors and over-the-top graphics; in content it was 1990s yuppie, with fashionable technology for the young, hip, and savvy. For the next five or six years, *Wired* played a major role in shaping attitudes that nourished the eruption of the dot-coms. When Advance Magazine Publishers, the parent company of Condé Nast, bought *Wired* for $75 million on May 8, 1998, it was clear that its time had passed. Throughout the mid-1990s countless less edgy publications devoted to the Internet, dot-coms, and the so-called new economy sprang up. Even staid and stogy publications like the *New York Times* tried to catch the wave by adding new sections devoted to technology like "Circuits."

While print played a noteworthy role in the emerging finance-entertainment complex, television took the hype to a new level. In 1989 NBC started CNBC, which, as Cassidy points out, "had started life as the Consumer News and Business Channel, presenting a combination of shopping tips and financial advice. In 1991 NBC purchased the assets of the rival Financial News Network, which had recently gone bankrupt, and folded its assets into the renamed CNBC. FNN had been a pioneer in business television. It was founded in 1981 by Glen Taylor, a former minister and children's television producer, and it started airing on three UHF stations in California with a stock ticker running across the screen. FNN never made any money, but it managed to get distributed to 30 million homes, which is why CNBC bought its remains."[28] It was not long before other stations like CNNfn devoted to financial news were launched. Even PBS could not resist the lure of finance and added *Wall Street Week* to its schedule. In several cases, these new programs changed the face of TV by transforming the screen. Following the lead of FNN, producers created television screens that looked more like terminals for Bloomberg.com than the nightly news. Stock prices and financial news were transmitted in real time for people with the speed and agility of someone adept at video games. The most important and innovative new shows were on cable stations. Programs like *Squawk Box, Street Signs, Market Week,* and *Market Wrap,* broadcast directly from NASDAQ headquarters in Times Square, were produced with all the glitz of the sports programs on ESPN, which broadcasts from the Zone, located next to NASDAQ on Broadway. One of the most important features of these new networks and shows was the invention of celebrity financial journalists like Ron Insana, coanchor of CNBC's *Street Signs* and *Business Center,* Mary Bartiromo, dubbed the "Money Honey," coanchor of CNBC's *Street Signs* and *Money Wrap,* Lou Dobbs, anchor of CNN's *Moneyline,* and Louis Rukeyser, host of PBS's *Wall Street Week.*

As these shows became more popular, celebrity journalists began to appear on regular network programs. Mary Bartiromo, for example, became a contributing commentator on NBC's *Today Show* and Ron Insana appeared regularly to comment on market matters on NBC's *Nightly News.* News, finance, and entertainment became further entangled by a series of mergers and acquisitions: General Electric acquired NBC, Disney bought ABC, Viacom purchased CBS, and AOL acquired Time Warner and CNN. When bits become the currency of the realm, everything is transcodable and print, television, and Internet begin to converge. While claiming to provide reliable news and information, these new financial news programs often were little more than infomercials, which were more about image than reality. Celebrity journalists created celebrity analysts like Morgan Stanley's Mary Meeker ("Queen of the Net") and Merrill Lynch's Henry Blodget. These "analysts" were always upbeat and rarely had anything negative to say about the market or individual stocks. Access to these analysts, in turn, raised the profiles of ambitious journalists. The glare of the lights, however, hid gathering shadows. As the 1990s unraveled, it became clear that the finance-entertainment complex was fraught with conflicts of interest. Analysts, who were supposed to provide reliable information for investors, were actually promoting companies on behalf of the investment banking branches of their firms, and journalists, who were supposed to be objective, were allowed to own stock in the companies they covered. In this world, it was obvious to everyone but the people running the SEC that the market is created by perception and manipulation. Lewis records an account of his meeting with Levitt and Walker.

> It was okay that Mary Meeker of Morgan Stanley and Henry Blodget of Merrill Lynch had plugged a portfolio of Internet company shares that, inside of six months, lost more than three quarters of their value at the same time they were paid millions of dollars, largely as a result of

the fees their firms raked in from the very same Internet companies. But it was . . . not okay for Jonathan Lebed to say that the FTEC would go from 8 to 20. When I asked *why* it was illegal, Walker had a pat answer.

"Because Jonathan Lebed was seeking to *manipulate* the market," he said.

But that only begged the question. If Wall Street analysts and fund managers and corporate CEOs who appear on CNBC and CNNfn to plug stocks are not guilty of seeking to *manipulate* the market, what on earth does it mean to *manipulate* the market?

The teenage JL understood what the chairman of the SEC failed to grasp: "Whether it is analysts, brokers, advisors, Internet traders, or the companies," JL observed, "everybody is manipulating the market. If it wasn't for everybody manipulating the market, there wouldn't be a stock market at all."[29]

By the late 1990s, the finance-entertainment complex was caught in an accelerating positive feedback loop with the media frenzy fueling the market, which was fueling the media frenzy. To keep the game going, journalists needed analysts as much as analysts needed journalists. The more TV hyped the market, the higher stock prices went; and the higher stock prices went, the more peopled watched financial news programs. Whether pumping iron in a fashionable Manhattan health club or pumping gas at the local filling station, people were watching financial news programs and checking their computers. From Wall Street to Main Street, lots of money was looking for a place to park.

COM GAMES) In the early 1990s, I began to realize that something important was happening. Though I watched the news and read a broad range of newspapers and magazines regularly, it was my students who alerted me to what was under way. As I listened to them, it became clear that the only way I was going to be able to understand the world of the Net was to become a student of my students. I am fortunate to have had an extraordinary group of students, to whom I remain deeply indebted for my understanding of new technologies.[30] The more I learned from them, the more obvious it became that the world of the kids was transforming the world of the grownups. With their guidance and support, I started experimenting with electronic and telematic technologies in my teaching and research. I began by teaching a global seminar with my Finnish colleague Esa Saarinen in 1992; this was the first time teleconferencing had been used for this purpose.³¹ In subsequent years, I developed courses in which students learned how to create multimedia hypertexts, and I started webcasting my classes to Williams College alumni/ae. Almost all of my colleagues greeted these efforts with indifference if not outright hostility. When I was unable to secure adequate support from the college for these experiments, I decided to accept Herbert Allen's generous offer to start a company to provide high-quality online education in the liberal arts, humanities, and sciences to all people of all ages all over the world. In November 1998, we cofounded the Global Education Network (GEN.com).³²

Only two months after the bailout of Long-Term Capital Management and a few months before the spectacular Priceline.com IPO, the launching of this initiative was caught in the cross-currents of the time. As we began developing plans over the next few months, we found ourselves in the midst of the overheated atmosphere of what seemed to be a revolution driven by kids but funded by adults. The investors who were smart, and there were a few, knew what they did not know and let twentysomethings take the lead. While biding their time and waiting for the inventions they eventually would buy and sell to be developed, many venture capitalists created incubators, which were playpens where young guys once dismissed as geeks did their thing. The strategy most venture capitals used was a variation of portfolio theory, which had become popular among investors: spread your bets by backing a broad range of companies. Everyone knew most of the start-ups would fail but gambled that one successful venture would more than make up for all the bad bets. At the height of the boom, it was hard to come up with an idea that could *not* find financial backing.

In the spring of 1999, we started interviewing technology companies to help us develop the software platform for GEN. These meetings often seemed like seminars with my students running the class; the kids were smart and had learned their lessons well. One presentation in particular stands out in my mind. With about ten twenty-year-olds, rummaging through their backpacks while sipping their bottled water, gathered around a big mahogany table surrounded by Norman Rockwell paintings and Frederick Remington sculptures at Allen & Company's Fifth Avenue offices, the tech company's CEO began his pitch with the obligatory PowerPoint presentation. The first slide was lime green and read DOMINATE OR DIE. These three words tell much of the story of the entire dot-com phenomenon. With all the insight and brashness of youth, this CEO, who owned neither a suit nor a tie, boiled down volumes of economic and network theory to a simple phrase, which might well have been a logo. The dot-com world, many argued, is a zero-sum game in which the winner takes all. As if they were reading from the same playbook, *every* technology company with which we met began the discussion by asking the same question: What's your exit strategy? From their point of view, there were only two possible answers to this question: IPO or buyout. The reason they asked this question first was that the answer determined the strategy they would recommend. Whatever the response, the time frame was the same: from conception to IPO or buyout could take no longer than *eighteen months.* The reason for this extraordinarily compressed time frame was the widely shared belief that the first one to the market wins. After all, how many people can name the second most popular online auction site? In a zero-sum game, it *is* dominate or die. In *New Rules for the New Economy: 10 Radical Strategies for a Connected World, Wired* founding editor and New Age guru Kevin Kelly summarizes the most basic economic assumption of dot-com entrepreneurs: "Increasing Returns. As the number of connections between people and things add up, the consequences of those connections multiply out even faster, so that initial successes aren't self-limiting, but self-feeding."[33] The correlative principles of increasing returns and positive feedback rest upon the network effect, which, as we have seen, suggests that the value of the network increases exponentially with the number of users. This leads to positive feedback loops, which result in increasing returns. In contrast to conventional wisdom, according to which scarcity increases value, the network effect suggests that plenitude increases value: more breeds more. Kelly offers a simplified graph (figure 25) and invokes no less an authority than *New York Times* columnist Paul Krugman to make this point.

> In the new order, as the law of plenitude kicks in and the nearly free take over, both of these curves are turned upside down. Paul Krugman, an economist at MIT, says that you can reduce the entire idea of the network economy down to the observation that "in the Network Economy, supply curves slope down instead of up and demand curves slope up instead of down." The more a resource is used, the more demand there is for it. A similar inversion happens on the supply side. Because of compounded learning, the more we create something, the easier it becomes to create more of it. The classic textbook graph is inverted.[34]

If one believes in this principle, two consequences follow, both of which have been very important for the Internet economy. First, in order to grow your network as fast as possible, it makes sense to give away your product

free of charge. If the product is bits rather than stuff, production costs after the first copy drop to almost nothing. Since increasing the number of
users on the network generates value, the prudent strategy is to give away
products that can only be used on the network. The fact that this approach
leaves unanswered the question of how to create the revenues necessary to
run a business did not quell the enthusiasm of entrepreneurs or investors.
Second, if first-to-market wins, time is more important than money. The
compressed development cycle led to huge burn rates and an extraordinary waste of capital. This approach worked only as long as venture capitalists were willing to place multiple bets on companies that had little
chance of success. But when money got tight, many start-ups could not
raise a second round of capital and crashed and burned.

What the companies with which we met never anticipated was that
we did not have an exit strategy because our aim was to produce a high-
quality product and we were in business for the long haul. Our plan is to
produce a quality product by retaining control of the company. Though it
is too early to tell if this strategy will work, GEN is still in business while
many of the companies advising us and others we thought would be our
competitors are not.

At times during the past several years, I have felt like an anthropologist
investigating a foreign tribe. My experiences as a participant-observer in

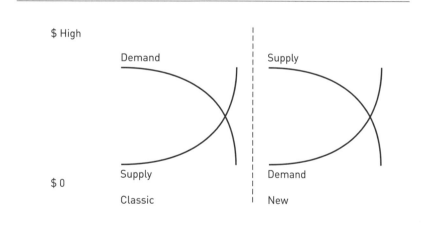

Figure 25

Adapted from *New Rules for the New Economy* by Kevin Kelly, copyright © 1998 by
Kevin Kelly. Used by permission of Viking Penguin, a division of Penguin Group (USA)
Inc. Reprinted by permission of HarperCollins Publishers Ltd. © Kevin Kelly 1998.

the worlds of investment banking and dot-coms have given me a unique opportunity to step behind the curtain of the financial world and look at recent economic developments from a perspective not usually available to "outsiders." The lessons I have learned have helped me understand the ways in which the dot-com boom and bust are symptomatic of the broader economic trajectories I have been tracing.[35]

As if to underscore the interrelation of the cyberculture of the 1990s and the counterculture of the 1960s, the dot-com era was born on the day the Grateful Dead icon Jerry Garcia died. On August 9, 1995, Mary Meeker orchestrated Netscape's IPO on the Equity Capital Markets trading floor of Morgan Stanley's Times Square building. The stock was offered at $28 a share, opened at $71, and closed at $58\frac{1}{4}$, giving it a $2.2 billion valuation after one day of trading.[36] The Netscape IPO marked the beginning of the dot-com gold rush and set the pattern for countless start-ups during the next five years. This venture was a joint undertaking of Jim Clark, founder of Silicon Graphics and Healtheon, and Marc Andreesen, a twenty-one-year-old graduate of the University of Illinois, Urbana-Champaign. Looking back on what Clark and Andreessen accomplished, it is undeniable that Netscape has in no small measure been responsible for the World Wide Web as we now know it. The ever-confident, if not arrogant, Clark observed, "People started drinking my Kool-Aid. Netscape obviously didn't create the Internet. But if Netscape had not forced the issue on the Internet, it would have just burbled in the background. It would have remained this counterintuitive kind of thing. The criticism of it was that it was anarchy. What the IPO did was give anarchy credibility."[37] By the mid-1990s, there were over twenty-five million Internet users, but it was difficult if not impossible to navigate the Net and find the information for which one was searching. By developing an intuitive graphical interface, Netscape made the Web both accessible and potentially ubiquitous. While at the University of Illinois, Andreessen had worked at the National Center for Supercomputing Applications (NCSA) and had been a member of the team that created Mosaic, which used simple graphic software. "When Mosaic appeared," Cassidy points out, "less that one percent of Internet traffic was on the World Wide Web. Two years later, the Web was the most popular thing on the Internet, accounting for about a quarter of all traffic. Mosaic was responsible for the transformation."[38] In 1994, Clark and Andreessen founded Mosaic Communications, which they later renamed Netscape as part of the settlement of a legal case the University of Illinois brought against the company. Clark provided initial funding of $3 million but

within a year took the company public. With a staff of eighty-five committed to the logic of increasing returns and thus willing to give away its
product free without any clear plan for generating profits, Netscape's stock
soared to $170 a share and the company was valued at $6.5 billion in less
than six months. Shortly after the IPO, Mary Meeker and Chris DePuy
published *The Internet Report,* which quickly became the bible for dot-com
entrepreneurs and investors. Morgan Stanley distributed over 300,000
copies of the report before HarperCollins issued a paperback edition.[39] The
lengthy study predicted that the explosive growth of information and
network technologies would create a period of unprecedented financial
opportunity. Sounding more like cheerleaders than analysts, Meeker and
DePuy summarized their conclusions:

> Due to technological advances in PC-based communications, a new
> medium—with the Internet, the World Wide Web and TCP/IP at its
> core—is emerging rapidly. The market for Internet-related products and
> services appears to be growing more rapidly than the early emerging
> markets for print, telephony, film, radio, recorded music, television and
> personal computers. . . . As the Internet continues to evolve, market
> opportunities for equipment/infrastructure providers should be huge.
> Opportunities for well positioned software/services companies and
> content/aggregation companies will also be significant.[40]

A few months after Meeker and DePuy's report appeared, a company
formed by two erstwhile Stanford graduate students, Jerry Yang and David
Filo, held its IPO. The name of the company was Yahoo. Yahoo had started
modestly as "Jerry's Guide to the World Wide Web" and by 1994 was at-
tracting thousands of users. The site was so successful that Yang and Filo
decided to establish a company one year later. While the reason they
named the site Yahoo has, to my knowledge, never been explained, Yang
has acknowledged in a private conversation that the inspiration came from
Jonathan Swift's *Gulliver's Travels.* In Swift's bitterly satirical tale, the Yahoos are human beings who appear to be animals and are enslaved to a
race of rational horses named the Houyhnhnms. For Swift, the Yahoos provide an image of human nature ruled by base instincts and unenlightened
by reason. By the end of the 1990s, many people were convinced that dot-
com fever had turned the United States into a nation of Yahoos.

Like Clark and Andreessen, Yang and Filo realized that for the Web to
become functional, better ways of organizing information and accessing

data had to be developed. In 1996, there were 200,000 sites on the World Wide Web, and Yahoo provided access to about six million Web pages a day.[41] Users were not charged and revenue was generated from advertising. Most of the companies that advertised on the Yahoo site were, predictably, other Internet companies. In spite of having raised $100 million from Japan's Softbank in the first part of 1996, Yang and then-CEO Tim Koogle decided that in order to keep its competitive edge, they had to pursue an IPO. On April 21, 1996, 2.6 million shares of Yahoo were offered at $13 a share. In the course of the first day's trading, the price rose to $43 and closed at $33, giving the company a value of $850 million. Less than three years later, Yahoo was selling for $500 a share and had a valuation of $35 billion.

Financial markets had *never* seen numbers like this. Faced with a rapidly changing situation, many analysts and investors conjured up new ways to evaluate Internet- and Web-based companies. According to the principles of traditional investing, the value of a company is determined by either an analysis of so-called "fundamentals" or the price/earnings (p/e) ratio. The fundamentals of a company include primarily expected dividends, cash flow, and assets. Some Internet companies tried to duck the critical issue of revenues by listing what they called "pro forma profits." In the wildly speculative world of Internet stocks, pro forma profits were more fiction than fact and thus were no more real than notional capital. In addition to this, many dot-coms engaged in questionable accounting practices that later returned to haunt them. Revenue-starved start-ups would swap advertising on their Web sites and credit the estimated value of the ads as income. Even though no money was exchanged, both companies participating in these round-trip trades booked revenue on the deal. For example, in 1999, iVillage Inc., a popular site aimed at women, disclosed that 20 percent of its "income" came from advertising swaps.

While new Internet companies had major expenses, almost none of them had any legitimate revenue streams; nor did they pay dividends or have many assets. Fundamental analysis, therefore, was extremely difficult if not impossible. The price/earnings ratio was no more helpful than fundamental analysis. The p/e ratio is determined by dividing the price of the stock by its earnings per share. Looking back to 1872, Yale economist Robert Shiller, who coined the phrase "irrational exuberance," established that for the S&P 500 stock index the p/e ratio fluctuated around a mean of 16 before the 1990s; the highest ratio during that time was 28. By 2000, however, the p/e ratio had risen to 45. While on NASDAQ, the p/e ratio was never more than 21 from 1973 to 1995, in 2000 it was 60.[42] For some of the high-profile stocks of the 1990s, the p/e ratio was astronomical. Yahoo, for example, at one point had a p/e ratio of 389, while the price of e-Bay soared to an incredible 1,600 times earnings. With no material assets underlying these evaluations, Internet stocks took the disappearance of the real to absurd levels. In the absence of plans for producing profits or fundamentals upon which to base judgments of value, evaluations were determined by what analysts called "eyeballs." In this scheme, the value of a company is calculated by the number of people who visit the site or the number of hits the site receives. As Cassidy correctly points out, "instead of being rewarded for cutting costs and increasing revenues, like most managers are, they were rewarded for increasing the number of page views. Not surprisingly, many of them would end up spending as much money as possible on marketing and promoting their sites, regardless of the cost."[43] And, it is important to add, regardless of whether companies had a proven product to sell. Not even Melville's confidence man could have come up with a scam this ingenious.

The problem of establishing reasonable valuations of Internet companies was further complicated by the difficulty of determining market capitalizations. While a company might issue several million shares of a stock, only a small number of these shares traded publicly. For example, when Amazon held its IPO, it issued twenty-three million shares, but only three million were traded on the open market. With vast amounts of liquidity available and the media creating an enormous buzz about the Internet, there was a huge amount of capital chasing a limited number of shares of stock during the late 1990s. In this case, the classical law of supply and demand still held: scarcity drove share prices up to unreasonably high levels. The market capitalization (or cap) of a company is determined by multiplying the total number of shares issued by the price per share. If the share price is artificially high, the market cap is also disproportionately exaggerated.

In 1996, the year of Yahoo's IPO, the market boom was in full swing. In the first four months of the year, $100 billion had flowed into stock market mutual funds, while investment banks were busy making $3 billion underwriting Internet IPOs. There were, however, voices cautioning that a bubble was emerging, which inevitably had to burst. When the Dow broke 6,500 in December 1996, Greenspan delivered his famous "irrational exuberance" speech and the next day, the Dow dropped 140 points. But the dip proved temporary; just two weeks after Greenspan's speech, Michael Mandel published an enthusiastic article in *Business Week* entitled "The Triumph of the New Economy: A Powerful Payoff from Globalization and the Information Revolution."

> Is the market crazy? Hardly. Underlying the equity boom is the emergence of a New Economy, built on the foundation of global markets and the Information Revolution. Starting in the early 1980s and accelerating in the past few years, the U.S. economy has been undergoing a fundamental restructuring. Exports and imports, once relatively insignificant, now amount to 26% of gross domestic product. Business investment in computers and communications hardware has soared by 24% over the past year alone, accounting for almost one-third of economic growth. From the Internet to direct-broadcast television, new companies are springing up almost overnight to take advantage of cutting-edge technologies.[44]

Less than seven months later, Greenspan himself changed his mind. Testifying before Congress on July 22, 1997, he remarked:

> What we may be observing in the current environment is a number of key technologies, some even mature, finally interacting to create significant opportunities for value creation. For example, the applications of the laser were modest until that later development of fiber optics engendered a revolution in telecommunications. Broad advances in software have enabled us to capitalize on the prodigious gains in hardware capacity. The interaction of both of these has created the Internet.

Exuberance, it seemed, might be rational after all. When Greenspan gave the green light, the party turned manic. The Dow quickly rose 150 points and closed at over 8,000 for the first time.[45] A media frenzy in early 1997 drove Internet stocks through the roof. On May 15, 1997, Mary Meeker took Amazon.com public, and by the end of the year its value had risen by 970 percent. At the same time AOL stock had increased 593 percent and Yahoo went up 584 percent.

During 1998, however, global events were threatening to spoil America's party. The debt crisis, which began with the bull market in 1982, had spread to Asia in the mid-1990s and then to Russia late in the decade. In August 1998, Russia devalued the ruble and defaulted on its loans. This triggered a cascade of events, which one month later drove Long-Term Capital Management, a huge hedge fund, to the brink of collapse (I will consider the case of Long-Term Capital Management and the role of the world debt crisis in its collapse in the next chapter). This crisis brought the entire global economy closer to meltdown than it had ever been. *Time* magazine expressed the fears of many with a cover September 14, 1998, story "Is the Boom Over?" This crisis in the global economy created an impossible dilemma for Greenspan. On the one hand, he should have raised interest rates to cool off the skyrocketing stock market, but on the other hand, raising rates would have exacerbated the global debt crisis and threatened the U.S. banking system, which was overextended in Asia and Russia. With many in the financial community calling for a rate increase, Greenspan not only deferred raising rates but actually cut rates three times. He went so far as to sanction the irrational exuberance he once had condemned.

> There is something else going on here, though, which is a fascinating thing to watch. It is, for want of a better term, the "lottery principle." What lottery managers have known for centuries is that you could get somebody to pay on a one-in-a-million shot more than the value of that chance. In other words, people pay more for a claim on a very big payoff, and that's where the profits from lotteries have always come from. So there is a lottery premium built into the price of Internet stocks.
>
> But there is at root here something far more fundamental—the stock market seeking out profitable ventures and directing capital to hopeful projects before the profits materialize [i.e., the invisible hand]. That's good for the system. And that, at the end of the day, probably is more of a plus than a minus.[46]

Once again, Greenspan's comments triggered a market surge.

With worries about the global economy and fears of an interest rate hike fading, the Internet boom did the impossible—it *increased* its momentum. Between 1998 and 2000, there were three hundred Internet IPOs. On March 30, 1999, Mary Meeker struck again with the Priceline .com IPO. The creation of a savvy pitchman named Jay Walker, Priceline.com is an online service that started by allowing users to bid on plane tickets that the airlines had not sold. Ten million shares were offered at $16 a share, but the price immediately rose to $85; by the end of the day, it closed at $68 and the company was valued at $10 billion—more than the total combined value of Continental Airlines and Northwest Airline. At one point, the price of the stock rose to $150 and the value of Priceline.com *exceeded the value of the entire airline industry.*[47] In the midst of the eu-

phoria, *Time* seemed to forget its doubts of a year earlier and named Jeff
Bezos its 1999 Person of the Year. Between October 1999 and March 2000,
investors borrowed record sums of money to purchase stock. At the same
time, the margin debt rose to a record $24 billion, up from the previous
record of $16.4 billion in April 1999. Not even worries about looming Y2K
problems could dampen investors' enthusiasm. While new Internet companies were starting up, "old" dot-coms were expanding. On January 10,
2000, AOL, which had acquired Netscape for $4.2 billion in 1998, an-
nounced the acquisition of Time Warner for $165 billion. Widely heralded
as the merger of "old" and "new" media companies, which would unleash
the wave of the future, this was the largest media deal in history. It was
generally assumed at the time that AOL's Internet business would quickly
absorb and transform Time Warner's traditional print, film, and TV businesses. Like many other Internet transactions at the time, this mega-deal
was done in vastly inflated stock rather than cash. Steve Case's timing
could not have been better and Gerald Levin's could not have been worse:
the deal was announced six days after the Dow closed at what is still its all-
time high of 11,723 and AOL stock was close to its peak price.

Three days later, Greenspan gave a speech in which he once again signaled concern about a stock market bubble created by what he now termed
"the wealth effect." With the world debt crisis somewhat stabilized and a
strategy for the Long-Term Capital Management bailout in place, the chairman of the Fed felt free to raise interest rates modestly in February (from
5.5 percent to 5.75 percent). Though the increase had no immediate impact on markets, this action actually signaled the end of the party. The
Dow started to decline but NASDAQ continued to rise and did not peak until March 10, when it closed at 5046.86. One week later, NASDAQ dropped
5 percent to close at 4798.13. Between March 10, 2000, and April 14, 2000,
the price of Amazon dropped 29.9 percent, AOL was down 6.2 percent,
e-Bay was off 27.9 percent, Priceline.com declined 38 percent, and Yahoo
lost 34.8 percent of its value.[48] Not only had the so-called Internet bubble
burst but the bull market that began in 1982 came to an end on March 17,
2000.

Looking back on the decade, it was a very strange party. Having started
GEN.com in 1998, I was fortunate enough to spend quite a bit of time in
New York in the late 1990s. Everywhere I went, euphoria was mixed with
a sense of foreboding. In spite of growing concern, most investors were reluctant to pick up their chips when the ante was still rising. While greed
was certainly a part of the motivation, the thrill of being in play was
equally important. Indeed, for many gamblers, the dicier the game, the

bigger the draw; the rush of risk sometimes can be an intoxicating high. By the end of the decade, Wall Street had become even more exciting than Vegas because the stakes were so much higher and the game so much faster. Nonetheless, an inescapable specter hung over the markets: virtually everyone quietly admitted that investing had become more of a confidence game than ever. From Wall Street to Main Street, people knew the boom was not real, but after two decades of a bull market, no one was any longer sure what really *was* real. As JR had observed twenty years earlier, "it's just different electric numbers on these checks and all which this computer reads them it doesn't give a shit if you're three years old just if there's money there." By the 1990s, questions had grown more urgent: Where *was* the money? What had money *become*? Was it *real*? Had it *ever* been real? Or was it merely an idea, a fiction, a notion, a consensual illusion? This is the specter that loomed over the new millennium. The problem of the disappearing real is not, of course, limited to the NYSE, NASDAQ, and global markets. As we have come to suspect, by the turn of the century, technology and finance had transformed both what we are and how we think. The arts and culture simultaneously reflected and promoted the emerging network economy. What had not yet become clear is that information, telematic, and network technologies have a different structure and operational logic, which, if not understood, threaten the very system they have created.

7

DIFFERENCE ENGINES

No but see that's the whole thing Bast see it's not money anyway it's just exchanging this here stock around in like this merging it with this here X-L subsidiary which it's worth like twenty times as much as, you know? See we just give these here Ray-X stock holders one share of X L preferred for their share of Ray-X only this here X-L's common stock capitalization is real low see so we have this here tremendous leverage see and . . . no well I don't exactly know but that's what this Mister Wiles said see he . . . No but . . . no I know but . . . No but I see I was just going to ask if you heard anything from U S Bureau of Mines see because . . . No I know I said that but . . . no I know but see we're just building up these here assets for like getting incorporated with these directors and all for this here stock issue see we can like exchange it around for these here other assets and get all this here borrowing power to . . . No wait I know I said that but . . . No but holy shit Bast I didn't invent it I mean this is what you do!

William Gaddis, *JR*

FROM WALL STREET TO LAS VEGAS) On August 1, 2001, the Guggenheim Museum in New York City issued a press release bearing the title "Solomon R. Guggenheim Foundation and The State Hermitage Museum to Open New Museum in September 2001 at The Venetian Resort-Hotel-Casino in Las Vegas." The alliance between the high-art culture of New York and the low culture of the Strip—to say nothing of joining St. Petersburg and Las Vegas—might initially seem unlikely. But, in fact, the Guggenheim's venture in Vegas is an integral part of the museum's long-term strategy and reflects the insight and vision of the director, Thomas Krens. Krens took over the Guggenheim just a few months before the collapse of the Berlin Wall in 1989. Bringing together art, commerce, and finance in unprecedented ways, the Guggenheim emerged as the museum of the future in the 1990s. The rise and fall of the Guggenheim's fortunes coincide precisely with the rise and fall of NASDAQ. There is no better laboratory for understanding the complex relation between art and finance in the late twentieth century than the Guggenheim. Krens's background in business as well as art taught him lessons in financial engineering that, he believed, were necessary to save museums during an era of dwindling government support and declining private contributions. Taking Warhol's adage—"Being good in business is the most fascinating kind of art"—as a mission statement for museums in the twenty-first century, Krens transformed the way museums do business.

It is no accident that one of the primary influences on Krens was Martin Shubik, professor of mathematical institutional economics at the Yale School of Management. From the time Krens arrived at Yale, he and Shubik gravitated toward each other. Shubik is an important economist whose monumental *Theory of Money and Financial Institutions,* upon which I have drawn and to which I will return, is the best book that has been written on the importance of game theory for financial economics. One of the things that makes Shubik's work so significant is his appreciation of the importance of complexity studies for understanding current economic processes. A long-time participant in the discussions at the Santa Fe Institute, Shubik has written seminal papers in this emerging field. Working with Shubik, Krens came to a deeper understanding of the ways in which technology and globalization are changing the very structure of markets and thereby transforming social, political, and economic life. The lines of influence between Shubik and Krens were not one way, for the teacher became a student of his student. Working with Krens increased Shubik's appreciation for art and has led to his effort to create a Museum of Money and Financial Institutions. The first stage of this project is a virtual museum, which is already complete (at http://www.museumofmoney.org), and planning for a bricks-and-mortar museum is well under way.

As Krens's understanding of the interrelation between art and economics took shape, he began designing two important projects that eventually had a major impact on the art world in the 1990s. The first was a plan to transform an abandoned electronics factory in a down-and-out New England mill town into the largest museum of contemporary art in the world. At the time, few took the idea seriously, but Krens persisted and today the Massachusetts Museum of Contemporary Art is a thriving cultural institution. The genius of Krens's plan was that from the beginning, he proposed Mass MOCA as an economic development rather than a cultural project. Only in this way was he able to win the political and financial support he needed. Though many were skeptical about his figures for projected revenues, the museum now plays a critical role in the regional economy. The second project seems unrelated to Mass MOCA but actually reveals its artistic and philosophical inspiration. In the late 1980s, Krens began planning a major exhibition of the art of the Soviet Union. Perhaps his upbringing in the Russian Orthodox tradition enabled him to understand the way in which the Russian avant-garde transformed religious mission into a comprehensive artistic project. As we have seen, Rodchenko and his fellow Constructivists took art from studio to factory in an effort to fulfill the avant-garde dream of transforming the world into a work of art. In the late 1980s, Krens already understood that in "the new world order," not only information but also culture would be the currency of the realm. Art and cultural institutions, in other words, would assume greater political and economic importance. In negotiating with the Soviet Union, Krens made the crucial strategic decision to work through the Soviet Foreign Ministry rather than the Ministry of Culture. Unexpected turns in Krens's career and world events delayed the exhibition until 1992. By the

time *The Great Utopia: The Russian and Soviet Avant-Garde, 1915–1932*
opened, the Soviet Union had collapsed and Krens was running the Guggenheim. In his preface to the catalogue accompanying the show, Krens
indirectly suggests the way in which his interpretation of Russian avant-
garde art has shaped his vision of the role of the museum in the twenty-
first century. "Somewhere between the absolute spiritual idealism of
Malevich's Suprematism and the dramatic reality of Tatlin's reliefs is that
utopian sensibility, within a historical context of political and social upheaval, which released Russian art from the studio and onto the street, and
which endowed it with a desire to pervade every aspect of life—even to become an agent of social change."[1] Incongruously, through Krens's efforts,
what begins in the studios of Moscow ends in the casinos and on the Strip
in Las Vegas.

Though it occurred by accident rather than design, it is difficult to
imagine a more appropriate Vegas partner for the Guggenheim than the
Venetian Resort-Hotel-Casino. After all, the Peggy Guggenheim Collection,
located on the Grand Canal, had long given the museum a presence in the
heart of Venice. Moreover, the growth of tourism and globalization of
theme parks in the 1980s steadily eroded the difference between the real
and the fake Venice. Since Venice itself has actually become a theme park
for foreign tourists, the Vegas copy might prove to be as good as, if not better than, the European original. But Krens's strategy is even more subtle
than this reversal of the real and the fake implies. By exhibiting "real" art,
which, at least since Plato, has been suspected of trafficking in semblance
rather than reality, in the global capital of the fake, Krens completely con-
founded the supposedly clear distinction between reality and image as
well as the real and the virtual. There is, however, a deeper motivation behind his initiative in Las Vegas, which echoes the aspirations of his Russian ancestors and precursors. Creating an alliance among St. Petersburg's
prestigious State Hermitage Museum (founded in 1764), the Guggenheim,
and the Venetian on the Strip, Krens effectively extends the avant-garde
project of collapsing high and low by bringing art to the masses.

The Hermitage-Guggenheim Museum and Guggenheim Las Vegas are
the latest additions to the network of museums Krens has been building
for more than a decade. While critics have charged him with "McDonald-
izing" the museum by creating a string of franchises that devalues the Guggenheim's cultural currency, this criticism completely misses the point of
his program. By the time Krens assumed the directorship, a decade of neoconservative policies was having a significant impact on museum funding
and was making it necessary for cultural institutions to devise new eco-

nomic models.[2] Krens not only has a sophisticated understanding of economics and globalization but understood the implications of information, telematic, and network technologies long before most people. The core of his strategy is to create a *global network* of museums. This approach rests upon an understanding of the importance, structure, and logic of networks in contemporary culture. The global network Krens is forming has four major components:

1. Different Guggenheim museums located in major cities around the world and alliances with other cultural institutions (in addition to New York, Venice, and Las Vegas, there are now Guggenheim museums in Bilbao, Spain, Berlin, and Rio de Janeiro as well as formal alliances with Kunsthistorische Museum in Salzburg, the Royal Academy in London, the Center for Art and Media Technology in Karlsruhe, the Shanghai Museum, and the Massachusetts Museum of Contemporary Art).
2. Guggenheim.com, an Internet company that provides cultural entertainment, information, news, cultural services, and commercial services like art sales, auctions, e-commerce, and retail.
3. GuggenheimTV, a cable TV network providing cultural education and entertainment.
4. GuggenheimInteractive, which supplies data, statistics, and information and functions as a travel planner.

Here art, finance, and entertainment form an alliance with global aspirations.

One of the great strengths of this plan is the way in which the real and the virtual are interrelated and reinforce each other. Unlike many cyberspace enthusiasts, Krens has always realized that the Internet and virtual reality complement rather than replace "real" paintings and actual museums. If Krens's strategy is to work, the museum's virtual presence must be as effective as its real presence. For the Guggenheim to become the first global cultural network, it would have to develop a Web site whose architecture is as impressive as the fabled Frank Lloyd Wright building on Fifth Avenue. To create this vital link in his network, Krens recruited the New York architectural firm Asymptote, whose principals are Hani Rashid and Lise Anne Couture. In recent years, Asymptote has experimented with photographic collage, digital modeling and imaging, video, and multimedia. The result is an impressive body of work ranging from finished buildings and interior design to installation art and interactive digital and virtual environments. All of these works imaginatively probe the "increasingly dense territory" between the real and the virtual.

The ambitious goal of the Guggenheim.com Web site was nothing less than to become "the first virtual gateway to global culture." One of the most innovative features of the site was the Guggenheim Virtual Museum, which is a multidimensional, real-time, interactive environment designed for new Internet art. Commenting on the ideas informing their design, Rashid and Couture indicate the intricate braiding of the real and the virtual in their work.

> Both the Guggenheim Virtual Museum (GVM) and the Guggenheim .com projects were thought of as spatial interfaces. However, the two projects' demands and criteria were different. Whereas the GMV is primarily thought of as a surrogate or augmented architectural experience that requires geometry, form, space, and time, Guggenheim.com is more informationally loaded, televisory, and encyclopedic. Simply stated, the GVM is thought of as an architectural experience on the Web while Guggenheim.com is a media experience exploring the spatial situation we have become accustomed to through television, film, the book, the billboard and so on.[3]

Developed for both broadband and narrowband, the site would allow users to access the Web sites of each Guggenheim museum and affiliated institutions as well as an image archive for works in the assembled collections. In this vision, the virtual Guggenheim enables the museum to extend its global reach in the "real" world (figure 26). In the emerging new world, the Guggenheim is not merely a place but is a space that is virtually boundless.

By 1999, Krens had established a downtown office for Guggenheim .com at One Wall Street. The apparent reason for the selection of this location for the new offices was that it overlooks the site where Krens had hoped to build a huge new museum designed by Frank Gehry.[4] While there were practical reasons for locating Guggenheim.com at One Wall Street, the symbolic significance of the address for Krens's vision was greater than even Andy Warhol could have imagined. From its earliest days, architecture has been essential to the success of the Guggenheim. Without Frank Lloyd Wright, Frank Gehry, and Rem Koolhaas, the Guggenheim would not be the world-class cultural institution it is today. In Asymptote, Krens found the ideal architectural firm for his virtual venture.

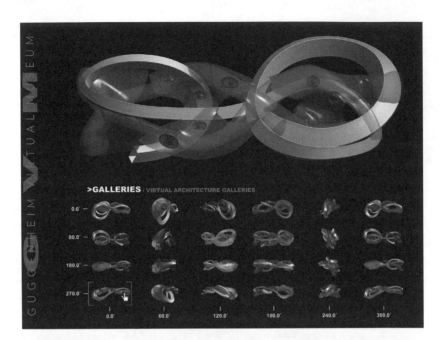

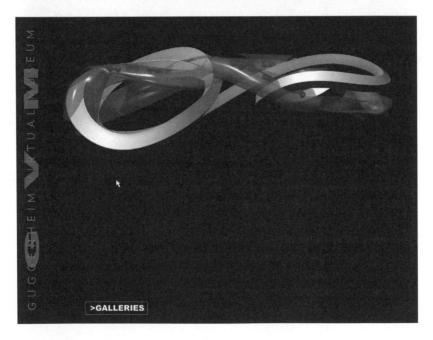

Figure 26
Hani Rashid and Lise Anne Couture, "Guggenheim Virtual Museum."

In 1998, the New York Stock Exchange commissioned Asymptote to fashion a virtual trading floor. In light of the differences that developed between the NYSE and NASDAQ during the 1980s and 1990s, this decision represented the belated acknowledgment that the future is undeniably virtual (figure 27). In their initial design of the Three-Dimensional Trading Floor (3DTF), Rashid and Couture attempted to re-create the physical trading environment with wireframe models. It quickly became apparent, however, that the actual trading floor had to be completely reconfigured to

Figure 27
Hani Rashid and Lise Anne Couture, "Three-Dimensional Trading Floor." Courtesy NYSE/SIAC/Asymptote.

function in a network environment in real time. We have already discovered that the networks relevant to today's markets are not only financial but also news and media networks. As the design went through numerous iterations, a complex multidimensional world began to emerge.

> The project took full advantage of opportunities in virtual space to manipulate spatial and temporal dimensions. The 3DTF allows one to occupy several virtual spaces, scales, and points of view simultaneously. Captured events can also be instantly replayed alongside real-time events, and the user is able to compress, stretch, distort, or overlap these as required. The importance of the temporal dimensions is evident as the inextricable relationships between financial "events" and media news-reporting of cause-and-effect is made transparent. The project posed an interesting opportunity to reconsider the "reality" of the actual trading floor: Asymptote's 3DTF version of the trading floor, although virtual and not intended to be constructed outside of a computer environment, is effectively a direction for possible future trading environments. The virtual trading floor as designed is both a reflection of the existing environment and a provocation for a new, physically augmented architecture.

The future projected in 3DTF arrived faster than anyone anticipated: the virtual realm began to "usurp the 'real' trading floor as a place." Today the virtual trading floor includes extensive data-mining capabilities, Internet connections for online trading, and television broadcasting facilities. Rashid and Couture confidently predict that "the general public soon will be able to navigate a virtual trading floor, check stock news and valuations, make trades, and meander about at will."[5]

Krens's dream for a new Guggenheim Museum on the East River went up in smoke on September 11, 2001. Mounting economic pressures and a new political climate threaten the network Krens has so carefully developed. In the following months, he was forced to pull the plug on the Guggenheim Virtual Museum, shut down Guggenheim.com's Wall Street office, close the SoHo Guggenheim, and cut his staff significantly. By the spring of 2003, the Guggenheim Las Vegas, which had opened only two weeks after 9/11, closed its doors. As the losses mounted, critics, who had never wanted Krens to succeed, gleefully asserted that the Guggenheim had been the Enron of the art world. Such smug satisfaction is, however, premature. Krens understands the future better than his critics. Though Guggenheim.com has, for the moment, ceased its operations, at the other end of the Street, virtual exchanges are transforming the world of finance in the artful ways Krens has long anticipated. When uptown is downtown and downtown is uptown, high and low become parts of the same game. Protests to the contrary notwithstanding, this game has just begun.

BALANCING THE BOOKS) The origin of the electronic computer and information age can be traced to three inventions of the nineteenth-century mathematician Charles Babbage: Difference Engines 1 and 2 and the Analytic Engine. None of these devices was built during Babbage's lifetime.[6] While it is commonly acknowledged that Babbage's calculating machines were the first prototypes of today's computers, it is rarely noted that he drew the inspiration for these inventions from Adam Smith's theory of the market. Furthermore, Babbage's appropriation of the Newtonian model underlying the Difference Engines and Analytic Engine indirectly informs some of the most important mathematical models in financial economics, which were widely used by investors from the 1970s through the 1990s. Not only, therefore, are computers used to model markets but the market was used as the model for the earliest computer.

Babbage was an extraordinarily creative and inventive person who, in addition to designing calculating machines, wrote books on subjects ranging from economics and manufacturing to theology and life insurance. His inventions included couplings for railroad cars, a submarine fueled by compressed air, an altimeter, a seismograph, and countless other mechanical novelties. An ardent gamesman, he was convinced that there is no game that cannot be played by an automaton and, to prove his point, he invented a mechanical chess player and card player.[7] When still a teenager, he betrayed what would prove to be characteristic hubris by inventing shoes that, he insisted, enabled one to walk on water. Though many of his ideas seemed quirky at the time, he was a highly regarded mathematician who, from 1828 to 1839, held the Lucasian Chair at Cambridge, once occupied by Newton. Babbage shared Newton's vision of a mechanical universe governed by universal laws whose beauty and rationality testify to the glory of the divine Creator.

Babbage's interest in calculating machines grew out of very practical concerns. In the early nineteenth century, people relied on long and complicated tables to do calculations about everything from navigation and life insurance to manufacturing, banking, and taxes. The calculations for these tables were done by "computers," who were people rather than machines. These computers were often women with little formal education who were trained to do the most basic arithmetic. Their calculations were first transcribed by hand, then typeset, and finally printed. The resulting tables were often filled with errors that, once printed, could not easily be corrected. Since humans introduced these errors, Babbage thought the only way to avoid mistakes was to remove people from the calculation process. He dreamed of creating a machine that would operate according to established rules and thus compute accurately without any human intervention. "The Difference Engine," Babbage explains, "is not intended to answer special questions. Its object is to calculate and print a *series* of results formed according to given laws."[8]

The inspiration for the structure of the first calculator came from an unlikely source. In 1819, Babbage traveled to France where he met Baron Gaspard Clair François Marie Riche de Prony. The French government had commissioned de Prony to develop "a definitive set of logarithmic and trigonometrical tables for the newly introduced metric system," which could be used to create tables for calculating taxes. Faced with this daunting task, de Prony borrowed the principle of division of labor from Adam Smith's *The Wealth of Nations.* Martin Campbell-Kelly, editor of Babbage's *Passages from the Life of a Philosopher,* explains that "the project made use of two small elite planning and executive staffs, which oversaw the work of between 60 to 80 'human computers,' who used the standard table-making known as the method of differences. The human computers needed to be capable only of the elementary operations of addition and subtraction and generally had only a minimal education."[9] Babbage eventually brought together his interest in machinery and economics in an influential study of then current industrial practices in England, entitled *On the Economy of Machinery and Manufacturers* (1832). What made Smith's analysis so intriguing for Babbage was his interpretation of the market as a *self-regulating machine.* When designing his calculating machine, Babbage borrowed his most important insights from Smith and de Prony. Recognizing that dumb parts could produce intelligent results, he broke down the calculation process into subroutines and distributed them among different components. To overcome the inevitable errors of human computers, he realized, it would be necessary to make a machine that was fully automated and, like market mechanisms, self-regulating (figure 28).

Babbage was not, of course, the first to build a calculating machine. Leibniz, for example, had created an impressive device for doing addition, called the "reckoner," in the 1670s. Babbage's Difference Engine was distinguished from previous calculators by the fact that it was *fully* automated

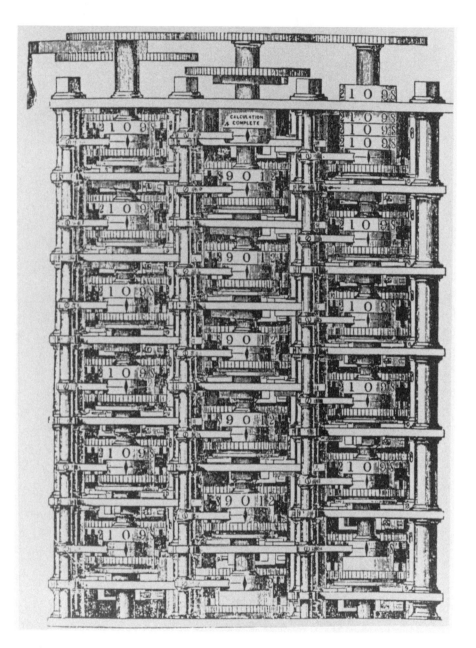

Figure 28
Charles Babbage, "Difference Engine No. 1" (drawing, 1823).

and used the latest *industrial* technology. The name of the machine refers to the method of differences, which is a technique to make it possible to multiply and divide by using the simpler procedure of addition. The conceptual problems Babbage faced were compounded by the practical difficulties of producing an exceptionally complex precision machine with nineteenth-century technology. Though he created a model in 1822 and eventually built part of the machine, he never completed it. One of the reasons for this failure was that he became distracted by a vision for an even more sophisticated calculating machine called the Analytic Engine. Babbage designed the Analytic Engine to do considerably more complex calculations. "The Analytic Engine," he explains, "consists of two parts."

1. The store in which all the variables to be operated upon as well as all those quantities which have arisen from the result of other operations, are placed.
2. The mill into which the qualities about to be operated upon are always brought.[10]

These two components correspond to the architecture of today's electronic computers: the store is the memory and the mill is the functional equivalent of the central processing unit (CPU).

Applying Smith's account of the market as self-regulating to machine design, Babbage planned the Analytic Engine to be self-correcting. In attempting to explain his vision, he invoked an ancient mythological symbol for infinity: the machine, he suggests, operates by "eating its own tail." Babbage envisioned feedback loops that would allow both the Difference Engines and Analytic Engine to bend back on themselves to correct mistakes before they were fed into later calculations and cascaded through the tables. The other prescient feature of the Analytic Machine was the use of punch cards to run it. Babbage borrowed this idea from the Jacquard loom, which had been invented in 1802 and by the 1820s was widely used in the British textile industry. He realized that in addition to affording a way to program calculations, punch cards also provided extended memory for the machine. The greater technical sophistication of the Analytic Machine expanded its calculating capacity beyond simple arithmetic functions. Babbage insisted that his new invention would give one "the entire control over the *combinations* of algebraic symbols."[11] One of the first to recognize the extraordinary implications of Babbage's machine was his sometime collaborator and the daughter of the poet Byron, Ada Lovelace. "Many persons," she writes, imagine that because the business of the Engine is to give its results in *numerical notation* the *nature of its processes* must consequently be *arithmetical* and *numerical,* rather than *algebraical* and *analytical.* This is an error. The engine can arrange and combine its numerical quantities exactly as if they were *letters* or any other general *symbols;* and in fact it might bring out its results in *algebraic* notation, were provisions made accordingly.[12]

Ada's mother, Lady Byron, went so far as to dub the Analytic Engine a "thinking machine." By designing a machine that could store algebraic symbols and operate on them through rules or algorithms, Babbage created what is, in effect, an all-purpose digital computer.

Babbage's inventions had no impact for almost a century. In the 1930s Alan Turing returned to the idea of a universal computational machine, and in 1945 John von Neumann developed the "von Neumann architecture," which provides the blueprint for most subsequent computers. What made the computer revolution possible was von Neumann's recognition of the importance of the same principle Babbage used to separation of data processing and memory functions. As we saw in chapter 1, von Neumann's contributions were not limited to computer technology. His 1944 book, *Theory of Games and Economic Behavior,* coauthored with Oskar Morgenstern, has had a significant impact on subsequent economic theory. Von Neumann interpreted economic systems as rule-governed games, which can be mathematically modeled. The players in these games are regarded as rational agents who assess alternative outcomes, calculate different means to achieve the preferred end, and freely choose the best action for the intended result. No less important for postwar economic theory was von Neumann's 1948 paper "The General and Logical Theory of Automata" in which he argues that with adequate organizational principles, unreliable components can be structured to form a reliable automaton with the capacity for self-replication. For von Neumann, as for Babbage, dumb parts can produce smart results. With the exponential growth in computing power during the latter half of the twentieth century, von Neumann's notion of automata has been used to model markets made up of autonomous agents whose unintentional interactions generate quantifiable behavioral patterns that, many argue, have predictive capabilities. As a result of his participation in the Macy conferences, many of von Neumann's most influential ideas were filtered through information theory and cybernetics. By the middle decades of the twentieth century, economists were beginning to argue that markets are actually information processing machines whose operational principles can be expressed in mathematical formulas and models.

We have discovered that during the 1950s and 1960s, game theory and cybernetics also shaped theoretical developments in the arts, humanities, and social sciences. The notion of rule-governed behavior at work in games was particularly appealing to structuralists who were looking for new interpretive models. According to theorists working in areas as different as literature, art, anthropology, and psychoanalysis, language was the privileged game. Structuralists, who read Saussure's linguistic theory through von Neumann's game theory, information theory, and cybernetic models of self-regulating mechanisms, concluded that language is, in effect, a difference machine. Just as Bateson had insisted that information is a "difference that makes a difference," so structuralists, following Saussure, maintain that "in languages there are only differences." Language, in other words, is a differential structure in which meaning emerges in and through a *network of differences.* The meta-structure, i.e., structure of structure, which constitutes the identity of differences and difference of identities, is binary opposition. Accordingly, each linguistic element assumes its specificity through its difference from other elements. Since structuralists are more interested in synchronic patterns than in diachronic development, they tend to bracket the historical development of the systems they consider. The structures underlying natural, social, and cultural processes, they believe, are closed and intrinsically stable. For structuralists, change and disruption always occur exogenously and are only temporary. While binary oppositions inevitably entail tensions, they nonetheless tend toward equilibrium and therefore create a certain stability.

When understood in this way, the systems structuralists identify bear marked similarities to the equilibrium models of classical economic theory. In an article entitled "A Model of General Economic Equilibrium," published in 1937, von Neumann examines the importance of the principle of equilibrium for economic theory.[13] The definitive statement of equilibrium theory during the postwar period was developed by Kenneth Arrow and Gerard Debreu.[14] It is not too much to say that the principle of equilibrium is the hinge upon which the scientific status of modern economics swings. According to Edmund Phelps, "it is no accident that the formal introduction of the concept into economics is associated with those very writers whose names are closely connected with the foundation of 'economic science.' It could even be argued that its introduction marks the foundation of the discipline itself."[15] Indeed, many economists, suffering an incurable case of physics envy, insist on trying to translate economic

relations into descriptive and predictive mathematical formulas. The notion of equilibrium was first introduced into economic theory by James
Steuart in 1769. From the eighteenth century until the present day, the
privileged science for economists has been physics. Steuart's use of equilibrium reflected the universe Newton described in his *Principia* (1687).
Nearly a century later, Adam Smith used the principle of equilibrium op-
erative in Newtonian mechanics to define the operation of the invisible
hand. "The natural price," he argues, "is, as it were, the central price, to
which the prices of all commodities are continually gravitating. Different
accidents may sometimes keep them suspended a good deal above it, and
sometimes force them down even somewhat below it. But whatever may
be the obstacles, which hinder them from settling in this center of repose
and continuance, they are constantly tending toward it."[16] It is important
to note that Smith does not claim that the economy operates at "this center of repose" but that it *tends* toward it. The realization of perfect equilibrium would actually bring an end to economic exchange. What allows
an equilibrium system to function is the disequilibrium or the *difference*
among forces—in the case of economics, these forces are called interests.
When the economy is understood in terms of the principle of equilibrium,
it is, in effect, a difference engine. We have already discovered that Smith's
notion of the invisible hand represents an economic version of divine
providence. Just as traditional Calvinist theology distinguishes general and
special providence, so Smith draws a distinction between the *general* tendency toward equilibrium and *special* cases of equilibrium. The overall
framework Smith established continues to set the terms for much analysis
today.

The modern version of equilibrium theory begins with the work of
the French economist Leon Walras's *Eléments d'economie politique pure,*
published in 1874 but not translated until 1954. Walras extended the account of dynamic forces in physical systems that Louis Poinsot developed
in *Eléments de statique* (1803) to formulate his analysis of economic equilibrium.[17] One of the most important contributions Walras made to the
discipline of economics was to develop a mathematical theory for equilibrium. According to Walras, competitive markets are governed by the differential forces of supply and demand, which inevitably tend toward equilibrium. Even its staunchest supporters admit that the general-equilibrium
theory is, like Newton's frictionless universe, idealized and therefore remains in important ways counterfactual. Noting the obvious shortcom-
ing of this perspective, Shubik points out that the model is static, timeless,
and inadequate for nonsymmetric information conditions.[18] In spite of

these obvious limitations, the general-equilibrium model remained largely unquestioned until the 1990s. In the years after World War II, mathematics became even more important for economists. Indeed, many economists seem to believe that if you cannot quantify something and express it in a mathematical equation, it is not real. The reliance on sophisticated mathematics led to a split between academic economists and financial analysts and traders: economists tended not to take markets and trading practices seriously and people involved in the markets regarded the theories and formulas of economists as misguided and thus irrelevant. However, this situation began to change in the 1950s and 1960s, when the new field of financial economics emerged. By the 1980s, the line dividing theory and practice had eroded considerably: analysts and traders were making investments on the basis of abstract mathematical formulas and models devised by the so-called "quants." Both the models and the ability to use them in trading were made possible by spread network technology as well as the exponential growth in the speed and data processing capacity of computers. Though it was not immediately evident to either the people involved in the markets for new financial products or many financial economists, these developments implied a fundamental shift in the understanding of models and how they work. As Jean-Pierre Dupuy points out in his discussion of von Neumann's neural networks:

> The model, which before had been hierarchically subordinated to a reality that it managed only to mimic, stood now as the equal of its referent. Consider the problem of trying to model a natural object whose complexity exceeds the critical threshold posited by von Neumann. The model, if it is to be faithful to what it represents, must also exceed this threshold. But then it will be not only a model of its object but also a model of itself, or rather of its own behavior.[19]

The model, in other words, creates the reality it also represents. When the model is equal to the referent, the real once again seems to disappear by being absorbed in the sign that is supposed to represent it.

As long as there have been markets, people have dreamed of developing models to guide investment. By the 1980s and 1990s, the volatility created by years of deregulation and the emergence of network technologies had created an urgent need for models that could lend a semblance of order to markets that often seemed chaotic. As we have seen, the necessity to manage risk led to the creation of new financial instruments that were extremely complicated. The networking of global markets created different trading conditions that in turn required new models and strategies. The theories and models that emerged between the 1950s and the 1970s, however, created as many problems as they seemed to solve. Far from the referent disappearing, the conflict between models and reality brought the global economy to the brink of collapse.

RANDOM WALKS) On March 29, 1900, Louis Bachelier presented his doctoral dissertation, "The Theory of Speculation," to his advisor, the famous French mathematician and physicist Henri Poincaré. Poincaré had created algebraic topology and, with Einstein and Hendrik Lorentz, had codiscovered the theory of relativity. The professor was expecting a dissertation on physics but Bachelier presented him with a study of the Paris bourse. Though Poincaré rejected the thesis and his student never achieved recognition during his lifetime, Bachelier's remarkable work transformed economic theory and financial practice during the latter half of the twentieth century. In 1964, Paul Cootner translated the work and published it as the lead essay in a collection of articles by prominent economists entitled *The Random Character of Stock Market Prices*. Bachelier discovered Brownian motion in the movement of stock prices and concluded that statistical methods could be used to determine the probability of market movements. Several decades later, Norbert Wiener formulated a mathematical theory for the phenomenon Bachelier identified. Bachelier's discovery pointed to unexpected similarities between the physical and economic worlds.

The first recorded observation of Brownian motion appeared in Robert Brown's article "A Brief Account of Microscopial Observations Made in the Months of June, July and August 1827, on the Particles Contained in the Pollen of Plants." Brown discovered that particles of pollen moved *independently and randomly*. The same phenomenon was later detected in microscopic particles suspended in liquids or gases. Investigators exploring this phenomenon formulated a heat equation showing that the motion of the molecules and particles increases with the rise in temperature. This notion of Brownian motion proved to be pivotal for the development of thermodynamics as well as information theory. In the 1870s, James Clerk Maxwell made a significant departure from the principles of classical physics when he applied statistical methods and probability to physical phenomena. Maxwell's innovation, according to Ilya Prigogine and Isabelle Stengers, "was to introduce probability in physics not as a means of approximation but rather as an explanatory principle, to use it to show that a system could display a new type of behavior to which the laws of probability could be applied."[20] This was the first time that a law of nature was cast probabilistically rather than deterministically. Ludwig Boltzmann extended Maxwell's analysis by arguing that heat is the function of the movement of the atoms and molecules comprising matter. Temperature, Boltzmann maintained, results from molecules' *average* rate of movement. While it is impossible to determine the temperature (i.e., the macrostate) precisely from the activity of any individual molecule (i.e., the microstate), temperature is a statistical phenomenon and as such is subject to probability. In his investigation of heat and temperature, Boltzmann's primary concern was to determine the mechanisms by which molecules move toward a state of equilibrium and systems thus become entropic. Using Maxwell's statistical methods, he argued that while the precise activity of individual particles cannot be ascertained, the overall trajectory of a population of molecules can be determined.[21]

Though Bachelier did not draw a direct analogy between the principles of thermodynamics and markets, his argument rests on an analogy between the two phenomena: as the random movement of molecules is to the overall trajectory of the molecular population, so individual stock prices are to the overall trajectory of the market. Inasmuch as activity at the micro level is random, movement at the macro level is probabilistic. In the introduction to his essay, Bachelier writes:

> The calculus of probabilities, doubtless, could never be applied to the fluctuations in securities quotations, and the dynamics of the Exchange will never be an exact science.
>
> But it is possible to study mathematically the static state of the market at a given instant, i.e., to establish the law of probability of price changes consistent with the market at that instant. If the market, in effect, does not predict its fluctuations, it does assess them as being more or less likely, and this likelihood can be evaluated mathematically.[22]

It is essential to understand that *random events are not arbitrary and therefore are not completely uncertain.* The whole point of financial economics is to devise ways to manage risk by reducing uncertainty to probability. In a move that proved decisive for later economic theory, Bachelier based his analysis of markets on games of chance like dice and roulette. This decision entailed two critical assumptions: first, individual gamblers and investors act independently of each other; and second, each bet or investment is independent of previous bets. The roll of the dice in the past does not influence outcomes in the future. Bachelier argues: "It seems that the market, the *aggregate* of speculators, at a given instant can believe in neither a market rise nor a market fall, since for each quoted price, there are as many buyers as sellers."[23] Just as the chance of heads or tails is always 50-50 regardless of previous results, so the likelihood of a stock going up or down is independent of previous performance. Because the market, like dice, has no memory, statistical analysis can be used to establish the probability of its movement at any given point in time. According to Bachelier, this calculation gives the gambler or investor a "mathematical advantage."

> The mathematical expectation shows whether a bet is advantageous or not; moreover, it tells what the bet logically must win or lose, but it does not give a coefficient in some manner representing the intrinsic value of the bet.
>
> This leads us to introduce a new concept, that of mathematical advantage.
>
> We shall call the "mathematical advantage" of a gambler that ratio of his positive expectations to the arithmetic sum of his positive and negative expectations.
>
> Mathematical advantage, like a probability, varies between zero and one. It is equal to 0.5 when the game is a fair game.
>
> *Principle of Mathematical Expectation.* The spot buyer may be compared with a gambler. In effect, the price of a security might increase after its purchase, a decrease is equally possible.[24]

When the odds can be calculated, the game for high-stakes players shifts from Las Vegas to Wall Street.

In 1958, M. F. M. Osborne delivered a paper entitled "Brownian Motion in the Stock Market" before the U.S. Naval Research Laboratory Solid State Seminar. The purpose of this paper, he explained, is "to show that the logarithms of common-stock prices can be regarded as an ensemble of decisions in a statistically steady state, and that this ensemble of logarithms of prices, each varying with the time, has a close analogy with the ensemble of coordinates of a large number of molecules. We wish to show that the methods of statistical mechanics, normally applied to the latter problem, may also be applied to the former."[25] Though he was unaware of it at the time, Osborne extends Bachelier's insights to develop what became known as the popular random walk theory of financial markets. A central tenet in the random walk interpretation of markets is the central limit theorem, according to which price changes follow a normal or Gaussian distribution (after German mathematician C. F. Gauss). Normal distribution, which is represented by what is called the bell curve, "is symmetrical about the mean, and the standard deviation measures the width of the central hump. Beyond this hump, on either side, the curve flattens out and soon becomes close to zero."[26] Since random events yield a bell curve or normal distribution, their *probability* can be accurately ascertained. This does not, of course, mean that individual events can be precisely predicted; but long-term trends or patterns can be anticipated. Short-term (e.g., daily) stock prices, by contrast, are not normal but are "fat-tailed." In other words, the probabilities of extreme high and extreme low values are higher than in normal distribution. Short-term changes do not occur over a long enough time period for the central limit theorem to apply; longer-term changes (e.g., over a year), by contrast, are more likely to be closer to normal distribution.

In his suggestive book *Fractals and Scaling in Finance: Discontinuity, Concentration, Risk,* Benoit Mandelbrot summarizes the principles that, according to Bachelier and Osborne, form the foundation of all statistical approaches to economics and finance. (Though Mandelbrot is best known for his discovery of fractals, his early work was in economics; he discovered fractals not only in natural phenomena and systems but also in economic activity.)

> *Independence of price increments.* Knowing the past brings no knowledge about the future.
>
> *Continuity of price variation.* A sample of Brownian motion is a continuous curve, even though it has no derivative anywhere. (A technicality deserves to be mentioned here at once: the above properties only hold almost surely and almost everywhere.)
>
> *Rough evenness of price changes.* . . . A record of Wiener Brownian price changes, over equal time increments . . . , is a sequence of independent Gaussian variables. . . .The eye sees it as a kind of evenly spread "grass" that sticks out nowhere.
>
> *Absence of clustering in time location of the large changes.*
> *Absence of cyclic behavior.*[27]

When all of these principles are taken together, they form the basis of what comes to be known as the efficient market hypothesis (EMH). Mandelbrot proceeds to give a concise definition of an efficient market, which, he argues, Bachelier anticipated: "A competitive market of securities, commodities or bonds may be considered efficient if every price already reflects all the relevant information that is available. The arrival of new information causes imperfections, but it is assumed that every such imperfection is promptly arbitraged away"[28] (I discuss arbitrage below). The key to the EMH is information and the speed of its dissemination. If stock valuations accurately reflect all available information at all times, price changes are unpredictable because they can be caused only by new and unexpected information. Change, in other words, is exogenous rather than endogenous. By way of anticipation, it is important to note that even when the market reacts very quickly to new information, it is impossible to completely eliminate all delay in absorbing information. Not even the newest communication technologies make information available infinitely fast, and therefore some people inevitably receive it later than others.

Eugene Fama coined the term "efficient market" in his 1965 article "Random Walks in Stock Market Prices." As the theory develops, it assumes three basic versions, which have different implications. In its weak form, the EMH

> asserts that prices fully reflect the information contained in the historical sequence of prices. Thus, investors cannot devise an investment strategy to yield abnormal profits on the basis of an analysis of past price patterns. . . . It is this form of efficiency that is associated with the term "Random Walk Hypothesis."
>
> The semi-strong form of EMH asserts that current prices reflect not only historical price information but also all publicly available information relevant to securities. If markets are efficient in this sense, then analysis of balance sheets, income statements, announcements or any other public information about a company . . . will not yield abnormal economic profits.
>
> The strong form of EMH asserts that all information that is *known* to any market participant about a company is fully reflected in market prices. Hence, not even those with privileged information can make use of it to secure superior investment results.[29]

From the 1960s through the late 1990s, the weak form of the EMH was widely accepted in most of the financial community. If prices immediately reflect all available information, future developments are discounted in the current prices of stocks. As a result of the speed with which information is disseminated, the market "knows" more than any individual at any given time. The market, in other words, has something like a mind of its own, which emerges from but is not reducible to the individuals who comprise it. Furthermore, the market is believed to incorporate all the information available at the moment and thus to be effectively omniscient. When understood in this way, the mind of the market appears to be the functional equivalent of the mind of God, whose all-knowing invisible hand creates and maintains order in what otherwise would be a chaotic universe.

Several additional assumptions informing the efficient market hypothesis are important but prove questionable. First, investors are assumed to be rational. In this context, *rational* conduct is defined as the effort to maximize expected returns for a given level of risk. Second, agents or investors are *homogeneous.* They all have access to the same information, which they interpret in the same way to make investments within the same time horizon. In addition to this, proponents of the EMH accept Bachelier's assumption that homogeneous investors act independently of each other. Economic agents, in other words, are like billiard balls or molecules that brush against and bump into each other but do not really interact. The information upon which investors base their decisions is, of course, often generated and transmitted by financial institutions and other news sources. Individual decisions, however, remain independent of each other. This understanding of the actions of individual investors implies that sequential moments of decision are also isolated from each other. Just as agents acting at a given moment are independent of each other, so the moments in a time series are discrete and independent. Markets, like dice, have neither memory nor history and thus cannot develop either upward or downward momentum.

It is, however, undeniable that markets are not always efficient. Indeed, markets can work only if there are inefficiencies. Inefficiencies are manifested in "mispriced" securities, which, for believers in the EMH, result from the inadequate distribution or availability of information. According to this model, efficient markets function something like difference engines, which, while tending toward equilibrium, create opportunities to make money on temporarily mispriced securities. Arbitrage, i.e., the practice of purchasing commodities or securities on one market for immediate resale on another market in order to profit from price discrepancies or differentials, is, of course, as old as markets themselves. What distinguishes arbitrage in financial markets since the late 1960s is the way in which complex mathematical formulas and models are used in structured finance and financial engineering to hedge bets by distributing risk. These trading strategies rely on the theory of *one price,* according to which accurate information results in securities in different markets trading at the same price. Just as systems that tend toward equilibrium eventually approach entropy, so markets whose efficiency increases approach a point where arbitrage becomes impossible. In other words, the more efficient the market, the shorter the period of time for arbitrage opportunities. For the arbitrageur, time is truly money: in arbitrage, money is made in the temporal gaps created by the delay in the equal distribution of relevant information, which results in one price. Inasmuch as different prices tend to converge, the EMH can be understood as a subset of general-equilibrium theory. It should be clear that the increased access to information and speed of its dissemination theoretically make markets more efficient by decreasing the spread in prices. Furthermore, the more efficient the market, the more difficult it is to make money. With computers and network technology distributing more information faster and faster, only the quick survive.

As these remarks suggest, the EMH has significant implications for investment strategies. Robert Shiller, whose influential *Irrational Exuberance* raises questions about the rationality of markets, explains:

> At its root, the efficient markets theory holds that differing abilities do not produce differing investment performance. The theory claims that the smartest people will not be able to do better than the least intelligent people in terms of investment performance. They can do no better because their superior understanding is already incorporated into share prices.
>
> If we accept the premise of efficient markets, not only is being smart no advantage, but it also follows immediately that being *not so smart* is not a *disadvantage* either. If not-so-smart people could lose money systematically in their trades, then this would suggest a profit opportunity for smart money: just do the opposite of what the not-so-smart money does. Yet according to the efficient markets theory, there can be no such profit opportunity for the smart money.[30]

Needless to say, this conclusion is not good news for stock analysts and brokers who claim to be smart and make their living selling information that is supposed to enable investors to outperform markets. Many analysts and traders reject the claim that the market is a random walk and insist that information properly interpreted can give investors an edge. The two most important versions of this position are fundamental analysis and technical analysis. Fundamentalists believe that it is possible to identify mispriced securities by analyzing earnings, dividend prospects, interest rates, and the competitive position of businesses. This information is supposed to determine the "intrinsic value" of the company, which serves as a measure by which to judge whether the stock is over- or underpriced. Technical analysts, who are sometimes also called chartists, are uninterested in corporate reports and balance sheets and concentrate on detecting patterns in past security prices. The most important variable to consider, they argue, is the activity of large institutional investors, who have important information about companies and economic trends. Chartists are convinced that accurate plotting of past price performances can uncover clues for the future direction of markets. However, if markets do not consistently exhibit such detectable trajectories, what is the best investment strategy?

In 1952, Harry Markowitz, a twenty-five-year-old graduate student at the University of Chicago, published a seminal paper entitled "Portfolio Selection." He eventually expanded the paper first into his doctoral dissertation and then into a book, *Portfolio Selection: Efficient Diversification of Investments* (1959). The notion of investment portfolios has become so popular that it is difficult to realize how revolutionary the idea was in the 1950s. Markowitz changed the way investors large and small think about markets and, by so doing, set the course of much financial economics for the next several decades. In 1990, he received the Nobel Prize in Economics. Though his conclusions were straightforward, his analyses were very complicated and highly mathematical. While a student at the University of Chicago, Markowitz had been a research associate at the Cowles Commission for Research in Economics. The director of the commission at the time was Tjalling Koopmans, who, like many so-called "quants," had been trained as a theoretical physicist. Koopmans is best known for work on the analytic method of computing known as linear programming. Linear programming, as Peter Bernstein points out, identifies combinations of inputs and outputs that maximize outputs for a given level of inputs and "then identifies the trade-offs required if one element is increased relative to the others."[31] While Markowitz's calculations would eventually require quadratic programming, his work at the Cowles Commission persuaded him of the importance of the new computational methods for creating alternative approaches to investing.

Though Markowitz developed his ideas more than two decades before the extraordinary market volatility created by political decisions, Federal Reserve policies, and global turbulence in the 1970s, he was already keenly aware of the importance of risk in investment strategies. His most important innovation was to shift from calculating risk in terms of individual stocks to assessing the risk of a portfolio made up of different stocks.

Rather than making investment decisions solely by referring to the fundamentals of a particular company or the actual performance of its stock in the past, Markowitz seeks to determine the *relative* volatility and hence risk of different securities in the portfolio. The efficiency of the portfolio is a function of the *differences* in the performances of its stocks. To achieve what came to be known as "Markowitz diversification," different stocks must move in different directions or stocks moving in the same direction must move by different percentage amounts. Markowitz, like many others at the time, used the standard deviation of stock price returns to calculate risk. It is possible to hedge risk, he argues, by buying and holding a diversified portfolio of securities. According to Markowitz, "the riskiness of a portfolio depends on the *covariance* of its holdings, not on the average riskiness of the separate investments."[32] By purchasing different kinds of stocks, one increases the chance that losses will be offset by gains. Obviously, this strategy also entails the possibility that big gains will be offset by losses. The central question for investors is how much risk they are willing to bear and how much they are willing to pay to hedge risk. For Markowitz, the differences and diversity of a portfolio create a certain stability, while similarities or the homogeneity of holdings breeds instability. A portfolio in which high volatility and low volatility balance each other is *efficient.* It is important to realize that a diversified portfolio of high-risk securities can actually be low-risk if it is hedged properly. In matters of risk, the whole is sometimes *less* than the sum of the parts. By proposing a new way to calculate risk, Markowitz attempts to give investors the basis upon which to choose either high or low risk.

At the time Markowitz formulated his theory, the use of computers had not spread much beyond the military and universities. It was therefore difficult if not impossible to do the calculations necessary to determine the covariance of risk in a variety of securities. One of Markowitz's students, William Sharpe, developed a simplified method for determining risk. Sharpe argued that it is not necessary to establish the covariance of the risk of countless individual securities because stocks tend to move with the market. The volatility and hence risk of a security can be ascertained by correlating it with the movement of a market portfolio. Theoretically, the market portfolio is supposed to include all assets, even real estate and human capital, but in practice stock market indexes are used. Sharpe named his theory the Capital Asset Pricing Model (CAPM). By removing the necessity to do many complex calculations to determine the efficiency of a basket of securities, the CAPM made it much easier for investors to use portfolio theory. With this simplification, it did not take long for Markowitz's strategy of buying and holding to become the mantra of both Wall Street and Main Street.

As we have seen, by the 1970s and 1980s the increasing volatility of markets made the need to find ways to manage risk much more urgent. The proliferation of financial instruments provided new investment opportunities but also created the necessity for new models for financial markets. In a world of options, futures, swaps, and repos, it was no longer enough to hedge risk by balancing the volatility of different stocks and bonds. For theory as well as practice, the problem became figuring out how to establish the value of all the new financial products. Faced with this daunting challenge, work done by three young economists at MIT and the University of Chicago during the late 1960s and early 1970s proved to be critically important.

In the spring of 1973, Fischer Black and Myron Scholes published "The Pricing of Options and Corporate Liabilities," in which they developed a mathematical formula for determining the fair-market value of call options. Nicholas Dunbar goes so far as to claim that what Black and Scholes discovered was nothing less than "the formula that changed the world."[33] While this claim is hyperbolic, there is no doubt that the Black-Scholes option theory marked a seismic event in financial economics whose reverberations are still being felt. The third participant in the discussions, which led to the revolutionary formula for pricing options, was Robert Merton, who was then writing his dissertation under Paul Samuelson at MIT. Shortly after the Black-Scholes paper appeared, Merton published "Theory of Rational Option Pricing." In 1997, Scholes and Merton were awarded the Nobel Prize for their discovery of "a new method to determine the value of derivatives" (Fischer Black had died by this time, and the Nobel is never awarded posthumously). The accomplishment of Black, Scholes, and Merton was all the more remarkable when one considers that in the 1960s options were a rarely used financial product.

While the Black-Scholes paper had little immediate impact, its timing was propitious. On April 23, 1973, a few weeks before the paper was published, the Chicago Board Options Exchange opened. Though the distance between *The Wealth of Nations* and the Black-Scholes options pricing theory is considerable, the underlying assumptions of economic thinking remain remarkably consistent over the intervening years. "The notion of equilibrium in the markets for risky assets," Black confesses, "had great beauty for me. It implies that riskier securities must have higher than expected returns, or investors will not hold them."[34] To calculate the appropriate balance between risk and return, it is of course necessary to know the value of different assets. In the case of derivatives, value can be determined only in relation to the underlying assets on which they are based. To assess the price of options, Black and Scholes used the latest version of stochastic calculus, which, as we have seen, originally had been introduced into economic theory by Bachelier. While the effort to price options can be traced to Charles Castelli's 1877 book, *The Theory of Options in Stocks and Shares,* little progress on this problem was made until the principles of statistical analysis were formulated. In his early efforts to work out a model for stock warrants, Black discovered that the formula for the variation of the price of the warrant in relation to time and stock prices was remarkably similar to a widely acknowledged heat-transfer equation.[35] When Black and Scholes teamed up, they quickly decided that the best way to approach the problem was to extend Sharpe's CAPM to options. The key factor in pricing options, they concluded, is the volatility of the underlying asset: the more volatile the asset, the more valuable the option. Therefore, if you know the volatility of the market, you should be able to calculate the value of the option. In order to make the formula work, however, Black and Scholes made several important assumptions, several of which are counterfactual:

1. Stocks pay no dividends during the life of the option.
2. Markets are efficient.
3. No commissions are charged.
4. Interest rates remain constant and are known.[36]
5. The percentage rate of change is normally distributed and the level of the asset price at the expiration of the option is lognormally distributed.

Though all of these assumptions are problematic, the final point turns out to be particularly troubling. Not only is the insistence on the normal distribution of returns an idealization of actual results but, more important, it is impossible to know in advance the volatility of the market. In an effort to overcome this limitation, most proponents of the Black and Scholes formula use the volatility of the underlying asset over some time just before the date for which the option price is being estimated. Needless to say, this does not solve the problem. As our analysis unfolds, it will become clear that the Black-Scholes formula is designed for a frictionless universe that bears little relation to the "real" world to which it was so enthusiastically applied.

By the time Merton turned his attention to this problem, many people realized that it was not necessary to use the CAPM in pricing options. Instead of simply calculating risk by pricing options in relation to volatility, Merton argued, in a manner reminiscent of Markowitz, it is possible to hedge risk by replicating the portfolio. Merton's theory assumes a hypothetical portfolio that replicates a call option. This strategy is much more complicated than simply purchasing stock. The portfolio involves selling short something like a Treasury bill and also buying some of the stock, but not necessarily one share of the stock for each option. How much stock one buys for the replicating portfolio depends on how one assesses the volatility of the underlying asset, which, of course, cannot be known with certainty. While the replicating portfolio can eliminate risk in theory, risk can never be completely eliminated in practice. This hedge does not have to involve a major capital expenditure because the asset serving as the counterbet can be purchased with borrowed money or the stock can be shorted. The aim of this strategy is to balance investments in a way that makes the portfolio as risk-free as possible.

When taken together, the Black-Scholes options pricing formula and Merton's method of portfolio replication create the possibility of using various securities and derivatives in arbitrage trades to hedge risk. Here, as elsewhere, arbitrage involves the interplay of difference and unity in markets that are difference machines tending toward equilibrium. Trading presupposes the law of one price according to which market inefficiencies are overcome as the dissemination of information, which creates price convergence.

An arbitrage opportunity arises when an investor can construct a *zero investment portfolio* that will yield a *sure* profit. . . . A zero investment portfolio means that the investor need not use any of his or her own money. Obviously, to be able to construct a zero investment portfolio one has to be able to sell short at least one asset and use the proceeds to purchase (go long on) one or more assets. . . . Even a small investor using short positions can take a large dollar position in such a portfolio.

An obvious case of an arbitrage opportunity arises when the law of one price is violated. . . . When an asset is trading at different prices in two markets (and the price differential exceeds transaction costs), a simultaneous trade in two markets can produce a sure profit (the net price differential) without any investment. One simply sells short the asset in the high-priced market and buys it in the low-priced market. The net

proceeds are positive, and there is no risk because the long and short positions offset each other.

A zero-investment portfolio is "established by buying and shorting component securities, usually in the context of an arbitrage strategy." When
shorting a stock, the shares are "not owned by the investor but borrowed
through a broker and later repurchased to replace the loan. Profit is earned
if the initial sale price is at a higher price than the repurchase price."[37] For
most traders and investors, the calculations required for such transactions
were prohibitively complex. The increasing sophistication of financial instruments and complexity of investment strategies created a widening gap
between average investors and traders and professionals who often were
trained in physics or computer science rather than economics or business.

Before proceeding to a consideration of the impact of these developments in financial economics on markets during the 1980s and 1990s, it is
important to pause to consider the implications of these new trading
strategies and their relation to other trajectories we have been following.
As we saw in chapter 5, throughout the 1980s and 1990s, new financial
products made possible by computers and networks vastly increased the
opportunity for leverage and thereby created a collateral crisis. More and
more money was being borrowed on the same collateral base. In addition
to this, the nature of collateral changed in ways that allowed investors to
use securities and derivatives as collateral for additional loans, which in
turn were used for yet further investments. This led to faster growth in the
financial sector than in the real economy and therefore to a shrinkage of
the latter *relative to the former.* The result of these developments was an inverted pyramiding process in which the foundation of financial markets
was virtually disappearing. At the same time, similar developments were
unfolding in the arts, philosophy, and critical theory. In postmodern art
and architecture, signs are not representational but are recycled in an ever-
expanding play of signifiers that has no end other than itself. The meaning and value of these circulating signs are not determined by their relation to independent referents but are a function of their differential
interrelations. For critical theorists, the world of the late twentieth century
was a culture of simulacra in which it is virtually impossible to distinguish
the real from the fake. Risk arbitrage takes these tendencies to another
level. With hedging portfolios and replicating portfolios in options pricing
theory, as well as strategies of borrowing and shorting stocks and derivatives, investments became more and more abstract until they appear to

have little to do with actual companies and processes in the productive economy. As the signs of finance proliferated, quants became invisible gods who seemed to allow traders to realize the ancient dream of creation out of nothing.

The deregulation of interest rates as well as the deregulation and privatization of banking and finance both nationally and internationally during the 1980s created unprecedented arbitrage opportunities. No one realized the far-reaching implications of these developments more quickly than John Meriweather. Meriweather and his legendary team of bond traders at Salomon Brothers served as the inspiration for Tom Wolfe's memorable *Bonfire of the Vanities* and were the subject of Michael Lewis's engaging best seller *Liar's Poker*. Meriweather's career was inadvertently launched by the Fed's 1979 decision to regulate the money supply and let the market determine interest rates. Before the late 1970s, the bond market, as we have seen, provided a relatively safe haven from the turbulence of other financial markets. Traditional investors tended to purchase bonds with fixed rates of return and hold them until maturity. Long before Markowitz developed his portfolio theory, bond investors followed a buy-and-hold strategy. Bond traders, however, were not interested in buying Treasuries and holding them until they matured; rather, they sought ways to make money by buying and selling bonds frequently between the time they were issued and their date of maturity. When Volcker decided to let interest rates float, previously stable bond markets turned volatile. In addition, the U.S. Treasury issued a broad range of bonds with different rates and maturities. Moreover, the securitization of debt with Mortgage Backed Securities created through Ginnie Mae and Fannie Mae provided additional investment opportunities. In the late 1970s and early 1980s, the bond market was becoming increasingly diversified and volatile. Where there are volatility and diversity, the arbitrageur smells the opportunity for profit. To appreciate what Meriweather did, it is necessary to recall how bond prices work. While bonds are fixed-income securities, with a preestablished rate of return at maturity, both their price and yield can move up or down between purchase and maturity. Though these fluctuations depend on a variety of factors, the relation between stock markets and bond markets is especially important. Sometimes the prices of stocks and bonds move in tandem, while at other times their movements are inversely proportional: as the stock market goes up, the bond market goes down, and vice versa. Furthermore, the prices and yields of bonds tend to be inversely though not necessarily proportionally related: as the price of bonds goes up, their yield goes down, and again vice versa. For Meriweather, these shifting price differentials created chances for profit.

During his early years, Meriweather's simplest trade involved "on-the-run" and "off-the-run" Treasuries. On-the-run Treasuries are newly issued and usually sell at slightly higher prices than older off-the-run Treasuries, which investors had bought earlier and continue to hold. These price differences are small and disappear quickly, but Meriweather realized that they created possibilities for arbitrage. Following yield curves and thus bond prices closely, his traders would look for the chance to make a profit on price differences. Because the spreads were small and lasted only briefly, they needed to make big bets quickly to realize relatively modest profits. The size of these wagers and the volatility of markets increased risks. Meriweather, however, had learned the lessons of the financial economists we have been considering and put their theories into practice with elaborate hedging strategies. Having realized that profits could be erased by fluctuations in the yield curve, he concluded that "the only way to escape this pitfall would be to buy or sell the mispriced bond, and at the same time take the exact opposite position on another bond sitting very close to it on the yield curve. For example, sell the on-the-run Treasury and buy an equal quantity of off-the-runs. By doing this, you could immunize yourself from the great wave of the yield curve."[38]

As new financial instruments began to emerge, Meriweather's hedging strategies became more complex. The deal that effectively transformed Wall Street occurred in September 1979.[39] As we have seen, by the late 1970s, years of inflation had considerably eroded financial assets. Growing worries about inflation led to concern about an increase in interest rates. These financial difficulties posed a dilemma for many investment banks. While banks had to underwrite businesses by selling corporate bonds to retain their competitive edge, the prospect of higher interest rates on bonds they had issued but not yet sold posed serious risks. If interest rates increased, the price of bonds would decrease, thereby forcing banks to sell more bonds to cover their underwriting expenses. In addition to this, underwriting sometimes involves an investment bank buying the new securities from the issuer and then reselling the securities in the market. In this case, the fall in prices causes a loss to the underwriter no matter how many bonds are sold. In fact, the more bonds are sold, the greater the loss. While the investment banking division of Salomon Brothers enjoyed a privileged status at the time, Meriweather's deal in the fall of 1979 marked a tectonic shift in the investment world. "In September 1979, while the U.S. was transfixed by the Iranian hostage crisis," Dunbar explains, "IBM issued a large, $1 billion bond through Salomon. Holding the bond as inventory while looking for buyers, the Salomon corporate finance department realized it was essentially making a huge bet that interest rates would not rise. How could it hedge the risk?" Calculating that hedging the corporate bond issue by shorting Treasuries would be too expensive, Meriweather proposed placing a counterbet on T-bill futures. On October 5, 1979, Salomon Brothers traders executed the ingenious plan Meriweather had proposed. The very next day, Volcker shifted direction by attempting to control the money supply and thus allowing interest rates to rise to the level determined by the market. When markets opened on Monday, interest rates immediately rose, thus allowing bond prices to drop 11 percent. In the following days, this pattern continued. All major banks were losing billions of dollars but Meriweather's bet on Treasury futures saved the day for Salomon.

Backed by this success, Meriweather's bond arbitrage desk played an increasingly important role at Salomon Brothers throughout the 1980s. According to Dunbar, "by 1990, the firm's balance sheet swelled above $150 billion . . . in size, most of it in the form of repoed government bonds. Like an inverted pyramid, this balance sheet sat on top of only $4 billion of equity capital—the value of Salomon's shares added together."[40] With trades becoming ever more complex, Meriweather and his team increasingly relied on the mathematical formulas and models developed by Markowitz, Black, Scholes, Merton, Sharpe, Ross, and others. Though Meriweather was astonishingly successful at Salomon Brothers, an investment impropriety of one of the traders under his direction eventually forced him to leave the firm. The SEC banned Meriweather from any involvement in financial markets for three months. By the time of his departure, he not only had changed bond trading forever but had transformed the way Wall Street does much of its business. The end of the Salomon Brothers chapter of his life, however, was the beginning of a new venture that proved even more important for Wall Street and beyond.

No sooner had Meriweather left Salomon Brothers than he began plotting how to reconstitute his trading team in a way that would allow them to operate independently and give him greater control over the operation. In August 1993, Meriweather started pitching a proposal for a new hedge fund to investors. In addition to four people from his Salomon group, the founding partners included Myron Scholes and Robert Merton. They hoped to raise $2.5 billion in start-up capital, which was one hundred times that of the average fund, and set the minimum investment at $10 million.[41] The fund would engage in arbitrage trades but would not be limited by the trading restrictions Salomon Brothers had imposed. In February 1994, Meriweather and his partners launched Long-Term Capital Management (LTCM). From the outset, the plan for LTCM had been to put into practice the mathematical theories financial economists had developed. Their investment strategy rested on an unwavering faith in the efficient market hypothesis. As market inefficiencies are overcome, they insisted, securities converge on one price. In this model, markets are difference engines tending toward equilibrium, which create the opportunity to make money in the delay between difference (in prices) and unity (convergence on one price). LTCM relied on the Black-Scholes formula for pricing options. So understood, the machinations of the market resemble the operation of Hegel's dialectical system. Extending Markowitz's portfolio theory, LTCM not only diversified trades within markets but also diversified their holdings by hedging in different markets. Their use of pairs trading was complicated by multiplying bets across global markets. As always in arbitrage, the trick of the trade is to assemble a portfolio balanced enough to be safe but unbalanced enough to yield a profit.

With new products and trading strategies becoming more popular, financial institutions as well as federal regulators had to find a way to assess the overall exposure to risk. Til Guldiman and Jacques Longerstaey, who were then working at JP Morgan, developed a relatively simple method to determine what they called "value-at-risk" (VAR). Once again, Markowitz's portfolio theory provided the inspiration. Assuming a normal distribution for returns, Guldiman and Longerstaey argued that the overall risk of a portfolio or institution can be calculated by adding the risks of particular investments and multiplying them by the size of the position. With the ethos of deregulation still in the air, in July 1993, the Basel Committee accepted the VAR calculation as a way for banks and financial institutions to regulate themselves.[42] Though this decision was crucial for LTCM's investment strategy, self-regulation eventually proved fatal for many individuals and institutions. The VAR formula created a false sense of security, which led LTCM partners to believe they could significantly increase leverage. As literature promoting the fund explained: "The reduction in the Portfolio Company's volatility through hedging would permit leveraging up of the resulting position to the same expected level of volatility as an unhedged position, but with a larger expected return."[43] LTCM planned to push leverage to levels not seen before or since.

LTCM's carefully devised strategy rested upon six important assumptions, several of which we have already encountered:

1. Markets are efficient and follow the One Price Law.
2. Risk can be quantified and therefore uncertainty eliminated through probabilistic statistical analysis. Volatility follows a Normal distribution . . .
3. Liquidity is always available, i.e. there will always be a buyer when one wishes to sell a security or derivative product.
4. Investors are rational and, in the long run, act in similar ways.
5. Investors act and markets move independently of each other.
6. Prices move in a continuous curve and are not subject to major leaps up or down. Seismic market shifts, sometimes called outliers, are so rare that they can for all practical purposes be disregarded.[44]

During its early years, the fund was enormously successful. In 1994, the partners achieved a 28 percent return and a year later the rate of return had risen to 59 percent. By 1997, the rate of return was 57 percent and profits were $2.1 billion. Even the overconfident partners were surprised when they accumulated an astonishing $134 billion in assets by 1998.[45] This unparalleled success was, however, a two-edged sword: the faster LTCM's profits grew, the more imitators it had, and these competitors made it much more difficult for LTCM's models to work effectively. As more players joined the game, spreads decreased and inefficiencies disappeared much more quickly. In any game of chance, there are basically two ways to turn a profit: make lots of money on a few bets, or make a little money on lots of bets. With fewer and fewer bets returning significant profits, LTCM had to increase the size of its positions. To finance these escalating positions, they increased their leverage. Since derivatives require little capital up front and can remain off-book, LTCM was able to increase its positions without much collateral and could conceal the higher risk of its portfolio from investors and regulators. Lowenstein explains how this scheme worked in one of the relatively simple on-run/off-run bond trades.

> No sooner did Long-Term buy the off-the-run bonds than it loaned them to some other Wall Street firm, which then wired cash to Long-Term as collateral. Then Long-Term turned around and used this cash as collateral on the bonds that *it* had borrowed. On Wall Street, such short-term, collateralized loans were known as "repo financing."

The beauty of the trade was that Long-Term's cash transactions were in perfect balance. The money that Long-Term spent going long (buying) matched the money it collected going short (selling). The collateral it paid equaled the collateral it collected. In other words, Long-Term pulled off the entire $2 billion trade *without using a dime of its own cash.*[46]

When collateral is reduced to nothing, anything remotely resembling a *real* economic base vanishes.

As increasing competition made it more difficult to make money using their original models, LTCM began to move into new areas. Entering equity markets they previously had avoided, they started to make directional bets on stock indexes without carefully hedging their positions. Using options to hedge drops in the market, LTCM's most common investment became the equity volatility trade, i.e., bets on the future volatility of stocks.[47] As we have seen, this strategy assumes that volatility can be accurately described by the standard deviation. Furthermore, diversified securities are supposed to move independently of each other or at significantly different rates. In 1997, LTCM had "$120 billion of borrowed bonds and $1.25 trillion of derivatives. According to partners Scholes and Merton," Dunbar reports, "the interlocking parts were now so perfectly engineered that these devices were virtually capable of perpetual motion. As the technology of risk management continued to improve, the tiny sliver of equity underneath the inverted pyramid would vanish completely. There would be no need for excess cash to lubricate the money machines, and no need for irritating shareholders. . . . At LTCM's zenith, they had a vision of zero capital and infinite leverage."[48] This scheme seems to make Marx's notion of capital as an infinitely productive self-reflexive loop operating like a perpetual motion machine a reality. But just when the money machines seemed to be functioning smoothly and at maximum efficiency, everything suddenly changed. Against all odds, the sequence of events that was never supposed to occur began to unfold in the late summer of 1997 and quickly spread throughout the global economy.

After three years of remarkable success, national and international events conspired to shatter the ideal of efficient markets and end the dream of risk-free arbitrage. In the previous chapter, we have considered the turbulence in markets created by the growing dot-com bubble. While the NYSE and NASDAQ continued to rise, there was increasing uneasiness among investors about a market bubble. On the home front, the burgeoning Monica Lewinsky scandal was creating growing problems for the

Clinton administration. At the same time, international financial markets were threatening to spin out of control. By 1997, the pattern of recurrent world debt crises, which, we have seen, began in Mexico in 1982, extended to Asia.[49] In the early 1990s, Thailand, at the urging of the IMF and World Bank, opened its economy to foreign investors who were eager to take advantage of new markets. However, when worsening economic conditions forced the Thai government to default on its loans in 1997, foreign capital fled as quickly as it had arrived. The Thai bank collapsed and what Thomas Friedman aptly labels "the electronic herd" fell into a full retreat. Fears that contagion would engulf all of Asia led to an IMF bailout of South Korea early in 1998. Aggressive intervention once again seemed to work and markets returned to what appeared to be a semblance of stability.

But while the situation in Asia appeared to be improving, conditions in Russia were rapidly deteriorating. In the years following the collapse of the Soviet Union, Western governments encouraged Russia's transition to private enterprise and capital markets. Though many urged slow and deliberate action, some, fearing a reversion to socialism, argued that the transition should be completed as quickly as possible. The most influential proponent of the latter position was Jeffrey Sachs, whose approach was known as "shock therapy." Sachs had some success in Poland during the late 1980s, but Russia posed special problems. Having labored under Soviet control for most of the century, Russia had neither the legal system nor the industrial and financial infrastructure to support a free market economy. Any hope for a smooth transition to capitalism and rapid improvement in economic conditions was crushed by corrupt politicians and ruthless oligarchs. Nevertheless, the IMF continued to encourage foreign investment in Russia. In 1997, short-term bonds were paying 40 percent annually and the newly opened Russian stock market rose 149 percent. With the prospect of such big returns, many individuals and institutions could not resist the temptation to invest in markets they knew were extremely volatile. The willingness of the IMF to bail out countries during the past two decades provided a sense of security in a situation that was increasingly unstable. When things became critical in July 1997, Secretary of the Treasury Robert Rubin and his deputy, Lawrence Summers, pressured the IMF and other countries to put together a $22.6 billion bailout. This action, however, only delayed the inevitable; much of the money was stolen by the oligarchs and a year later the Russian economy was on the verge of collapse.[50]

Mesmerized by their models, the partners at LTCM were not as pessimistic as many other investors. In fact, they thought people were *overes-*

timating market volatility and thus they sold options to institutions that wanted insurance to protect them from a precipitous drop in share values. If, as LTCM predicted, the market did not plummet, investors would realize their mistake and the price of options would fall. To finance these transactions, LTCM shorted the options. This meant that if, contrary to their expectations, the market actually dropped, they would have to close their option contracts. The options had been shorted and therefore it would be necessary to buy back the options they had already sold in order to close out their positions. Since the prices of the options had gone up, they had to buy them back at a higher price than that at which they had sold them. In 1979, Meriweather had bet right—in 1998, he bet wrong.

As I have noted, LTCM models were predicated on the assumption that major market jumps are so rare that they need not be figured in their calculations. But the data upon which the models depended did not even go back to 1992, to say nothing of the 1987 market collapse, which, in retrospect, offered a clear warning of things to come for anyone with eyes to see. Ten years later, another crisis occurred, which this time threatened the entire global economy. On August 17, 1997, Russia devalued the ruble, thereby effectively defaulting on their Treasury bills. A year earlier, the IMF had come to the rescue of Russia, but by this time it was clear that the fledgling democracy "lacked the basic component of market economics, including viable commercial banking systems, stock and bond markets, and laws to protect private property and enforce contracts." Contrary to all expectations the IMF did not orchestrate another bailout loan. Paul Blustein goes so far as to insist that the resulting crisis "created a threat more destabilizing to the West than anything the friends of communism had ever concocted during the decades in the Kremlin." [51] The impact of the Russian default and the refusal of the IMF to come to the rescue of investors sent shock waves through global markets. Liquidity quickly dried up and investors fled risk.

While the crisis of 1997 bore marked similarities to the meltdown in 1987, changes that had occurred in the intervening decade made the situation much more perilous. New financial instruments, pyramiding leverage, markets more closely connected and operating in real time, the instantaneous transmission of news and information as well as a significant increase in the number of people in the market made the potential for extraordinary damage much more likely. For LTCM, these developments were nothing less than catastrophic. In August 1997, the outlier they thought could never occur hit with unexpected speed and force. Four days after Russia's default, the hedge fund lost $553 million. By the end of August, LTCM had lost $1.9 billion in assets and 45 percent of their capital. More important, the carefully crafted models that had been guiding their investments as well as those of all the banks and financial institutions that had tried to imitate them had broken down. Rather than converging, as the models assumed, spreads were increasing. From the point of view of the partners, this was totally irrational. They remained convinced that in the long run, rationality would return, markets once again would become efficient, and equilibrium would be restored. But as Keynes once wisely observed, "in the long run we're all dead." The question was whether LTCM could survive long enough for conditions to return to what they regarded as normal.

LTCM's hedging strategies mistakenly assumed that all markets would not move in the same direction at the same time. Furthermore, they thought there would always be adequate liquidity in the market, i.e., there would always be buyers when they wanted to sell. But in a perfect storm, everybody heads for cover. With no one buying and option contracts being called, LTCM did not have the capital to meet its obligations. Not only were their models flawed but the strategy of leveraging as much as possible returned to haunt them. LTCM faced an unprecedented collateral crisis. Most of their assets were held by creditors as collateral for loans that had been made to purchase additional assets. In the absence of buyers, the only thing LTCM could do was sell their holdings to raise the capital they needed. However, because these positions were so large, when they sold assets, their actions depressed prices still more, thereby creating the need to sell additional holdings. Several decades earlier, Paul Samuelson had observed that you can't lose more money than you invest. But this is not true because you *can* lose more than you invest *if* you are highly leveraged. At the time of the crisis, LTCM was leveraged 33 : 1! Losing all bets simultaneously and forced to sell more of their assets, a positive feedback loop with negative results began to form and quickly approached the tipping point. The situation was all the more alarming because some of the major banks and financial institutions at home and abroad were deeply invested in LTCM. The massive loans they had made to the collapsing hedge fund were "secured" by collateral that suddenly was disappearing. In addition to this, many other individuals and institutions were using similar models and thus also faced the prospect of ruin.

With events spinning out of control during the lazy days of August 1998, William McDonough, head of the New York Federal Reserve Bank, realized that something had to be done quickly. Since many people in government as well as the private sector had become concerned that bailouts by either the IMF or federal government were encouraging reckless investor behavior, McDonough and his colleagues were reluctant to propose government funding to solve the problem. McDonough convened a meeting of the players most deeply involved to address the crisis. After several days of heated discussions and complex negotiations, the group formed a consortium that included JP Morgan, Merrill Lynch, Morgan Stanley, Goldman Sachs, Salomon Smith Barney, Bankers Trust, Chase Manhattan, Lehman Brothers, Credit Suisse, Deutsche Bank, Barclays Capital, Union Bank of Switzerland Société Générale, and Paribas.[52] Each member of this group agreed to contribute between $100 and $300 million to create a bailout package totaling $3.625 billion. Meriweather and his partners were not fired but they lost control of the fund and their actions were carefully monitored by an oversight committee of the consortium.[53] While members of the consortium avoided financial ruin, their stock values dropped significantly. Merrill Lynch's stock, for example, fell two-thirds by October before leveling off. With catastrophic problems for the house of cards they had so carefully constructed looming on the horizon, Scholes and Merton journeyed to Stockholm on December 10, 1997, to receive the Nobel Prize in Economics "for a new method to determine the value of derivatives." Two years later LTCM was dissolved. Global meltdown had been avoided, but it had become obvious that something had fundamentally changed.

Though the next few years would see crises ranging from the collapse of the dot-coms and the sharp drop in global financial markets to corporate and accounting improprieties, the economy of the 1980s and 1990s effectively ended with the failure of Long-Term Capital Management. What makes this particular case so revealing is the way in which it brings together the multiple trajectories we have been tracing. As Lowenstein correctly points out:

> The supreme irony is that the professors were trying to deconstruct and ultimately to minimize risk, not—they believed—to speculate on overcoming it. In this, the fund was not unique. Long-Term was in fact the quintessential fund of the late twentieth century—an experiment in harnessing the markets to the twin new disciplines of financial economics and computer programming. The belief that tomorrow's risks can be inferred from yesterday's prices and volatilities prevails at virtually every investment bank and trading desk. This was Long-Term's basic mistake, and its stunning losses betrayed the flaw at the very head— the very brain—of modern finance.[54]

Many of the assumptions upon which the models developed by financial economists were based had proven to be wrong. The lessons to be learned from LTCM, however, are not only negative. To the contrary, the collapse of the largest hedge fund in history revealed a new financial infrastructure in which networks are organized and operate according to a different logic. One of the primary reasons for the crisis in the global economy during the late 1990s was that the models investors were using were at odds with the new realities of the emerging network economy.

8

IN-SECURITIES

Whole God damned problem tastes like apricots, whole God damned problem listen whole God damned problem read Wiener on communication, more complicated the message more God damned chance for errors, take a few years of marriage such a God damned complex messages going both ways can't get a God damned thing across, God damned much entropy going on say good morning and she's got a Goddamned headache thinks you don't give a God damn how she feels.

William Gaddis, *JR*

UNBALANCING THE BOOKS) Isaac Newton (1642–1727) is, of course, best known for his contributions to optics, physics, mathematics, and astronomy. But he also played an important role in the economic history of England. His most influential scientific work was done between 1669 and 1687, while he held the Lucasian professorship at the University of Cambridge. This period culminated in the 1687 publication of his epochmaking work, *Philosophiae naturalis principia mathematica.* He retired from scientific research in 1673, though he published *Opticks* in 1704. The end of Newton's scientific career marked the beginning of his political life. The policies of James II thrust Newton into a political career that began at the university but eventually led to Parliament. In an effort to take control of the university, the king insisted that all positions at Cambridge University had to be filled by Roman Catholics. An ardent Protestant who believed in the independence of the university, Newton led the resistance to this royal intrusion. When William of Orange defeated James II, faculty colleagues elected Newton to represent them at the Convention Parliament in 1689. Though he did not formally resign from Cambridge until 1701, he was never again an active member of the university community.

In what seems like an unexpected turn of events, Newton was appointed warden of the mint in 1696; three years later, he was elevated to the influential position of master of the mint. While this new position brought Newton considerable wealth, he was not content to serve only as a figurehead; rather, he played an active role in helping England through the difficult period of recoinage. As master of the mint, Newton found himself at the center of London's economic life at a time when new forms of paper currency and unprecedented speculative markets were rapidly emerging. Faced with a surge in counterfeiting occasioned by the introduction of paper currencies, Newton was instrumental in establishing safeguards to secure the value of money. He could not, however, protect himself or others from the volatility of the speculative markets that were springing up in London's coffeehouses and gaming parlors. Newton actually became caught up in the famous South Sea bubble, which led to the first great stock market crash in 1720. An observation by one of the investors in the South Sea Company might well serve as sage advice for gullible investors in the late 1990s: "The additional rise above the true capital will only be imaginary; one added to one, by any stretch of vulgar arithmetic will never make three and a half, consequently all fictitious value must be a loss to some person or other first or last. The only way to prevent it to oneself must be to sell out betimes, and so let the Devil take the hindmost."[1] Newton also could have profited from this advice. Though he first sold his shares in the South Sea Company for a profit of £7,000, he was consumed by the mania of the moment, reinvested his money, and eventually lost £20,000. Reflecting on his experience, Newton commented, "I can calculate the motions of heavenly bodies, but not the madness of people."[2] As a result of the financial disaster caused by the collapse of the South Sea Company, Parliament passed the Bubble Act (June 11, 1720), which required all joint-stock companies to secure a Royal charter.

Newton's experience in speculative markets taught him a lesson financial economists and the investors who followed their advice would learn almost three centuries later: there *is* a difference between physical and mechanical systems, which can be understood as inherently rational equilibrium systems, and markets, which are complex systems where interacting agents make unpredictable moves. The sophisticated mathematical models and programs developed during the last half of the twentieth century were no more able to account for bubbles than was Newtonian physics in the eighteenth century. And the reasons for this failure were the same: their models were at odds with the way the "real" world works much of the time. Just when the real seems to have slipped away, it unexpectedly returns—often transformed—to disrupt the models, strategies, and systems constructed to deny it.

As the different trajectories we have been tracking become ever more entangled, the complexity of networks of all kinds rapidly increases. New computer and telematic technologies, and real-time financial news, media, and entertainment create conditions for networks to expand and become more and more interrelated. The greater the connectivity, the greater the volatility. History shows that by the end of the 1990s, crises had become much more frequent: 1873, 1929, 1962, 1979, 1982, 1987, 1989, 1994, 1997, 2000, 2001. . . .

As we have seen, it is precisely such volatility that new financial products, market models, and investment strategies developed in the 1980s and 1990s were designed to manage. The irony, of course, is that many of these innovations actually *increase* the volatility they are supposed to reduce. Just as Babbage dreamed of eliminating errors by creating a difference engine that would get rid of human computers, so the financial economists we have been considering wanted to create mathematical models and computer programs that would reduce uncertainty to calculable risk. Computerized trading systems operating according to rational models were not supposed to make the mistakes ignorant and biased human calculators inevitably made. Theorists' fundamental assumptions about the rationality and efficiency of markets rest upon a view of the universe as quantifiable and calculable, which can be traced to the equilibrium system Newton describes in *Principia.*

By 1997, it had become undeniable for anyone willing to consider the evidence that the efficient market hypothesis and related theories were wrong on virtually every count. At the most basic level, the efficient market hypothesis and the practices it promotes presuppose not only the accessibility but also the *reliability* of information. Investors must have confidence in the reports issued by companies and financial analysts. As the 1990s drew to a close, however, it became obvious that much of the information upon which people were basing their decisions was not just mistaken but intentionally misleading. While many factors contributed to this tendency, three are important in this context. First, during the 1980s and 1990s, companies began using stock options as compensation. This practice began with higher-level executives and managers but with the explosive growth of dot-com companies spread to almost all employees. From the CEO to the entry-level programmer, employees received stock options as part of their compensation package. At the height of the dot-com craze, the options game got completely out of control. In many cases, inexperienced and mediocre executives were given huge salaries as well as hundreds of thousands of stock options to manage companies that had little or no prospect of becoming profitable in the foreseeable future. The rationale for this policy had been developed in the early 1970s by two University of Chicago graduates, Michael Jensen and William Meckling, who both had studied with Milton Friedman. Instead of assessing the value of companies in terms of their size and assets, Jensen and Meckling followed economists and investors who concentrated on profits and, most important, stock prices to determine how much a company is worth. To maximize the performance of executives, they concluded, it is necessary to align their interests with the interests of shareholders. This can be done by including a large number of stock options in compensation packages. With thousands of stock options, executives had a vested interest in driving up stock values. Since these options do not have to be expensed until they are exercised, huge compensation packages did not show up on either income statements or balance sheets. The primary argument in support of not listing stock options on company balance sheets is that the Black-Scholes formula notwithstanding, it is impossible to know their value until they are actually exercised. Certain restrictions, which affected their value, were also placed on options. The ability to exercise options was tied to the duration of employment. In most cases, contracts included a schedule for exercising options. People had to work for a predetermined period before they could begin cashing in their chips and even then were limited to exercising a specified number of options per week or month of work. In addition to this, these options were nontransferable and thus recipients could not trade their options in any market. Even if one accepts the Black-Scholes model as appropriate for market-tradable options, nontransferable options significantly complicate the valuation problem.

Once again, a carefully crafted theory had unintended consequences. While granting executives a large number of options in the company aligned his or her interests with the interests of stockholders, it also created a significant incentive to drive up the value of the stock by any means necessary. Long-range strategies vanished in the flurry of short-term tactics for increasing stock prices. As long as share values were rising, the actual performance of the business did not really matter. John Cassidy underscores the importance of these developments.

> The rise of the stock option revolutionized the culture of corporate America. The chief executives of blue-chip companies, who in the nineteen eighties had portrayed Icahn, Pickens, and their ilk as vandals, now embraced the values of the raiders as their own. For decades, the Business Roundtable, a lobbying group that represents C.E.O.s of dozens of major companies, had stressed the social role that corporations played in their communities, as well as the financial obligations they owed their stockholders. In 1997, the Business Roundtable changed its position statement to read, "The paramount duty of management and board is to the shareholder."
>
> In many cases, C.E.O.s turned into corporate raiders themselves, albeit internal raiders. Companies liked I.B.M., Xerox, and Procter & Gamble, acting on their own volition, fired tens of thousands of workers. Their chief executives insisted that "downsizing" was necessary to

compete effectively, and that was sometimes true. But once the C.E.O.s were in possession of mega-options, they had another motivating factor: an enormous vested interest in boosting their firm's stock price.[3]

In this new world, if disinformation increases share values, it appears to be justifiable. In other words, there was considerable incentive to conceal any information that would have an adverse effect on stock prices.

Gaps in the federal government's regulatory policies as well as practices of investment banks and securities analysts made it easier for companies to mislead investors. As I have noted, derivatives are off-book and therefore do not have to be included in a company's financial reports. Since there are minimal margin requirements for derivative investments, it is extremely difficult and often impossible for investors to know the actual risk exposure of the companies in which they are investing. In addition to this, stock analysts had little incentive to distribute accurate information and make reliable buy-hold-sell recommendations. During the 1990s, investment banks reaped huge profits by underwriting IPOs. Firms considering an IPO often shopped around for an investment bank that would be sure to publish a favorable analysis at the time of or just prior to the public offering. Thus, stock analysts were tempted to present overly optimistic evaluations of companies in the hope of securing highly lucrative business for the investment bank division of their firms. Further conflicts of interest were created for older mature firms long after their IPOs, because investment banks were involved in their issue of new securities and in their merger and acquisitions activities.

With increasing financial incentives for concealing or distorting important information about companies, the financial press might have been expected to present a more balanced perspective for investors. For the most part, however, journalists were irresponsible and actually contributed to the problem. As we have seen, the emerging finance-entertainment complex created conflicts of interest, which fed the speculative frenzy. Almost three years after the bubble burst, James Ledbetter, business editor of Time Europe, belatedly confessed:

> The late 1990s witnessed an explosion of business media. CNBC became the most profitable cable channel in America. New magazines and Web sites sprang up: Business 2.0, Red Herring, The Street.com and the publication I worked for, the Industry Standard. All purported to untangle the mysteries of the burgeoning Internet economy.
>
> Yet for all that increased attention, it's difficult to say that the en-

larged business media played a decisive role in exposing the shortcomings of American corporate practices. Indeed, too often the new magazines and Web sites acted as incurious cheerleaders, championing executives and innovative companies without questioning their books. . . .

The mainstream media, too, did its share of hyping the technology boom, but no one did as much evangelizing as the so-called new economy publications. They preached about how technology created new paradigms. But they were frequently slow to note when technology didn't work, or markets didn't exist, and they relied far too much on a handful of self-interested bankers for information.[4]

With the insatiable demand for news created by new media operating 24/7, financial journalists gathered information wherever they could. In many cases, the businesses they were covering were so new that the only ones who understood them were the entrepreneurs, analysts, and venture capitalists who had the most to gain by favorable press. All too often, what was supposed to be responsible news coverage amounted to little more than publicity for companies that were more image than substance.

Looking back on the 1990s, what is most startling is how few people at the time seemed to be concerned about what was happening. Ignorance is no excuse because many of the players realized they were promoting a house of cards that would inevitably collapse. When taken together, the policies and actions of company executives, investment banks and securities analysts, and the financial media created a complex confidence game that duped many credulous shareholders. When investors finally caught on, there was a crisis of confidence in markets, which introduced the very psychological uncertainties that mathematical formulas and models had been created to avoid.

In addition to being mistaken about the accuracy and distribution of information, the EMH and related economic theories were wrong about the rationality of investors. Investors *are not* always rational but frequently trade on the basis of intuition, whim, and rumor as much as reason and reliable information. Furthermore, people are not always risk averse; to the contrary, sometimes investors take unreasonable risks without hedging their bets. During such periods, the more dicey the game, it seems, the bigger its draw. As I have argued, at the height of the dot-com craze, major financial institutions, venture capitalists, and many small investors knew that the companies they were betting on had very little chance of success yet were willing to gamble on the big payoff as long as others were in the game. In addition to acting irrationally at times, investors are not as similar as they appear to be according to both the random walk theory and EMH. Instead of homogeneous billiard balls or gas molecules whose independent actions collide to generate probable patterns, human actors have different interests, intentions, and biases, which inevitably color the interpretation of information upon which they make decisions. At the most basic level, the time horizon for investment plays a significant role in how information is processed. What the long-term investor regards as important is often insignificant for the day trader and vice versa. It is also necessary to acknowledge that though electronic technologies and federal legislation have improved communications, investors still do not all have equal access to the best information at the same time. Even media and networks operating in real time cannot completely overcome the unequal distribution of information relevant to investors. Large investment firms with big staffs as well as expensive machines and programs for gathering and storing data have an undeniable advantage over small investors whose resources are limited.

If information is not quickly and widely distributed, markets cannot be efficient. The more carefully one ponders markets, the more suspect the whole notion of efficiency becomes. In more general terms, the search for efficiency usually involves the effort to eliminate excess, surplus, and waste. In industrial processes, for example, so-called scientific management studies often analyze the activity of workers in an effort to eliminate excess motion and precisely coordinate man and machine. Obviously, the notion of efficiency does not function in exactly the same way in the efficient market hypothesis. Nonetheless, it is not difficult to discern the image or metaphor of an industrial machine at work in theories of efficient market machinations. Strip away whatever is not needed so well-oiled wheels can turn more smoothly. Waste and efficiency, however, are not always objective but are often in the eye of the beholder. What is efficient for management sometimes seems wasteful to workers, and vice versa. For example, when a manufacturing company downsizes and outsources work to reduce operating expenses and thus improve its balance sheet, it might appear to become more efficient. Or when an investment bank lays off high-salaried employees in pursuit of higher profits, the principle of efficiency might seem well served. But in the longer run, these moves might turn out to be inefficient. With higher unemployment, it is more difficult for consumers to purchase the products of supposedly efficient companies. And when experienced employees are released, they take with them a wealth of knowledge and experience, which are very expensive to replace. Lean is often mean but mean is not always good business.

As the 1980s and 1990s wore on, the eager pursuit of efficient markets led to further paradoxes. While preaching the gospel of efficiency, companies created excesses on a scale never before seen. Money begat money in feedback loops that seemed to be endless. Whether the much-touted creative destruction was more creative or more destructive depended on one's place in the economic system. What seems puzzling in the sober light of the morning after is how little resentment excessive wealth provoked. Many workers on the lower rungs of the socioeconomic ladder actually seemed to buy into the ideology of trickle-down economics. As money became more and more unreal, everybody seemed to think it was within their grasp. With a vested interest in keeping the game going, the media irresponsibly promoted the myth of the democratization of wealth. While kids wanted to be like Mike, their parents wanted to be like Bill. But people pumping gas, punching the time clock, or teaching school had no more chance of cashing in on the market than most inner-city kids had of reaching the NBA. The dream of wealth on the part of people who had no realistic possibility of attaining it led them either to support or not to protest policies that were not in their best interests. The "efficiency" of markets presupposes such irrational behavior.

It becomes clear, then, that for the mathematical formulas and models financial economists and engineers were using during the 1980s and 1990s to work, it was necessary to assume an idealized state, which is at odds with the way much of the real world operates. Like Newton's closed system, markets in these models appear to represent a frictionless world far removed from the reality of markets and traders. This impression was reinforced by influential textbook presentations of some of the most abstract theoretical models, which went so far as to ignore taxes and transaction costs. In addition to this, to financial economists markets seem, as the world did in classical physics, to move toward equilibrium. By the late 1980s, Kenneth Arrow, who, we have seen, developed one of the most influential formulations of equilibrium theory, had begun to recognize its limitations.

The general perspective of mainstream (so-called neoclassical) economic theory has certainly had some empirical successes. From a very broad perspective, there is a considerable degree of self-maintenance or homeostasis. What appear to be major shocks, especially wars, are absorbed, not immediately, of course, but in the sense that after a relatively few years the economy appears to be about where it would be if the shock had not occurred. . . . But it is clear that many empirical phenomena are not covered well by either the theoretical or empirical analyses based on linear stochastic systems, sometimes not by either. The presence and persistence of cyclical fluctuations in the economy as a whole of irregular timing and amplitude are not consistent with the view that the economy tends to return to equilibrium after any disturbances. . . . The securities markets have always shown great volatility, while the international financial markets, on which currencies are exchanged, have shown virtual disorganization since exchange rates were allowed to float, although most economists would have regarded free-exchange rate movements as an aid to stabilization. These empirical results have given impetus to the closer study of dynamic models and the emphasis on the application of new results on nonlinear dynamic models.[5]

Arrow concludes that the application of the principle of equilibrium to the entire economy all the time results in idealized models that are counterfactual. To rely on these models, therefore, can lead to unexpected results and possibly even devastating mistakes. The problems Arrow and his colleagues detect in the foundational assumptions of much traditional economic theory had already been identified at the beginning of the century but were consistently overlooked until circumstances and events forced theorists to reconsider their models.

While Bachelier anticipated the use of the heat equation and probability statistics to model markets, his teacher, Poincaré, recognized problems in Newtonian physics, which anticipated criticisms of neoclassical economics almost a century later. Poincaré's argument turns on what is known as the three-body problem. Using Newton's law of universal gravitation, it is possible to develop a formula to determine the position of two interacting bodies as a function of time. When a third body is introduced, however, matters become considerably more complicated. Three-body systems tend to be chaotic because of the way nonlinearities enter the differential equations that describe them. To calculate the eventual positions of bodies, it is necessary to determine the initial conditions of the system to an extremely high degree of accuracy. The longer the time interval of the prediction, the greater the computational power necessary to solve the equations. While such systems are in principle predictable, in practice the difficulty of determining the original conditions and required computational power and time make chaotic systems effectively unpredictable. Eight years after Bachelier submitted his unacceptable thesis, Poincaré published *Science and Method,* in which he maintained that Newtonian physics cannot solve the three-body problem "because of the nonlinearities inherent in the system. A very small cause which escapes our notice," Poincaré argues, "determines a considerable effect that we cannot fail to see, and then we say that the effect is due to chance . . . it may happen that small differences in the initial conditions produce very great ones in the final phenomena. A small error in the former will produce an enormous error in the latter. Prediction becomes impossible."[6] The phenomenon Poincaré notices is what contemporary chaos theorists describe as extreme sensitivity to initial conditions. In complex dynamic systems, the factors influencing any event are so numerous and interrelated that they cannot all be taken into account and thus prediction is impossible. In *Chaos and Order in the Capital Markets,* investment strategist Edgar Peters explains that "the unpredictability occurs for two reasons. Dynamic systems are feedback systems. What comes out goes back in again, is transformed, and comes back out, endlessly. Feedback systems are much like compounding interest except the transformation is exponential; it has a power higher than 1. Any differences in initial values will grow exponentially as well."[7] If economic systems are understood in this way, they become both dynamic and nonlinear. By the end of the twentieth century, reality had caught up with Poincaré's theories.

Looking back at the 1990s, the problems with the efficient market hypothesis and the models built upon it seem so obvious that it is difficult to understand why it took so long for economists and investors to acknowledge them. Lawrence Summers, a former secretary of the treasury and the current president of Harvard University, has gone so far as to claim, "The efficient market hypothesis is the most remarkable error in the history of economic theory."[8] Why then were these models not discarded sooner? The answer, it seems, is that people from universities and Wall Street to Main Street *wanted to believe* in the models. Paradoxically, these economic formulas and models were symptoms of the very desires and emotions they were designed to eliminate. Rationality, order, and predictability become all the more desirable in a world that appears to be increasingly irrational, chaotic, and unpredictable. The greater the uncertainty and irrationality of the real world, the greater the desire to believe in an ideal world where investors are rational and markets are efficient. But in the complexities of emerging network culture, such illusions have no future.

While many of the mistakes economists and investment strategists made in the 1980s and 1990s now seem obvious, what has not yet been recognized is that their theories and models also rested upon several fundamental *philosophical* errors. The theories of leading financial economists in the last half of the twentieth century have an inadequate understanding of human selfhood or subjectivity and misconstrue the nature of time and historical development. These two errors are actually different versions of the same mistake. Contrary to the presuppositions of leading financial economists, reality is not an aggregate of separate entities, individuals, or monads that are externally and contingently related; it is an emerging *web* consisting of multiple *networks* in which everything and everyone come into being and develop through ongoing interrelations. Within these webs, subjects and objects are not separate from each other but coemerge and coevolve. As this process unfolds, there is no subject without an object and vice versa. In the world of finance, for example, there can be no investor (subject) without something in which to invest (i.e., a commodity, security, bond, derivative, etc.), and, obviously, there are no investments without investors (figure 29). Furthermore, individual

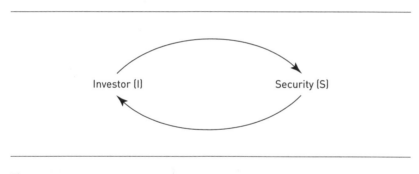

Figure 29

agents never act independently of each other but are reciprocally related and in such a way that their actions condition each other. All action is interaction. In the game of poker, for example, my wagers are always responses to the bets of other players. The successful player keeps his eyes on other players even when they do not seem to be engaged in the game. The more skillful the player, the better he reads the faces of others while always maintaining his own poker face. In a similar manner, an individual investor inevitably acts in a context shaped by the concurrent decisions and actions of other investors—be they individual or institutional. These

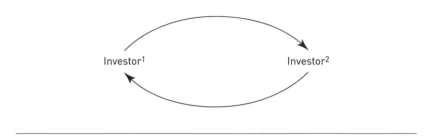

Figure 30

actions, in turn, condition but do not completely determine the actions of other investors (figure 30).

Shifting from the status of the self to the question of time, temporal moments, like the actions of human subjects, are intrinsically interrelated. Accordingly, time is not an infinite series of isolated moments in which the past, present, and future are separate and events are disconnected (figure 31). Rather, the moments of time are interrelated in such a way that the past accumulates to establish a trajectory into the future and the future impinges upon the present in a way that requires a constant recasting and refiguring of the past (figure 32). The poker player must both remember the past actions of other players and anticipate future moves. Does George bluff in this situation? If I up the ante, what will Alan do? Patterns remembered from previous games often help a player understand what is going on. Moreover, time is a two-way street: the past not only conditions the future but the future also influences the past. The past, after all, exists only in our memory of it. This memory is not set in stone but is constantly revised in light of changing expectations. If I expect George to hold rather than fold, his earlier moves look one way; if, on the other hand, I expect

Figure 31
Serial time.

him to up the ante even if he is only holding two pairs, the past appears different. When understood in this way, the moment of decision or action is poised at the intersection of past/memory and future/expectation. Time as well as history, therefore, has a direction or trajectory, though neither is probabilistic or determined.

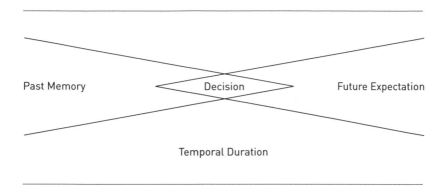

Figure 32

To understand individual agents and temporal moments as immersed in emerging webs of relations where everything is inextricably interrelated is to interpret reality as inescapably relative. Relativity, as I have already suggested, does not involve arbitrary subjectivity; to the contrary, the relativity of reality is a function of networks of activity and constraint in and through which individuals assume and develop their specific identities. This is the philosophical principle Simmel discovered in money. Money, he argued, discloses "the interdependence of things, which relativism establishes as their essence." His understanding of the interconnectivity of being lies at the heart of his interpretation of money and markets and, conversely, his understanding of the relativity of money informs his account of the relativity of reality. Money, Simmel concludes, "is nothing but the symbol of this relativity."

> *Money as reification of the general form of existence according to which things derive their significance from their relationship to each other.*
> The philosophical significance of money is that it represents within the practical world the most certain image and the clearest embodiment of the formula of all being, according to which things receive their meaning through each other and have their being determined by their mutual relations.[9]

In this scheme of things, to be is to be related, or, in a more contemporary idiom, to be is to be connected. Far from a machine in which parts are independent of each other and are organized only by the imposition of a design from without, the economy is a growing web of relations in which order episodically emerges from within. To complete a model that can effectively guide theory and practice in a network economy, it is necessary to open closed equilibrium systems and move beyond stochastic calculus to a more sophisticated understanding of the structure and function of complex adaptive systems.

COMPLEXITY AND CONTRADICTION IN MARKETS) In 1966, Robert Venturi published what proved to be a prophetic work—*Complexity and Contradiction in Architecture.* By presenting a sustained critique of modern architecture, Venturi laid the groundwork for his postmodern manifesto, *Learning from Las Vegas,* published with Denise Scott Brown and Steven Izenour six years later. Modern architecture, he argues, turns away from the complexities and contradictions of the contemporary world in search of an idealized realm of timeless forms and permanent structures. In his opening salvo, Venturi identifies what he regards as the most misleading errors of modernists.

> Orthodox Modern architects have tended to recognize complexity insufficiently or inconsistently. In their attempt to break with tradition and start all over again, they idealize the primitive and elementary at the expense of the diverse and the sophisticated. As participants in a revolutionary movement, they acclaimed the newness of modern functions, ignoring their complications. In their role as reformers, they puritanically advocated the separation and exclusion of elements, rather than the inclusion of various requirements and juxtapositions.[10]

For all the sophistication of their structures, modern architects remain simpleminded. Instead of exploring complex interrelations, they attempt first to separate and segregate elements and then reduce their differences to simple rules or principles. Rejecting this approach, Venturi cites August Heckscher, whose book, *The Public Happiness,* deeply influenced him: "Amid simplicity and order rationalism is born, but rationalism proves inadequate in any period of upheaval." In contrast to modernism's desire for simplicity, Venturi revels in complexity.

I am for richness of meaning rather than clarity of meaning; implicit function as well as the explicit function. I prefer "both-and" to "either-or," black and white, and sometimes gray, to black or white. A valid architecture evokes many levels of meaning and combinations of focus: its space and its elements become readable and workable in several ways at once.

But an architecture of complexity and contradiction has a special obligation toward the whole: its truth must be its totality or its implications of totality. It must embody the difficult unity of inclusion rather than the easy unity of exclusion. More is not less.[11]

And, it is important to add, *more is different.* (The principle of "both-and" lies at the heart of Hegel's dialectic. Hegel's system issues in precisely "the difficult whole" for which Venturi is searching.)

By the time Venturi and his colleagues published their study of Las Vegas, his understanding of and appreciation for complexity had grown considerably. As we have seen, Vegas becomes the prism through which one can understand the ways in which proliferating media networks transform reality into image. What Venturi realized in 1972 that he did not fully appreciate in 1966 is that modernism and postmodernism not only represent two historical periods but also reflect different technological eras. Whereas modernism is inseparable from "19th-century industrial vision," postmodernism, Venturi, Brown, and Izenour argue, emerges with "20th-century communication technology."[12] Though industrial machines might be complicated, they are not complex. Countless separate parts can function according to fixed rules to create operational systems that are as linear as a Mies van der Rohe building. But these structures, Venturi insists, both misrepresent and distort contemporary reality. The challenge is not to flee from complexity and contradiction but to learn how to figure them in everyday life.

It should be clear that true believers in the efficient market hypothesis and proponents of modern architecture share a common vision of the world. Like buildings modeled after ideal Platonic forms, the pristine models of financial markets are symptomatic of the desire for order in a messy world that no longer seems rational. To avoid chaos, they believed, complexity must be reduced to simplicity. By the middle of the 1980s, however, it was becoming clear that this dream of simplicity and order is a dangerous illusion.

Many economists and investors gradually came to realize that there were problems with the mathematical formulas and models driving much market activity. In an effort to address the questions emerging markets were raising, the Santa Fe Institute sponsored a workshop, "The Evolutionary Paths of the Global Economy," from September 8 through 18, 1987. One year later, the proceedings of the meetings were published in a volume entitled *The Economy as an Evolving Complex System,* edited by Kenneth Arrow, Philip Anderson, and David Pines. The timing of the workshop could not have been more fortuitous: one month later the stock market suffered its worst crash since 1929. Ten years after this crash, just as Long-Term Capital Management was pushing the global economy to the brink of collapse, SFI published a follow-up volume, which both reported on the work of the past decade and set the direction for future research. The crises of 1987 and 1997 are precisely the kind of outliers for which the efficient market hypothesis cannot account. By 1998, the price of this failure and the urgency to develop alternative models had become undeniable.

As the center of the rapidly developing field of complexity studies, the Santa Fe Institute brings together researchers in the physical, biological, and social sciences to examine problems of self-organization in complex systems. In *The Self-Organizing Economy,* Princeton economist and *New York Times* columnist Paul Krugman underscores the importance of the work being done at SFI for the study of economics: "some of the ideas that come out of the interdisciplinary study of complex systems—the attempt to find common principles that apply across a wide variety of scientific fields, from neuroscience to condensed matter physics—are, in fact, useful in economics as well."[13] In their introduction to the 1997 volume, Brian Arthur, Steven Durlauf, and David Lane argue that "the complexity perspective" or "the process-and-emergence approach," which sometimes is labeled the "Santa Fe approach," differs from the standard neoclassical or equilibrium approach: "In the equilibrium approach, the problem of interest is to derive, from the rational choices of individual optimizers, aggregate-level 'states of the economy' (prices in general equilibrium analysis, a set of strategy assignments in game theory with associated payoffs) that some aggregate-level consistency condition (market-clearing, Nash equilibrium), and to examine the properties of these aggregate-level-states. . . . However, the equilibrium approach does not describe the mechanism whereby the state of the economy changes over time—nor indeed how an equilibrium comes into being."[14] In this way as well as many others, the equilibrium model is similar to structuralist models. Just as the equilibrium approach does not describe the mechanism by which the economy changes, so structuralists analyze synchronic systems but ignore diachronic processes. Complex adaptive systems differ from equilibrium systems in almost every way. The model of markets that grows out of complexity studies overcomes the philosophical problems inherent in the efficient market hypothesis and suggests an interpretation of relational webs and interconnected networks that extends from the economy to society and culture as a whole.

One of the leaders in the sciences of complexity is John Holland, professor of psychology, electrical engineering, and computer science at the University of Michigan. Holland's development of genetic algorithms, which I will consider below, and mathematical models for the phenomenon of emergence in complex adaptive systems have been very influential in a variety of fields.[15] At the 1987 workshop, Holland presented a paper entitled "The Global Economy as an Adaptive Process," in which he identifies what he regards as the primary features of the global economy.

1. The overall direction of the economy is determined by the interaction of many dispersed units acting in parallel. The action of any given unit depends upon the state and actions of a limited number of other units.
2. There are rarely any global controls on interactions—controls are provided by mechanisms of competition and coordination between units, mediated by *standard operating procedures,* assigned roles and shifting associations.
3. The economy has many levels of organization and interaction. Units at any given level typically serve as building blocks for constructing units at the next higher level. The overall organization is more than hierarchical, with all sorts of tangling interactions (associations, channels of communication) across levels.
4. The building blocks are recombined and revised continually as the system accumulates experience and adapts.
5. The arena in which the economy operates is typified by many *niches* that can be exploited by particular adaptations. . . .
6. Niches are continually created by new technologies and the very act of filling a niche provides new niches. . . . Perpetual novelty results.
7. Because the niches are various, and new niches are continually created, the economy operates far from an optimum.[16]

Holland's account of the structure of the emerging global economy summarizes the primary characteristics and operational logic of complex adaptive systems. By considering the presuppositions and implications of this alternative interpretation of systems, it is possible to construct a model that more adequately reflects the structure and function of the network economy at the beginning of the twenty-first century.

Markets are network phenomena. To understand their operational logic, I will consider the stock market as an emerging complex adaptive system. It is important to note that the actors or agents in this system can be either human beings or computer programs. While obviously differing significantly, humans and information processing machines nonetheless function in surprisingly similar ways in webs and networks of different kinds. When understood as complex adaptive systems (CASs), webs and networks are *self-reflexive structures.* That is to say, individual agents and systems—be they social, political, religious, or economic—are interrelated in such a way that neither can exist without the other. This is an important point whose significance can easily be misunderstood. As we have come to suspect, individuals do not first exist in isolation from each other and then come together to form groups; to the contrary, individuals become what they are through their participation in communities, parties, churches, synagogues, mosques, and markets. Paradoxically, there can be no individuals without the group and no group without individuals. As a result of this interconnection, subjects and groups are bound in loops of mutual influence. Since the relation between the individual and the whole is two-way, they form a system that is nonlinear. Instead of separated and isolated, as conceived in neoliberal economic theory and much recent financial economics, agents are interconnected members of networks in which all action is interaction. The interrelation of investors creates the market, which, in turn, creates possibilities for investors to play their games. The logic of these networks of exchange appears to be circular but is not vicious.

Notorious hedge fund manager George Soros was one of the first to recognize the importance of the reflexive structure of markets. According to Soros, one of the fundamental mistakes proponents of the EMH make is the use of outmoded scientific models in which subject and object or agent and system are independent of each other and thus do not interact in mutually conditioning ways. Explicitly acknowledging his debt to philosophers like Hegel and Marx, Soros develops an analysis of reflexivity in which agent and system are thoroughly interactive. He distinguishes the passive function in which agents attempt to understand the context of their decisions from the active function through which their thinking has an impact on the "real world."

When both functions operate at the same time, they interfere with each other. Functions need an independent variable in order to produce a determinate result, but in this case the independent variable of one function is the dependent variable of the other. Instead of a determinate result, we have an interplay in which both the situation and the participants' perceptions are dependent variables so that an initial change precipitates further changes both in the situation and in the participants' views. I call this interaction "reflexivity," using the word as the French do when they describe a verb whose subject and object are the same.[17]

Reflexivity is a nonlinear relation in which cause and effect are interdependent: the thoughts and actions of agents influence the operation of the system, which, in turn, influences the thoughts and actions of agents. When the agent is an investor and the system is the market, this interactivity is mediated by the interplay of expectations.

Soros sometimes suggests that the critical consideration is the difference between natural systems, in which subjects and objects are independent, and social systems, in which they are interdependent. Elsewhere, however, he acknowledges that according to the principles of quantum mechanics, such a separation between subjects and objects is impossible. If he were familiar with complexity theory, he would find even more support for the position he tries to develop. Though Soros's language is complex, his insight is simple: investors act in response to their expectations of the thoughts and actions of other investors. As Keynes once observed, competitive prices "are based on expectations about expectations, or expectations about expectations about expectations."[18] We have already seen this dynamic in our consideration of playing poker. The canny poker player bets on his expectation of the other players' expectations. The game—be it poker or the market—becomes a speculative hall of mirrors. For complexity theorists, what Soros describes as reflexivity creates recursive patterns, which are coemergent and coevolve. In a richly suggestive article with the formidable title "Asset Pricing under Endogenous Expectations in an Artificial Stock Market," Brian Arthur, John Holland, and their colleagues argue, "Asset markets . . . have a recursive nature in that agents' expectations are formed on the basis of their anticipations of other agents' expectations, which precludes expectations being formed by deductive means. Instead, traders continually hypothesize—continually explore—expectational models, buy or sell on the basis of them that perform best, and confirm or discard these according to their performance. Thus, individual beliefs or expectations become endogenous to the market, and constantly compete with an ecology of others' beliefs or expectations. The ecology of beliefs coevolves over time."[19] Several points in this seminal observation deserve emphasis. First, it is clear that these theorists are extending models derived from the biological sciences to develop a view of the market as something like a coevolving ecosystem. Holland has already suggested the importance of the ecological and evolutionary notion of niches in competitive environments for his understanding of the global economy. Second, *belief* is endemic to markets. In the absence of objective criteria, interpretive models rest upon faith as much as knowledge. While reason is not absent from economic deliberations, it is far from the only relevant variable. Finally, while agents in ecological economic systems are always interacting, they are not subject to any centralized control. To the contrary, complex adaptive systems are decentralized structures for processing distributed information.

In an effort to understand how distributed networks operate, investigators have conducted a variety of experiments, using what computer scientists call cellular automata, to create simulations of markets. A cellular automaton is "a computer program or piece of hardware consisting of a regular lattice array of cells. Each cell is assigned a set of instructions by means of an algorithm that tells it how to respond to the behavior of adjacent cells as the automaton advances from one discrete step to the next. Cellular automata are inherently parallel computing devices."[20] In the absence of any overall program or design, each cell evolves according to simple rules that respond to altering circumstances created by changes in surrounding cells. As the cells interact, complex forms and patterns begin to merge. To understand how cellular automata work, consider a flock of birds. As the flock flies through the air, it maintains its pattern even when confronting unexpected obstacles. There is no pilot directing the flock; rather, each bird communicates with the other birds immediately around it and adjusts its movements in a coordinated way. Though no bird knows the overall pattern or the precise direction of the flock, the flock "knows" where it is going. In other words, a "mind of the flock" emerges from the birds, which remain ignorant of it. There are many examples of such behavior in nature. Schools of fish, herds of animals, beehives, and colonies of ants and termites all act like cellular automata. In addition to these natural phenomena, social activity also exhibits similar behavior. The clearest example of people functioning as cellular automata is the activity of crowds, whose dynamics can be seen in the popular wave fans create in a crowded stadium. The wave seems to emerge spontaneously and, once it has started, each spectator acts independently yet in response to his or her neighbor. While no single fan can see the wave, someone watching the crowd as a whole observes a coherent pattern.

As scientists and social scientists developed an understanding of such phenomena, they began to write computer models to analyze and perhaps predict behavior. In 1968, John Conway, a mathematician who was then at Cambridge University, put von Neumann's theory of cellular automata into practice by developing what he called the Game of Life. The rules of this computer game are as simple as its results are complex. The space of the game is a grid with each square forming a cell that is either occupied or empty. Every cell is governed by rules, which determine the parameters for responding to the state of the surrounding cells. Conway discovered that local interactions of relatively simple rules produce complex dynamic global patterns that emerge, evolve, and disappear unpredictably. Emergent patterns are neither infinite nor arbitrary; to the contrary, a limited range of forms regularly appears. This does not, however, mean that the patterns are predictable. The pattern that actually emerges depends on initial conditions that can never be sufficiently specified to determine the outcome.

The Game of Life attracted considerable attention both within and beyond the university. As economists began to understand the implications of cellular automata, they quickly saw that the Game of Life provides a useful model for financial markets and economic behavior. Investors, like the individual cells in the game, act independently by following rules that are adaptable to the rules other investors are using. From the interactions of these agents, the pattern of the market emerges. If, as Conway maintains, free rule-governed behavior generates a limited range of patterns, it might be possible to identify the parameters within which markets move.

Insofar as conscious or unconscious rules guide the behavior of investors, their expectations or hypotheses function like anticipatory schemata. These schemata entail implicit or explicit models that compete in a process that is formally identical to Darwin's survival of the fittest. Agents, Arthur and Holland argue, "continually form individual, hypothetical, expectational models or 'theories of the market,' test these, and trade on the ones that predict best. From time to time, they drop hypotheses that perform badly, and introduce new ones to test. Prices are driven endogenously by these induced expectations. Individuals' expectations, therefore, evolve and 'compete' in a market formed by others' expectations. In other words, agents' expectations coevolve in a world they cocreate."[21] It is important to remember that the investing agent can be a computer program as well as a human actor. As software becomes more sophisticated, programs can adapt to the changing landscape of the market.

(While the recognition of the ways in which economists have long appropriated evolutionary theory to explain economic process is widespread, few cultural critics realize the extent to which Darwin's theory is indebted to population studies and economic speculation. Indeed, it was only after reading Smith's discussion of the division of labor that Darwin formulated his account of the survival of the fittest.)

One of the most significant innovations of the 1980s and 1990s was the introduction of widespread programmed trading in securities markets. This new investment strategy obviously required a great increase in computer power and speed as well as the development of networked markets. The integration of genetic algorithms and neural networks proved to be an important breakthrough for computerized trading. In many ways, the use of genetic algorithms in finance marks the synthesis of Babbage's difference engine and his friend and colleague Darwin's theory of evolution. In *Genetic Algorithms and Investment Strategies,* Richard Bauer explains: "Genetic algorithms are software procedures modeled after genetics and evolution. GAs are designed to efficiently search for attractive solutions to large, complex problems. The search procedures in survival of the fittest shape future generations by gradually manipulating a population of potential problem solutions until the most superior ones dominate the population."[22] Genetic algorithms are used to simulate how networks learn. Modeled on the operation of the human brain and nervous system, nonlinear neural networks are made up of multiple nodal layers in which output at one level becomes input at another level. The architecture of such networks is sometimes described in terms of "parallel distributed processing models, adaptive systems, self-organizing systems, neurocomputing, connectivist/connectionist models and neuromorphic systems."[23] When genetic algorithms are processed through neural networks, the result is an operational system that is virtually identical to the structure of the market as a whole. Since output at one level of the neural network can be used as input at another level, the system can actually learn from its "experience." The changing code of the algorithm functions as the DNA of the operational system. In this way, genetic algorithms can adapt and evolve or more precisely coevolve in relation to other genetic algorithms, which are operating according to the same principles. Frances Wong and Clarence Tan offer a helpful diagram (figure 33) of how these nonlinear neural networks operate in trading activity. As systems of genetic algorithms and neural networks enter into competition with each other, a coevolutionary process develops in which only the fittest models survive. The key variable in survival is adaptation, which requires effective responses to other algorithmic agents circulating in the system.

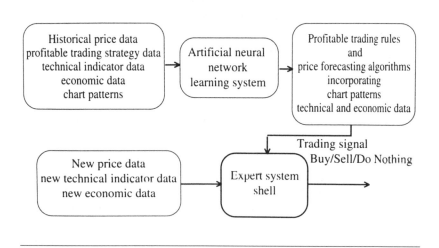

Figure 33
Genetic algorithms and neural networks. From Francis Wong and Clarence Tan, "Hybrid Neural, Genetic, and Fuzzy Systems," *Trading on the Edge: Neural, Genetic, and Fuzzy Systems for Chaotic Financial Markets*, ed. Guido Deboeck (New York: Wiley, 1994), 259. Copyright © 1994 by John Wiley & Sons, Inc. Reprinted by permission of John Wiley & Sons, Inc.

Throughout the 1980s, genetic algorithms, neural networks, and programmed trading remained the restricted domain of quants trained in computer science and financial economics. Trading, it turned out, was indeed rocket science. But this situation changed in 1989, when Bruce Babcock published his *Guide to Trading Systems.* In addition to explaining the complexities of computational trading in layman's terms, Babcock provided easy-to-use software programs for investors. By the time Babcock's book appeared, the use of high-powered workstations had become widespread on Wall Street. With new machines to run the most recent trading programs, the speed, volume, and complexity of trading on networked financial markets increased dramatically.

The reflexivity or recursivity of complex adaptive systems has further implications for the development of markets. Since the efficient market hypothesis is an extension of equilibrium models, it assumes continuous change and therefore cannot account for abrupt discontinuities in either an upward or a downward direction unless there is evidence of discontinuous information flows. Models related to or derived from the EMH presuppose a negative feedback system in which disequilibrium is checked before so-called outliers occur. Complex adaptive systems, by contrast, are not limited to negative feedback, but also involve positive feedback, which makes discontinuities unavoidable. In "Self-Reinforcing Mechanisms in Economics," Brian Arthur elaborates the difference between these two types of feedbacks.

> Conventional economic theory is built largely on the assumption of diminishing returns on the margin (local negative feedbacks); and so it may seem that positive feedback, increasing-returns-on-the margin mechanisms ought to be rare. Yet there is a sizeable literature on such mechanisms, much of it dating back to the 1920s and 1930s, particularly in international trade theory, industrial organization, regional economics, and economic development. Self-reinforcement goes under different labels in these different parts of economics: increasing returns, cumulative causation, deviation-amplifying mutual causal processes; virtuous and vicious circles; threshold effects; and non-convexity. The sources vary. But usually self-reinforcing mechanisms are variants of or derive from four generic sources: large set-up or fixed costs (which give the advantage of falling unit costs to increased output); learning effects (which act to improve products or lower their cost as their prevalence increases); coordination effects (which confer advantages to "going along" with other economic agents taking similar actions); and adaptive expectations (where increased prevalence on the market enhances beliefs of further prevalence).[24]

The nonlinearity of self-reinforcing mechanisms creates positive feedback loops, which form or strengthen inclinations or biases of interacting agents. Expectations feed expectations at an accelerating rate, creating a network effect in which *more becomes different*. At a certain juncture the market reaches a "tipping point," which results in something like a discontinuous phase shift. To see how this dynamic works out in markets, it is helpful to consider how it appears in physical systems.

Per Bak, who was a professor in the physics department at the Brookhaven National Laboratories, has developed an analysis of phenomena as different as the formation of landscapes, evolution, neural activity, and the triggering of avalanches, which sheds considerable light on the movement of markets. In each case, Bak observed what he described as "the tipping point" or, in more scientific terms, "self-organized criticality." "Complex behavior in nature," he argues, "reflects the tendency of large systems with many components to evolve into a poised, 'critical' state, way out of balance, where minor disturbances may lead to events, called avalanches, of all sizes. Most of the changes take place through catastrophic events rather than by following a smooth gradual path. The evolution of this very delicate state occurs without design from any outside agent. The state is established solely because of the dynamical interactions among individual elements of the state: the critical state is *self-organized.* Self-organized criticality is so far the only known general mechanism of complexity." [25] Four points in this description of self-organized criticality are relevant in this context. First, as the term implies, self-organized criticality is a state resulting from the interactions among agents or components rather than from the intervention of any external forces or agents. Second, in the state of self-organized criticality, nonlinear events can have effects disproportionate to their causes. In other words, the accumulation of small events eventually can have major consequences. Third, the dynamic interaction among individual agents or elements of the system generates global events that require a holistic description. Such events cannot be reduced to an account of the individual elements and their separate actions. Finally, at the tipping point, the effect of any specific individual event becomes unpredictable. While it is possible to know that something will trigger a "catastrophic event," it is never possible to be sure what specific occurrence will tip the balance and thereby upset the equilibrium. Bak uses the example of a pile of sand shaped like a cone or a pyramid. As grain after grain of sand is added, the pile gradually approaches the critical point at which an avalanche becomes inevitable but not precisely predictable. It is impossible to know which particular grain of sand will cause the pile to collapse. When the avalanche occurs, the effect seems to be completely disproportionate to the cause of one more tiny grain of sand in the pile.

The notion of self-organized criticality helps to explain the dynamics of extreme market volatility as well as the increasingly frequent occurrence of bubbles. Investors are not simply independent individuals but are interactive agents whose decisions can become self-reinforcing. When this occurs, positive feedback loops form, thereby creating an accelerating momentum that can result in herdlike behavior triggering an avalanche, which issues in an abrupt shift up or down in the price of a stock. In certain situations, this pattern of behavior spreads rapidly and the whole market shifts abruptly. For theorists and traders committed to the notions of equilibrium and rationality embedded in the efficient market hypothesis, investors poised at the tipping point appear to be acting irrationally. Instead of carefully assessing their situation and making independent judgments, they go with the accelerating flow. It is important to stress that such irrationality can take opposite forms. Positive feedback, in other words, can have a negative effect on individual stocks as well as the whole market. Bubbles, therefore, can be both positive and negative. In his prescient *Manias, Panics, and Crashes: A History of Financial Crises,* originally published in 1978, Charles Kindleberger identifies five recurrent stages in bubbles: euphoria, overtrading, revulsion, discredit, and despair.[26] Market hype leads to excessive investment, which drives up stocks beyond reasonable evaluations. Paradoxically, the higher the market goes, the more people invest and the more they invest, the higher it goes. Even when people realize what is going on, they often remain caught up in the frenzy and continue pouring money into the market. Eventually, however, the market reaches the tipping point, where everything turns around. In a fit of panic, everyone rushes for the exits and the market drops as fast or faster than it had risen. In this cycle, excessive optimism inevitably leads to excessive pessimism, creating a despair that is as irrational as the exuberance it displaces. In moments of panic, investors do not conform to the principles of the EMH by acting rationally and independently but act like a herd. As Shiller argues in his influential book, *Irrational Exuberance:* "If millions of people who invest were all truly independent of each other, any faulty thinking would tend to average out, and such thinking would have no effect on prices. But if less-than-mechanistic or irrational thinking is in fact similar over large numbers of people, then such thinking can indeed be the source of stock market booms and busts."[27] As markets become more and more interconnected, herdlike behavior increases. Indeed, in networked markets, booms and busts are as much the rule as the exception.

In addition to providing a more accurate model of markets in a network economy, the theory of complex adaptive systems also overcomes the philosophical shortcomings of the efficient market hypothesis. As we have seen, devotees of the EMH have an inadequate understanding of human selfhood as well as time and history. Far from acting independently, investors are caught in webs of mutual influence and codetermination. Instead of a series of disconnected moments, time is a complex process in which past/memory and future/expectation intersect in the present moment of decision. The interplay of recollection and anticipation lends time a direction. In other words, there is an "arrow of time" whose trajectory is not completely random. The direction of this arrow is not simply the result of the memories and expectations of individual investors in the market. In complex adaptive systems, part and whole are interrelated in such a way that the whole emerges from but cannot be reduced to the sum of its parts. The interrelational structure of the complex whole has attributes that cannot be detected in or deduced from the individual members from which it arises. It is helpful to recall the examples of a flock of birds and colony of ants. Though the flock and colony have no pilot or director, order emerges through the interaction of each individual with others around it. The pattern emerging from these interactions bends back on itself and directs individual birds and ants toward ends of which they remain unaware. When the order of the whole is understood in this way, it makes perfect sense to talk about "the mind of the flock" or "the mind of the colony." In a similar way, the market, which emerges from the activity of individual investors, loops back to direct them toward ends of which they are not always aware. Since the market operates like a complex adaptive system, there is a mind of the market in more than a metaphorical sense. In systems formed by human agents, the collective mind both remembers and anticipates things of which individual investors remain unaware. Accordingly, the market does not resemble a game of chance in which each roll of the dice or spin of the roulette wheel is independent of previous occurrences. To the contrary, the "arrow of time" makes markets *path dependent.* Since markets *do* have both a short-term and long-term memory, the past establishes the parameters of future investment decisions without completely determining outcomes in advance. It is important to remember, however, that the future also conditions the past. Expectation influences memory as much as memory effects expectation. As Soros, whose book bears the subtitle *Reading the Mind of the Market,* insists, the reflexive interplay of memory and expectation establishes an inescapable "bias" in the market. Over against supporters of the EMH, Soros goes so far as to claim: "I believe that market prices are always wrong in the sense that they present a biased view of the future. But distortion works in both directions: not only do market participants operate with a bias, but their biases can also influence the course of events. . . . The participants' perceptions are inherently flawed, and there is a two-way connection between flawed perceptions and the actual course of events, which result in a lack of correspondence between the two."[28] In contrast to the financial models driving the market throughout the 1980s and 1990s, in which the price always tends to be right, Soros insists that *the price is always wrong.*

Far from consistent and continuous, the interrelation of past and future in the present creates a temporal trajectory marked by repeated *disconti-*

nuities. The historical development of markets is characterized by what biologist Stephen Jay Gould in another context describes as "punctuated equilibrium."[29] Like living organisms, economic systems coevolve through a long process in which periods of equilibrium are punctuated by catastrophic events, which are both creative and destructive. The gradual accumulation of quantitative changes eventually leads to a qualitative leap in which new organizational patterns suddenly emerge. Mandelbrot goes so far as to insist that "the possibility of sharp discontinuity is an essential ingredient that sets finance apart from classical physics."[30] When such abrupt changes occur, the reconfiguration of the competitive landscape creates new niches for agents able to adapt quickly and effectively. Individuals, institutions, and organizations that cannot adjust and adapt do not survive.

Moments of discontinuity are sites of what complexity theorists describe as *emergence.* In complex adaptive systems, new patterns of order emerge from within and are not imposed from without. According to Hayek, in biological, social, and economic systems, there are "two sources of order." On the one hand, order is an "exogenous" construction that imposes external constraints; on the other hand, order grows from within and thus is "self-generating, . . . endogenous, or *spontaneous.*"[31] Hayek, we have seen, interprets the economy as a decentralized information processing machine, which operates according to the principles of distributed parallel processing. The market simultaneously forms and is formed by the interrelations of investors acting according to rules, schemata, and programs, which they constantly adjust to changing conditions. There can no more be a market without the operational schemata and rules of investors than there can be investors without the implicit and explicit rules and regulations governing the market. The interrelation of investors and market creates the necessity for adaptive coevolution. "Adaptation to the unknown," Hayek explains,

> is the key in all evolution, and the totality of events to which the modern market order constantly adapts itself is indeed unknown to anybody. The information that individuals or organizations can use to adapt to the unknown is necessarily partial and is conveyed by signals (e.g. prices) through long chains of individuals, each person passing on in modified form a combination of streams of abstract market signals. Nonetheless, *the whole structure of activities tends to adapt, through these partial and fragmentary signals, to conditions foreseen by and known to*

no individual, even if this adaptation is never perfect. That is why the structure survives, and why those who use it survive and prosper.

There can be no deliberately planned substitutes for such a self-ordering process of adaptation to the unknown. Neither his reason nor his innate "natural goodness" leads man this way, only the bitter necessity of submitting to rules he does not like in order to maintain himself against competing groups that had already begun to expand because they had stumbled upon such rules earlier.[32]

In ways that are not immediately obvious, this principle of emergent self-organization is a further articulation of ideas and structures we have discovered in our exploration of the theological and aesthetic prefigurations of markets. The notion of self-organization represents a reinterpretation of Calvin and Smith's invisible hand in terms of complex adaptive systems. For Calvin, as we have seen, order is imposed from without by a providential God. Smith transforms this external governor into an internal principle of self-regulation to form an account of markets. This principle of self-regulation, I have argued, is a further refinement of the inner teleology articulated in Kant's notion of beauty and elaborated in Hegel's philosophical idea as well as Marx's account of capital and Simmel's interpretation of money. The theory of complex adaptive systems explains how such internal governance works. The market can be understood as a self-regulating system in which the interactivity of a network of individual agents gives rise to organizational patterns, which, in turn, guide these agents toward ends that are not always their own. By the end of the twentieth century, this network was embodied in realities that were becoming increasingly virtual. In those complex networks, the invisible hand is no longer omniscient and omnipotent. To the contrary, the order governing the network economy emerges from the internal relations of human and machinic agents whose knowledge is always mistaken and memories as well as expectations are inescapably incomplete.

Not only do markets no longer seem omniscient, but recent developments in a new field known as artificial life also suggest that the principle of equilibrium, which lies at the foundation of classical economics, has severe limits. While systems of all kinds might sometimes tend toward equilibrium, in self-organizing systems, order invariably emerges *far from equilibrium,* between too much and too little order. In contrast to equilibrium systems in which stability is maintained through negative feedback, positive feedback tends to disrupt equilibrium by increasing both the operational speed and the heterogeneity of the components and connections in a system. As positive feedback increases the speed of interaction among more and more agents, linear causality gives way to recursive relations in which effects become disproportionate to the causes from which they emerge. In 1984, Christopher Langton was conducting research in artificial life, when he made a crucial discovery while attempting to build an artificial von Neumann universe with interacting cellular automata. We have already seen how cellular automata can be used to develop models of markets. At the time Langton began experimenting with cellular automata, he was working with the physicist Stephen Wolfram at the University of Michigan, under the direction of John Holland, who had been a student of von Neumann. Wolfram had discovered that cellular automata could be classified according to four typical patterns of behavior: (1) rigid structures that do not change; (2) oscillating patterns that change periodically; (3) chaotic activity that exhibits no stability; and (4) patterns that are neither too structured nor too disordered, which emerge, develop, divide, and recombine endlessly in complex ways.[33] Langton found the fourth category of automata particularly interesting. Though the principles governing this intermediate domain remained obscure, he suspected that activity in this region would be characterized by "a phase transition between highly ordered and highly disordered dynamics, analogous to the phase transition between solid and fluid states of matter."[34]

As Langton studied the dynamics of phase transition in more detail, he noticed that the four patterns of behavior fall into a regular sequence. He describes the activity occurring between order and disorder as "complex."

...Order $\rightarrow$ Complexity $\rightarrow$ Disorder $\rightarrow$ Complexity $\rightarrow$ Order...

The interstitial domain between order and disorder is *the edge of chaos,* where self-organization emerges in unpredictable ways. Summarizing Langton's conclusion, Stuart Kauffman writes: "Just near this phase transition, just at the edge of chaos, the most complex behavior can occur—orderly enough to ensure stability, yet full of flexibility and surprise."[35] Kauffman draws on Bak's work to argue that coadapting landscapes evolve to a point of self-organized criticality where minor changes in one landscape can trigger an avalanche of changes that ripple through the entire network. In an argument as reflexive as the phenomena it analyzes, Kauffman appropriates Smith's notion of the invisible hand to describe biological systems, which he then uses to model markets.

The edge-of-chaos image arises in coevolution as well, for as we evolve, so do our competitors; to remain fit, we must adapt to their adaptations. In coevolving systems, each partner clambers up the fitness landscape toward fitness peaks, even as that landscape is constantly deformed by the adaptive moves of its coevolutionary partners. Strikingly, such co-evolving systems also behave in an ordered regime, a chaotic regime, and a transition regime. It is almost spooky that such systems seem to coevolve to the regime at the edge of chaos. As if by an invisible hand, each adapting species acts according to its selfish advantage, yet the entire system appears magically to evolve to a poised state where, on average, each does as best as can be expected.[36]

As a result of the intricacy of the interrelations among agents and between agents and landscapes, not all things are possible at all times in complex webs and networks. This is not to imply that the future trajectory of coevolving actors and systems is completely determined by the past. Interacting agents create landscapes that establish parameters of constraint, which simultaneously limit and open possibilities. These possibilities can be realized only through genuinely unpredictable decisions and actions. The arrow of time in path-dependent systems does not erase events occurring by chance; therefore, history always holds surprises. The improbable, in other words, not only can happen but actually does happen repeatedly.

During the 1990s, there were repeated attempts to use the theory of complex adaptive systems to predict market movements. The most interesting and promising of these efforts is the work being done by the Prediction Company, a spin-off of the Santa Fe Institute founded in 1991 by Doyne Farmer, Norman Packard, and Jim Gill. According to the company prospectus, "Based on their earlier work in chaos theory and complex systems, Drs. Packard and Farmer felt the financial markets were an example of highly complex systems that would be amenable to predictive technology."

> The world of financial trading is changing rapidly. Market integration and consolidation, decimalization, 24-hour trading sessions, regulatory changes, online trading, rapid information dissemination—these and other forces create an ever-changing environment. This environment makes it difficult for the traditional trader or investment manager, even armed with the best in commercial technology, to deliver consistent positive results.

Prediction Company is bringing two main forces to bear against this changing environment: world-class technology and world-class science. Our technology allows us to build fully automated trading systems, which can handle huge amounts of data, react and make decisions based on that data and execute transactions based on those decisions—all in real time. Our science allows us to build accurate and consistent predictive models of markets and the behavior of financial instruments traded in those markets.[37]

With this understanding of the structure of complex adaptive systems and the dynamics of emergent self-organization, it is possible to complete the depiction of the way in which investors and securities interact in markets. Suppose each of three investors, I_A, I_B, and I_C, invests in a different security, S_X, S_Y, and S_Z,respectively (figure 34). Investors and securities, we have seen, are corelative—each emerges and changes through the other: I—S. Since value is relative, the price and movement of any security is a function of its place within a web of relations with other securities:

$$S_X \leftrightarrow S_Y \leftrightarrow S_Z \leftrightarrow S_X.$$

Investors, like securities are joined in reflexive loops of mutual determination:

$$I_A \leftrightarrow I_B \leftrightarrow I_C \leftrightarrow I_A$$

Investors' interpretations of particular securities as well as the market as a whole are conditioned by their interpretations of other investors' interpretations of the same factors. In addition to this, temporal duration must be calculated in modeling markets. It is, therefore, necessary to add a temporal vector: T^1, T^2, T^3. The market has a history and evolves in a direction conditioned by the mutual determination of memory and expectation (the superscript numbers represent temporal order):

$$I_B^1 \leftrightarrow S_Y^1 \leftrightarrow I_B^2 \leftrightarrow S_Y^2 \leftrightarrow I_B^3 \leftrightarrow S_Y^3.$$

Since investors and securities at any given moment are interrelated, the historical development and future expectations of other investors and securities also shape the present in which decisions are made:

$$I_A^1 \leftrightarrow S_X^1 \leftrightarrow I_B^2 \leftrightarrow S_Y^2 \leftrightarrow I_C^3 \leftrightarrow S_Z^3;\ I_C^1 \leftrightarrow S_Z^1 \leftrightarrow I_B^2 \leftrightarrow S_Y^2 \leftrightarrow I_A^3 \leftrightarrow S_X^3.$$

When understood in this way, both the deciding subject and the moment of decision are something like nodes in constantly changing webs. Not all nodes within a network, of course, are equal; some are more important and powerful than others. The stronger the node, the greater the propensity of other nodes to cluster around it. The clustering of nodes sets up a

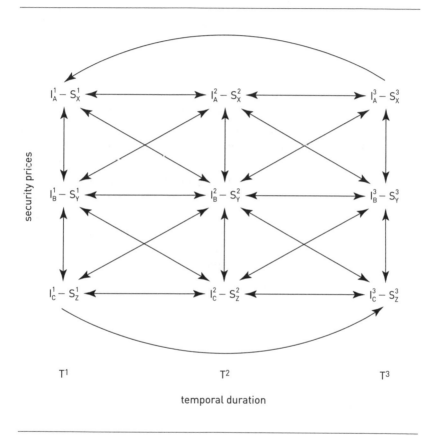

Figure 34
Market as complex adaptive system.

distinction between strong and weak relational links within as well as among networks. For example, the decision by a leading brokerage house to buy or sell stock in a leading company in a sector can quickly spur other investors to follow suit, thereby triggering a sudden shift in the stock's price. Or an unexpectedly poor earnings report by a leading company can trigger a rapid sell-off. If analysts regard the company as a leading economic indicator, the effect of the stock's movement can have an impact on the entire market. In this case, the leading company is something like a strong node, which has a significant impact on smaller companies or weaker nodes in the market network. This dynamic is not limited to securities in a single market. With the expansion of global trading networks operating in real time, shifts in one market are immediately felt in others. Thus, impact of the price movement of a particular stock in one market rapidly rippling through real-time networks can have a disproportionate effect on the entire global economy.

If the economy is interpreted as a complex adaptive system, it is a relational web or network in which order spontaneously emerges from within and is not imposed from without. This emergent self-organizing system is neither planned nor programmed and therefore is not the creation of any overarching agent or centralized agency. While agents—be they individuals, institutions, or machines—within these networks never act independently, they nonetheless retain the capacity to make decisions within the parameters created by market conditions. Since "the mind of the market" influences the agents from whose actions it emerges, investors and market are bound in a reflexive relation of codetermination and coevolution. Having emerged from the interplay of investors, the market folds back on itself in recursive loops to condition the activities of the agents whose actions continually create the market.

As we survey the past, it becomes clear that history does have a direction: there is a discernible movement toward increasing interrelatedness or interconnectedness. As everything and everybody become more interconnected, the complexity of the networks joining us increases. The course of this trajectory is neither steady nor continuous; to the contrary, it is punctuated by unexpected disruptions and surprising twists and turns. As complexity increases, the rate of change accelerates and disruptions become more frequent. In other words, when webs and networks extend their reach, volatility and therefore instability increase. This instability comes from *within* rather than without. This is not to imply, of course, that networks are not also disrupted by factors that seem to be exogenous. Markets, for example, can be adversely affected by unexpected political developments or even natural disasters. The networks influencing markets are not only financial but extend to natural, social, and cultural phenomena. *Everything is networked;* thus, what is outside one network is inside another. Transitions within, between, and among these networks occur at the edge of chaos and tend to be both unexpected and disruptive. Creative destruction occurs at the edge, border, margin of order and disorder, where insecurity is unavoidable. In such a world, to call investments *securities* is to misunderstand the dynamics of markets.

In the early twenty-first century, the world has become more complex than it has ever been and the rate of change continues to accelerate. Many people still do not understand the far-reaching implications of this growing complexity. Greater complexity brings more volatility and instability, which in turn create unavoidable uncertainty and insecurity. As uncertainty and insecurity increase, there is an understandable desire for certainty, stability, and world order—be it new or old. During the 1990s, the longing for simplicity and clarity manifested itself in a resurgence of market fundamentalism. According to the models financial economists devised, investors are rational and markets operate efficiently in a world where there is no event that is unexplainable and no risk that is unmanageable. While claiming to be realists, these true believers imagine an ideal world at odds with the new realities emerging in network culture. Their dream of a rationally ordered world where every risk can be hedged is as old as time itself. All such schemes are designed to escape time and history and thereby overcome the inescapable insecurity of life. In the final analysis, this dream is a religious vision in which the market is a reasonable God providentially guiding the world to the Promised Land where redemption finally becomes possible.

9

RUSTLING RELIGION

—Money . . . ? in a voice that rustled
—Paper, yes.
—And we'd never seen it. Paper money.
—We never saw paper money till we came east.
—It looked so strange the first time we saw it. Lifeless.
—You couldn't believe it was worth a thing.
—Not after Father jingling his change.
—Those were silver dollars.
—And halves, yes and quarters, Julia. The ones from his pupils. I can hear them now . . .
—Sunlight, pocketed in a cloud, spilled suddenly broken across the floor through the leaves of the trees outside.

William Gaddis, *JR*

RETURN OF THE REPRESSED)

Rustle (Middle English *rustlen, rustelen,* akin to Frisian *rus-selje,* Dutch *ridselen*—imitative): To move with soft whispering sounds. To steal (cattle).

Pecuniary (Latin *pecuniarius,* from *pecunia,* wealth in cattle): Consisting of or pertaining to money. Requiring payment in money.

Religion is one of the most powerful and dangerous forces in the world today. Four decades ago, anyone looking ahead to the next millennium never would have imagined this turn of events. In the 1960s the death of God, the secular city, and the demythologization of the Bible sent traditional religion into full retreat. At that time, there was widespread agreement among historians, sociologists, and even many theologians that modernization led to secularization. Expanding media networks exposed people to different cultural traditions with a vitality and plausibility it was difficult to deny. As new technologies transformed traditional societies and populations became more urbanized, long-held traditional beliefs lost their hold on many followers. Instead of a fall from grace, many people regarded the disappearance of religion as the liberation from age-old superstitions, prejudices, and ideologies that had long divided humankind and threatened the future.

In retrospect, the role of religion in emerging network culture appears to be considerably more complicated. Religion as such did not simply disappear as analysts had insisted; rather, alternative forms of spirituality temporarily displaced traditional religious beliefs and practices. Protests to the contrary notwithstanding, the 1960s counterculture was a spiritual, if not overtly religious, phenomenon. Disillusioned with domestic social policies and the escalating war in Vietnam, many people young and old sought inspiration in long-overlooked traditions of social protest and political activism in Judaism and Christianity. Neither the civil rights nor the antiwar movement would have been possible without the support of churches and synagogues throughout the country. Thousands of other young people, who had become alienated from what they understood to be Western values, turned to the East in search of spiritual visions and practices that promised to change the world by changing consciousness. Politically, these latter-day mystics and militants were far to the left of center; ethically, they tended to be humanists, relativists, and libertarians. The only thing about which rebels and resisters were certain was that moral absolutes were as dead as the traditional God. As absolutes faded and foundations crumbled, there was a loss of clarity and growth of uncertainty; the logic of the world seemed to have become undeniably fuzzy.

By the mid-1970s, this situation began to change dramatically. Repressed forms of religious belief and practice unexpectedly began to return to transform the social, political, and economic landscape. In the past two decades, the spread of global capitalism has been accompanied by the rise of global fundamentalism. Religious fundamentalism, however, takes different forms and has different functions in different historical, social, and cultural contexts. In the most general terms, outside the U.S., religious fundamentalism often provides a way to resist the expansion of global capitalism and American power, while within the United States, religious fundamentalism tends to legitimize market fundamentalism and sanctify American power.

In 1976, *Newsweek* declared that "the most significant—and overlooked—religious phenomenon of the 70s" was "the emergence of evangelical Christianity into a position of respect and power."[1] For those with ears to hear, this religious revival had been rustling just beneath the surface of ostensibly secular culture for several years. As early as 1972, Billy Graham had given an indication of things to come in an address at West Point on the occasion of his receipt of the Sylvanus Thayer Award for his promotion of the traditional values of Duty, Honor, and Country "during a decade when many Americans seemed to have abandoned them." Anne C. Loveland summarizes Graham's address to the officers and cadets:

> "The very survival of the American democratic way of life is at stake," Graham warned. "Demonstrations, pickets, marches, protests, and bombings" all threatened to undermine the "delicate balance between freedom and order" on which American society was based. "Whether we

like to admit it or not, there is an increasing moral darkness in our nation and a gathering political storm that threatens our very survival," he
observed. Graham declared that he looked not to "the dropouts and the
copouts" to save the country but to "the men and women who believe in
duty, honor, and country—and have a strong faith in God."

In the following decades, Graham's diagnosis was repeated again and
again until it became the governing orthodoxy of a new generation of political and military leaders. Having lost its way during the 1960s, the argument goes, America faced the challenge of reestablishing a firm religious foundation for its war on godless communism. In his concluding
remarks, Graham cast this struggle in the apocalyptic terms of a battle between the forces of light and darkness: "So let's not spend our time curs-
ing the darkness. Let's light a candle! Let's light a candle that will banish
moral and spiritual blight. Let's light a candle that will guide men into
tomorrow. Let's light a candle that will roll back fascism and social injustice. Let's light a candle that will warn our enemies that we will die so that
our children and grandchildren can have the freedom that we've had. Let's
light a candle that by God's grace will never be put out."[2] These images and
words still echo through the halls of power.

While Jimmy Carter was the first modern president who claimed to be
a born-again Christian, the "holy" alliance of evangelical Christianity, neoconservative politics, and neoliberal economics did not really take shape
until the presidency of Ronald Reagan. Though not an active churchgoer,
Reagan identified himself as an evangelical Christian. In an interview during the 1976 presidential campaign, he claimed to have had a born-again
experience, which brought him to realize "a hunger in this land for a spiritual revival; a return to a belief in moral absolutes—the same morals
upon which the nation was founded." Confessing his faith in divine providence and "the divine origin" of Scripture, Reagan declared, "The Bible
contains an answer to just about everything and every problem that con-
fronts us, and I wonder sometimes why we don't recognize that one Book
could solve a lot of problems for us." While it is easy to dismiss such gestures as political theater staged to court favor with a growing constituency,
it is a mistake to overlook the far-reaching political implications of the return of conservative Christianity. By making religion an instrument for
promoting his policies, Reagan began eroding the long-established separation of church and state, which was one foundational principle he chose
to ignore. His support for school prayer, creationism, and the right to life
were only the most obvious examples of the broader agenda to moralize

politics in the struggle for redemption, which inspired his defense policy. Translating the battle between light and darkness into the contest between capitalism and communism, Reagan transformed politics and economics into a religious campaign. The more fervent Reagan became, the more actively the new religious right supported him. Jerry Falwell went so far as to declare that President Reagan and Vice-President Bush were "God's instruments in rebuilding America."[3]

What most united Reagan and the religious right was a Manichaean view of the world in which the powers of good and evil are locked in a life-and-death struggle. The defining image of the Reagan presidency was "the evil empire," which combined apocalyptic Christianity with George Lucas's film *Star Wars* to create a script as simple as black and white. Reagan first introduced the notion of the evil empire in a 1983 speech to the National Association of Evangelicals. The USSR, he warned, is "the focus of evil in the modern world."[4] While challenging Soviet president Gorbachev to tear down the Berlin Wall, Reagan proposed building a wall as high as the heavens. Members of the religious right supported his Strategic Defense Initiative (i.e., Star Wars) by forming the Religious Coalition for a Moral Defense Policy, which quickly became a well-oiled lobbying machine with considerable influence on Capitol Hill as well as in the Pentagon. Though appearing to extend the logic of the Cold War, Reagan's strategy was actually to destroy the balance of terror, which had brought a semblance of stability for half a century. A world with one rather than two superpowers, he and his advisors believed, would be safer and more secure. But contrary to expectation, the eventual success of his policies contributed to uncertainty at home and instability abroad. The dissolution of the bipolar world created a multicentric world, which proved very unstable. When the opposition between Right and Left was no longer clear, the difference between right and wrong often seemed fuzzy. The geopolitical map, which had ordered the globe for half a century, had been torn up without a new one having to be drafted. On the domestic front, the collapse of the evil empire left America unsure of its mission. When the world is understood as a battlefield between good and evil, the disappearance of the powers of darkness creates a personal as well as a political void, which cries out to be filled. To restore order in a world that seemed to be edging toward chaos, America needed to invent a new evil other over against which it could define and defend itself. The name of this evil other was radical Islam; its face was Saddam Hussein, who, it is important to note, was not an Islamist.

Twenty years after Reagan delivered his "evil empire" speech, George W. Bush used the occasion of a campaign debate to declare Jesus to be the most influential philosopher in his life. In the years following his controversial election, it became clear that Bush meant what he said perhaps even more than he realized at the time. Offering reassurances about the looming war with Iraq, Bush asked the American people to have confidence not only in him but also in "the loving God behind all of life, and all of history." Shortly thereafter, he addressed the National Prayer Breakfast in February 2003: "Events aren't moved by blind change and chance. Behind all of life and all of history, there's a dedication and purpose, set by the hand of a just and faithful God."[5] The hand of providence, it seems, is not invisible to George W. Bush.

For Bush, as for Reagan, evangelical Protestantism inspires neoliberal economic policies and a neoconservative political agenda whose compassion is a matter more of word than of deed. Bush's policies on tax cuts, privatization, and deregulation are actually much more aggressive than were those of the Reagan administration. Not even financial and corporate scandals from Houston to Wall Street have deterred him from pursuing his crusade to privatize Medicaid and Social Security and to weaken the Securities and Exchange Commission and the Federal Communications Commission. Like Reagan, Bush's religious mission is most obvious in his defense policy and military strategy. By casting the "war on terror" in terms of the struggle between good and evil, he simultaneously lends it a religious aura and revives the ideology (and the military budgets) of the Cold War era. This religio-political vision is not limited to Bush but is shared by many important members of the Republican Party. The majority leader of the House, Tom DeLay, for example, has asserted, "Only Christianity offers a way to live in response to the realities that we find in this world—only Christianity." Paul Krugman reports that DeLay confessed that he is "on a mission from God to promote a 'biblical worldview' in American politics."[6] DeLay's religious views are shared by such other influential denizens of Capitol Hill as Senators Trent Lott and Don Nickels as well as Attorney General John Ashcroft.

Changes in the political landscape during the past twenty years reflect a country that is becoming more conservative politically and religiously. Surveys conducted in 2002 indicate that 47 percent of all Americans claim to attend religious services at least once a week. In Western Europe, by contrast, only 20 percent of people go to services regularly and in the so-called "New Europe," the number slips to 14 percent. These differences on the issue of religion go a long way toward explaining the growing political divide separating the United States and Europe. In the U.S., the religious organizations that have been gaining power in recent years are not formerly mainline denominations like the Lutherans, Methodists, Presbyterians, and Episcopalians but Southern Baptists, Pentecostals, and Evangelicals. Though differing in many ways, the groups whose numbers and influence are growing are all Protestant, share roots in the so-called red states, i.e., the South and Southwest, and have memberships that are predominantly white. As the country is becoming more diverse, the religions with political power are becoming less diverse.[7]

One of the reasons for the increasing power of religions that have not traditionally been in the American mainstream is that their leaders are unusually media savvy and highly entrepreneurial. There are now over 200 cable TV networks, 1,700 radio stations, many media distributors, and numerous publishing houses dedicated to promulgating the gospel of the religious right. Unlike many European countries, where religion is supported by the state, American religion has always been a private enterprise attractive to true believers and avid promoters. In this highly competitive religious marketplace, effective advertising increases market share. Skilled in the latest sales strategies, members of the religious right effectively spread their views to a mass audience. This commodification of religion is the inverse of the sacralization of the commodity: rather than turning the commodity into a sacred object soliciting desire, confidence men market religion as a precious commodity, which promises certainty, security, and finally redemption. This brand of religion is perfectly suited to the country's first born-again CEO president.

By assuming Reagan's mantle, Bush's political crusade has also extended the culture wars that began in the 1960s. With latter-day Straussians educated at the University of Chicago by Alan Bloom determining defense policy, there has been a regime change in Washington that few could have imagined in 1968. According to today's true believers, we finally have the chance to correct the errors of the past so graphically embodied in President Clinton and his administration.

Just as we lost our religious and moral moorings and became trapped in a morass of relativism, self-indulgence, and liberalism in the 1960s, so in the 1990s we lost certainty about right and wrong as well as good and evil and therefore had no sense of personal values or national purpose. While the excesses of the 1960s were primarily sexual and those of the 1990s were largely financial, they led to the same result: the disappearance of the clarity, discipline, and purpose without which people lost their way and were left to err aimlessly in pursuit of personal gratification at the expense of social good. For those who have confidence in providence, however, God works in unexpected ways to bring good out of evil. Just as God can save an individual from drink, so He can save a country from its spiritual degeneracy and moral laxity. The threat posed by representatives of the axis of evil provides the opportunity for America to redeem itself.

Bush is not always the most articulate spokesperson for his own beliefs and policies. In the wake of September 11, William Bennett, former director of the National Humanities Center, head of the National Endowment for the Humanities, and secretary of education, emerged as a leading defender of Bush's moral vision and political program. In his recent book, *Why We Fight: Moral Clarity and the War on Terrorism,* Bennett argues, "It took George W. Bush, a 'cowboy' president like Ronald Reagan, to revive the language of good and evil. Like Reagan before him, the president did so with precision and justification." Nothing less than the return to moral absolutes can prepare the country for the crises that lie ahead. Bush declared to nations around the world, "Either you are with us or against us"; Bennett explains, "The war we were being invited to join was a war over ultimate and uncompromising purposes, a war to the finish. Like World War II, like our war with Soviet communism, this is a war about good and evil."[8] As Bennett's argument unfolds, it becomes clear that Bush's war on terrorism has as much to do with the 1960s as it has to do with the problems of the twenty-first century. According to Bennett, the legacy of the 1960s was a moral relativism that, he insists, inevitably led to anti-Americanism. He traces the moral decline of America to " 'the adversary culture' of the 1960s." This polemic is, of course, familiar from the culture wars of the 1980s and 1990s, which Bennett fueled and Lynne Cheney fanned while serving as the head of the National Endowment for the Humanities. By the late 1990s, Bennett argues, moral decline had spread from college campuses to society as a whole: "I am not just talking about the politics of a radical or revolutionary fringe. As contemporary historians have well documented, the ideas and opinions promulgated by the 1960s New Left and counterculture were echoed, in however diluted a form, throughout the institutions of the liberal mainstream, particularly the universities and the media." Even more disturbing for the emerging moral majority is the way in which "the relativist ethos of the cultural Left" trickled down to "educators on the primary- and secondary-school levels."[9] The only way out of this moral impasse and the political paralysis it brings, Bennett insists, is a return to religious, moral, educational, and economic fundamentals. Though the message was clear, the messenger was not; a few weeks after Bush declared victory in his war with Iraq, Bennett declared failure in his war on vice. William Bennett turns out to have been a confidence man all along. While promoting moral clarity and family values, he was losing millions of dollars gambling. Not even Hollywood could have imagined a script in which the nation's self-appointed moral czar lost it all in Las Vegas—the capital of the very postmodernism to which Dr. Right had attributed the country's woes.

The faults and foibles of individual players should not overshadow the important issues at stake in the return of the religious. For many people, there is a profound longing for clarity, certainty, and security in a world where they are quickly slipping away. What often goes unnoticed, however, is the contradiction between the cultural values of religious and political conservatives and their economic policies. Bennett's downfall is a parable of these tensions. If, as I have suggested, Las Vegas has something to teach us about the postmodern economy, then Bennett's inability to resist its lure, while at the same time preaching from his *Book of Virtues*, tells us something about the contradictions between neoliberal economics and neofundamentalist religion. Indeed, the rapid spread of global capitalism creates the instabilities and insecurities that undercut traditional moral and religious values. In an increasingly connected world, rapid change is not only unavoidable but is a necessary survival strategy. As mobility transforms all aspects of life, ideas become as fluid as the media in which they circulate. With everything in rapid flux and becoming more complex, the desire for simplicity, which is characteristic of every version of fundamentalism, religious and otherwise, is understandable. This search for simplicity in a world of complexity is one of the primary reasons there has been a worldwide resurgence of religious fundamentalism in recent decades. While obviously differing in important ways, evangelical Christianity and Islamic fundamentalism are actually mirror images of each other. By promising moral clarity grounded in religious absolutes, they hold out the prospect of a return to the secure world of walls in a world of increasingly volatile and risky webs. This strategy is both misguided and dangerous. If we have learned anything from the economic crises of the late 1990s, it is that *models matter.* When the models informing policies and guiding strategies are at odds with new emerging realities, the consequences can be devastating. Whatever their faiths, true believers seeking redemption through a return to religious, moral, political, and economic fundamentals court the very disaster they claim to be struggling to avoid.

Religion is inescapable but its form is not. In recent decades, the religious right in many societies has hijacked religion to promote partisan political agendas. Islamic fundamentalism no more represents the rich diversity of Islam than evangelical Christianity represents the complexity of Christianity. In an increasingly networked culture, it is necessary to cultivate an appreciation for the resources and limitations of many religious traditions. Religious visions that remain stuck in the oppositions and contradictions of the past pose a threat to the future. Simplistic beliefs are dangerous in an ever more complex world and therefore must be confronted directly and criticized vigorously. But criticism alone is not enough. It is also necessary to develop alternative types of religious vision that might lead to new social, political, economic, and cultural realities.

THREE TYPES OF THEOLOGY OF CULTURE)   Alfred North Whitehead once suggested that everyone is born either a Platonist or an Aristotelian. In 1946, Paul Tillich published "The Two Types of Philosophy of Religion," in which he maintained that every philosophy of religion developed in the Christian tradition can be understood as either Augustinian or Thomistic. The former he labels the ontological type, the latter the cosmological type. The distinction between the two types of the philosophy of religion is based on the differences between the two classical arguments for the existence of God, the ontological and cosmological arguments. Tillich regards the teleological argument or the argument from design as a variation of the cosmological argument, which argues from effect (i.e., world) to cause (i.e., God as creator, governor, and designer). The essay opens with a description of the most important differences between the two types.

> One can distinguish two ways of approaching God: the way of overcoming estrangement and the way of meeting a stranger. In the first way man discovers *himself* when he discovers God; he discovers something that is identical with himself although it transcends him infinitely, something from which he is estranged, but from which he never has been and never can be separated. In the second way, man meets a *stranger* when he meets God. The meeting is accidental. Essentially they do not belong to each other.[10]

Since Tillich's concern is the philosophy of religion, he focuses on the problem of the knowledge of God. In the ontological type, the knowledge of God and the knowledge of Truth are identical, and this knowledge is immediate or direct. From this point of view, "*God is the presupposition of the question of God*" (13). One cannot ask about God if one does not already possess an implicit knowledge of God. This argument is obviously Platonic: knowledge of truth is the condition of the possibility of distinguishing between true and false and as such cannot be derived from experience. The ontological argument, Tillich maintains, "is the rational description of the relation of our mind to Being as such. Our mind implies *principia per se nota,* which have immediate evidence whenever they are noticed: the transcendentalia, *esse, verum, bonum.* They constitute the Absolute in which the difference between knowing and the known is not actual. This Absolute as the principle of Being has absolute certainty. It is a necessary thought because it is the presupposition of thought" (15). Tillich's argument hinges on the identification of God and Being, or in his own terms, the power of Being. In a move that has far-reaching consequences, he claims that in the ontological type, epistemology and ontology are inseparable. "The Augustinian tradition," he confesses, "can rightly be called mystical, if mysticism is defined as the experience of the identity of subject and object in relation to Being itself" (14). If God is being or the power of Being, then everything that exists is, in some way, united with the divine. God, in other words, is immanent in self and world.

In the cosmological type, by contrast, the relation between the human and divine is mediated or indirect. God is not immanent but is transcendent to self and world. Since nothing is grounded in itself, everything that exists is a sign referring beyond itself first to other things and ultimately to the divine origin, which is the truth of all reality.

> For Thomas all this follows from his sense-bound epistemology: "The human intellect cannot reach by natural virtue the divine substance, because, according to the way of the present life the cognition of our intellect starts with the senses." From there we must ascend to God with the help of the category of causality. This is what the philosophy of religion can do, and can do fairly easily in cosmological terms. We can see that there must be pure actuality, since the movement from potentiality to actuality is dependent on actuality, so that an actuality, preceding every movement, must exist. (18)

In the cosmological type, knowledge of God is a posteriori rather than a priori; God or truth, therefore, is the conclusion rather than the presupposition of argumentation. Because God is transcendent, human reason alone cannot reach the final truth of the divine. At the limit of human understanding, faith must supplement reason.

In contrast to the ontological type in which God is Being as such, in the cosmological type, God is *a* being. Tillich traces this shift in the understanding of the divine to the medieval Scottish Catholic theologian John Duns Scotus.

> The first step in this direction was taken by Duns Scotus, who asserted an insuperable gap between man as finite and God as the infinite being, and who derived from this separation that the cosmological arguments as *demonstrations ex finito* remain within the finite and cannot reach the infinite. They cannot transcend the idea of a self-moving, teleological universe. . . . The concept of being loses its ontological character; it is a word, covering the entirely different realms of the finite and the infinite. God ceases to be Being itself and becomes a particular being, who must be known, *cognitione particulari*. Ockham, the father of later nominalism, calls God a *res singularissima*. (19)

Given our analysis of the theological origins of eighteenth-century political economy, it is significant that Duns Scotus was a Scot. While Tillich emphasizes the role of Thomas Aquinas in promoting the cosmological type, his acknowledgment of the importance of Ockham suggests the significance of this alternative for the form of Protestantism that was so influential for early political economists.

Tillich gives absolute priority to the ontological type. Indeed, he goes so far as to argue that the cosmological type represents "a destructive cleavage" that establishes oppositions that inevitably lead to human estrangement. In this analysis, unity is not only primal but is always *present* beneath or behind every form of separation. "The ontological principle in the philosophy of religion," he concludes, "may be stated in the following way: *Man is immediately aware of something unconditional which is the prius of the separation and interaction of subject and object, theoretically as well as practically*" (22). To overcome the cleavage between the finite and the infinite, it is necessary to return to the unity of the divine, which is never really absent.

Tillich's typology is a variation of the romantic scheme we have already discovered in thinkers as different as Schleiermacher, Hegel, and Marx. Though the terms of analysis differ and emphases vary throughout the modern tradition, there is a recurrent effort to rewrite the biblical narrative of creation, fall, and redemption as the movement from unity into opposition and then either back to reunion or forward to a new union. In recent years, such metanarratives have come under serious attack from a variety of critical perspectives. All too often, however, these criticisms are ideological and fail to do justice to the complexities involved in both theology and contemporary cultural analysis. With careful refinement, qualification, and expansion, Tillich's account of two types of the philosophy of religion provides a useful framework for drawing together the strands of the argument we have been considering by suggesting an alternative theology of culture.

As we have discovered, network culture emerging at the beginning of the twenty-first century is the result of the dialectical interplay of religion, art, and economics. Throughout the course of modernity and postmodernity, art displaces religion as the source of spiritual vision and inspiration and then, in turn, is displaced by money and markets, which come to embody human desire. When taken together, religion, art, and economics form a dialectic without synthesis in which later stages displace without replacing earlier stages in such a way that each shadows the other. While momentarily repressed, earlier stages can always return to disrupt what seemed to have replaced them. With this understanding of social, cultural, and economic development, it is possible to place Tillich's typology in a historical perspective in two distinct but related ways. First, Tillich's two types of philosophy of religion are not atemporal but are so situated that they can emerge only in a particular historical situation. While anyone can be a Platonist after Plato, Plato could not have developed Platonism before the emergence of the historical conditions that make Platonism possible but not necessary. With this insight in mind, it is necessary to revise and expand Tillich's typology in a second way. Philosophical and theological visions are inseparably bound to changes in the broader cultural and economic landscape and vice versa. In other words, religion, art, and economics are caught in complex webs of mutual implication and coevolution. Since these loops are nonlinear, every form of reductive analysis is inadequate; to understand one, it is always necessary to understand the other two (see figure 13, in chapter 3).

To understand the interrelation of religion, art, and economics, it is helpful to expand Tillich's analysis from two types of philosophy of religion to three types of theology of culture (figure 35). For reasons that will become clear as the analysis unfolds, these three types can best be described as monistic, dualistic, and complex. While the first two types represent refinements of Tillich's ontological and cosmological categories, the third type moves beyond the limits of his argument to suggest a spiritual and ethical vision better suited to life in a networked world than any of the

	Monistic	Dualistic	Complex
Locus of the Real	Present Immanent	Absent Transcendent	Neither absent nor present Neither transcendent nor immanent
Relation of Identity and Difference	Identity-without-difference Negation epiphenomenal	Identity-in-opposition-to-difference Affirmation-by-negation	Identity-in-difference/ Difference-in-identity Affirmation of affirmation and negation
Source of Order	Implicit Unfolds gradually	External Imposed from without	Emergent Spontaneous self-organization
Status of Time and History	Archaeo-teleological process	Struggle between closed systems	Interplay of open systems
Relation of Self to World	Primordially unified At home in the universe	Primordially divided Estranged from the world as it is	Nodular Infinite restlessness
Possibility of Redemption	Realized eschatology Always already redeemed (actual)	Apocalyptic eschatology Redemption certain but in the future (possible)	Virtual eschatology Redemption impossible

Figure 35

Three types of theology of culture.

currently reigning faiths and ideologies. This three-part typology not only delineates alternative religious and theological perspectives but also provides the parameters for describing different forms of currencies as well as contrasting understandings of the role of art. While my primary concern will be with religion, I will briefly indicate the way in which this typological analysis illuminates the surprising isomorphism of religion, art, and money. In order to establish the differences among the three types of theology of culture, I will consider the position of each on six important issues: the locus of the real, the relation of unity and difference, the source of order, the status of time and history, the relation of self to world, and the prospect of redemption. It is, of course, necessary to stress that these types are not intended to describe exhaustively particular historical religions. Moreover, within each type there can be many subtle variations, which have important implications for a variety of issues. Though the focus of my analysis is primarily Christianity, the typology could be applied to other religions. It is often surprising to discover that strands in different religious traditions are often more similar than different versions of a single tradition.

One of the most important tasks of theology is to articulate what members of a particular religious tradition believe to be real. Though the real can assume countless guises, it is always necessary to ask where the real—however it is imagined or conceptualized—is located. Is it here or elsewhere? Above or below? Inside or outside? In the past, present, or future? In the first type of the theology of culture, the real is *present* here and now. At the earliest stages of human development, the real, understood as the sacred, is not yet a separate sphere but pervades everything. Since the world as such is fraught with mystery, it appears to be holy. In this form of experience, the relation to the real is immediate and direct and thus requires no intermediaries. While later philosophers and theologians translate this primal form of religion into elaborate doctrines and systems, its basic contours remain unchanged. This type of theology of culture generally corresponds to Tillich's ontological type of philosophy of religion. Since the real, understood as Being or the power of Being, is *immanent* in natural and historical processes, those with eyes to see realize that the cosmos is enchanted.

Within this framework, difference, diversity, and multiplicity are ultimately epiphenomenal. What is most real is an original unity that is antecedent to and a condition of the possibility of all separation and division. Though differences once articulated can become oppositions, the unity grounding them is never completely lost. This primal unity is also the source of world order, which is implicit and unfolds gradually. To invoke a familiar metaphor, the oak is in the acorn or, in a more contemporary idiom, temporal development is programmed before it begins. Inasmuch as the end is the realization of the original program, history is an archaeo-teleological process like the one described by T. S. Eliot's memorable words in "Little Gidding":

> We shall not cease from exploration
> And the end of our exploring
> Will be to arrive where we started
> And to know the place for the first time.[11]

Though the future often seems uncertain, retrospectively it is clear that things could not have been otherwise.

Since the real is immanent in nature and history, the self is at home in the universe. The challenge facing individual subjects is not so much to change the world as to accept what is as what ought to be. This framework implies an ethics of acceptance or even compliance rather than resistance. Forever at one with the real, the self is always already redeemed. This is a realized eschatology in which salvation is at hand here and now.

While the first type of the theology of culture tends to be monistic, the second type is dualistic. The real is not present here and now but is absent or, more precisely, elsewhere. In theological terms, the real is transcendent. Such transcendence can be expressed spatially or temporally; accordingly, the real is believed to be above, or below, on the one hand, and in the past or in the future, on the other. From the perspective of the first type of the philosophy of culture, the transcendence of the real establishes what Tillich labeled "a destructive cleavage," which eventually infects all aspects of the world and every dimension of experience. The foundational opposition between the real and the not-real grounds a series of related structural oppositions, which simultaneously provide order and harbor the threat of disorder. At the most rudimentary level, the relation—or nonrelation—between the real and the not-real entails the noncontradictory logic of either/or in which identity is established by opposition to difference. Instead of implicitly one, identity and difference are constituted oppositionally: something or someone is either this or that. The logic of either-or is always precise, and therefore it is possible to make theoretical and practical distinctions with clarity and certainty.

Since there is no direct, essential, or implicit association with the real, the relation to or awareness of it is not immediate but must be mediated.

Insofar as the religious imagination conceives the real in terms of God, awareness of and relation to the real must be given or revealed through intermediaries like prophets, saints, or messiahs, or in oral and written sacred texts. The history of religions is, in large measure, the story of competing narratives about various intermediaries, which are constructed to establish and maintain the relation between the real and the not-real. Though details obviously vary, the binary structure of all such schemes remains the same. Since the real is transcendent rather than immanent, the relation to it is contingent instead of necessary. Moreover, the constitution of this relation must be initiated by the real itself. The difference between the real and everything else leads to the opposition between those who are chosen and those who are not. In other words, the opposition between the transcendent and the immanent translates into intraworldly oppositions between good and evil, believers and nonbelievers, redeemed and condemned, etc.

Within the Protestant tradition, which, we have seen, was critical to the formulation of what eventually became the modern understanding of markets, the real is conceived as a transcendent creator God whose providential wisdom and power govern the world. Both the order of things and episodic disruptions are external or imposed from without. While the history of Protestantism has resulted in many sects and subsects, each of these departures represents a variation of two theological alternatives with significantly different implications. On the one hand, God's omnipotent will ultimately remains a secret even for those to whom it is revealed. While believers are certain that God governs the universe, the principles by which He rules remain shrouded in mystery. From this point of view, the order of things remains a matter of faith rather than knowledge. On the other hand, God limits His absolute power by freely ordaining certain laws by which He governs the universe. God can, in principle, suspend these rules and regulations but in fact never does so. These divine principles provide the foundation of all reality. Though order remains exogenous, it can be known through divine revelation. Since God reveals these principles to the elect, faith and knowledge are not antithetical; rather, knowledge based on faith can disclose the true order of things. Inasmuch as this foundational knowledge is a gift of the real itself, believers can be certain of its truth.

When meaning and order are not intrinsic but are extrinsic, the significance and purpose of things and events can be established only by referring beyond themselves. For those with eyes to see, everything becomes a sign referring to a transcendent referent, which secures the foundation of knowledge and basis of action. In a more contemporary idiom, if one knows the algorithms God prescribes, it is possible to decode the program of both personal and cosmic history.

To true believers armed with such certainty, history becomes a comprehensible struggle between the forces of light and darkness, right and wrong, and good and evil. The logic of either-or leads to closed systems in which negotiation and compromise are unacceptable. The situation can become perilous when equally self-certain uncompromising closed systems encounter each other. Faced with this dilemma, there are four alternatives: conversion of one side to the other, a standoff between opponents, domination of one system by the other, or, finally, the destruction of one of the systems. When conversion no longer seems possible, the situation becomes more complicated and more dangerous. The subsequent standoff can be the result of either the failure of one system to control or destroy the other or a calculated strategy for maintaining a balance of power. When successful, the latter approach establishes a temporary equilibrium, which preserves a certain degree of stability and order. Such order, however, is inevitably fragile because it is always threatened by true believers on each side, who share a Manichaean view of the world and seek to destroy each other. In this polar or binary universe, opposites mirror one another. The structure of each system is the same but the signs are reversed: what is positive in one is negative in the other and vice versa. Both sides subscribe to a vision of history as the tale of war on the evil other. As long as the forces of evil—however they are conceived—are not vanquished, things are not as they ought to be. If the real is not fully present here and now, it must be affirmed by negating what currently exists. Individuals and communities find meaning and purpose by participating in the struggle to destroy the darkness of the present age so that the new world order can be born. In this theological narrative, history is a three-part story (i.e., creation, fall, and redemption) whose final chapter is the apocalyptic struggle to realize the Kingdom of God. The struggle might be long, but the outcome is certain: redemption will surely occur in the future. You can bet on it!

Though apparently clear and precise, the logic of either-or is inherently fuzzy and finally self-contradictory. Whether conceived religiously, politically, socially, or psychologically, opposites need each other in order to be themselves. The effort to affirm one by negating the other eventually reverses itself by affirming the other without which it cannot be itself. If identity is oppositional, the negation of the other necessarily results in self-negation. In a Manichaean universe, then, victory is defeat. Faced with this unexpected turn of events, there are two alternatives. First, one can find or invent a different other over against whom one reasserts one's own identity. Throughout history, when the evil other is vanquished, another other repeatedly arises to take its place. Second, one can recognize the futility of such ceaseless warfare and acknowledge that complex interrelations are necessarily constitutive of everything and everybody. In other words, nothing can ever be itself by itself. With this insight, systems and structures that seemed to be closed begin to open or, more precisely, now appear always to have been open.

The third type of the theology of culture is complex. In contrast to the monistic and dualistic types, the real in this case is neither present nor absent. Rather, it is irreducibly interstitial or liminal and as such is *virtual*. It is important to understand the precise meaning of virtual reality in this context. *Virtual* derives from the Latin *virtus* (capacity or virtue) by way of the Middle English *virtuall* (effective, powerful). Among its many meanings, one that is obsolete remains the most suggestive: "capable of producing a certain effect or result; effective, potent, powerful." Far from merely possible, imaginary, or unreal, the virtual is the elusive real in and through which everything that exists comes into being and passes away. Always betwixt and between, it is neither immanent nor transcendent, neither here and now nor elsewhere and beyond. Since the virtual is never present as such, it cannot be represented but can only be traced in its aftereffects. It approaches by withdrawing and withdraws by approaching.

With the emergence of complexity, it becomes clear that the three types of theology of culture bear a complicated relation to time. As connectivity increases and differences proliferate, the arrow of time follows a trajectory from simplicity to greater complexity. Accordingly, one type emerges after the other but their relation is not strictly linear. In the first place, an earlier type can persist after a later type emerges. It is, after all, possible to be a committed monist or dualist in an era of complexity. In the second place, the third type is not the culminating synthesis of the other two. The complex type is the nonsynthetic third, which bends back on itself to inscribe the margin of difference between monism and dualism. The virtual reality articulated at the third stage is both the result and the presupposition, which is not to say the foundation, of the first and second stages in this evolutionary process. As a result of the nonlinearity of this complex structure, types one and two are already inscribed through type three even before it emerges. While obviously impossible within the framework of linear time, type three is simultaneously after and before types one and two.

The nonlinearity of complexity suggests why the virtual is the condition of the possibility of all structural oppositions. As the medium in which opposites fold into and emerge from each other, virtual reality complicates (Latin: *complicare,* to fold together) everything. In the third type of the theology of culture, nothing is either simple or self-identical because everything is parasitic upon something other than itself. Identity and difference, for example, are not oppositional but are thoroughly relational: each is relative to and thus inhabits the other. Instead of wrapping identities in a solipsistic shroud, such relativity draws them out of themselves to create a play of differences in which everything and everybody becomes itself in and through others. Identity, therefore, is always differential; to affirm one is always already to affirm an other. In this scheme, to be is to be related or, in more current terms, *to be is to be connected.* When connectivity increases, differences proliferate and the network of relations becomes more complex.

As the condition of the possibility of differences, virtual reality eludes the very structural oppositions it nonetheless enables. Neither present nor absent, here nor there, the virtual is *spectral.* To understand the importance of this point, it is helpful to note that the word *specter* harbors a tale with an intriguing web of associations. A specter is, of course, an apparition, phantom, or ghost. The word derives from the Latin *spectrum* (appearance, image, apparition) whose stem, *spek,* means to see or regard. *Spek* is also the root of *speculate* as well as *species. To speculate* means both to meditate or reflect and to engage in buying or selling something with an element of risk on the chance of making a profit. The Latin *species* means, among other things, shape, form, outward appearance, and, by extension, representation, image, and appearance. While the English word *species* is used most often to designate the fundamental taxonomic category that ranks after genus, consisting of organisms capable of interbreeding, a less common meaning is more suggestive in this context. In the Roman Catholic Church, *species* designates the outward appearance or form of the eucharistic elements that is retained after their consecration. *Specie,* in contrast to *species,* is coined money. As I have already noted, in the medieval Catholic liturgy, one of the forms of the eucharistic wafer was a coin bearing a sacred insignia and inscription. The words of the priest effect a process of transubstantiation through which the fiat currency of the wafer becomes the body of Christ, who is the absolute mediator between God and man. Within this economy of salvation, the divine mediator incarnate in the eucharistic coin is the currency of exchange, which makes redemption possible for human beings. When Christ dies and ascends to heaven, the divine does not disappear but remains to haunt the community of believers as a ghost or specter now deemed holy.

Within the emerging global economy, this specter unexpectedly returns as the virtual reality whose shade leaves every set fuzzy. Everything that seems to be clear and precise is really shadowed by a double, which can be thwarted but not destroyed. The repressed inevitably returns to disturb and displace systems and structures designed to exclude it. This disruption pushes systems toward the edge of chaos, where order sometimes emerges spontaneously. Neither implicit nor imposed from without, order in complex networks is emergent. Through the interactions of individual agents, structures, and systems, an order that is not designed or programmed unexpectedly takes shape. This order, which is endogenous yet aleatory, can emerge only if subjects and systems are open rather than closed. Since interactive agents and linked systems make adjustments and adaptations, which often lead to surprising results, relational networks do not always operate smoothly or evolve consistently. Disruption, like order, is endogenous. When dislocation occurs, equilibrium gives way to creative destruction through which new organizational patterns, structures, and systems are formed. This is the tipping point at which new realities emerge.

NEW REALITIES)   "All things are," as Nietzsche insists, "entwined, enmeshed," even if not always "enamored." As expanding networks create greater connectivity, which, in turn, results in increased complexity, it becomes ever more important to understand how various natural, social, and cultural systems are woven together to form the fabric of contemporary life. The financial and economic theories that were so influential in the 1980s and 1990s, we have discovered, were based upon a notion of equilibrium systems that is of only limited use in a network economy. The commitment to models that did not reflect newly emergent realities was a major factor contributing to the financial disruption in markets in the late 1990s. By showing the limitation of closed systems, the recent turmoil in financial markets points to the growing importance of theories of complex adaptive systems for understanding and negotiating the intricacies of the global economy. In a wired world, the economy is a global network with a distinctive structure and operational logic, which can be understood only by extending analysis beyond the domain of economics to broader natural, social, and cultural processes.

Our investigation has made it clear that modern markets are not merely a function of economic factors. Just as agents are not separate actors, so the economy is not an isolated system but is a node in multiple networks and worldwide webs (figure 36). Financial markets and networks are entangled in media, entertainment, technology, information, and even transportation networks ranging from the local to the global. These networks extend beyond the social, cultural, and economic domains to the realm of nature. Nature, we are discovering, is also a complex information-processing network that shapes and is shaped by social and cultural processes. Within this complex of networks, systems and subsystems are open and continually coevolve. Periods of relative stability are punctuated by endogenous disruptions, which provide the occasion for creative destruction. Since the relation among these systems is nonlinear, all determination is codetermination. Nature, society, and culture, in other words, are interrelated in such a way that each arises from and shapes the other and none can be simply reduced to the other. In ways rarely noted, economic developments during the last half of the twentieth century have both grown out of and influenced religious, artistic, and philosophical developments, which date

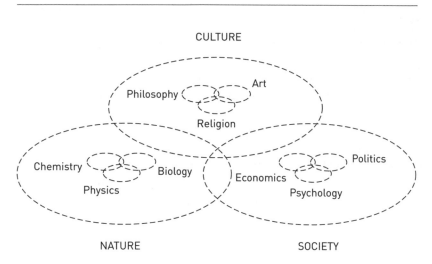

Figure 36
Networks of networks.

back to the Reformation. During the past four decades, religion, art, and finance have been joined in subtle feedback and feedforward loops of mutual influence and transformation. Each of these networks is itself a complex adaptive system; moreover, the interrelation of all the networks forms a complex adaptive system. The structure of networks, in other words, is fractal: part and whole are isomorphic. The iteration of the microstructure generates the macrostructure and the operation of the macrostructure sustains the microstructure. Within this network of networks, everything is relative because all things are interrelated.

The fractal structure of networks can be discerned in the isomorphism of the religious, monetary, and artistic systems we have been considering (see above, pp. 316–17). Just as there are three types of theology of culture, so there are three types of currency, which can take forms as different as commodities, representational money, and virtual/spectral currencies. Far from separate or independent, the three forms of currency and three types of theology of culture directly mirror each other (see above, p. 117).[12] As one moves from exchanging goods directly in the face-to-face situation of barter through exchange mediated by representational money (e.g., paper backed by precious metals) to the exchange of spectral currencies, which are immaterial, there is a shift from immanence (actual things) through transcendence (referential signs) to relational signifiers, traded on virtual networks, which are neither immanent nor transcendent. The transition from commodity money to representational money is marked by the emergence of the general equivalent (e.g., gold), which is the economic equivalent of God. The value of referential money is constituted by the reference of a signifier to an ostensibly independent or transcendent signified, which is the general equivalent without which exchange is impossible. The transition from representational money to spectral currency, in turn, occurs when the general equivalent disappears in the relational play of floating signifiers backed by nothing other than themselves. This play or, more precisely, interplay is what I have labeled the economic absolute. The notion of the economic absolute inverts and subverts the traditional understanding of the absolute. The word *absolute,* derived from the Latin *absolutus* (completed, unfettered, unconditional, from the past participle of *absolvere,* to free from), means not mixed, pure, unadulterated; not limited by restrictions; unconditional; and, most important, unrelated to and independent of anything else. The absolute, then, is precisely that which *is not related* and therefore *is not relative.* The economic absolute, by contrast, is *absolute relativity.* If being is relational, there is nothing that is absolute in the traditional sense of the term because there is nothing that is not relative. Relativity is what makes everything what it is and as such is absolute. The economic absolute, then, is the relational medium in and through which the relative values of floating currencies are constituted. As the condition of the possibility of exchange, this absolute is the virtual matrix, which is neither precisely inside nor outside the economy.

Just as the three forms of currency and three types of theology of culture mirror each other, so there are three corresponding types of art, which can be described as premodern, modern, and postmodern (figure 37). The advent of modernism is coterminous with the invention of the notion of high or fine art. While there were obviously creative works of remarkable artistic accomplishment prior to the modern era, the differentiation of art as a distinct cultural practice or special domain was a long and slow process. It was not until the end of the eighteenth century that a clear opposition between art and nonart was finally established. At this time, the critical variable in defining art sensu strictissimo was the relation between creative activity and market forces. In contrast to craft, low art, or kitsch, which is produced for profit, high art is not supposed to be made for the market but is created for its own sake. Fine art is neither practical nor utilitarian but is useless and therefore nonutilitarian. As such it is indepen-

Premodernism	Modernism	Postmodernism

Art and Non-Art
    Not clearly differentiated
	Art and Non-Art
	    Opposed
		Art and Non-Art
		    Not clearly differentiated

Craft = Art	Art vs. Craft High Art vs. Low Art Art vs. Commodity Art vs. Finance Autonomous vs. Utilitarian	World as Work of Art High Art–Low Art Commodity as Art/ Art as Commodity Art of Finance

Use Value	Transcendent Value of Art
	    Avant-Garde
	    a) Abstract Art
	        Self-referential
	    b) Utopian Art
	        Otherworldly
	        Futuristic
		Circulating Simulacra
		    Webs: Images of Images
		    Networks: Signs of Signs
		
		Endlessness of Art

Figure 37
Three types of art.

dent of the market and resolutely self-referential; its distinguishing trait is *autonomy*. Just as God is the unmoved mover who creates de novo, so the artist creates original works whose self-referentiality directly reflects or even embodies their divine prototype.

The autonomy of the work of art sets it apart from the everyday world. Art, like the divine in whose image it is made, is transcendent. This transcendence can take two forms: advanced art can be abstract or utopian. What unites these two forms of art is their negative relation to the world as it is. Abstraction—whatever its form—and utopianism are both committed to escaping from or overturning the established order. These two strategies are alternative versions of the modern avant-garde agenda. The term "avant-garde" is a military metaphor, which suggests one who leads his or her followers into battle. We have seen that at the end of the eighteenth century, art displaced religion as the focus of human moral vision and spiritual aspiration. The avant-garde artist became the prophet who would lead the human race into the New Age or Promised Land. This new territory could be either experiential or mental on the one hand or, on the other, sociopolitical. Instead of repeating everyday experience or satisfying familiar desires, abstract art is calculated to provide the occasion for an alternative experience that resists common interests by calling into question familiar modes of representation. In some cases, the altered form of consciousness resulting from the encounter with the work of art can transport one out of time and space and into what seems another realm. In such moments, art becomes spiritual and is effectively indistinguishable from what many describe as religious experience. There is, however, a danger in such art. Art and the experience it occasions can become so otherworldly that they are for all practical purposes irrelevant. Just as the religious mystic, wrapped in a shroud of silence, retreats from the world, so art can become hermetic by withdrawing into itself and losing its social and political relevance.

In contrast to abstraction, which often turns people inward, utopian art turns people outward by projecting another world intended to surpass the limitations of contemporary experience. Instead of mystical, this tradition is militant and can take two forms. First, the artist can project a world that is so ideal that it can never be realized in time and space. Like religious utopias past and present, this artistic vision bears a thoroughly negative relation to the world as we know it. The second alternative is for art to provide the vision for social and political change. From this point of view, the challenge is not to escape or negate the world but to transform it into a work of art. True art is not otherworldly and therefore should not be set apart by placing it on a pedestal, hanging it on a wall, or enclosing it in a museum. To the contrary, art should be *in* the world. The artist must leave the studio and move to the factory or take to the Street in order to lead the way to the Promised Land. When the utopia arrives or the Kingdom comes, the world will be redeemed by becoming artful.

Postmodernism is the unexpected realization of the modern avant-garde's dream of transforming the world into a work of art. When department store windows and digital signs on urban streets become art galleries and snow shovels and soup cans become artworks, art and nonart become indistinguishable. A urinal placed in an art exhibition asks not only "What is art?" and "Who is an artist?" but, more important, "What is not art?" and "Who is not an artist?" The distinction between high and low art collapses and all of culture becomes a work of art. Far from resisting market forces, art becomes a commodity, and artists in turn become businessmen and entrepreneurs skilled in the art of finance.

The disappearance of the autonomy of the work of art can also be seen in its mode of production and reproduction. The myth of originality dies with the disappearance of transcendence. The artist is no more autonomous than the works she or he produces. The creative process involves the recycling of figures and images in works that are deliberately signs of other signs. As the technologies of production and reproduction change, the networks on which these images and signs circulate are transformed. In network culture, works of art dematerialize and become codeable bits flowing on worldwide webs at the speed of light.

From one perspective, these developments mark the end of art. Art is no longer a separate domain but now appears to be nothing special. When indistinguishable from nonart, art appears to be dead. From another point of view, however, postmodernism announces the infinite expansion of art. If art and nonart cannot be clearly distinguished, there is nothing that is not art. The transformation of the world into a work of art is not so much the end of art as the advent of the endless process of its creation. Because art is endless, which is not to say eternal, the processes of its production remain open rather than closed. The modernist challenge to "make it new!" pushes art beyond modernism itself. Always operating far from equilibrium, this creative destruction keeps everything off balance and makes everyone and everything inescapably insecure.

The emergence of network culture transforms old realities and creates new realities we are only beginning to understand. In this uncharted territory, *maps matter.* The financial meltdown in the late 1990s should alert us to the economic, social, and political problems created when people in positions of power remain ideologically committed to outdated models. As everything becomes more interconnected and therefore more complex, certainty, security, and stability disappear. This loss is so disruptive and disturbing that it drives many people to try to find refuge in the simplicities of a bygone era. Armed with the certainty that clarity—moral and otherwise—supposedly brings, true believers of every stripe set out on missions to redeem the world and thus save people from the powers of chaos, confusion, and darkness. This struggle is as dangerous as it is futile; the inevitable result of such misguided ventures eventually will be the very disaster true believers claim they are trying to avoid.

Religion, however, does not always function in such pernicious ways; it can also be salutary even if not salvific. Instead of providing certainty, clarity, and security, religion can engender uncertainty, leave things fuzzy, and make people insecure. If reality turns out to be virtual, who can really be sure what is real and what is not? While undeniably disconcerting, such uncertainty can also be liberating. Whereas certainty closes the mind and makes the new as well as the other threatening and incomprehensible, uncertainty opens one to the unexpected and transforms the difference of others into an unexpected gift that enriches oneself.

A complex time needs a complex vision. In emerging network culture, selves have become intricate nodes in expanding webs of countless relations. As the fibers of this network become more interconnected, different nodes are drawn into coevolutionary webs. Though this developmental process neither is grounded in nor refers to anything beyond itself, it is not closed. The virtuality of the real keeps everything braided in worldwide webs open and makes creative development possible. The openness of the nodular subject is the space-time of desire. When desire is creative, it does not seek satisfaction but cultivates perpetual restlessness. The endless rustle of desire, which keeps things in constant motion, is strangely pleasurable. Though seeming to seek satisfaction, when it is vital, *desire desires desire.* In emerging networks, satisfaction is as undesirable as it is unattainable. Since redemption presupposes closure as well as satisfaction, however it is figured, the ceaseless flux of life in network culture renders redemption impossible. Rather than the sign of certain death, the impossibility of redemption is the mark of endless life. To affirm this life is to embrace the infinitely complex networks that make us what we are and are not.

Did you ever say "Yes" to one joy? Oh my friends, then you said "Yes" to *all* pain. All things are entwined, enmeshed, enamored—

—did you ever want Once to be Twice, did you ever say "I love you,
bliss—instant—flash—" then you wanted *everything* back.
—Everything anew, everything forever, everything entwined, enmeshed, enamored—oh, thus you love the world—
—you everlasting ones, thus you love it forever and for all time; even
to pain you say: Refrain but come again! *For joy accepts everlasting
flow!*[13]

Virtual reality is the current guise of what once was called sacred or perhaps even God. Virtuality, however, is a strange God. In a world where reality is virtual, nothing is certain or secure. Purpose and meaning are as
elusive and shifty as the constantly morphing networks in which they
emerge. The openness of the future is not subject to the calculations of
probability; indeed, the improbable not only can happen but does happen
repeatedly. In the face of the truly improbable, risk cannot be completely
hedged. Who would want it otherwise? Risk, uncertainty, and insecurity,
after all, are pulses of life. Though there might be an arrow of time, the entropic tendencies of equilibrium and satisfaction can be resisted at least
for a while. For the canny player, life is not a crapshoot but a game of poker.
Since one can never be sure the chips can be redeemed, the best strategy
is to keep the game going as long as possible. In the final analysis, the
problem is not to find redemption from a world that often seems dark but
to learn to live without redemption in a world where the interplay of light
and darkness creates infinite shades of difference, which are inescapably
disruptive, overwhelmingly beautiful, and infinitely complex.

NOTES

INTRODUCTION

1. William Gaddis, *JR* (New York: Penguin, 1993).

CHAPTER ONE

1. Gwyon was a Celtic god whose name also recalls the medieval tale, *Sir Gawain and the Green Knight*. Camilla was the virgin queen of the Volscians and a follower of Diana. Gaddis draws many of his accounts of religious myths and rituals from Sir James Frazer's *The Golden Bough: A Study in Magic and Religion*. For helpful annotations to Gaddis's work, see "A Reader's Guide to William Gaddis's *The Recognitions*," www.williamgaddis.org.

2. William Gaddis, *The Recognitions* (New York: Penguin, 1993), 3. Throughout the remainder of this section, references to this book are given in the text.

3. Ulrich Zwingli (1484–1531) was the Swiss Protestant reformer whose work prepared the way for Calvin.

4. Gaddis, *The Recognitions*, 495.

5. For a more complete discussion of Melville's treatment of these issues, see Mark C. Taylor, "Discrediting God," *About Religion: Economies of Faith in Virtual Culture* (Chicago: University of Chicago Press, 1999), 7–28.

6. During this period he wrote *Billy Budd*, which was not published until 1924.

7. The *New York Times* obituary referred to him as "Henry Melville," and another death notice listed his name as "Hiram Melville."

8. See Glenn Porter, ed., *Encyclopedia of American Economic History: Studies of the Principal and Movements of Ideas* (New York: Charles Scribner's Sons, 1980), 1:426.

9. Larry Allen, *Encyclopedia of Money* (New York: Checkmark, 2001), 151.

10. For Melville, as for Gaddis, proper names bear symbolic significance. The cosmopolitan is neither frank nor particularly good. John Irwin points out that "'Goodman' was the Puritan title of address." Through a character named Charley

Noble, Melville notes that "Goodman" is also "a cant term for a thief . . . and a Scottish title for the Devil." John Irwin, *American Hieroglyphics: The Symbol of the Egyptian Hieroglyphics in the American Renaissance* (Baltimore: Johns Hopkins University Press, 1983), 336.

11. Herman Melville, *The Confidence-Man: His Masquerade* (New York: Norton, 1971), 213–14.

12. See, for example, Fredric Jameson, *Postmodernism: or, The Cultural Logic of Late Capitalism* (Durham: Duke University Press, 1991); Fredric Jameson and Masao Miyoshi, *The Cultures of Globalization* (Durham: Duke University Press, 1998); and Antonio Negri and Michael Hardt, *Empire* (Cambridge: Harvard University Press, 2000).

13. In his recent study, Robert Nelson examines the relationship between post–World War II economic theory and religious belief. "Economists think of themselves as scientists," he notes, but "they are more like theologians." According to Nelson, economics has in effect become a secular religion that is ignorant of its theological roots. Summarizing his argument, Nelson concludes:

> As religious hopes for a secular salvation increasingly turned to economic events in this world—and from the mid-nineteenth century onward many people sought a secular salvation through abolishing economic scarcity and arriving at a state of complete material abundance on earth—economists became the preeminent social scientists, the proselytizers of those forms of secular religion and in fact served as the main religious focus for efforts in the West to defeat opportunism, to establish strong implicit contracts, and to solve other transaction costs and collective action problems.

In order to create a successful economic system, Nelson argues, it is necessary to establish "a set of values in society that offer vigorous encouragement to self-interest in the market and yet maintain powerful normative inhibitions on the expression of self-interest in many other less socially acceptable areas." Since economists are not equipped to address value questions, theologians must play a major role in formulating economic policies. Indeed, he goes so far as to suggest that "it might not be economists but theologians who are the most important members of society in determining economic performance."

While Nelson is surely correct in his insistence on the important relationship between economics and religion, he has an unsophisticated understanding of religion, which limits the value of his analysis. He assumes that religion is best understood in terms of the traditional theism characteristic of naïve Protestant believers. At no point in the argument does he give any indication of understanding the sophistication of the Western theological tradition or its complex relationship to philosophical ideas, which have played a critical role in the development of influential theories of the market. Furthermore, Nelson has no appreciation for the important changes in so-called traditional religion during the period he studies. He does not even seem to have heard of postmodernism. No less problematic than these assumptions and oversights is the lack of any consideration of changes in financial markets and instruments during the last four decades. In sum, Nelson's view of religion is too simplistic to do justice to its intricate interplay with economics and other aspects of culture. Robert Nelson, *Economics as Religion: From Samuelson to Chicago and Beyond* (University Park: Pennsylvania State University Press, 2001), 266, 6, 8.

14. See Thomas J. J. Altizer, *The Gospel of Christian Atheism* (Philadelphia: Westminster Press, 1966), and Harvey Cox, *The Secular City: Secularization and Urbanization in Theological Perspective* (New York: Macmillan, 1966). For a sociological analysis of secularization, see Peter Berger, *The Sacred Canopy. Elements of a Sociological Theory of Religion* (New York: Doubleday, 1967) and *The Homeless Mind: Modernization and Consciousness* (New York: Random House, 1973). I have considered these issues in detail in *Erring: A Postmodern A/theology* (Chicago: University of Chicago Press, 1984).

15. Quoted in Marc Shell, *Art and Money* (Chicago: University of Chicago Press, 1995), 179 n. 63.

16. Quoted in Mary Portas, *Windows: The Art of Retail Display* (New York: Thames and Hudson, 1999), 14.

17. William Leach, *Land of Desire: Merchants, Power, and the Rise of a New American Culture* (New York: Random House, 1993), 136–37.

18. Walter Benjamin, *The Arcades Project,* trans. Howard Eiland and Kevin McLaughlin (Cambridge: Harvard University Press, 1999), 37.

19. Quoted in Leach, *Land of Desire,* 60.

20. Ibid., 156. In developing this account, I have for the most part followed Leach's fine history of this period.

21. Portas, *Windows,* 8.

22. Simon Doonan, *Confessions of a Window Dresser: Tales from a Life in Fashion* (New York: Penguin, 1998), 111.

23. Ibid., 108.

24. Ibid., 116.

25. Andy Warhol, *The Philosophy of Andy Warhol* (New York: Harcourt Brace, 1975), 92.

26. Clement Greenberg, "Modernist Painting," in *Modernism with a Vengeance, 1957–1969,* ed. John O'Brien (Chicago: University of Chicago Press, 1993), 4:85.

27. Serge Guilbaut, *How New York Stole the Idea of Modern Art: Abstract Expressionism, Freedom, and the Cold War,* trans. Arthur Goldhammer (Chicago: University of Chicago Press, 1984), 177.

28. Ibid., 185.

29. Quoted in David Galenson, *Painting outside the Lines: Patterns of Creativity in Modern Art* (Cambridge: Harvard University Press, 2001), 131. Galenson presents a fascinating analysis of a different aspect of the economy of art by carefully plotting the relationship between the age of artists and the price of their work.

30. Bruce Glaser, "Questions to Stella and Judd" (interview), in *Minimal Art: A Critical Anthology,* ed. Gregory Battcock (Berkeley: University of California Press, 1969), 158.

31. Quoted ibid., 136.

32. Ibid.

33. Quoted in Adachiara Zevi, *Sol LeWitt: Critical Texts* (Rome: Editrice Inonia, 1994), 123.

34. Ibid., 32.

35. Andy Warhol, "What Is Pop Art? Answers from 8 Painters," *Artnews* 62 (November 1963), 26.

36. Quoted in Glaser, "Questions," 138.

37. Ibid., 139. In his recent book, Alexander Alberro considers the relationship of conceptual art in the 1960s and early 1970s to emerging information technologies and new communications systems. He concentrates on a small group of New York artists, which includes Sol LeWitt, Carl Andre, Douglas Huebler, Robert Barry, Joseph Kosuth, and Lawrence Weiner. Alberro's primary thesis is that the New York art dealer Seth Siegelaub played a critical role in the development and promotion of conceptual art. The insistence on the centrality of Siegelaub detracts from what might otherwise have been a useful account of conceptual art in relation to broader social and cultural currents. Moreover, Alberro's analysis is limited by his exclusive reliance on the work of Marshall McLuhan for the theoretical underpinnings of his interpretation of new media. Finally, Alberro asserts but does not adequately explain or demonstrate connections between conceptual art and financial practices. See Alexander Alberro, *Conceptual Art and the Politics of Publicity* (Cambridge: MIT Press, 2003).

38. To a remarkable extent, art in the twentieth century follows the course Hegel charted in the nineteenth century. Representation dissolves in concept, transforming art into philosophy. Because Hegel's system is closed, the range of possible moves is finite and history—artistic and otherwise—can come to an end. If, however, systems are open rather than closed, the end of art is not the end of the story.

39. Jean-Pierre Dupuy, *The Mechanization of the Mind: On the Origins of Cognitive Science,* trans. M. B. DeBevoise (Princeton: Princeton University Press, 2000), 66.

40. John von Neumann and Oskar Morgenstern, *Theory of Games and Economic Behavior* (Princeton: Princeton University Press, 1947), 1, 47. For an exhaustive account of the role of game theory in economics, see Robert Aumann and Sergiu Hart, *The Handbook of Game Theory with Economic Applications* (New York: Elsevier, 2000). Though game theory has had a noteworthy influence on economic theory and practice in the last half century, it is important not to overemphasize its significance. What is of particular interest in this context is the way in which von Neumann's theory has influenced humanists and social scientists as well as economists.

41. Von Neumann and Morgenstern, *Theory of Games,* 49, 33.

42. *Stanford Encyclopedia of Philosophy,* http://plato.stanford.edu/entries/game-theory.

43. As we will see, there are other ways to understand von Neumann's argument that lead to an account of markets as complex adaptive systems operating far from equilibrium. This line of analysis marks a significant departure from the perspective of leading financial economists whose models presuppose probability statistics derived from Brownian motion and the heat equation to develop models for programmed trading.

44. Martin Shubik, *The Theory of Money and Financial Institutions* (Cambridge: MIT Press, 1999), 1 : 17, 9.

45. Dupuy, *The Mechanization of the Mind,* 67.

46. F. A. Hayek, *The Fatal Conceit: The Errors of Socialism,* ed. W. W. Bradley (Chicago: University of Chicago Press, 1989), 146.

47. Richard Macksey, "Lions and Squares: Opening Remarks," *The Structuralist Controversy: The Languages of Criticism and the Sciences of Man,* ed. Richard Macksey and Eugenio Donato (Baltimore: Johns Hopkins University Press, 1970), 7–8.

48. Quoted in Dupuy, *The Mechanization of the Mind,* 18. Dupuy is, to my knowledge, the only other person to have recognized the close relationship between structuralism and cybernetics.

49. Jacques Lacan, "Psychoanalysis and Cybernetics, or On the Nature of Language," *Seminar XXIII,* trans. Sylvana Tomaselli (New York: Norton, 1988).

50. Jacques Derrida, *Margins of Philosophy,* trans. Alan Bass (Chicago: University of Chicago Press, 1982, 10.

51. Jean Baudrillard, *Symbolic Exchange and Death,* trans. Ian Grant (London: Sage, 1993), 6.

52. Gregory Bateson, *Steps to an Ecology of Mind* (New York: Ballantine, 1972), 453.

53. Baudrillard, *Symbolic Exchange and Death,* 13.

54. Jacques Derrida, "Structure, Sign, and Play in the Discourse of the Human Sciences," *Writing and Difference,* trans. Alan Bass (Chicago: University of Chicago Press, 1978), 279.

55. For a fuller account of these systems, see Mark C. Taylor, *The Moment of Complexity: Emerging Network Culture* (Chicago: University of Chicago Press, 2001).

CHAPTER TWO

1. Whenever he is surprised or upset, JR's favorite expression is "Holy shit!"

2. Georg Simmel, *The Philosophy of Money,* trans. Tom Bottomore and David Frisby (New York: Routledge, 1990), 236.

3. Aristotle, *Nicomachean Ethics,* trans. Roger Crisp (New York: Cambridge University Press), bk. 5, chap. 8.

4. R. Glenn Hubbard, *Money, the Financial System, and the Economy* (New York: Addison-Wesley, 1997), 20.

5. Martin Shubik, *The Theory of Money and Financial Institutions* (Cambridge: MIT Press, 1999), 1:282.

6. Simmel, *The Philosophy of Money,* 441.

7. See Jean-Christophe Agnew, *Worlds Apart: The Market and the Theater in Anglo-American Thought, 1550–1750* (New York: Cambridge University Press, 1986).

8. Norman O. Brown, *Life against Death: The Psychoanalytic Meaning of History* (New York: Random House, 1959), 243.

9. Julia Kristeva, *Powers of Horror: An Essay on Abjection,* trans. Leon Roudiez (New York: Columbia University Press), 4.

10. See, inter alia, Jacques Derrida, "From Restricted to General Economy: A Hegelianism without Reserve," *Writing and Difference,* 250–77.

11. As will be discussed later, it is important to note that the restricted economy is supposed to be an intrinsically stable system and the general economy approximates a complex adaptive system.

12. Georges Bataille, "The Notion of Expenditure," *Visions of Excess: Selected Writings, 1927–1939,* ed. Allan Stoekl (Minneapolis: University of Minnesota Press, 1985), 118. The classic treatment of the subject is Marcel Mauss, *The Gift: Forms and Functions of Exchange in Archaic Societies,* trans. Ian Cunnison (New York: Norton, 1967).

13. Bataille, "The Notion of Expenditure," 119–20.

14. Bataille, "The Practice of Joy before Death," *Visions of Excess,* 238.

15. Simmel, *The Philosophy of Money,* 187.

16. In developing the following analysis of the relationship between money and religion, I have drawn on William H. Desmonde, *Magic, Myth, and Money: The Origin of Money in Religious Ritual* (New York: Free Press, 1962); Paul Einzig, *Primitive Money: In Its Ethnological, Historical, and Economic Aspects* (London: Eyre and Spottiswoode, 1948); Pierre Klossowski, *La Monnaie vivante* (Paris: Eric Losenfeld, n.d.); Jürgen Harten and Horst Kurnitzky, *Museum des Geldes: Über die seltsame Natur des Geldes in Kunst, Wissenschaft und Leben* (Düsseldorf: Städtische Kunsthalle, 1978); Denis W. Richardson, *Electric Money: Evolution of an Electronic Funds-Transfer System* (Cambridge: MIT Press, 1970); and Lawrence Weschler, *Shapinsky's Karma, Boggs' Bills, and Other True-Life Tales* (San Francisco: North Point Press, 1988).

17. Joseph T. Shipley, *The Origins of English Words: A Discursive Dictionary of Indo-European Roots* (Baltimore: Johns Hopkins University Press, 1984), 248; Desmonde, *Magic, Myth, and Money,* 124.

18. Horst Kurnitzky, "Das liebe Geld—die wahre Liebe," *Museum des Geldes,* 39.

19. While it is obvious that this economic relationship continues to inform religious practice, it is rarely noted that there is a close connection between pecuniary offerings and ritual sacrifice. The intersection of economics and sacrifice can be seen most clearly in economic theories of atonement. Anselm's account of salvation in terms of the payment of a ransom is the classic example of this symbolic exchange. See *Why God Became Man: A Scholastic Miscellany,* ed. Eugene Fairweather (Philadelphia: Westminster, 1966), 100–183.

20. Desmonde, *Magic, Myth, and Money,* 104–5, 124.

21. For instructive extensions of Freud's analysis of ritual sacrifice, see René Girard, *Violence and the Sacred,* trans. Patrick Gregory (Baltimore: Johns Hopkins University Press, 1981); Girard, *The Scapegoat,* trans. Yvonne Freccero (Baltimore: Johns Hopkins University Press, 1986); and Eric Gans, *The Origin of Language: A Formal Theory of Representation* (Berkeley: University of California Press, 1981).

22. Marc Shell, *Art and Money* (Chicago: University of Chicago Press, 1995), 16–19. Shell points out that such tokens can be found in the United States as late as 1825. See also Shell, *The Economy of Literature* (Baltimore: Johns Hopkins University Press, 1978), and Shell, *Money, Language, and Thought: Economies from the Medieval to the Modern Era* (Baltimore: Johns Hopkins University Press, 1993).

23. Shell, *Art and Money,* 13.

24. Shubik, *The Theory of Money,* 1 : 142.

25. In the current financial lexicon, a market maker attempts to keep order in financial markets by maintaining "firm bid and offer prices in a given security." This is accomplished by a commissioned agent "standing ready to buy or sell

round lots at publicly quoted prices." In return for serving as a buyer of last resort, the market maker receives a commission on each transaction in the securities for which he is responsible. See www.forbes.com/tools/glossary.

26. Agnew, *Worlds Apart*, 20. In developing the following account of the emergence of markets in Greece, I have followed Agnew's analysis.

27. Ibid., 20.

28. Ibid., 25, 21.

29. Shubik, *The Theory of Money*, 1:224–25.

30. Agnew, *Worlds Apart*, 41.

31. Fernand Braudel, *Civilization and Capitalism: 15th–18th Century*, vol. 2, *The Wheels of Commerce*, trans. Sian Reynolds (Berkeley: University of California Press, 1992), 227, 228.

32. Karl Polanyi, *The Great Transformation: The Political and Economic Origins of Our Time* (Boston: Beacon, 1992), 67–68. This view of the relation between foreign and domestic trade recalls Aristotle's fear that chrematistic exchange threatens the household economy.

33. Aristotle, *Politics*, trans. Ernest Barker (New York: Oxford University Press, 1962), 28–29.

34. The other passages are Leviticus 25:35–37, Deuteronomy 23:21–22, and Psalm 15:5.

35. Jacques Le Goff, *Your Money or Your Life: Economy and Religion in the Middle Ages*, trans. Patricia Raum (New York: Zone Books, 1988), 28, 35.

36. Quoted in Le Goff, *Your Money or Your Life*, 37. For an illuminating example of Jewish abjection, see Sander Gilman, *The Body of the Jew* (New York: Routledge, 1991).

37. A second criticism of usury is also related to time. In usury, money never stops working and therefore violates the Sabbath.

38. R. H. Tawney, *Religion and the Rise of Capitalism* (New York: Harcourt Brace, 1926), 40, 41.

39. Quoted in James Buchan, *Frozen Desire: The Meaning of Money* (New York: Welcome Rain, 2001), 67–68.

40. Braudel, *The Wheels of Commerce*, 390, 392. In developing the following account of banking in the Middle Ages, I have been guided by Braudel's rich study.

41. Ibid., 393–95. The Fuggers were a German merchant and banking dynasty during the fifteenth and sixteenth centuries who played an important role in developing capitalism. Their economic wealth gave them considerable political power. The Fuggers joined other influential merchants and financiers in urging the pope to relax or rescind the prohibition of interest. Jakob Fugger was the target of a vehement attack by Luther for his support of interest payments.

42. Ibid., 101–2, 495.

43. F. A. Hayek, *The Fatal Conceit: The Errors of Socialism,* ed. W. W. Bradley (Chicago: University of Chicago Press, 1989), 146.

44. See Max Weber, *The Protestant Ethic and the Spirit of Capitalism,* trans. Talcott Parsons (New York: Scribner, 1958).

45. Quoted in Brown, *Life against Death,* 228.

46. Tawney, *Religion and the Rise of Capitalism,* 89–90.

47. Brown, *Life against Death,* 226.

48. Quoted in Tawney, *Religion and the Rise of Capitalism,* 105. See also Georges Bataille, *The Accursed Share,* trans. Robert Hurley (New York: Zone Books, 1988), 1:122–24.

49. Thomas Aquinas, *Introduction to St. Thomas Aquinas,* ed. A. C. Pegis (New York: Random House, 1948), 193, 215.

50. For an imaginative exploration of the implications of Ockham for recent philosophy and literary theory, see the work published pseudonymously by Derrida's son, Pierre: Pierre Alferi, *Guillaume d'Ockham Le Singular* (Paris: Le Editions de Minuit, 1989).

51. Meyrick H. Carré, *Realists and Nominalists* (New York: Oxford University Press, 1967), 115.

52. John Calvin, *Institutes of the Christian Religion,* trans. Ford L. Battles (Philadelphia: Westminster, 1960), 1:197.

53. Ibid., 199, 201, 208.

54. Ibid., 721.

55. Robert Reich, introduction to Adam Smith, *The Wealth of Nations* (New York: Modern Library, 2000), xviii.

56. Adam Smith, *The Theory of Moral Sentiments,* ed. D. D. Raphael and A. L. Macfie (Oxford: Clarendon Press, 1976), 179. Arthur Herman, *How the Scots Invented the Modern World: The True Story of How Western Europe's Poorest Nation Created Our World and Everything in It* (New York: Crown, 2001), presents a useful account of this period of Scottish intellectual history.

57. Smith, *The Theory of Moral Sentiments,* 185.

58. Anthony, earl of Shaftesbury, *Characteristics of Men, Manners, Opinions, Times, Etc.,* ed. John Robertson (Bristol: Thoemmes Press, 1995), 2:141.

59. Francis Hutcheson, *An Inquiry into the Original of Our Ideas of Beauty and Virtue* (New York: Georg Olms Verlag, 1990), 1:15.

60. David Hume, *A Treatise of Human Nature* (London: Longmans, Green, and Co., 1886), bk. 3, pt. 2, sec. 2.

61. Smith, *The Wealth of Nations,* 15.

62. Quoted in Albert O. Hirschman, *The Passions and the Interests: Political Arguments for Capitalism before Its Triumph* (Princeton: Princeton University Press, 1997), 28.

63. Ibid., 98.

64. Quoted ibid., 64–65.

65. Bernard Mandeville, *The Fable of the Bees: or, Private Vices, Publick Benefits* (Oxford: Clarendon Press, 1924).

66. Alexander Pope, "Essay on Man," in *The Norton Anthology of English Literature,* ed. M. H. Abrams et al. (New York: Norton, 1964), vol. 1.

67. Smith, *The Theory of Moral Sentiments,* 183.

CHAPTER THREE

1. Stuart Kauffman, *At Home in the Universe: The Search for the Laws of Self-Organization and Complexity* (New York: Oxford University Press, 1995), 69.

2. In addition to using the notion of emergent self-organizing systems to model markets, some economists also use this theory to account for the development of money. This line of analysis was anticipated by Karl Menger in an 1892 article entitled "On the Origin of Money." Against theorists who argue that money originates through the deliberate institution of practices and procedures crafted by legislators to meet requirements for exchange, Menger maintains that money emerges "spontaneously" from "the practice of everyday life."

> Putting aside assumptions which are historically unsound, we can only come fully to understand the origin of money by learning to view the establishment of the social procedure, with which we are dealing, as the spontaneous outcome, the unpremeditated resultant, of particular, individual efforts of the members of a society, who have little by little worked their way to a discrimination of the different degrees of saleableness in commodities. ("On the Origin of Money," *Economic Journal,* 2, no. 6 [June 1892]: 250)

Lawrence White appropriates Menger's theory to develop an interpretation of the evolution of money from its commodity form to new virtual currencies. See White, *The Theory of Monetary Institutions* (New York: Blackwell, 1999), 1–25.

3. Pierre Bourdieu, *The Rules of Art: Genesis and Structure of the Literary Field,* trans. Susan Emanuel (Stanford: Stanford University Press, 1995), 142. In a series of insightful works, Bourdieu has presented rich historical and sociological analyses of the trajectory I am tracing. See, inter alia, *The Field of Cultural Production: Essays on Art and Literature,* ed. Randal Johnson (New York: Columbia University Press, 1993), and *Distinction: A Social Critique of the Judgment of Taste,* trans. Richard Nice (Cambridge: Harvard University Press, 1984).

4. Bourdieu, *The Rules of Art,* 142.

5. Ibid., 81.

6. Friedrich Schiller, *On the Aesthetic Education of Man: In a Series of Letters,* trans. Reginald Snell (New York: Frederick Ungar, 1965), 26, 40.

7. Immanuel Kant, *Critique of Judgment,* trans. James Meredith (New York: Oxford University Press, 1973), pt. 2, p. 21.

8. Friedrich Schiller, *On the Aesthetic Education of Man: In a Series of Letters,* trans. Elizabeth Wilkinson and L. A. Willoughby (New York: Oxford University Press, 1967), 45, 27, 87, 80.

9. Friedrich Schleiermacher, *On Religion: Speeches to Its Cultured Despisers,* trans. John Oman (New York: Harper, 1958), 39, 55, 36.

10. G. W. F. Hegel, *Science of Logic,* trans. A. V. Miller (New York: Humanities Press, 1969), 826, 736.

11. Ibid., 836.

12. G. W. F. Hegel, *Phenomenology of Spirit,* trans. A. V. Miller (New York: Oxford University Press, 1977), 10, 12.

13. G. W. F. Hegel, *The History of Philosophy,* trans. E. S. Haldane and Frances Simson (New York: Humanities Press, 1968), 3:378.

14. G. W. F. Hegel, *Philosophy of Right,* trans. T. M. Knox (New York: Oxford University Press, 1969), 122.

15. Ibid., 123, 152.

16. Ibid., 129–30.

17. Quoted in Martin Nicolaus, foreword to Karl Marx, *Grundrisse: Foundations of the Critique of Political Economy,* trans. Martin Nicolaus (New York: Penguin Books, 1973), 26.

18. Marx, *Grundrisse,* 271.

19. Karl Marx, "On the Jewish Question," *The Marx-Engels Reader,* ed. Robert Tucker (New York: Norton, 1978), 50.

20. Marx, *Grundrisse,* 221, 146.

21. Karl Marx, *Writings of the Young Marx on Philosophy and Society,* trans. Lloyd Easton and Kurt Guddat (New York: Doubleday, 1967), 266, 267; Marx, *Grundrisse,* 225.

22. Karl Marx, *Capital,* ed. Friedrich Engels (New York: International Publishers, 1967), 3:86, 105, 95.

23. Marx, *Grundrisse,* 226.

24. Marx, *Capital,* 1: 104–5, 111.

25. Marx, *Grundrisse,* 255, 261.

26. Ibid., 270, 188, 258, 259–60, 261, 516; Marx, *Capital,* 1:130.

27. Quoted by David Frisby in his introduction to *The Philosophy of Money,* 33.

28. Georg Simmel, *The Philosophy of Money,* trans. Tom Bottomore and David

Frisby (New York: Routledge, 1990), 484–85. Throughout this section, references to this work are given in the body of the text.

29. Douglas Hofstadter, *Gödel, Escher, Bach: An Eternal Golden Braid* (New York: Vintage, 1980), 17. The Epimenides paradox is a version of the liar's paradox.

30. Warhol, *The Philosophy of Andy Warhol* (New York: Harcourt Brace, 1975), 92.

CHAPTER FOUR

1. Edgar Allan Poe, "The Gold-Bug," *Poe: Poetry and Tales* (New York: Library of America, 1984), 562.

2. David Carpenter, "Gold and Silver," *The Encyclopedia of Religion,* ed. Mircea Eliade (New York: Macmillan, 1987), 6:67–69.

3. Bernhard Laum, *Heiliges Geld* (Tübingen: Mohr, 1924), 128–29. See also Norman O. Brown, *Life against Death: The Psychoanalytic Meaning of History* (New York: Random House, 1959), 247.

4. Peter Bernstein, *The Power of Gold: The History of an Obsession* (New York: Wiley, 2000), 3.

5. Carpenter, "Gold and Silver," 67.

6. Quoted in Walter Benn Michaels, *The Gold Standard and the Logic of Naturalism: American Literature at the Turn of the Century* (Berkeley: University of California Press, 1987), 154–58.

7. John Williams, ed., *Money: A History* (New York: St. Martin's, 1997), 16. In assembling this brief account of coinage, I have drawn on Williams's helpful work, which accompanied an 1997 exhibition at the British Museum's HSBC Money Gallery.

8. Karl Marx, *Capital,* ed. Friedrich Engels (New York: International Publishers, 1967), 1:126.

9. Friedrich Nietzsche, "On Truth and Lie in an Extra-moral Sense," *The Portable Nietzsche,* ed. Walter Kaufmann (New York: Penguin, 1980), 46–47.

10. Martin Shubik, *The Theory of Money* (Cambridge: MIT Press, 1999), 1:390.

11. Lawrence White, *The Theory of Monetary Institutions* (New York: Blackwell, 1999), 40. I have rephrased and abbreviated White's points.

12. Williams, *Money: A History,* 26–27.

13. Kevin Dowd, *The State and the Monetary System* (New York: St. Martin's, 1989), 166.

14. John Maynard Keynes, *A Treatise on Money* (New York: Harcourt Brace, 1930), 2:291–92.

15. "Staff Review," *Bretton Woods: Looking to the Future,* A-2.

16. William Greider, *Secrets of the Temple: How the Federal Reserve Runs the Country* (New York: Simon and Schuster, 1987), 230–31.

17. Quoted in Joel Kurtzman, *The Death of Money: How the Electronic Economy Has Destabilized the World's Markets and Created Financial Chaos* (New York: Simon and Schuster, 1993), 51.

18. Greider's exhaustive study, *Secrets of the Temple,* is the most complete account of events surrounding the Fed in the 1970s and 1980s. Throughout this section I have drawn on the wealth of data he accumulates. Unless otherwise noted, figures and statistics come from Greider.

19. White, *The Theory of Monetary Institutions,* 71.

20. It is important not to confuse the use of the term "liberal" in the political and the economic sense. The neoliberal economic program is actually closer to what most people associate with the conservative political agenda and political liberalism represents many of the positions economic neoliberals resist. In the most general sense, economic liberalism involves the freedom of the individual and, correlatively, the minimization of governmental interference and regulation. These twin pillars lead to support for free markets and laissez-faire policies, which, of course, can be traced to Adam Smith. In the neoliberalism of the Chicago school, these basic principles traditionally lead to support for open financial and capital markets, the relaxation or elimination of currency exchange restrictions, lower corporate and personal taxes, a balanced budget, and the deregulation of businesses. While not representative of the Chicago school, members of the Austrian school, of whom Hayek is the most influential, and financial economists, who are proponents of the efficient market hypothesis, also support much of the neoliberal agenda. It is important to note that many neoliberals no longer oppose fiscal deficits but have come to see them as a useful political strategy for limiting the size of government. Large deficits, they argue, inhibit Democrats from increasing expenditures and expanding the size or role of the government.

21. My colleague Chris Geiregat kindly provided this figure.

22. White, *The Theory of Monetary Institutions,* 204.

23. Quoted in Greider, *Secrets of the Temple,* 14.

24. Ibid., 333–35.

25. Ibid., 76.

26. See Jacob Schlesinger, "The Deregulators: Did Washington Help Set the Stage for Economic Woe?" *Wall Street Journal,* October 17, 2002, 1.

27. Sten Thore, *The Diversity, Complexity, and Evolution of High Tech Capitalism* (Boston: Kluwer, 1995), 167.

28. Ken Auletta, *Greed and Glory on Wall Street: The Fall of the House of Lehman* (New York: Warner, 1987), 241, 43.

29. Quoted ibid., 240.

CHAPTER FIVE

1. Karl Marx, *Manifesto of the Communist Party,* in *The Marx-Engels Reader,* 473.

2. Quoted in Camilla Gray, *The Russian Experiment in Art, 1863–1922* (New York: Henry Abrams, 1962), 249.

3. Jacques Derrida, *Specters of Marx: The State of the Debt, the Work of Mourning, and the New International,* trans. Peggy Kamuf (New York: Routledge, 1994), 45.

4. F. A. Hayek, *The Fatal Conceit: The Errors of Socialism,* ed. W. W. Bradley (Chicago: University of Chicago Press, 1989), 9.

5. Quoted in Thomas Bass, *The Predictors: How a Band of Maverick Physicists Used Chaos Theory to Trade Their Way to a Fortune on Wall Street* (New York: Henry Holt, 1999, 13.

6. Martin Shubik, *The Theory of Money* (Cambridge: MIT Press, 1999), 1:142.

7. George Soros, *On Globalization* (New York: Public Affairs, 2002), vii.

8. Frederic Pryor, *Economic Evolution and Structure: The Impact of Complexity on the U.S. Economic System* (New York: Cambridge University, 1996), 104.

9. In an effort to chart these changes, I have developed a time line, running from 1921 to 2003. See http://www.press.uchicago.edu/books/taylor.

10. Dan Schiller, *Digital Capitalism: Networking the Global Market System* (Cambridge: MIT Press, 1999), 1. In developing the following account, Schiller's fine study has been an invaluable source of information.

11. Ibid., 10.

12. Ibid., 5–6.

13. Ibid., 32.

14. For a penetrating critique of the IMF and the World Bank, see Joseph Stiglitz, *Globalization and Its Discontents* (New York: Norton, 2002). I will return to the issue of world debt in chapter 7.

15. Schiller, *Digital Capitalism,* 47.

16. *Framework for Global Electronic Commerce,* July 1, 1997, http://cmcnyls.edu/Papers/WHGIIFra.HTM.

17. See, for example, Schiller, *Digital Capitalism;* and Don Tapscott, David Ticoll, and Alex Lowry, *Digital Capital: Harnessing the Power of Business Webs* (Boston: Harvard Business School Press, 2000).

18. Schiller, *Digital Capitalism,* 37, 38.

19. Hiromi Hosoya and Markus Schaefer, "Bit Structures," *Harvard Design School Guide to Shopping,* ed. Rem Koolhaas (New York: Taschen, 2001), 158.

20. Sze Tsung Leong, "Ulterior Spaces," *Harvard Design School Guide to Shopping,* 767.

21. Elinor Harris Solomon, *Virtual Money: Understanding the Power and Risks*

of Money's High-Speed Journey into Electronic Space (New York: Oxford University Press, 1997), 68.

22. *Business Week,* June 12, 1996, 66.

23. Some analysts see great advantages in privately issued money. Indeed, Hayek goes so far as to propose extending market principles to the creation of money. See Hayek, *Denationalization of Money* (London: Institute of Economic Affairs, 1990), 13–14.

24. Solomon, *Virtual Money,* 41–42.

25. Ibid., 203, 202.

26. It is important to note that even investing in U.S. Treasuries involves certain risks like inflation and market price fluctuations as interest rates change.

27. Clifford W. Smith and Charles W. Smithson, *The Handbook of Financial Engineering* (New York: Harper and Row, 1990), 583.

28. Hedge funds do not, of course, exist only to hedge risk but employ a variety of investment strategies to maximize returns.

29. Bass, *The Predictors,* 15.

30. Nicholas Dunbar, *Inventing Money: The Story of Long-Term Capital Management and the Legends behind It* (New York: Wiley, 2000), 24–25.

31. John Marshall and Kenneth Kapner, *Understanding Swaps* (New York: Wiley, 1993), 19–20.

32. Smith and Smithson, *Handbook,* 45.

33. Dunbar, *Inventing Money,* 31.

34. U.S. options markets received a major boost in 1973 when the law prohibiting pension funds and endowments from investing in options was lifted. This created a major influx of capital that contributed to the growth of these new markets.

35. Bass, *The Predictors,* 13–14.

36. Dunbar, *Inventing Money,* 171. I will explain how dynamic hedging works in the next chapter. At this point, suffice it to say that it is another strategy of counterbetting, which assumes the relativity of values.

37. Smith and Smithson, *Handbook,* 19.

38. Marshall and Kapner, *Understanding Swaps,* 3.

39. Ibid., 4.

40. Ibid., 3.

41. Smith and Smithson, *Handbook,* 204.

42. Ibid., 609.

43. Dunbar, *Inventing Money,* 104.

44. Bass, *The Predictors,* 265.

45. Robert Venturi, Denise Scott Brown, and Steven Izenour, *Learning from Las Vegas* (Cambridge: MIT Press, 1988), 13.

46. Ibid., 9.

47. Quoted in Bass, *The Predictors,* 87. I have drawn on Bass's account of Thorpe's relation to Claude Shannon. See 84–87.

48. Michael Lewis, *Liar's Poker: Rising through the Wreckage on Wall Street* (New York: Penguin, 1989), 162.

49. Ibid., 222.

50. Maria Bartiromo, *Use the News: How to Separate the Noise from the Investment Nuggets and Make Money in Any Economy* (New York: Harper Business, 2001), 102.

51. Quoted in Roger Lowenstein, *When Genius Failed: The Rise and Fall of Long-Term Capital Management* (New York: Random House, 2000), 106.

52. John Geanakoplos, "Promises Promises," *The Economy as an Evolving Complex System, II,* ed. W. Brian Arthur, Steven Durlauf, and David Lane (New York: Addison-Wesley, 1997), 288–90.

53. See Bass, *The Predictors,* 160–65.

54. Ibid., 162–63.

CHAPTER SIX

1. See www.nynyhotelcasino.com.

2. Though rarely noted, there is a direct line from the Vegas Strip to the AT&T building. Johnson borrows the signature feature of the building, the curved roofline designed to resemble the top of a Chippendale highboy, from the Vanna Venturi House. Venturi, in turn, based his design on "the sign for the Motel Monticello" on the Vegas Strip.

3. *Frank Gehry: The Complete Works,* ed. Kurt Foster (New York: Monacelli, 1998), 580.

4. Paul Goldberger, "Busy Building: Post-iconic Towers Invade Times Square," *New Yorker,* September 4, 2000, 90.

5. David Dunlap, "The Great Red, Green, and Blue Way," *New York Times,* December 30, 2001, 6.

6. Herbert Muschamp, "The Guts of Times Square," *New York Times Magazine,* October 22, 2000, 68.

7. Guy Debord, *Society of the Spectacle* (Detroit: Black & Red, 1983), aphorisms 20, 34, and 14.

8. Jayson Blair, "Turning Pixels into Panache," *New York Times,* February 17, 2000, B1. A few years after publishing this article, Jayson Blair was exposed for being a confidence man. Mixing fact and fiction, he fabricated information in numerous articles he wrote for the *New York Times.* None of the media excesses of the 1990s did more damage to confidence in the press than Blair's deceit.

9. Though rarely noted, one of the ways Nokia has been able to retain its com-

petitive edge is by listening to kids. Their researchers regularly give grade-school children new devices in order to discover what they do with them. The widely popular instant messaging on cell phones, which most Americans have not yet mastered, was invented by children as a way of communicating with friends in school.

10. Gaddis, *JR*, 26. Throughout this section, references to *JR* are given in the text.

11. Michael Lewis, *Next: The Future Just Happened* (New York: Norton, 2001), 27–28. Throughout this section, references to this book are given in the text. My account of this case is drawn from Lewis's book.

12. "Swallow Me, Swallow," *The Economist*, May 11, 2002, 71. In the wake of the problems caused by the dot-com collapse and the decline of technology stocks, this planned merger, as well as NASDAQ's other plans for expansions, have been cancelled.

13. Mark Ingebretsen, *NASDAQ: A History of the Market That Changed the World* (New York: Forum, 2002), 42. This is the best book on the development and operation of NASDAQ. In developing my account in the following pages, I have drawn on much of the information that Ingebretsen has gathered.

14. Ibid., 37.

15. Ibid., 66.

16. Ibid., 177.

17. Ibid., 183.

18. Quoted from http://forbes.com/tools/glossary/glossary.jhtml.

19. Ingebretsen, *NASDAQ*, 21.

20. Ibid., 81.

21. Ibid., 101–102.

22. Ibid., 141.

23. Marc Friedfertig and George West, *The Electronic Day Trader* (New York: McGraw-Hill, 1998), 18.

24. Ingebretsen, *NASDAQ*, 9–10.

25. Friedfertig and West, *The Electronic Day Trader*, 10–11.

26. John Cassidy, *Dot.Con: The Greatest Story Ever Sold* (New York: Harper-Collins, 2002), 225, 229–30.

27. Quoted in Theodore Roszak, *The Cult of Information: The Folklore of Computers and the True Art of Thinking* (New York: Pantheon, 1986), 150. Paulina Borsook is one of the few writers to have noted the important relationship between Internet culture and forms of spirituality, which grew out of the 1960s counterculture. She identifies two contrasting spiritual styles: "ravers and Gilders," whose chief representatives are Net denizen and erstwhile Grateful Dead lyricist John Perry Barlow and George Gilder respectively. "Ravers," she explains, "are neohip-

pies whose antigovernment stance is more hedonic than moral, more lifestyle choice than policy position. Keep your laws off my body: Let's hear it for drugs, sex, and rock 'n' roll!" Gilders, by contrast "are most similar to those of the conservative branch of the Republican Party and are suspicious of the government for many of the same reasons." Borsook correctly recognizes a strange symmetry between these two seemingly opposite perspectives. Borsook, *Cyberselfish: A Critical Romp through the Terribly Libertarian Culture of High Tech* (New York: Public Affairs, 2000), 16–17.

28. Cassidy, *Dot.Con,* 167.

29. Lewis, *Next,* 67, 53.

30. Among my students who are making important contributions to new technologies are: Steve Case, who founded AOL; José Marquez, an artist and social critic, who created South to the Future; Bo Peabody, who founded Tripod, later bought by Lycos; Dylan Tweeny, who publishes the Tweeny Report, devoted to technology and the Internet; Chris Tweeny, who is engaged in online social work; John Kim, an erstwhile programmer for financial institutions, who is now completing a Ph.D. in communication studies at Stanford; Matt Sly and DeWitt Clinton, who created the technology platform for Eziba; Suela Nako, currently a financial analyst; Noah Peeters, now a lawyer; and many others who are involved in different parts of the Internet world.

31. For an account of this seminar, see Mark C. Taylor and Esa Saarinen, *Imagologies: Media Philosophy* (New York: Routledge, 1994).

32. See Mark C. Taylor, "The Currency of Education," *The Moment of Complexity,* 233–70.

33. Kevin Kelly, *New Rules for the New Economy: 10 Radical Strategies for a Connected World* (New York: Viking Penguin, 1998), 160.

34. Ibid., 55–56.

35. One of the puzzles of the dot-com phenomenon is why so many companies offered their stocks at such undervalued prices. Michael Casey points out that "in doing so, they effectively failed to maximize their profits by leaving a great deal of money 'on the table,' money that might have prolonged their corporate lives" ("Dot-Com IPO Pricing Baffles Economists," *Wall Street Journal,* September 9, 2002). This strategy seems to contradict the orthodox assumptions about the rationality of investors. The only possible explanation seems to be that company representatives assumed that the value of the buzz created by a highly successful IPO was greater than the money they could have made by issuing the stock at a higher price.

36. Cassidy, *Dot.Con,* 80–88. Cassidy's excellent book is the most complete account of the dot-com phenomenon yet to have appeared. I have drawn most of my figures in this section from this book.

37. Michael Lewis, *The New New Thing: A Silicon Valley Story* (New York: Norton, 2000), 85.

38. Ibid., 52.

39. Cassidy, *Dot.Con,* 95.

40. Mary Meeker and Chris DePuy, *The Internet Report* (New York: Harper-Business, 1995), I-2.

41. Ibid., 98.

42. Ibid., 286.

43. Ibid., 96.

44. Michael Mandel, "The Triumph of the New Economy: A Powerful Payoff from Globalization and the Information Revolution," *Business Week,* December 30, 1996.

45. Cassidy, *Dot.Con,* 158–59.

46. Quoted ibid., 202–3.

47. Ibid., 3, 8.

48. Ibid., 293. For a comprehensive list of Internet stocks and their performance during this tumultuous period, see 348–63.

CHAPTER SEVEN

1. Thomas Krens, preface to *The Great Utopia: The Russian and Soviet Avant-Garde, 1915–1931* (New York: Guggenheim Museum, 1992), x.

2. By the 1980s and 1990s, the practice of corporate sponsorship of museum exhibitions was widely accepted. One of Krens's most controversial tactics was to extend this practice by actually mounting exhibitions devoted to the products of the sponsors. In 1998, the Guggenheim opened its wildly popular BMW motorcycle show, which later traveled to the Las Vegas Guggenheim; in 2001, an exhibition of Armani fashions was held. The Armani show was particularly controversial because it coincided with a significant financial "contribution" by the designer.

3. Hani Rashid and Lise Anne Couture, *Flux* (New York: Phaidon, 2001), 59.

4. On February 28, 2000, Mayor Rudolph Giuliani held a press conference at the uptown Guggenheim to announce the designation of the Guggenheim as the developer of the East River site and to pledge $70 million of city support for the project.

5. Rashid and Couture, *Flux,* 36–37.

6. The Difference Engine was first built under the direction of Doron Swade, director of the Museum of Science in London, to commemorate the two-hundredth anniversary of Babbage's birth. Swade presents an engaging account of the struggle to complete Difference Engine 2 in the midst of the cutbacks in funding for the arts under Margaret Thatcher's neoconservative government. See Doron Swade, *The*

Difference Engine: Charles Babbage and the Quest to Build the First Computer (New York: Viking, 2000).

7. Ibid., 177–80.

8. Charles Babbage, *Passages from the Life of a Philosopher,* ed. Martin Campbell-Kelly (New Brunswick: Rutgers University Press, 1994), 35–36.

9. Martin Campbell-Kelly, introduction to *Passages from the Life of a Philosopher,* 13.

10. Babbage, *Passages from the Life of a Philosopher,* 89.

11. Ibid., 93.

12. Quoted in Swade, *The Difference Engine,* 170.

13. John von Neumann, "A Model of General Economic Equilibrium," *Review of Economics Studies* 13 (1945):109.

14. Kenneth Arrow and Gerard Debreu, "Existence of an Equilibrium for a Competitive Economy," *Econometrica* 54 (1954): 265–90.

15. Edmund Phelps, "Equilibrium: Development of the Concept," *New Palgrave: A Dictionary of Economics,* ed. John Eatwell, Murray Milgate, and Peter Newman (New York: Macmillan, 1987), 2:180.

16. Adam Smith, *The Wealth of Nations* (New York: Modern Library, 2000), 65–66.

17. Donald Walker, "Leon Walras," *New Palgrave,* 4:853–63.

18. Martin Shubik, *The Theory of Money* (Cambridge: MIT Press, 1999), 99–100.

19. Jean-Pierre Dupuy, *The Mechanization of the Mind: On the Origins of Cognitive Science,* trans. M. B. DeBevoise (Princeton: Princeton University Press, 2000), 142–43.

20. Ilya Prigogine and Isabelle Stengers, *Order Out of Chaos: Man's New Dialogue with Nature* (New York: Bantam, 1984), 123.

21. Claude Shannon used the principles of thermodynamics to develop his information theory. See Claude Shannon and Warren Weaver, *The Mathematical Theory of Information* (Urbana: University of Illinois Press, 1949).

22. Louis Bachelier, "Theory of Speculation," *The Random Character of Stock Market Prices,* ed. Paul Cootner (Cambridge: MIT Press, 1964), 17.

23. Ibid., 26 (emphasis added).

24. Ibid., 26–27.

25. M. F. M. Osborne, "Brownian Motion in the Stock Market," *The Random Character of Stock Market Prices,* 100.

26. Nicholas Dunbar, *Inventing Money: The Story of Long-Term Capital Management and the Legends behind It* (New York: Wiley, 2000), 7.

27. Benoit Mandelbrot, *Fractals and Scaling in Finance: Discontinuity, Concentration, Risk* (New York: Springer, 1997), 25.

28. Ibid., 493.

29. Burton Malkiel, "Efficient Market Hypothesis," *New Palgrave*, 2:120. See also Burton Malkiel, *A Random Walk down Wall Street* (New York: Norton, 1999).

30. Robert Shiller, *Irrational Exuberance* (Princeton: Princeton University Press, 2000), 173–74.

31. Peter Bernstein, *Capital Ideas: The Improbable Origins of Modern Wall Street* (New York: Free Press, 1992), 46. Bernstein's book is the best study of the impact of quantitative analysis and mathematical models on economic theory and financial markets during the last three decades.

32. Ibid., 54 (emphasis added).

33. Dunbar, *Inventing Money*, 32.

34. Quoted ibid., 33.

35. Kevin Rubash, "Black-Scholes Option Pricing Models," http://bradley .bradley.edu/~arr/bsm.

36. Ibid.

37. Zvi Bodie, Alex Kane, and Alan Marcus, *Investments* (New York: McGraw Hill, 1996), 289.

38. Dunbar, *Inventing Money*, 58. In developing my account of Meriweather's activity at Salomon Brothers and Long-Term Capital Management, I have been guided by Dunbar's analysis and by Roger Lowenstein, *When Genius Failed: The Rise and Fall of Long-Term Capital Management* (New York: Random House, 2000). Unless otherwise indicated, the figures cited are gathered from these two works. I have, however, also collected some relevant data from newspaper and magazine accounts.

39. I am following Dunbar's account at this point. See Dunbar, *Inventing Money*, 64–66.

40. Ibid., 106.

41. These figures are from ibid., chap. 6.

42. Ibid., 138, 140.

43. Quoted ibid., 140.

44. Lowenstein, *When Genius Failed*, 65, 127. Lowenstein points out that the LTCM partners' calculations "implied that it would take a so-called ten-sigma event—that is, a statistical freak occurring one in ten to the twenty-fourth power times—for the firm to lose all of its capital in one year."

45. See Dunbar, *Inventing Money*, and Lowenstein, *When Genius Failed*.

46. Lowenstein, *When Genius Failed*, 45.

47. Ibid., 128.

48. Dunbar, *Inventing Money*, 190.

49. The clearest and most comprehensive treatment of the two-decade world

debt crisis is Paul Blustein, *The Chastening: Inside the Crisis That Rocked the Global Financial System* (New York: Public Affairs, 2001).

50. Lowenstein, *When Genius Failed,* 139.

51. Blustein, *The Chastening,* 239, 238.

52. Lowenstein, *When Genius Failed,* provides the best account of the details of these discussions.

53. Dunbar, *Inventing Money,* 223–24.

54. Lowenstein, *When Genius Failed,* 235.

CHAPTER EIGHT

1. Quoted in Charles Kindleberger, *Manias, Panics, and Crashes: A History of Financial Crises* (New York: Wiley, 2000), 31. For an engaging fictional account of this remarkable era, see David Liss, *A Conspiracy of Paper* (New York: Ballantine, 2000).

2. Kindleberger, *Manias, Panics, and Crashes,* 31.

3. John Cassidy, "The Greed Cycle," *New Yorker,* September 23, 2002, 69.

4. James Ledbetter, "The Boys in the Bubble," *New York Times,* January 2, 2003.

5. Kenneth Arrow, "Workshop on the Economy as an Evolving Complex System: Summary," *The Economy as an Evolving Complex Adaptive System,* ed. Philip Anderson, Kenneth Arrow, and David Pines (New York: Addison-Wesley, 1988), 278. Other works that consider the importance of complexity studies for economic systems and financial networks include Uwe Cantner, Horst Hanusch, and Steven Klepper, eds., *Economic Evolution, Learning, and Complexity* (New York: Springer-Verlag, 2000); Francis Heylighen, Johan Bollen, and Alexander Riegler, eds., *The Evolution of Complexity* (London: Kluwer, 1999); Edgar Peters, *Complexity, Risk, and Financial Markets* (New York: Wiley, 1999); Edgar Peters, *Patterns in the Dark: Understanding Risk and Financial Crisis with Complexity Theory* (New York: Wiley, 1999); and Sten Thore, *The Diversity, Complexity, and Evolution of High Tech Capitalism* (Boston: Kluwer, 1995).

6. Quoted in Edgar Peters, *Chaos and Order in the Capital Markets* (New York: Wiley, 1996), 137.

7. Ibid.

8. Quoted in Roger Lowenstein, *When Genius Failed: The Rise and Fall of Long-Term Capital Management* (New York: Random House, 2000), 74n.

9. Georg Simmel, *The Philosophy of Money,* trans. Tom Bottomore and David Frisby (New York: Routledge, 1990), 127–29.

10. Robert Venturi, *Complexity and Contradiction in Architecture* (New York: Museum of Modern Art, 1966), 17.

11. Ibid.

12. Robert Venturi, Denise Scott Brown, and Steven Izenour, *Learning from Las*

Vegas (Cambridge: MIT Press, 1988), 118. Over the years, Venturi has developed a more sophisticated understanding of communications technologies. See *Iconography and Electronics: Upon a Generic Architecture, A View from the Drafting Room* (Cambridge: MIT Press, 1996).

13. Paul Krugman, *The Self-Organizing Economy* (Malden, MA: Blackwell, 1996), 2.

14. Brian Arthur, Steven Durlauf, and David Lane, introduction to *The Economy as an Evolving Complex System, II* (New York: Addison-Wesley, 1997), 2–3.

15. See John Holland, *Emergence: From Chaos to Order* (Reading, MA: Addison-Wesley, 1998), and Holland, *Hidden Order: How Adaptation Builds Complexity* (New York: Addison-Wesley, 1995).

16. John Holland, "The Economy as an Adaptive Process," *The Economy as a Complex Adaptive System,* 117–18.

17. George Soros, *The Alchemy of Finance: Reading the Mind of the Market* (New York: Wiley, 1994), 42.

18. Quoted in Benoit Mandelbrot, *Fractals and Scaling in Finance: Discontinuity, Concentration, Risk* (New York: Springer, 1997), 506.

19. Brian Arthur, John Holland, Blake LeBaron, and Richard Palmer, "Asset Pricing under Endogenous Expectations in an Artificial Stock Market," *The Economy as an Evolving Complex System, II,* 15.

20. Peter Coveney and Roger Highfield, *Frontiers of Complexity: The Search for Order in a Chaotic World* (New York: Fawcett Columbine, 1995), 425.

21. Arthur and Holland, "Asset Pricing," 18.

22. Richard Bauer, *Genetic Algorithms and Investment Strategies* (New York: Wiley, 1994), 9.

23. Ibid., 22.

24. Brian Arthur, "Self-Reinforcing Mechanisms in Economics," *The Economy as an Evolving Complex System,* 9–10.

25. Per Bak, *How Nature Works: The Science of Self-Organized Criticality* (New York: Springer-Verlag, 1996), 1–2. See also Henrik Jensen, *Self-Organized Criticality: Emergent Complex Behavior in Physical and Biological Systems* (New York: Cambridge University Press, 1998).

26. Kindleberger, *Manias, Panics, and Crashes,* chap. 2. See also Robert Brenner, *The Boom and the Bubble: The US in the World Economy* (New York: Verso, 2002).

27. Robert Shiller, *Irrational Exuberance* (Princeton: Princeton University Press, 2000), 148.

28. Soros, *The Alchemy of Finance,* 14. See also Leon Levy, *The Mind of Wall Street* (New York: Public Affairs, 2002).

29. See, inter alia, Stephen Jay Gould, *Hen's Teeth and Horse's Toes* (New York:

Norton, 1983), and *Wonderful Life: The Burgess Shale and the Nature of History* (New York: Norton, 1989).

30. Mandelbrot, *Fractals and Scaling in Finance,* 52.

31. F. A. Hayek, *Rules and Order* (Chicago: University of Chicago Press, 1973), 36-37.

32. F. A. Hayek, *The Fatal Conceit: The Errors of Socialism,* ed. W. W. Bradley (Chicago: University of Chicago Press, 1989), 76.

33. Wolfram has recently published an impressive tome in which he attempts to reinterpret all of science on the basis of the principles of complexity. While there is much of interest in Wolfram's argument, his most important ideas have been anticipated by other thinkers working in the area of complexity studies. In his eagerness to stake out his claim for originality, Wolfram refuses to acknowledge the contributions of others without whom his own work would have been impossible. See Stephen Wolfram, *A New Kind of Science* (Champaign, IL: Wolfram Media, 2002).

34. Quoted in Peter Coveney and Roger Highfield, *Frontiers of Complexity: The Search for Order in a Chaotic World* (New York: Fawcett Columbine, 1995), 274. See also Christopher Langton, ed., *Artificial Life* (New York: Wiley, 1989, 1994).

35. Stuart Kauffman, *At Home in the Universe: The Search for the Laws of Self-Organization and Complexity* (New York: Oxford University Press, 1995), 87.

36. Ibid., 27.

37. For a thorough account of the Prediction Company, see Thomas Bass, *The Predictors: How a Band of Maverick Physicists Used Chaos Theory to Trade Their Way to a Fortune on Wall Street* (New York: Henry Holt, 1999). Lawrence David develops an informative account of Prediction Company's use of genetic algorithms in their models and trading strategies. See "Genetic Algorithms and Financial Applications," in *Trading on the Edge,* 133-147.

CHAPTER NINE

1. Quoted in Anne C. Loveland, *American Evangelicals and the U.S. Military 1945-1993* (Baton Rouge: Louisiana State University Press, 1996), 211. See also Martin Marty and R. Scott Appleby, *Accounting for Fundamentalisms: The Dynamic Character of Movements* (Chicago: University of Chicago Press, 1994); and Gabriel Almond, R. Scott Appleby, and Emmanuel Sivan, *Strong Religion: The Rise of Fundamentalisms around the World* (Chicago: University of Chicago Press, 2003).

2. Loveland, *American Evangelicals and the U.S. Military,* 165-66.

3. Ibid., 211-13.

4. Ibid., 215

5. Ibid.

6. Paul Krugman, "Gotta Have Faith," *New York Times,* December 17, 2002.

7. For a highly informative study of the new religious diversity in the United States, see Diana Eck, *A New Religious America: How a "Christian Country" Has Now Become the Most Religiously Diverse Nation* (New York: Doubleday, 2001). See also David Barrett, George Kurian, and Todd Johnson, *World Christian Encyclopedia: A Comparative Survey of Churches and Religions in the Modern World,* 2 vols. (New York: Oxford University Press, 2001).

8. William Bennett, *Why We Fight: Moral Clarity and the War on Terrorism* (New York: Doubleday, 2002), 45. It is interesting to note that *Why We Fight* was also the title of a series of propaganda films during the Second World War. For passionate and insightful analysis of the historical propensity to justify military action by sanctifying conflict, see Chris Hedges, *War Is a Force That Gives Us Meaning* (New York: Anchor, 2002).

9. Ibid., 138, 139, 68.

10. Paul Tillich, "The Two Types of Philosophy of Religion," *Theology and Culture,* ed. Robert Kimball (New York: Oxford University Press, 1959), 10. Though Tillich associates the ontological type with Augustine and the cosmological type with Thomas Aquinas, these categories are roughly parallel to Whitehead's distinction between Plato and Aristotle. Throughout this section, page references to this essay are given in the text.

11. T. S. Eliot, "Little Gidding," *Collected Poems, 1909–1969* (London: Farber & Farber, 1963), 222.

12. In his influential work, *Symbolic Economies: After Marx and Freud,* Jean-Joseph Goux uses the principles of Lacanian psychoanalysis to frame an interpretation of exchange. He identifies four forms of value: elementary or accidental form, total or extended form, general form, and money form. While these categories bear a certain resemblance to the three types of theology of culture I have described, the preoccupation with bringing together Marx and Freud, which Goux shares with so many postwar European intellectuals, limits the value of his analysis. There is a significant difference between the trajectory Goux plots and the one I am suggesting. For Goux, there is a movement from duality (reciprocal exchange) through multiplicity (generalized exchange) to unity (general equivalent). In contrast to this, I am proposing a scheme that moves from unity through duality to differential complexity. Goux's misleading argument on this point is at least in part the result of his lack of appreciation for the subtleties of Western religious and theological traditions. Finally, while he suggests the importance of what he describes as "a nonphallocentric, noncentralized conception, as yet unconceived, of a network, a polynodal, nonrepresentative organization" in the context of his discussion

of Bataille's effort to move "beyond the formation of *monocephalous* societies," he does not develop the implications of this potential insight. See Jean-Joseph Goux, *Symbolic Economies: After Marx and Freud,* trans. Jennifer Curtiss Gage (Ithaca: Cornell University Press, 1990), 46.

13. Friedrich Nietzsche, *Thus Spoke Zarathustra,* trans. Marianne Cowan (Chicago: Regnery, 1957), 335.

INDEX

abjection, 61, 73, 340n36

absolute, economic, 5, 100, 105, 109, 116–17, 326

Absolute Idea, Hegelian, 5, 100–102, 103; Marx and, 104–5, 108, 109; network economy as, 159, 295; Simmel and, 110, 115

abstract art, 39, 40–42, 95, 118, 328

Abstract Expressionism, 39, 41, 42, 48

accounting: of dot-coms, 216; double-entry, 74–75; scandals of, 138

adaptation: in markets, 294–95; by neural networks, 289. *See also* complex adaptive systems; evolution

aesthetics: Calvin's theology and, 4, 84; gold and, 123; Hegel's system and, 4–5, 105; Kantian (*see* Kantian aesthetics); markets and, 4, 80, 100, 104; money and, 5, 31, 100, 106; Schiller on, 97, 98–99; Schleiermacher's theology and, 99; Scottish moral philosophy and, 4, 12, 77, 80, 84–86, 87, 88–89, 94; Simmel's philosophy and, 110, 112, 117–18; utility and, 94. *See also* art

after-hours trading, 201

Agnew, Jean-Christophe, 68, 71, 340n26

Alberro, Alexander, 336n37

alchemy, 61, 126, 163

Alchemy of Finance (Soros), 163

algorithms: Babbage's Analytic Engine and, 237; of cellular automata, 286; Conceptualism and, 3; genetic, 283, 288–89, 356n37; structuralism and, 46

Allen, Herbert, xv–xvi, 8, 139, 211

Althusser, Louis, 48

Amazon.com, 217, 218, 220

Amsterdam Stock Exchange, 4, 76–77

Analytic Engine, 233, 236–37

Anatomy of Greed (Cruver), 147

Anderson, Philip, 282

Andre, Carl, 336n37

Andreesen, Marc, 214

Andy Warhol Museum, 37

Anselm, Saint, 339n19

anti-Semitism, 73

AOL, 189, 195, 196, 218, 220

Aquinas, Thomas, 80–81, 313, 314, 315, 357n10

arbitrage, 193, 245, 246–47, 252–56, 257, 259

architecture: of Asymptote, 10, 228–29, 231–32; crisis of confidence and, 1; Guggenheim Museum and, 229; modernism in, 173, 280–81; of NYSE virtual trading floor, 10;